MANAGERIAL ECONOMICS
Readings, Cases, and Exercises

MANAGERIAL ECONOMICS
Readings, Cases, and Exercises

R. CHARLES MOYER
University of New Mexico

JAMES R. McGUIGAN
Wayne State University

GEORGE W. TRIVOLI
Hillsdale College

West Publishing Company

St. Paul
New York
Los Angeles
San Francisco

To the memory of my father—RCM

To my mother and the memory of my father—JRM

To my daughter Jennifer Rene—GWT

COPYRIGHT © 1979 By WEST PUBLISHING CO.
50 West Kellogg Boulevard
P.O. Box 3526
St. Paul, Minnesota 55165

All rights reserved
Printed in the United States of America

Library of Congress Cataloging in Publication Data
Main entry under title:
    Managerial economics.
    1. Managerial economics—Addresses, essays, lectures. 2. Managerial economics—Case studies.
I. Moyer, R. Charles, 1945–   II. McGuigan, James R.   III. Trivoli, George.
HD30.22.M36   658.4   78–15479
ISBN 0–8299–0157–4

CONTENTS

Matrix of Selection vii
Preface ix
Acknowledgments xi

Part One Introduction 1

Chapter 1 Scope and Methodology of Managerial Economics 3

1. Reading: *William J. Baumol,* What Can Economic Theory Contribute to Managerial Economics? 3

Chapter 2 Goals and Objectives of the Organization 8

2. Reading: *Wilbur G. Lewellen and Blaine Huntsman,* Managerial Pay and Corporate Performance 8
3. Case: Setting Objectives at the Maritime Administration 17

Part Two Decision Making in the Private Sector 25

Chapter 3 Demand and Forecasting 27
4. Reading: *Thomas F. Hogarty and Kenneth G. Elzinga,* The Demand for Beer 27
5. Reading: *Geoffrey H. Moore,* The Analysis of Economic Indicators 31
6. Reading: *Thomas D. Hopkins,* Higher Education Enrollment Demand 39
7. Case: The Demand for Roses 50
8. Case: A Demand Study of Bus Ridership in the City of Detroit 52
9. Exercises 54

Chapter 4 Production and Cost Analysis 58

10. Reading: *William A. Longbrake,* Statistical Cost Analysis 58
11. Reading: *John Riew,* Economies of Scale in High School Operation 66
12. Reading: *Haim Barkai and David Levhari,* The Impact of Experience on Kibbutz Farming 73
13. Case: Break-even Analysis for Lockheed's Tri-Star: A Case on Application of Financial Techniques 81
14. Exercises 88

Chapter 5 Pricing 93

15. Reading: *J. Fred Weston,* Pricing Behavior of Large Firms 93
16. Reading: *Joseph P. Newhouse,* A Model of Physician Pricing 108
17. Reading: *Bruce T. Allen,* Why Does Gasoline Cost More in Charlevoix Than It Does in Detroit? 117
18. Case: A Rate Increase for the Alabama Power Company 121
19. Exercises 130

Chapter 6 Capital Budgeting 134

20. Reading: *J. Fred Weston,* Investment Decisions Using the Capital Asset Pricing Model 134
21. Case: *General Medical Center Capital Budgeting Problems of an Urban Hospital* 143
22. Exercises 152

Part Three Issues in Regulation, Market Structure, Conduct, and Performance 155

Chapter 7 Regulating the Private Corporation 157

23. Reading: *George J. Stigler,* The Theory of Economic Regulation 157
24. Reading: *Donald R. Fraser and Peter S. Rose,* Bank Entry and Bank Performance 176
25. Case: Product Liability: What Are the Limits? 188

Chapter 8 Merger Regulation 191
26. Case: Proctor & Gamble-Clorox Merger: A Landmark Decision 191
27. Case: Bank Mergers and Antitrust: Provident National Bank and Central-Penn National Bank Merger 194
28. Case: Antitrust Assault on Conglomerateness: U.S. vs. Ling-Temco-Vought, Jones & Laughlin Steel, and Jones & Laughlin Industries Case 199

Part Four Decision Making in the Public Sector 203

Chapter 9 Cost-Benefit Analysis 205

29. Reading: *Walter I. Garms,* A Benefit-Cost Analysis of the Upward Bound Program 205
30. Reading: *Thomas Peterson,* Cost-Benefit Analysis for Evaluating Transportation 234
Proposals: Los Angeles Case Study 217
31. Case: Benefit-Cost Analysis of a Curbside Recycling Program 224

Chapter 10 Externalities and Income Distribution 226

32. Reading: *Robert E. Kohn,* Price Elasticities of Demand and Air Pollution Control 226
33. Reading: *W. Lee Hansen and Burton A. Weisbrod,* The Distribution of Costs and Direct Benefits of Public Higher Education: The Case of California
34. Case: Calculation of an Effluent Charge: Case of PPG Industries in Barberton, Ohio 248
35. Case: The Cost of Pollution Control at the Timken Company 255

MATRIX OF SELECTION—CHAPTER CROSS REFERENCES

Book Selection	McGuigan Moyer	Brigham Pappas	Leftwich	Haynes Henry	Spencer Seo Simkin	Hirschleifer	Mansfield	Watson	Ferguson Gould
1	1	1	1	1	1	1, 2	1	1	Intro.
2	2	1	1, 2	1	1, 9	9	1, 5	8	——
3	2	1	1, 2	1	1, 9	9, 17	1	8	——
4	5, 6, 7, 8	4, 5, B	5, 6	3	5, 6	5, 6	4	2, 3, 4	3, 4
5	6	4, 5, B	3, 5, 6	4	4	5, 6	4	3	3, 4
6	5, 6, 7, 8	4, 5, B	3, 5, 6	3, 10	5, 6	5, 6	4	3, 4	3, 4
7	6, 8	4, 5, B	6	4, 10	4, 6	5	——	3, 4	3, 4
8	6, 8	4, 5, B	6	4	4-6	5	——	3, 4	4
9	5, 6, 7, 8	4, 5, B	3, 5, 6	3, 4	4-6	3-6	2-4	2-4	1-4
10	10, 11	8, 9	9	6	8	9, 10, 14	6	11	7
11	10, 11	8, 9	9	6	8	9, 10, 14	6	11	7
12	9, 11	6	8	6, 7	7	9, 10, 14	5, 7	9, 10	5, 6
13	10	8	9	5	10	9, 10	6	11	7
14	9, 10, 11	6, 8, 9	8, 9	5-7	7, 8, 10	9, 10, 14	5-7	9-12	5-7
15	12, 13, 14	10, 11	11, 12	8, 9	12	10-12	9, 11	16, 17, 19, 20	9, 10, 12
16	12	10, 11	11, 12	8, 9	12	10-12	9-11	16, 20	9, 10, 12
17	13	11	12	8, 9	10, 12	10-12	11	19, 20	12
18	12, 21	10, 11	11	9	12	10-12	9, 11	16, 17	9, 10
19	12, 13, 14	10, 11	10-13	8, 9	12	10-12	8-11	13-20	8-12
20	15, 16	13	——	11	14, 15	16	16	21	——
21	15	13	——	10, 11	14, 15	16	16	21	——
22	15, 16	13	——	11	14, 15	16	16	21	——
23	18, 19, 21	12	15	8, 9	13	11, 13, 17	9	16, 17	16
24	18	12	15	8, 9	13	11, 13, 17	9, 11	18, 20	9-12
25	19	12	15	——	13	11, 13	9-11	15, 23	12
26	19	12	15	9	13	17	11	16	9, 12
27	19	12	15	9	13	17	11	16	9, 12
28	19	12	15	9	13	17	11	16	9, 12
29	17	13	18	12	14	17, 18	17	15, 23	16
30	17	13	18	12	14	17, 18	17	15, 23	16
31	17	13	18	12	14	17, 18	17	15, 23	16
32	20, 5, 8	4, 5	18	12	5	17	15	15	16
33	17, 20	——	17	12	——	15	15	15	16
34	20	——	18	12	——	17	15	15	16
35	20	——	18	12	——	17	15	15	16

TEXTS INCLUDED IN CROSS-REFERENCE MATRIX

1. James R. McGuigan and R. Charles Moyer, *Managerial Economics*, 2nd edition (St. Paul, Minn.: West Publishing Co., 1979)

2. Eugene F. Brigham and James L. Pappas, *Managerial Economics*, 2nd edition (Hinsdale, Ill.: Dryden Press, 1976).

3. Richard H. Leftwich, *The Price System and Resource Allocation*, 6th edition (Hinsdale, Ill.: Dryden Press, 1976).

4. W. Warren Haynes and William R. Henry, *Managerial Economics: Analysis and Cases*, 3rd edition (Dallas, Tex.: Business Publications, Inc., 1974).

5. Milton H. Spencer, K. K. Seo, and Mark G. Simkin, *Managerial Economics*, 4th edition (Homewood, Ill.: Irwin, 1975).

6. Jack Hirshleifer, *Price Theory and Applications* (Englewood Cliffs, N.J.: Prentice-Hall, 1976).

7. Edwin Mansfield, *Micro Economics: Theory and Applications*, 2nd edition (New York: Norton, 1975).

8. Donald S. Watson, *Price Theory and Its Uses*, 4th edition (Boston: Houghton-Mifflin, 1976).

9. C. E. Ferguson and J. P. Gould, *Microeconomic Theory*, 4th edition (Homewood, Ill.: Irwin, 1975).

PREFACE

This book provides a series of readings, cases, and exercises to be used in conjunction with a course in managerial economics, applied microeconomics, or intermediate microeconomic theory. The ultimate test of the economic discipline is the extent to which its analytical tools and theoretical models can be applied to real-world economic problems. Our objective in this book is to illustrate the breadth of problem areas to which economic analysis can be fruitfully applied.

This book is unique among supplementary text materials in that it combines readings, cases, and exercises into one integrated package. The readings that we have selected, we feel, clearly illustrate applications of economic theory and tools of managerial economics. We have attempted to keep the level of sophistication of mathematics and statistics on a plane consistent with the background of most students who are taking courses in managerial economics or intermediate microeconomic theory; i.e., only elementary statistics (including OLS regression) and some basic calculus are used in the selected articles. In addition to illustrating the applicability of economic tools and theory, the chosen readings also introduce students to the type of materials that may be found in the better economic and financial academic journals.

The cases presented give students an opportunity to apply their newly acquired tools and theoretical models directly to real-world problems. Similarly, the problems and exercises provide for further student interaction and application of skills. This combination of cases and exercises, in addition to the readings, should be an attractive supplement to those who use case and problem-oriented books as a primary text.

Part One of the book discusses the scope and methodology of managerial economics in an insightful article by Baumol. In addition, goals and objectives of an organization are discussed in the Lewellen and Huntsman article, and illustrated in the Maritime Administration case.

Part Two deals with private-sector decision making. The general areas of demand and forecasting, production and cost, pricing, and capital budgeting are illustrated in a series of readings, cases, and exercises.

Part Three focuses on social and regulatory constraints on business. Through the use of cases and readings, issues dealing with regulation, market structure- conduct-performance, and social responsibility are examined.

Part Four looks at decision making in the public sector. Readings and cases are provided to show the applicability of economic tools to solving problems of cost-benefit analysis, externalities, and income distribution.

To assist students and teachers in choosing appropriate readings, cases, and exercises, a cross-reference matrix is provided, which shows the relationship between the materials in this book and specific chapters in leading managerial economics and intermediate microeconomics textbooks.

We wish to thank the authors and publishers of the articles for their permission to reprint them in this volume. Similarly, for those cases not prepared exclusively by us, we thank the authors for their permission to use the material. We also wish to acknowledge the assistance of our students and colleagues who made many helpful suggestions with respect to our ultimate choice of readings. Finally, we are most appreciative of our students who provided useful feedback on the cases and exercises as they were being developed.

ACKNOWLEDGMENTS

William J. Baumol, "What Can Economic Theory Contribute to Managerial Economics," *American Economic Review* (May, 1961), reprinted with permission of the American Economic Association and the author.

Wilbur G. Lewellen and Blaine Huntsman, "Managerial Pay and Performance," *American Economic Review* (September, 1970), reprinted with permission of the American Economic Association and the authors.

Thomas F. Hogarty and Kenneth G. Elzinga, "The Demand for Beer," *Review of Economics and Statistics* (May, 1972), reprinted with permission of North Holland Publishing Co. and the authors.

John Riew, "Economies of Scale in High School Operation," *Review of Economics and Statistics* (August, 1966), reprinted with permission of North Holland Publishing Co. and the author.

Haim Barkai and David Levhari, "The Impact of Experience on Kibbutz Farming," *Review of Economics and Statistics* (February, 1973), reprinted with permission of North Holland Publishing Co. and the authors.

Robert E. Kohn, "Price Elasticities of Demand and Air Pollution Control," *Review of Economics and Statistics* (November, 1972), reprinted with permission of North Holland Publishing Co. and the author.

Geoffrey H. Moore, "The Analysis of Economic Indicators," *Scientific American* (January, 1975), reprinted with permission. Copyright 1974 by Scientific American, Inc. All rights reserved.

J. Fred Weston, "Pricing Behavior of Large Firms," *Western Economic Journal* (March, 1972), reprinted with permission of the Western Economic Association and the author.

Thomas D. Hopkins, "Higher Education Enrollment Demand," *Economic Inquiry* (March, 1974), reprinted with permission of the Western Economic Association and the author.

William A. Longbrake, "Statistical Cost Analysis," *Financial Management* (Spring, 1973), reprinted with permission of the Financial Management Association and the author.

J. Fred Weston, "Investment Decisions Using the Capital Asset Pricing Model," *Financial Management* (Spring, 1973), reprinted with permission of the Financial Management Association and the author.

Joseph P. Newhouse, "A Model of Physician Pricing," *Southern Economic Journal* (October, 1970), reprinted with permission of the Southern Economic Association.

Donald R. Fraser and Peter S. Rose, "Bank Entry and Bank Performance," *Journal of Finance* (March, 1972), reprinted with permission of the American Finance Association and the authors.

Uwe E. Reinhardt, "Break-Even Analysis for Lockheed's Tri Star: An Application of Financial Theory," *Journal of Finance* (September, 1973), reprinted with permission of the American Finance Association and the author.

George J. Stigler, "The Theory of Economic Regulation," *Bell Journal of Economics and Management Science* (Spring, 1971). Copyright 1971, The American Telephone and Telegraph Co., 195 Broadway, New York, New York 10007. Reprinted with permission.

Walter I. Garms, "A Benefit-Cost Analysis of the Upward Bound Program," *Journal of Human Resources*, vol. 6, no. 2 (1971). Copyright 1971 by the Regents of the University of Wisconsin. Reprinted with permission of the University of Wisconsin Press and the author.

W. Lee Hansen and Burton A. Weisbrod, "The Distribution of Costs and Direct Benefits of Public Higher Education: The Case of California," *Journal of Human Resources*, Vol. 4, no. 2 (1969). Copyright 1969 by the Regents of the University of Wisconsin. Reprinted with permission of the University of Wisconsin Press and the authors. This article is an extension of material used in their book, *Benefits, Costs and Finance of Public Higher Education* (Chicago: Markham, 1969).

Thomas Peterson, "Cost-Benefit Analysis for Evaluating Transportation Proposals: Los Angeles Case Study," *Land Economics*, Vol. LI, No. 1 (1975). Copyright 1975 by the Regents of the University of Wisconsin. Reprinted with permission of the University of Wisconsin Press and the author.

Thomas M. Tole, "Case of the Alabama Power Company," reprinted with permission of the author.

J. Daniel Williams and George W. Trivoli, "General Medical Center"; reprinted with permission of the authors.

Bruce T. Allen, "Why Does Gasoline Cost More in Charlevoix Than It Does in Detroit?" *Michigan State Economic Record*, Vol. 14, No. 6 (November-December, 1972); reprinted with permission of the author and Michigan State University Bureau of Business and Economic Research.

Part One Introduction

Chapter 1 Scope and Methodology of Managerial Economics

READING

1 WHAT CAN ECONOMIC THEORY CONTRIBUTE TO MANAGERIAL ECONOMICS?

William J. Baumol
PRINCETON UNIVERSITY

What to me is one of the most significant aspects of economic theory for management science was brought out very clearly in a talk I had some time ago with a biologist friend of mine. This biologist is an eminent authority on clock mechanisms in animals. There is a remarkable and well-known periodicity in the behavior of a large variety of animal species—in fact, probably among all of them. To illustrate the point, the emergence of adult fruit flies from their pupae usually occurs shortly after dawn. Even if the flies are placed in a darkened room whose temperature, humidity, and other evidences of passage of time are carefully controlled, they will continue to emerge from the pupae at just about the same time day after day. However, if after being kept under these controlled laboratory conditions they are suddenly shown some light in order to produce the effect of a false dawn, there is a permanent shift of phase and, after some transient behavior, they will change the time at which they emerge from the pupae to that corresponding to the dawn which they were last shown. This suggests that there is a very definite way in which these animals can tell the time; that is to say, in which they can recognize when twenty-four hours are over, even though there is nothing conscious about it.

Of course a clock mechanism suggests periodicity, and periodicity, to any good cycle theorist, suggests difference or differential equations. And in fact, after this biologist had been working on the subject for some time, he became aware of this possibility and set out to find a mathematician who could help him to determine an appropriate equation. This was done, a relationship was fitted by statistical methods, and it turned out that it was appropriate to use a nonlinear differential equation. It was found that one such equation could fit a great variety of the data which this man had available. Not only could it do that, but with the aid of the equation he was able to make a number of interesting predictions which were subsequently very closely confirmed by data which he was able to collect.

Here is where we come to the point of the story—the contrast between the situation of the biologist and that of the economic theorist—for the biologist who had obtained a very nice relationship on the basis of empirical data was totally unable to give any sort of analytical ex-

Introduction

planation of what he had. He had absolutely no model on which he could base a derivation of his mathematical relationship. We may, perhaps, generalize by remarking that biologists, with some notable exceptions, have data without models, whereas we in economic theory have models which usually are created without data. And in this way we have summarized one of the economic theorist's greatest weaknesses and one of his greatest strengths.

I would now like to emphasize the latter, the more pleasant, side: the fact that the economist is an expert model builder. Indeed, there are very few disciplines which produce model builders with such practice and such skill. This, I think, is one of the most important things which the economic theorist can contribute to the work of management science. In management science it is important—in fact, absolutely essential—to be able to recognize the structure of a managerial problem. In order to be able to analyze it at all and to be able to do so systematically, it is necessary to do several things: first of all, to undertake a judicious simplification—an elimination of minor details which are peripheral to the problem and which, if included in the model, would prevent any successful and systematic analysis. Second, it is important to capture in a formal statement the essence of all the interrelationships which characterize the situation, because it is only after stating these interrelationships so explicitly that we can hope to use the powerful techniques of rigorous analysis in the investigation of a managerial problem. It is the model which incorporates both these features; it is the central focus of the entire analysis which must capture the essence of the situation which is being investigated.

Thus, in any of the complex situations which are encountered in the systematic analysis of management problems, model building is a critical part of the investigation. Problems as diverse as the optimal size and composition of a department store product line or the location of a company's warehouses have one thing in common: their complexity—which arises to a large extent out of the network of interrelationships among their elements. An increase in the number of items carried in a store reduces the capacity for carrying stocks of other items: on the one hand it makes it more likely that the customer will find what she wants when she enters the store; on the other she may find more often that although the store usually carries what she desires, it happens to be out of it temporarily. The length of time a customer must search for an item is affected by a change in product line; the likelihood of "impulse" purchases is also affected, etc. The drawing together of such a diversity of strands is the major function of the model, without which most of our tools will not function. Moreover, in my experience it is not atypical that nearly half of the time spent in the investigation of such a problem is devoted to model building—to capturing the essence of the situation in a set of explicit relationships. For there are no cut and dried rules in model building. It is essentially a matter of discovery, involving all of the intangibles of discovery—hunch, insight, and intuition, and no holds are barred. Only after the model has been built can the problem sometimes be reduced to a routine by use of standard rules of calculation.

To my knowledge there are few classroom courses in this critical skill of model building, and, because it has no rules, it cannot be taught like trigonometry or chemistry. But apparently it can be learned by experience. And, as I have said, the economic theorist has had a great deal of experience in the construction and use of such models. When he employs some differential equations, you can almost be certain that he has derived them from a model which he built, not, like the biologist, from some data which he has collected.

This, then, is one of the major contributions which the economic theorist can, in my opinion, make to managerial analysis. It is, however, a skill and a predisposition that he brings with him, not a series of specific results.

This takes me to the second major point that I wish to make: the other way in which I think economic theory can be helpful to management science. I believe the most important thing a managerial economics student can get out of a course in economic analysis is not a series of theorems but rather a set of analytical methods. And for that reason I think it is far more important for him to learn the basis of these theorems, their assumption and their methods of derivation, than to end up with a group of conclusions. I can say quite categorically that I have never encountered a business problem in which my investigation was helped by any specific economic theorem, nor, may I add, have I ever met a practical problem in which I failed to be helped by the method of reasoning involved in the derivation of some economic theorem.

One of the major reasons that the propositions of economic theory are not directly applicable to management problems is that the theory does not deal with the major concerns of the businessman. Product line, advertising, budgeting, sales force allocation, inventory levels, new product introduction are all relative strangers to the idealized firm of value theory whose major concern is price-output policy. Certainly there is little in the theoretical literature which refers directly to the warehouse location or the department store product line problems which were mentioned previously.

Even where more familiar theoretical matters, such as pricing problems, arise in practice, the results of the theory provide only limited help. This is because theorems in economic analysis deal with rather general abstract entities, with firms which have the peculiar and most interesting characteristics of actual companies eliminated from them in order to enable the analyst to draw conclusions which apply to the entire economy and not just to one or several particular firms. As a result, when attempting to apply these theorems, one finds that they have abstracted some of the features it is most essential to retain in order to analyze the specific situation with which one is faced in the market. The theory offers us fairly general admonitions, like the one which tells us that marginal cost must equal marginal revenue if we are to maximize profits—surely a statement which is not very much of a guide in application. I repeat that in my applied work I have never found any occasion to use either this theorem or any other such specific proposition of economic analysis.

But I have often found it absolutely essential to use the techniques of marginal analysis as it occurs in the theory of the firm, the theory of production, and in welfare economics. Several times I have even found it helpful to use the techniques and derivations of some of the elasticity theorems. This last illustration perhaps merits a little expansion. It may appear extraordinary that the elasticity theorems were of any use in application at all for they would seem to provide the ultimate illustration of tools whose use requires the availability of exten-

Introduction

sive data. However, the point I am making is that it was not the theorems but the methods of analysis and derivation which were employed. For example, an analogue of the elementary proposition that unit elasticity is the borderline between increasing and decreasing total revenue in response to a decrease in price can be applied in other situations. In fact, it is precisely because of the lack of data that it often becomes necessary to decide just where such break-even points occur, and in a number of cases I have found that the ability to prove that this critical point is sufficiently beyond what may reasonably be expected is an adequate substitute for the availability of data. Thus knowledge of the method of derivation of the theorems—and, indeed, of the spirit of the theorems themselves—often enables one to do things without data which otherwise would be pretty much out of the question.

But this is not the major point. If it is true—and it certainly has been true in my experience—that every firm and every managerial situation requires a model which is more or less unique, none of the standard theorems is going to fit in with it. It will be necessary, in effect, to derive special theorems which enable one to deal with that specific situation. Here one is helped, then, not by the generalized propositions which have been developed by the theorist, but by the methods which have enabled him to achieve his results which show us how analogous conclusions or analogous analyses can be conducted for the problems at hand. It is for this reason that I make my plea about the teaching of economics and economic theory to the managerial economist. This plea is not only that economic theory should be taught to the business student but that it should be presented to him pretty much as it is taught to the liberal arts student, with the emphasis not on a series of canned conclusions but on the methods of investigation on the derivations behind the results—on the analytic tools and methods.

There is a third way in which economic theory can help in managerial analysis—and, perhaps strangely, here the more elementary concepts of economics are primarily involved or, rather, concepts which though relatively sophisticated are used in a very elementary way. These elementary concepts can imbue the economist with habits of thought which enable him to avoid some significant pitfalls. For example, consider the case of external economies and diseconomies. How much can familiarity with this concept tell us about the dangers involved in directing one branch of an enterprise to maximize its profits in disregard of the effects of its actions on other parts of the firm! Similarly, we economists are made very sensitive by marginal analysis to the perils of resource allocation by average cost and profit—resource allocation rules of thumb which are so frequently encountered in business practice. Such bits of reasoning once led one of my colleagues, who was reviewing some of the cases cited in the literature of managerial analysis, to remark that he was amazed at how often this reading had forced him to recall his sophomore economics!

To summarize, then, I have suggested very little by way of concrete contribution from economic theory to managerial economics. With some exceptions, I have not said that this particular result or that particular body of discussion is essential or even particularly helpful for the managerial economist. I have been able to offer no illustrations of managerial problems in which I was able to use very specific pieces of the body of economic analysis. But this is right in line with the very nature

Scope and Methodology of Managerial Economics

of my major point: the assertion that a managerial economist can become a far more helpful member of a management group by virtue of his studies of economic analysis, primarily because there he learns to become an effective model builder and because there he acquires a very rich body of tools and techniques which can help him to deal with the problems of the firm in a far more rigorous, a far more probing, and a far deeper manner.

Chapter 2 Goals and Objectives of the Organization

READING
2   MANAGERIAL PAY AND CORPORATE PERFORMANCE

Wilbur G. Lewellen and Blaine Huntsman[*]

At the core of most economic analyses of industrial behavior is the proposition that the managers of an enterprise guide its activities in such a way as to maximize the monetary well-being of its owners. The theory of the firm in its conventional form depends heavily on this presumption, and the alleged allocative efficiency of the private enterprise system is founded on its implications. Corporations can, of course, simultaneously pursue a variety of goals, with different top management groups placing differing degrees of importance on a range of alternative objectives. If, however, it should turn out that profit-related goals are consistently subordinated, the relevance of much of our received economic doctrine would become suspect.

That doctrine notwithstanding, the possibility has been raised in recent years that goals other than maximization of profits or share prices may well govern managerial behavior. The dissenting point of view can be traced to the descriptive arguments advanced by Adolph A. Berle and Gardiner C. Means nearly forty years ago. They asserted, in substance, that the rise of the giant corporation was increasingly serving to separate control from ownership. The natural corollary of this contention is that management is not necessarily constrained to act with the owners' welfare in mind, but can be expected instead to serve primarily its own economic self-interest. More recently, William J. Baumol (1958, 1962, 1967) has suggested that management can—and, in fact, does—cater to such self-interest by maximizing the total sales revenues of the enterprise, with profit increases being but a secondary issue. Baumol's argument is based at least in part, on the observation that executive salaries appear to be " . . . far more closely correlated with the scale of operations of the firm than with its profitability" (1967, p. 46). However, it is not clear a priori that the economic self-interests of ownership and management *can* be neatly separated. For example, most top executives have substantial stock holdings in their own firms and receive a sizeable fraction of their total compensation in the form of stock options and other stock-related pay arrangements (see Wilbur G. Lewellen 1968, 1969a).

The intent of the present paper is to examine empirically the question of whether the financial rewards reaped by high level corporate executives are more strongly influenced by company performance as measured by total corporate revenues or—alternatively—as measured by either of two standards of shareholder welfare. The results should provide a basis for drawing at least some tentative conclusions as to the ex-

---

[*] The authors are, respectively, associate professor of industrial management at Purdue University and associate professor of finance at the University of Utah. The research was supported with funds supplied by the National Bureau of Economic Research, the Purdue Research Foundation, and the Ford Foundation's grant for research in business finance to the Sloan School of Management at the Massachusetts Institute of Technology. The advice and counsel of Professors Frank Bass, George Horwich, Robert Johnson, and Edgar Pessemier of Purdue, Professor John Lintner of Harvard, and Professor Bruce Baird of Utah are gratefully acknowledged. The computations were performed at the computer centers of Purdue University and the Massachusetts Institute of Technology. Of course, the opinions and conclusions presented are solely the authors'.

pected nature of managerial behavior in the contemporary industrial environment.

We are aware that several previous empirical studies have been conducted with the same stated objective. Typically, the methodology has been to compare the respective degrees of correlation between executive compensation and firm sales on the one hand, and executive compensation and firm profits on the other. Perhaps the most thorough of these studies is that by Joseph W. McGuire, John S. Y. Chiu, and Alvar O. Elbing[1] who concluded that sales and compensation were more highly correlated than were profits and compensation, and interpreted those results as supportive of the Baumol hypothesis. The findings presented in the current paper lead to interpretations that run counter to those of McGuire, et al., and are based on tests of a multivariate regression model which is designed to reduce the effects of various statistical and measurement biases. Our findings also reflect the use here of more comprehensive indices both of executive remuneration and shareholder welfare than have been characteristic of earlier investigations.

I. *The Sample*

The very large firm is obviously the one in which the phenomenon of the separation of ownership from control—and its possible consequences in terms of managerial behavior—is likely to be most severe. For that reason, the sample examined consists of 50 firms drawn from the top of the *Fortune* magazine list of the nation's 500 largest industrials. Virtually all the firms involved would be regarded as "blue chips" in the language of the investment community, all enjoy a very wide public distribution of their common stock, and a broad spectrum of industry categories is represented.

While data on such items as company sales and profits are readily accessible in published financial statements, certain other information which is essential to the proper execution of a study of the sort undertaken here is not so easily obtained. In particular, a truly comprehensive measure of managerial remuneration requires that the worth of *all* the major constituents of the relevant pay packages be recognized, including, in addition to cash salaries and bonuses, the full range of indirect, deferred, and contingent compensation arrangements that executives enjoy. The raw material for an evaluation of these devices for senior management is publicly available only in the proxy statements which corporations must submit in conjunction with their annual shareholders' meetings. Because of variations in the manner in which firms present these data, however, and because of changes in the SEC's reporting rules over the years, it is not always possible to put together an adequate record of top executive rewards for every large company one might care to inspect.[2] As a result, it became necessary to dip down as far as the corporation ranked 94th on *Fortune*'s most recent tabulation[3] in order to assemble a sample of 50 whose executives' earnings histories could be compiled accurately for any length of time. Those 50 firms currently account for approximately one-fourth of the total sales and profits of the entire manufacturing sector. They are listed in the Appendix.

The study examines the cross-sectional relationships between executive compensation and company performance at three-year intervals, beginning with 1942 and ending with 1963. This period was chosen because the requisite figures were available on total executive remuneration from an earlier investigation of the components of managerial pay by one of the authors (Lewellen 1968). Since similar information would have been exceedingly expensive to duplicate for other periods, as shown in Section III, its existence seemed a compelling argument in favor of exploiting that resource for our present purposes. The entire time span was analyzed in order to detect any inter-temporal evolution in the underlying relationships which might have arisen from phenomena such as continuing corporate growth. The years examined also encompass an era of significant structural change in the economy, especially in the tax environment, and include the pervasive influence of several business cycles and two wars.

II. *The Model*

The major hypotheses which have been advanced to explain observed levels of senior executive compensation can be summarized in their simplest forms as follows: (i) A firm's top management is rewarded primarily on the basis of its ability to increase the profits of the enterprise; or (ii) The compensation of top executives depends upon the vol-

---

[1] Others include those of Arch Patton, David R. Roberts, and Oliver E. Williamson.

[2] A discussion of the methods of compiling the data is contained in Section III.

[3] The 1968 list was the latest one available at the time the analysis here was initiated.

Introduction

ume of sales generated by the corporation whose affairs they administer. Given the widely accepted proposition that the market value of a firm's equity at any point in time is approximately equal to the discounted worth of the future returns anticipated by actual and potential owners, (i) can be interpreted as the analogue of the share price maximization precept.

Of these hypotheses, (i) conforms with the behavioral assumptions underlying the conventional theory of the firm, while previous empirical findings (McGuire, Chiu, and Elbing, Patton, Roberts) appear to support (ii). Other possible viewpoints include the propositions that executives are rewarded according to *both* profit and sales performance, or, at the opposite extreme, that neither item is relevant. The model developed here is designed to test this range of alternatives.

The Basic Model

Abstracting, for the moment, from potential statistical and measurement problems, and in the absence of theoretical reasons to specify an alternative form of functional relationship, we may begin by postulating that a top executive's compensation is related in linear fashion to both the profits and sales of the firm he manages. The structural form of the relationship can be written:

$$(1) \quad C_{it} = a_0 + a_1 \pi_{it} + a_2 S_{it} + u_{it}$$

Where, C, π, and S represent executive compensation, corporate profits, and corporate sales, respectively, and u is a random disturbance term. Subscript i denotes the firm and subscript t the period to which the measure applies.

By supplying a basis for observing the magnitude of the coefficients a_1 and a_2 and the levels of statistical significance attaching thereto, the above specification provides a natural vehicle for inferring the relative influence of the two independent variables upon compensation, and thereby testing the alternative hypotheses. The emergence of a positive value for the constant term a_0 would imply, in effect, that executive rewards rise less than in proportion to company sales and/or profits. Thus, it seems probable that a $50 thousand difference in annual profits between two firms in the $100 million profit range would result in a smaller difference in the pay of their respective chief executives than would the same dollar profit difference in the case of two firms whose yearly earnings were in the $100 thousand range. Represented graphically, the compensation vs. profits or compensation vs. sales relationship would therefore be expected to be concave downward for a sample of enterprises differing widely in size, and the linear approximation to any segment of such an underlying relationship would necessarily include a positive intercept value. It follows, then, that a_1 and a_2 must be interpreted in marginal—although constant for the sample range—terms throughout.

Statistical Problems

Unfortunately, direct application of equation (1) to any generalized sample of cross-sectional data can be expected to encounter several possible sources of statistical bias. For one thing, the efficiency of least square estimates depends upon the variances of the disturbance terms being constant. Examination of scatter diagrams of pilot regression runs using equation (1) revealed, as anticipated, that the error terms were *not* constant but were approximately in proportion to the dependent variable. Moreover, and as one might also suspect, those firms relatively large by virtually any scale criterion were also characterized by relatively high sales and profits levels. This scale-associated linkage between the independent variables poses the threat of serious collinearity,[4] with resultant difficulties in estimating the separate influences of those variables. The regression coefficients produced by fitting data to (1) were characterized by inordinately large standard errors, suggesting that the correlation between the independent variables was indeed too high to permit the generation of reliable estimates.

An approach which attacks both these problems is the weighted regression technique.[5] Since scatter diagrams of equation (1) indicated that the error terms (u_{it} for all i)

---

[4] The high degrees of correlation between the independent variables in their natural form were indicated by the presence of simple correlation coefficients which in most cases, exceeded .9. This high degree of observed correlation is consistent with the results of a prior study by Bevars D. Mabry and David L. Siders, which employed correlation analysis to investigate the relationship between profits and sales.

[5] An alternate approach commonly used to ameliorate scale-related problems, given that there are no a priori grounds for specifying a linear vis-à-vis a multiplicative relationship, is to convert the natural values of the variables into logarithms. Results of the tests of the *log* transform of (1) were in fact characterized by somewhat lower simple correlation coefficients between *log* π_{it} and *log* S_{it}, but the scatter diagrams still suggested the presence of excessive heteroscedasticity. The *log* transform was therefore rejected as a device for testing the hypothesis.

tended to vary directly with the dependent variable, an appropriate weighting procedure is to divide each variable in (1) by any one of several scale-related deflators, provided there are acceptable grounds for expecting that the variances of the deflators bear a proportionate relationship to those of the u_{i_t}. Moreover, by creating ratios in which both numerator and denominator are associated with the firm's size, the weighted regression approach eliminates the basic reason for expecting high degrees of correlation between the variables as a consequence of a common scale factor. Following the Miller and Modigliani precedent, book value of total assets was the weighting factor chosen because the resulting deflated variables have "... natural and useful economic interpretations in their own right" (Merton H. Miller and Franco Modigliani 1966, p. 350).[6] Deflating (1) by total book assets, denoted by A, yields the following form:

$$(2) \quad \frac{C_{it}}{A_{it}} = a_0 \left(\frac{1}{A_{it}}\right) + a_1 \left(\frac{\pi_{it}}{A_{it}}\right) + a_2 \left(\frac{S_{it}}{A_{it}}\right) + u^*_{it}$$

Since the variances of the deflator selected are hypothesized to be roughly proportional to those of the u_{i_t}, the error terms in the original equation, we would expect the variances of the new error terms ($u^*_{i_t} = u_{i_t}/A_{i_t}$) to be approximately constant over the sample range. Examination of scatter diagrams indicated that the requisite least squares assumption of homoscedasticity was in fact met by (2). As to the collinearity problem, tests of the model evinced materially smaller standard errors of the coefficient estimates in addition to producing consistently high t-values in conjunction with tests of significance. Both these phenomena suggest that the deflated variables are not sufficiently collinear as to interfere with the formation of reliable coefficient estimates.[7]

---

[6] That "natural and useful interpretation" in the present context relates to the fact that equation (2) now implicitly describes a process whereby management is viewed as maximizing company sales or profits per dollar of resources employed, i.e., maximizing subject to the available resource constraint.

[7] It might be noted that the model (2) is now linear homogeneous. Accordingly, consistency in interpretation requires that it be tested with the constant term suppressed. In order to check this specification, we first ran the regression with a constant term added and found it in no case to be significantly different from zero.

III. Measurement

An empirical test of the model necessitates that meaningful measures of the separate variables be obtained. This section defines the measures chosen and discusses the rationale underlying their selection.

Executive Compensation

Previous studies seeking to determine the influence of corporate performance on executive compensation merit some skepticism in the sense that only *partial* indices of compensation, typically, cash salary plus bonus payments alone were employed (McGuire, Chiu, and Elbing, Patton, Roberts). Other forms of remuneration such as pension benefits, deferred pay, qualified profit-sharing plans, and stock options have been ignored entirely. These latter items, however, frequently result in annual after-tax increments to executives' wealth that are of magnitudes many times the concurrent salary and bonus awards.

The proper treatment of deferred and contingent elements represents a task of major proportions. Lewellen's 1968 study embodies the relevant analysis and provides comprehensive measures of total executive earnings within the sample companies. The approach employed in appraising the worth of the noncash components of managerial remuneration was to calculate, for each individual senior executive and for each year in which he appeared in his firm's proxy statements, what might be termed the "current income equivalent" of his various deferred and contingent pay schemes. This consisted of the amount of additional direct cash income he would have required from his company to be as well rewarded after taxes as he was by all the supplemental compensation arrangements he actually enjoyed. In the case of a pension plan, for example, the procedure was to determine the additional salary or bonus the executive would have needed if he were to be enabled, with those additions, to purchase for himself an individual retirement annuity from an insurance company similar in form and equal in value to the benefits promised him under his employer's retirement plan. Similar calculations were made for other fringe benefits and the aggregate worth of his entire compensation package established. The total remuneration figures used in the present study therefore represent the sum of all such estimated current income equivalents plus salary and bonus.[8]

---

[8] The relevant computations were made by matching

Introduction

As a matter of both convenience and efficiency, the compensation of the single highest-paid executive in each firm for each year is taken into account here as the dependent variable measuring the size of the firm's managerial pay package. While it may seem more appropriate that the remuneration of *all* the senior policy-making individuals in a corporation be tested for a relationship to company performance, it happens that the pay of a firm's top man is a suitable surrogate for the pay of his closest subordinates in terms of their relative standing vis-à-vis corresponding officials in other firms.[9]

For comparability with prior empirical work, the model was initially tested using only the salary and bonus receipts of the senior officer of each company as the dependent variable, and then tested again using the more comprehensive total compensation measure instead. The symbol C_{i_t} is employed below to denote the salary plus bonus, and $C_{i_t}^*$ to denote the total remuneration, of the top executive of firm i in year t.

Measurement of Profitability

The model was also subjected to two different sets of tests, each using a separate index of shareholder welfare as an independent variable. The first set incorporated a direct measure of book profits while the second employed an equity market value measure. The book profit choice is perhaps the more conventional, and provides a basis for comparing our findings with those of earlier writers. Nevertheless, some caution must be exercised in interpreting regression results which depend on such a measure.

There are statistical drawbacks associated with the use of reported profit which stem from both its determination and behavior as contrasted with the same features of the other hypothesized performance criterion—namely, corporate sales revenues. While relatively uniform bases exist for recording revenues,[10] profit measurement is conditioned by a range of accounting options which are much less uniform. The areas of depreciation policy and inventory valuation offer prominent examples. Additionally, an examination of the year-to-year changes in reported corporate profits vis-à-vis sales changes indicates that the former measure is much more sensitive to short-run economic influences than is the latter, and consequently is more volatile. Profits therefore are more apt to depart from their "true" or "normal" values when observed in any given year than are sales, giving rise to the likelihood that the profits coefficients in regression equations of the form being tested here will tend to be biased downward.[11] But, because in our tests profits proved consistently to be a more powerful explanatory variable than did sales, steps either to adjust the profit measure for accounting disparities among firms or to remove some of the random noise by various normalization procedures were not taken. If they had been, the only likely effect would be to increase further the size and, presumably, the significance of the profits coefficients. Such an effect would in no way alter the interpretation of our results.

Besides these statistical problems, the use of reported profits for any particular year as the index of corporate achievement implies that no conflict exists between short- and long-run maximization strategies by management, i.e., that there is no real trade-off between increasing the current year's net income and increasing the current value of future income. There are, however, a variety of circumstances which could lead to such a conflict. For example, a cutback in expenditures for the proper maintenance of plant and equipment can produce very favorable current profit results, but at the sacrifice of subsequent earnings because of the deterioration of physical assets. Conversely, expensed outlays for research into new product opportunities will reduce immediate reported profits but can provide the foundation for sizeable future earnings. Growth-oriented decisions, depending on the market expectations they generate, may furnish substantive

---

throughout the after-tax present value of the actual compensation arrangement being considered on the one hand, and its contrived current income equivalent on the other. For the details, see Lewellen (1968, ch. 2-6). A similar computational approach can be found in a study by Leonard R. Burgess.

[9] When the sample corporations were ranked in selected years first according to the total compensation of their top executive alone, then the total for their top three executives combined, and finally the total for their top five executives combined, the Spearman rank correlation coefficients between the three schedules were consistently on the order of .95 and were significant at the .0001 level in all instances (see Lewellen 1968, pp. 227-28).

[10] The definition employed here is the standard one of gross sales, less discounts, returns, and allowances.

[11] A well-publicized single-equation model which is characterized by two independent variables, one subject to both measurement errors and random fluctuations, is that commonly used to test the relative influence of dividends and retained earnings on share prices. For a detailed discussion of the procedures for dealing with these phenomena in the context of the dividend policy equation, see Irwin Friend and Marshall Puckett.

Goals and Objectives of the Organization

current benefits to shareholders by increasing the market value of their holdings. The recent literature of business finance is, of course, rich in its emphasis on the maximization of share prices as the correct managerial goal (see David Durand, Myron J. Gordon, Lewellen (1969 b), John Lintner, Modigliani and Miller (1958), Alexander A. Robichek and Stewart C. Myers). It was for this reason that the retests using equity market value (denoted below by V_{i_t}) in place of profits were conducted.

Measurement of Assets

As will be recalled, a measure of total book assets was introduced into the final version of the model (2) as a deflator. The asset measure used, denoted A_{i_t}, is defined net of depreciation for firm i as of the beginning of year t.

Summary of the Variable Definitions

The notation adopted, then, is as follows:

C_{i_t} = Salary plus bonus payments received by the chief executive of firm i during year t;

$C_{i_t}^*$ = Total after-tax compensation of that executive, including the equivalent value of all major deferred and contingent compensation arrangements;

π_{i_t} = Reported total after-tax profits of firm i during year t;

S_{i_t} = Total sales revenues of the firm, net of discounts, returns, and allowances;

V_{i_t} = Total market value of the firm's outstanding common stock as of the beginning of year t;

A_{i_t} = Total book value of the assets of the firm, net of depreciation, at the beginning of year t.

These measures, as formulated from the data gathered from the 50 corporations in the sample, were fitted to the model developed in the preceding section.

IV. *The Empirical Results*

Table 1 shows the results of the initial tests which were conducted using profits and sales as the measures of corporate performance. Table 2 displays the results of the retests in which equity market value was substituted for profits. Both tables are divided into two panels. The left-hand panel records the findings when salary plus bonus payments alone are adopted as the measure of chief executive compensation, while the right-hand side indicates the results when total executive pay is the dependent variable.

Profits, Sales, and Compensation

The evidence in Table 1 provides strong support for the hypothesis that top management's remuneration is heavily dependent upon the generation of profits. In particular, the signs of the coefficients of the profit measure are positive for each cross-section regardless of the compensation measure employed. Moreover, the profit variable proves highly significant for all runs in which the dependent variable consists of executive salary plus bonus payments, and for six of the eight years in the case of total compensation as the dependent variable. By contrast,

TABLE 1—REGRESSION RESULTS: PROFITS, SALES, AND COMPENSATION

	Regression Equation: $\frac{C_{i_t}}{A_i} = a_0\left(\frac{1}{A_{i_t}}\right) + a_1\left(\frac{\pi_{i_t}}{A_{i_t}}\right) + a_2\left(\frac{S_{i_t}}{A_{i_t}}\right) + u_{i_t}^*$								Regression Equation: $\frac{C_{i_t}^*}{A_{i_t}} = a_0\left(\frac{1}{A_{i_t}}\right) + a_1\left(\frac{\pi_{i_t}}{A_{i_t}}\right) + a_2\left(\frac{S_{i_t}}{A_{i_t}}\right) + u_{i_t}^*$					
Year	a_0	t	a_1	t	a_2	t	R^2	a_0	t	a_1	t	a_2	t	R^2
1942	95.3[a]	8.86	5039.5	2.35	−86.6	1.20	.806	40.1[a]	13.99	1928.1	3.37	−28.6	1.49	.912
1945	101.0	6.52	3307.2	1.98	−50.8	.81	.744	41.9	7.52	1610.8	2.68	−27.6	1.21	.798
1948	86.7	8.38	1413.9	2.48	12.6	.30	.833	73.0	9.63	447.7	1.07	6.6	.20	.830
1951	109.9	12.89	1397.0	3.04	−5.6	.20	.927	68.1	9.58	1202.9	3.14	−14.6	.65	.880
1954	129.3	9.68	1192.5	3.27	−23.1	.97	.910	85.8	4.55	1188.7	2.13	−8.7	.26	.751
1957	112.9	7.59	963.5	3.89	6.6	.40	.929	146.6	1.96	461.6	.37	30.6	.37	.439
1960	121.3	6.65	660.7	3.12	15.1	.88	.919	130.5	3.40	1181.2	2.65	1.8	.00	.761
1963	155.3	9.24	677.5	3.91	−15.6	1.08	.932	71.8	2.35	875.8	2.77	17.4	.66	.737

[a] Times 10^3. For purposes of the regression runs, executive compensation was measured in actual dollars and all other variables were measured in millions of dollars. The economic interpretation of the profit coefficient (a_1) listed for 1963—to take an example—therefore is as follows: For corporations in the size range encompassed by the sample, every $1 million differential in reported company profit was, on the average, accompanied by a $677.50 differential in the annual pre-tax salary and bonus earnings of the firm's chief executive.

Introduction

the sales measure is in no instance statistically significant, and the sales coefficients are approximately equally divided among years with respect to sign.

In view of the previously cited findings of earlier studies (see McGuire, Chiu, and Elbing, Roberts) in which the compensation measure adopted was essentially the same as our C_{i_t} (top executive salary plus bonus), we were more than mildly surprised at the apparent strong influence of π_{i_t} on C_{i_t} here, as well as at the accompanying lack of any statistically significant relationship between C_{i_t} and S_{i_t} (the left-hand panel of Table 1).[12] Those earlier studies had led us to anticipate an initially weak relationship between profits and remuneration—or perhaps none at all—and, in addition, to expect that corporate sales would show up as the variable more strongly influencing managerial rewards. In other words, we were prepared to find that our first attempts would at best provide a basis for comparing the results of subsequent runs using more highly developed measures of the relevant variables, and that any major insights would stem from the introduction of such improved measures.

It is not likely that differences in either the sample bases tested or the time periods examined can account for the substantive differences between the findings presented here and those of Roberts and of McGuire, Chiu, and Elbing. All three samples were drawn from the nation's largest industrial firms, and the time span covered in the current study encompasses the years tested in both of the previous investigations. A more plausible explanation lies in the fact that the tests here were conducted within the framework of a more completely developed multivariate model designed to cope with the serious statistical problems discussed in Section II.

A second unexpected feature of the test results was the lack of improvement in fit upon substitution of total executive compensation for salary plus bonus as the dependent variable (right-hand panel of Table 1). Rather, both the levels of statistical significance associated with profits and the coefficients of multiple correlation *diminished* slightly for most years when C_{i_t} was replaced by $C_{i_t}^*$. There are at least two possible explanations for this phenomenon: (i) The performance of the model using the partial compensation measure, C_{i_t}, was substantially better than anticipated, leaving relatively little room for improvement; (ii) A sizeable proportion of $C_{i_t}^*$, especially in the later years tested, is attributable to compensation arrangements whose values depend importantly on short-term fluctuations in employer-company share prices—stock options, for example. Because these short-term fluctuations reflect a host of random influences, the total compensation figures embody a considerable "noise" component.[13]

The general pattern of changes in both sets of results over time highlights an additional point. Looking again at the left-hand panel of Table 1, it can be seen that the *size* of the profit coefficients shows a marked year-to-year decrease for seven of the eight periods tested (a_1 shows a very slight increase between 1960 and 1963). Similarly, in the right-hand panel, excluding the only two runs for which the profit variable is not statistically significant (1948 and 1957), a corresponding secular decline is evident. Since the companies in the sample have grown over time, the simultaneously decreasing size of the profit coefficients supports our earlier expectation that the compensation vs. profits relationship is concave downward. The increasing values of a_0 displayed in the Table reflect the same phenomenon.

To summarize: the results shown in Table 1 indicate that equations utilizing salary plus bonus payments alone as a measure of executive remuneration yield slightly better regression fits than do those employing total compensation. But regardless of which compensation measure is adopted, reported company profits appear to have a strong and persistent influence on executive rewards, whereas sales seem to have little, if any, such impact.

Market Values, Sales, and Compensation

Because of the possible conceptual and measurement difficulties that are associated with annual book profit as a direct index of shareholder welfare, the model was retested using the alternative measure discussed in

---

[12] We were also surprised—especially in the light of the scaled nature of our model—at the rather high degree of explanatory power it displayed. The coefficients of multiple correlation exceeded .9 for the five most recent years tested, and were nowhere lower than .737.

[13] In the early years shown, the bulk of senior executive compensation consisted of salary and bonus payments. Consequently, for these early years the results of the tests employing $C_{i_t}^*$ do not differ materially from those in which C_{i_t} is the dependent variable. However, as the disparity between the partial and total compensation measures widens over time, i.e., as rewards other than salary and bonus become progressively more important in the total pay package, the regression results also diverge. For a discussion of the indicated shift in emphasis within the managerial compensation package, see Lewellen (1968).

Goals and Objectives of the Organization

TABLE 2—REGRESSION RESULTS: MARKET VALUES, SALES, AND COMPENSATION

| | Regression Equation: $\frac{C_{i_t}}{A_{i_t}} = a_0\left(\frac{1}{A_{i_t}}\right) + a_1\left(\frac{V_{i_t}}{A_{i_t}}\right) + a_2\left(\frac{S_{i_t}}{A_{i_t}}\right) + u^*_{i_t}$ ||||||| Regression Equation: $\frac{C^*_{i_t}}{A_{i_t}} = a_0\left(\frac{1}{A_{i_t}}\right) + a_1\left(\frac{V_{i_t}}{A_{i_t}}\right) + a_2\left(\frac{S_{i_t}}{A_{i_t}}\right) + u^*_{i_t}$ |||||||
Year	a_0	t	a_1	t	a_2	t	R^2	a_0	t	a_1	t	a_2	t	R^2
1942	98.0[a]	9.72	339.2	2.82	−25.3	.48	.815	41.5[a]	15.08	109.9	3.35	− 1.5	.10	.912
1945	98.9	6.63	263.9	2.78	−33.5	.63	.762	41.8	7.61	103.3	2.95	−13.6	.70	.803
1948	86.9	8.75	239.9	3.25	9.0	.24	.846	73.3	9.66	51.9	.92	12.9	.45	.829
1951	111.1	12.81	105.3	2.73	14.1	.58	.925	69.1	9.35	78.1	2.37	6.8	.33	.870
1954	128.6	9.78	101.0	3.55	− 4.3	.22	.913	85.2	4.49	88.6	2.16	13.6	.47	.748
1957	118.8	7.63	39.8	3.13	19.4	1.20	.922	148.7	2.01	26.6	.44	33.5	.44	.440
1960	126.7	6.99	23.5	3.07	17.7	1.05	.919	138.1	3.93	59.7	4.03	− 4.4	.14	.796
1963	160.1	9.68	28.9	4.12	−10.1	.74	.934	78.3	2.72	45.6	3.73	19.1	.81	.766

[a] Times 10^3. Again for these runs, compensation was measured in dollars, and all other variables in millions of dollars. As indicated in connection with Table 1, the economic interpretation of the market value coefficient for, say, 1963 in the left-hand panel would take the following form: For companies in the relevant size range, a differential of $1 million in the firm's total equity market value was accompanied by a $28.90 differential in the annual pre-tax salary plus bonus enjoyed by its top executive.

Section III, the total market value of the firm's outstanding common stock. This measure was chosen because it presumably incorporates the investing public's evaluation of future as well as current returns to owners, and also avoids the potential statistical problems that arise from differences in accounting procedures among firms.

The results of the retests are set forth in Table 2 and parallel those of the initial tests in virtually all relevant respects, with market value now appearing to be a major factor in the determination of compensation levels. Specifically, the coefficients of the market value variable have positive signs for all cross-sections no matter which measure of compensation serves as the dependent variable. In addition, the market value measure proves highly significant for all eight years when salary plus bonus is the dependent variable, and for six of the eight years when the performance measures are regressed against total compensation. Again, the sales variable is statistically insignificant in all cases and the sales coefficients vary in sign.

The total explanatory power of the equations containing equity market value as a control variable roughly matched that of the corresponding equations in which book profit was employed. The historical pattern of the retest results is also similar to that of the initial tests in that the secularly declining size of the market value coefficients and the secularly increasing a_0 values suggest downward concavity in the underlying relationship. Thus, the substitution of equity market value for profits in the equations has no material impact on either the nature or the interpretation of the findings.

V. Summary and Conclusions

The question of whether a corporation's profitability or its sales revenue has the stronger influence on the rewards of its senior officers has been examined here by means of a multivariate analysis. The underlying issue is that of the personal payoff to the professional manager for pursuing operating objectives that enhance the monetary well-being of shareholders. Because the results of the study persistently indicate that both reported profits and equity market values are substantially more important in the determination of executive compensation than are sales—indeed, sales seem to be quite irrelevant—the clear inference is that there is a greater incentive for management to shape its decision rules in a manner consonant with shareholder interests than to seek the alternative goal of revenue maximization. The evidence presented therefore can be interpreted as support for the notion that a highly-industrialized economy characterized by a diverse set of suppliers of capital, sizeable aggregations of productive resources, and a professional managerial class can in large measure still be analyzed by models which are based on the assumption of profit-seeking behavior.

APPENDIX

Companies in the Sample

Allied Chemical
American Can
American Cyanamid
American Metal Climax
American Tobacco

Introduction

Anaconda
Bendix
Bethlehem Steel
Boeing
Borden
Caterpillar Tractor
Cities Service
Continental Can
Continental Oil
Douglas Aircraft
Dow Chemical
DuPont
Eastman Kodak
Firestone Tire
General Electric
General Foods
General Motors
General Tire
B.F. Goodrich
Goodyear Tire
Gulf Oil
Inland Steel
IBM
International Harvester
International Paper
IT&T
Jones and Laughlin Steel
Lockheed Aircraft
National Dairy Products
North American Aviation
Phillips Petroleum
Procter & Gamble
RCA
Republic Steel
Reynolds Tobacco
Shell Oil
Sinclair Oil
Standard Oil (Indiana)
Swift
Texaco
Tidewater Oil
United Aircraft
U.S. Rubber
U.S. Steel
Westinghouse Electric

REFERENCES

W. J. Baumol, "On the Theory of Oligopoly," *Economica*, Aug. 1958, *25*, 187–98.
———, "On the Theory of Expansion of the Firm," *Amer. Econ. Rev.*, Dec. 1962, *52*, 1078–87.
———, *Business Behavior, Value, and Growth*, rev. ed., New York 1967.
A. A. Berle and G. C. Means, *The Modern Corporation and Private Property*, New York 1934.
L. R. Burgess, *Top Executive Pay Package*, New York 1963.
D. Durand, "Costs of Debt and Equity Funds for Business: Trends and Problems of Measurement," *Conference on Research in Business Finance*, New York 1952, 215–47.
I. Friend and M. Puckett, "Dividends and Stock Prices," *Amer. Econ. Rev.*, Sept. 1964, *54*, 656–82.
M. J. Gordon, *The Investment, Financing, and Valuation of the Corporation*, Homewood 1962.
W. G. Lewellen, *Executive Compensation in Large Industrial Corporations*, New York 1968.
———, 1969a, *The Cost of Capital*, Belmont, Calif. 1969.
———, 1969b, "Management and Ownership in the Large Firm," *J. Finance*, May 1969, *24*, 299–322.
J. Lintner, "The Valuation of Risk Assets and the Selection of Risky Investments in Stock Portfolios and Capital Budgets," *Rev. Econ. Statist.*, Feb. 1965, *47*, 13–37.
B. D. Mabry and D. L. Siders, "An Empirical Test of the Sales Maximization Hypothesis," *Southern Econ. J.*, Jan. 1967, *33*, 367–77.
J. W. McGuire, J. S. Y. Chiu, and A. O. Elbing, "Executive Incomes, Sales, and Profits," *Amer. Econ. Rev.*, Sept. 1962, *52*, 753–61.
M. H. Miller and F. Modigliani, "Some Estimates of the Cost of Capital to the Electric Utility Industry," *Amer. Econ. Rev.*, June 1966, *56*, 333–91.
F. Modigliani and M. H. Miller, "The Cost of Capital, Corporation Finance, and the Theory of Investment," *Amer. Econ. Rev.*, June 1958, *48*, 261–97.
A. Patton, *Men, Money, and Motivation*, New York 1961.
D. R. Roberts, *Executive Compensation*, Glencoe, Ill., 1959.
A. A. Robichek and S. C. Myers, *Optimal Financing Decisions*, Englewood Cliffs 1965.
O. E. Williamson, *The Economics of Discretionary Behavior*, Englewood Cliffs 1964.
Fortune, "The Fortune Directory of the 500 Largest U.S. Industrial Corporations," June 1968, *77*, 186–204.

CASE 3 SETTING OBJECTIVES AT THE MARITIME ADMINISTRATION*

BACKGROUND

The Merchant Marine Act, 1936 Prior to 1936, several attempts had been made to assist merchant shipping through mail contracts and construction loans. However, in 1936, a new law known as the Merchant Marine Act, 1936, declared that the national policy would be to foster the development and to encourage the maintenance of a merchant marine fleet sufficient to carry the domestic waterborne commerce of the U.S. and a substantial portion of the foreign commerce of the country in essential trades, as well as being capable of serving as a naval and military auxiliary in time of war. The merchant marine fleet would be owned and operated insofar as practicable by citizens of the United States, and composed of the best equipped, safest, and most suitable types of vessels constructed in the United States, as well as being manned by a trained and efficient citizen personnel.

To obtain such a fleet, the Act provided for construction and operating subsidies to be paid by the government to shipping lines. These subsidies were designed to equalize the differences between the cost of building and operating ships under the American flag and the much lower costs under foreign flags.

The New Maritime Program On October 23, 1969, a Presidential Message was transmitted to Congress outlining programs to revitalize the U.S. maritime industry. The message resulted in the Merchant Marine Act of 1970—the most important and far-reaching maritime legislation since 1936. The Act marked a turning point for the U.S. merchant marine fleet after a long period of steady decline and has received the enthusiastic support of both management and labor.

The 1970 Act, which received almost unanimous approval from Congress, incorporates all the major maritime recommendations made to Congress. It is designed to redirect U.S. policies to deal effectively with problems that afflict the operation and building of American ships. An innovative ship construction program designed to restore the United States to a first class maritime nation is the core of the legislation.

The New Maritime Program is intended to reverse the steady erosion of the nation's maritime strength. In 1950, the fleet of U.S.-flag-carrying vessels consisted of 1,145 modern vessels, and by 1971 the active fleet numbered under 700 vessels, with two-thirds at or near 25 years of age. These older vessels will become scrap candidates within several years because old age reduces the fleet's competitive edge. U.S.-flagship participation in carriage of U.S. foreign commerce fell from 42 percent in 1950 to 5.6 percent by 1971 (See Table 1).

The purpose of the new program is to produce a modern, efficient fleet that will be built in the U.S. and operated with U.S. personnel, but with far less dependence on Federal financial support than in the past. The Presidential message to Congress stated:

> Our program is one of challenge and opportunity. We will challenge the American shipbuilding industry to show that it can rebuild our Merchant Marine at reasonable expense. We will challenge American ship operators and seamen to move toward less dependence on government subsidy. And, through a substantially revised and better administered government program, we will create the opportunity to meet the challenge.

There are two major thrusts of the new program. The first one is to develop an American Merchant Marine fleet that is capable of carrying a substantial portion of this nation's international trade and providing support in times of national emergency. The second one is to improve competitiveness and productivity of U.S. shipping and shipbuilding industries through application of advanced technology, innovative management and aggressive shipping programs. By assuring firm governmental support, the program seeks to provide for the maritime industry's growth and stability.

---

*This case was developed by R. Charles Moyer and adapted from: Robert J. Blackwell, *Current Status and Future Requirements of the U.S. Maritime Program* (December, 1972; U.S. Maritime Administration); *Review of the Maritime Subsidy Program* (December, 1972; U.S. Maritime Administration); and R. Charles Moyer and Harold Handerson, "A Critique of the Rationales for Present U.S. Maritime Programs," *Transportation Journal* (Winter, 1974).

Introduction

Table 1   U.S. Flag Carriage of U.S. Trade

Percent of Total

	1969 Total	1969 Export	1969 Import	1970 Total	1970 Export	1970 Import	1971 Total	1971 Export	1971 Import
Liner	22.6	22.3	23.0	23.5	23.6	23.2	21.0	21.8	20.3
Nonliner	2.1	3.1	0.7	2.2	2.5	1.8	2.2	3.1	.9
Tanker	3.2	9.9	2.5	4.4	10.2	3.8	4.9	11.0	4.4
Percent of Total Tons	4.5	6.5	3.3	5.3	16.4	4.6	5.6	6.7	4.6

U.S. Flag Tonnage (thousands of long tons)

	1969 Total	1969 Export	1969 Import	1970 Total	1970 Export	1970 Import	1971 Total	1971 Export	1971 Import
Liner	9,271	5,041	4,230	11,817	6,905	4,912	10,259	5,419	4,840
Nonliner	4,371	3,709	662	5,364	3,664	1,700	4,700	3,862	838
Tanker	5,486	1,481	4,005	8,049	1,797	6,252	9,388	1,615	7,773
Total Tons	19,128	10,231	8,897	25,230	12,366	12,864	24,347	10,896	13,451

The Merchant Marine Act of 1970 The program developed under The Merchant Marine Act of 1970 provides an extensive array of subsidies and other support to virtually every sector of the maritime industry. The shipbuilding sector receives direct construction differential subsidies (CDS) designed to equalize the U.S. cost to buyers with foreign construction costs. In addition, under provisions of the Jones Act of 1920, no waterborne domestic cargo of the U.S. may be transported on any vessel other than one that is U.S. constructed, owned and operated. This provision of the Jones Act guarantees to U.S. shipyards the entire market for ships used in domestic commerce. The Maritime Administration (MarAd) also undertakes a sizeable research and development program that is designed to provide indirect technological assistance to U.S. yards. Shipowners and operators may receive operating differential subsidy (ODS) that compensates them for the higher costs of American crews, maintenance, insurance, and so on. In addition, government loan guarantees under Title XI of the 1970 Act may be secured for up to 87.5 percent of the required financing for a new ship. These guarantees result in significant savings in the financing of a ship that may cost in excess of $100 million.

Taxes on income generated from shipping may be deferred, sometimes indefinitely under the Capital Construction Fund (CCF) provision of the Merchant Marine Act of 1970. A wide range of cargo preference laws provide further assistance by generally requiring: (1) that all military cargo be shipped aboard U.S. bottoms; (2) that agricultural exports (or at least a large percentage of them) be moved on U.S. flagships; (3) that other U.S. export cargo get preferential treatment; and (4) that all domestic coastwise trade be aboard U.S. built, owned and operated ships. While this enumeration of government programs supporting the U.S. merchant marine is not exhaustive, it does outline the major types of available assistance.

Prior to 1970, the major emphasis of MarAd programs was on providing support to scheduled liner operators carrying general cargo (and increasingly containerized cargo) on trade routes determined by MarAd to be essential to U.S. interests. The 1970 Act made it possible for the first time to provide CDS and ODS to tankers and other bulk carriers operating in the foreign commerce of the U.S. Thus, emphasis has shifted sharply within the Maritime Administration away from general cargo trade to the bulk trade. As can be seen below, most new CDS funds have been going to support the construction of oil tankers, many in the very large crude carrier category (VLCCs), combination oil, bulk, and ore carriers (OBOs) and liquid natural gas carriers (LNGs). Similarly, the government backed Title XI loan guarantees have also been heavily concentrated in the energy-carrying ship category. The extent of this policy change is further evidenced in recent policy statements in support of current and future MarAd programs, which have come to focus almost exclusively on the critical role shipping will play in meeting America's short-term energy import needs.

Maritime Programs and U.S. Energy Needs
The increasing energy orientation of MarAd programs is evidenced both in the ship mix for CDS awards and in the ship mix receiving Title XI ship mortgage guarantees. Table 2 provides data on the Funded Ship Construction Program for fiscal years (FY) 1970-71 thru 1973, with estimates for FY 1974 and FY 1975. As the table shows, the program has been transformed substantially since 1971. In that year, nearly all the ships built were either barge carriers (LASH), containerships, or cargo-container conver-

Goals and Objectives of the Organization

Table 2   Funded Ship Construction Program 1971-1974 (dollars in thousands)

	1971		1972		1973		1974 (est.)		1975 (est.)	
Ship Type	No.	CDS Cost	No.	CDS Cost	No.	CDS Cost	No.	CDS Cost	No.	CDS Cost
Barge Carrier (LASH)	7	$88,328	2	$23,655	—	—	—	—	—	—
Roll-on/Roll-off (Ro/Ro)	—	—	2	$33,312	2	$31,115	—	—	—	—
Ore-Bulk-Oil Carrier (OBO)	2	$27,461	—	—	—	—	—	—	—	—
Tanker—up to 40,000dwt	—	—	4	$32,463	3	$25,912	2	$15,600	1	$7,800
Tanker—up to 100,000dwt	—	—	1	$12,051	3	$34,462	7	$78,500	2	$23,200
Very Large Crude Carrier (VLCC)	—	—	5	$139,775	4	$123,402	3	$135,000	4	$156,100
Liquified Natural Gas Carrier (LNG)	—	—	—	—	9	$193,511	2	$34,000	5	$85,000
Containership	3	$21,496	—	—	—	—	—	—	—	—
Dry Bulk Carrier	—	—	—	—	—	—	—	—	—	—
Conversions	11	$31,896*	5	$10,046*	3	$948*	3	$29,300**	1	$9,700**
Total	23	$169,181	19	$251,302	24	$409,350	17	$292,400	13	$281,800

* Cargo and container conversions.
**Tanker conversions.
Source: Division of Budget, Maritime Administration, December 20, 1973.

sions. The 1974 and 1975 budgets project total supported construction to consist solely of tankers and LNGs.

The Title XI Ship Mortgage Guarantee Program has also been strongly influenced by the increased energy transportation orientation of MarAd. The Title XI program permits a shipowner to receive a government guarantee on the debt used to finance either 87.5 percent of the cost of a ship (in cases where no CDS assistance is received) or 75 percent (in cases where CDS has been used). Thus, the full faith and credit of the U.S. Government is placed behind the debt issued by a shipowner, resulting in lower interest rates and substantial financing savings. The shift in program emphasis may be seen in Table 3.

Total commitments of guarantee authority increased from $1.2 billion in 1970 to $3.1 billion in 1973, and of this $1.9 billion increase, nearly $1.3 billion, or 67 percent, went to finance the construction of energy oriented vessels such as LNGs, offshore drilling rigs, OBOs, and tankers.

These two key indices of the thrust of MarAd programs—CDS grants and Title XI mortgage guarantees—clearly indicate the dramatic shift in program emphasis which has occurred since 1970, the year in which the new MarAd Program commenced.

FACTORS INFLUENCING THE DETERMINATION OF OBJECTIVES

The purpose of our national shipping policy is put forth in general terms in Section 101 of the Merchant Marine Act of 1936 (as amended), which is still the basic legislative policy statement in the U.S. maritime field:

> It is necessary for the national defense and development of its foreign and domestic commerce that the United States shall have a merchant marine (a) sufficient to carry its domestic water-borne commerce and a substantial portion of the water-borne export and import foreign commerce of the United States and to provide shipping service essential for maintaining the flow of such domestic and foreign water-borne commerce at all times, (b) capable of serving as a naval and military auxiliary in time of war or national emergency, (c) owned and operated under the United States flag by citizens of the United States insofar as may be practicable, (d) composed of the best equipped, safest, and most suitable types of vessels, constructed in the United States and manned with a trained and efficient citizen personnel, and (e) supplemented by efficient facilities for shipbuilding and ship repair.

Thus, it is argued that gains to the nation from its maritime program divide into two principal streams, those that strengthen the economy and those that

Table 3   Title XI Commitments ($ millions)

	Cumulative June 30, 1970		Cumulative June 30, 1973	
	Commitments ($)*	% of Programs	Commitments ($)*	% of Programs
River/Ocean Tug Barges	25	2	162	5
Cargo Ships	692	57	1,172	38
Tankers	487	41	925	30
Bulk/OBO	—	—	75	2
Oil Drilling/Drill Service	—	—	184	6
LNG's	—	—	575	19
Total	1,204	100	3,093	100

*Not including amortization and terminations.
Source: Maritime Administration, Division of Ship Financing Guarantees.

Introduction

contribute to the national security. These benefits arise both from operating ships under the U.S. flag and from building them in domestic shipyards.

A. Economic Benefits

1. Ship Operating

Employment aboard privately operated U.S. merchant ships has declined steadily during the past decade, from 44,423 individuals in April, 1962 to 27,474 individuals in April, 1972. Employment aboard ships receiving operating differential subsidies (ODS) declined more rapidly than employment on nonsubsidized ships. In 1962 employment on ships receiving ODS payments represented 43 percent of total employment on privately operated U.S. flagships; by 1972 that share had dropped to about 35 percent.

The employment effects of ODS payments are not easily isolated for scrutiny because such payments vary in response to differences in operating costs arising from dissimilarities in the ships themselves, the trade routes they serve, cargoes carried, and so forth. Higher labor costs on American flagships account for much of the cost differentials between the U.S. and foreign-flag operators, but ODS levels still do not correlate closely with crew sizes. The only generalizations that can be made in this regard relate to the number of sea-going jobs provided for each ship subsidized, rather than to the relationship between employment and ODS expenditures.

Because of necessary crew rotation, each position aboard ship normally provides employment for 2.4 people. A modern containership carries a crew of 35 to 40 individuals. ODS payments for such a ship thus provides employment for a crew of 85 to 96 people. Tankers generally operate with crews of 25 to 30 individuals, with only minor variations because of ship size. The employment generated by ODS for tankers thus falls in the range of 60 to 72 jobs per ship.

Freight charges account for a significant portion of the total cost of goods carried in oceanborne trade. This is especially true for bulk cargoes with low value-to-weight ratios. The use of U.S. flagships in place of foreign vessels to carry U.S. foreign trade cargoes contributes to the country's balance of payments to the extent of the freight payments that otherwise would have gone to foreign ship owners, adjusted for net changes in foreign-exchange balances incident to port charges and other navigation expenses.

U.S. imports of bulk commodities are increasing at a rapid pace, and imports of major bulk items are expected to increase by more than 250 percent from 1970 to 1985.

The imports forecast for 1985 would require the following shipping capacity (note DWT = *dead weight tons*):

Tankers	Number
80,000 DWT	112
250,000 DWT	284

LNG Carriers	Number
225,000M	92

Bulk Carriers	Number
120,000 DWT	75

The net difference to the U.S. balance of payments between carrying all of these imports of bulk commodities in U.S. flagships and foreign flagships can be estimated at $259 million for 1975, $1,374 million for 1980, and $2,290 million for 1985.

Foreign trade shipments of general cargoes of the types commonly carried by container ships and barge carriers offer additional opportunities for balance-of-payments savings from the use of American flagships. While the tonnages involved in these trades are much lower, unit freight charges are much higher, and potential balance-of-payment gains are thus disproportionate to the physical volume of trade.

The existence of U.S. flag-shipping capacity offers an element of protection against possible exploitation by foreign ship owners of the advantages that would be inherent in their monopolistic control of U.S. foreign-trade shipping. Participation in conferences serving U.S. trade routes grant American shipping companies a voice in the determination of conference rates and strengthen the hand of the Federal Maritime Commission in regulating those rates.

Perhaps even greater importance should be attached to maintaining U.S. flag participation in the oil trades. The potential threat to the country's economic and security interests posed by greatly increased dependence on overseas sources for petroleum, as now appears imminent, requires no elaboration. Total, or near total, dependence on foreign flagships to carry those imports would compound both the economic and national-security risks involved. In 1971, U.S. flag tankers carried less than 5 percent of the nation's petroleum imports, and as imports from more distant sources in the Middle East and Africa increase, that share would likely drop even farther, unless programs to stimulate U.S. flag tanker operations are pursued.

2. Shipbuilding

The major shipyards of the United States currently employ approximately 83,000 people, of which about 60,000 are production workers engaged in shipbuilding and repair. Naval programs account for a little more than one-half of these production workers, and of the remainder about 13,000 individuals are employed in private commercial shipbuilding and 15,500 people are engaged in projects supported by the Maritime Administration. Construction differential subsidies (CDS) are thus responsible for some 23 percent of shipyard employment of production workers. However, that share has varied widely during the past decade, ranging from a high of 23 percent in January, 1963 to a low of 4 percent in January, 1970.

Each million dollars of ship construction provides an estimated 28 work years of direct shipyard employment and an equal amount in various support activities. A dollar of CDS expenditure is matched by $1.5 to $3 in private funds at current CDS rates. As these rates decline, the employment effects per dollar of CDS increase.

Perhaps even greater significance is to be found in the nature of the employment gain generated through shipbuilding. A relatively large proportion of shipyard positions are filled with low-skilled workers whose alternative opportunities are very limited and who make up a significant share of total unemployment. Moreover, several important shipyards are located in regions of the country where unemployment rates have been above average. Unemployment among minority groups exceeds average unemployment by 50 to 80 percent in the regions most affected. In contrast, most shipyards employ relatively large numbers of minority workers, and minority participation in shipyard work forces generally exceeds regional averages for total employment and for blue-collar skills. This is especially true for Atlantic-Coast shipyards. Minority employment in white-collar positions is still low, but it is growing rapidly, having doubled in the last three years.

The total income effects of CDS expenditures cannot be determined with precision, but if an investment multiplier of 3 is assumed, each dollar of CDS expenditure would produce $7.50 to $12 in GNP gains. Applying an average tax rate of 20 percent to such income gains would yield an estimated $1.50 to $2.40 to the Treasury for each dollar of CDS expenditure.

Shipbuilding contributes positively to the country's balance of payments. Ships operated under the American flag enhance foreign exchange balances arising from U.S. seaborne foreign trade whether they carry imports or exports. When engaged in trade between foreign ports, they yield no foreign exchange earnings. Building such ships in the United States aids the balance of payments to the extent of their capital costs if purchased abroad.

B. National Security Benefits
  1. Ship Operating
    a. National Security Requirements
      The primary national security requirements for U.S.-flag merchant shipping are expressed in the

Goals and Objectives of the Organization

Defense Planning and Programming Guidance (DPPG) promulgated by the Secretary of Defense. In this document the Secretary of Defense defines the level of and location of wars that the U.S. must be prepared to fight in order to maintain national security. The U.S. Merchant Marine fleet must be capable of delivering unit equipment, accompanying supply, and resupply to our military forces as promptly as needed.

The latest analytic definition of ship requirements can be found in a multi-agency study called Sealift Procurement and National Security (SPANS). The Department of Defense, Federal Maritime Commission, and MarAd participated in the study effort. The report was published August 2, 1972. SPANS was a four-part study that examined the history and current practices of sealift procurement by the military to determine whether inequities were being created by the procurement system.

One of the four parts was a definitive analysis of the sealift requirement based on the current DPPG guidance. The predominant planning scenario was a conventional war in Europe followed by an Asian contingency. The SPANS analysis developed the sealift capability required by military needs and determined the ability of a projected merchant fleet to meet them. If the merchant fleet was insufficient, selected additions were made and the fleet was reexamined relative to its ability to satisfy the demands posited.

The basic merchant fleet consisted of the current U.S. merchant fleet less any ships phased out by ship-life rules (25-year life or 10-year additional life after major rebuilding). The National Defense Reserve Fleet (NDRF) was activated, added to the current U.S. merchant fleet, and together these two components were considered the base level of sealift available.

There was a combined mix of ships that totaled 439 including 309 vessels in the active merchant fleet and 130 ships considered capable of activation from the NDRF. At the time selected for the scenario (1976) the average age of ships in the NDRF exceeded 30 years.

The ship types were divided into 11 types for calculation purposes; each of these ship types was characterized by its ability to carry a specific type of cargo. Table 4 shows all container ships to be limited to carriage of resupply. Except for resupply, all military units require large amounts of unit equipment (vehicles plus aircraft) of various types for initial deployments. Most previous studies have also indicated that container ships are not suitable for carriage of unit equipment.

In the primary scenario examined, heavy attrition of ships was calculated to occur during the first 90 days due to submarine action by the enemy.

The SPANS scenario was limited to the first 90 days

21

Introduction

Table 4 — Fleet Characterization and Capability (units of carriage)

Notional Number	1	2	3	4	5	6	7	8	9	10	11
Ship Type	Breakbulk (>20 knots)	Breakbulk (<20 knots)	Container Self Sustaining	Container Nonsustaining (<20 knots)	Container Nonsustaining (>20 knots)	Combo RO/RO Container	Small RO/RO	Large RO/RO	LASH	Sea Barge	NDRF
Number of Ships	81	82	20	30	56	4	3	4	18	3	130
Average Speed (Knots)	8.4	20.4	11.2	16.5	23.7	23.5	18.3	25.3	22.3	20	15.7
Infantry (S/T)	1,853	1,933				1,796	2,093	3,855	4,031	5,070	1,086
Airmobile	646	667				854	806	1,476	1,661	2,303	351
Amount/Mechanized	2,797	2,956				2,578	3,057	5,678	5,894	6,990	1,639
Marine	3,530	3,731				3,420	3,873	7,197	7,679	9,200	2,079
Support	2,095	2,172				1,830	2,266	3,889	4,301	5,042	1,228
Resupply	8,060	9,063	10,079	8,423	15,305	12,610	6,204	11,565	18,780	21,043	4,721

of requirements because the assumption was that after the initial deployment, the conflict would either escalate to nuclear exchange or stabilize at a lower level of intensity. SPANS indicated that the resupply required for the first 90 days would be calculated at an intensive level of conflict, while beyond that time period, resupply should be calculated at a sustained level that is approximately 50 percent less intense as the first 90 days. The resupply requirements for shipping are therefore considerably less than the initial deployment requirements. An additional significant assumption was that following the initial 90-day period, attrition of shipping by enemy submarine attack would become nil, as Table 5 indicates.

Table 5 — Ship Losses

Time Span	Numbers of Dry Cargo Sailings Eastbound	Ships Sunk
0-30 days	328	130
31-60 days	211	40
61-90 days	43	15
Total	582	185

With this attrition level the basic fleet would fall short of achieving the required objective. The augmentation program that was considered most capable of meeting the objective at lowest cost was the utilization of NATO ships, with a total of 198 NATO ships presumed available for this augmentation.

2. Shipbuilding

The amount of shipyard capability needed for direct national security purposes is a function of three separate requirements. They are as follows:

a. Breakout of the National Defense Reserve Fleet. This operation requires that the ships be placed in drydocks for a short period and that all hull, machinery, and electronic equipment be restored to normal operating condition.

b. Replacement of vessels lost to enemy action. During the initial stages of NATO reinforcement, the attrition rate of ships lost due to enemy action is calculated to be very high. Attrition can also be expected to affect ships engaged in essential U.S.-foreign trade, and it will be equally imperative to replace any losses of ships in this category. If a short conventional war is followed by a major nuclear exchange, the need to replace ships lost during initial mobilization will not be great. However, some ships would be required for postnuclear hostilities and for the rehabilitation of damaged areas. On the other hand, military scenarios do admit that the initial conventional conflict could stabilize into a long conventional war without a nuclear exchange, and under such circumstances, the United States will need to continue to build ships for NATO resupply, at least until the war is contained and positive control of the ocean has been established. This need will be particularly acute if European shipyards are not available.

This wartime capability to maintain and replace the merchant fleet reveals a critical problem with any policy that relies heavily upon the foreign purchase of U.S. flagships. This is due to the fact that ships take long periods of time for construction, and at any given time a large percentage of the tonnage under foreign construction could be denied. Since wartime capability is almost always needed on a short notice, both the trained labor force and facilities must be in place in peacetime as well. It is from just such a nucleus that the U.S. was able to respond during World War II to the largest shipbuilding demands ever placed on any nation.

c. Repair of Merchant Vessels. A U.S. shipyard capability will also be important both to the repair of battle damage and to provide normal maintenance. This will maintain the U.S. merchant fleet at the highest level of efficiency and permit the maximum use of this resource. Some repair capability will also be applied to the repair of allied vessels, particularly those damaged in water adjacent to the United States.

None of the above requirements for shipyard capability have addressed the need for naval construction and repair. While some of this can be done in naval shipyards, the Navy's present policy is that all new surface ship construction be carried out in commercial shipyards. Commercial yards will undoubtedly be used additionally for repair, especially those normally performing a large percentage of Navy work.

It must be noted at this point that neither the Navy nor the Department of Defense has furnished the Department of Commerce with specific requirements for shipyards. Repeated formal requests for such information have only resulted in very general answers, the most recent being forwarded by the Navy on October 24, 1972. This reply confirmed the scenario used in the Sealift Procurement and National Security (SPANS) Study, which involves a brief conventional war with sealift attrition falling to nominal rates within a few months after initial mobilization.

Goals and Objectives of the Organization

While the possibility of a stabilized conventional war of long duration is recognized, the Navy holds the position that its control of the seas would still keep attrition at low levels.

Questions for Discussion

1. Evaluate the employment arguments in support of the U.S. Merchant Marine subsidy program. Does your analysis change depending upon the level of unemployment? What other factors should be considered in deciding on the validity of the employment argument?
2. Evaluate the balance-of-payments arguments in support of the U.S. Merchant Marine subsidy program. Does the existence of fluctuating exchange rates alter these arguments? Under what circumstances would you be willing to impute any "real" economic value to these balance-of-payments benefits?
3. Given the national security arguments presented in support of American maritime programs, how consistent do you find the direction of emphasis of current programs with these defense justifications?
4. What impact do you expect the "energy crisis" will have upon the future direction of maritime programs? What direction would you recommend that these programs take over the next five years?

Part Two Decision Making in the Private Sector

Chapter 3 Demand and Forecasting

READING
4 THE DEMAND FOR BEER
Thomas F. Hogarty and Kenneth G. Elzinga*

I Introduction

This note presents estimates of the price and income elasticities of beer. Aside from the usual academic and commercial interest in learning of demand characteristics, knowledge of the demand for beer also has public policy implications due to the heavy taxation of the product. About 35 per cent of the price of a glass of beer represents tax revenue with federal and state taxes on beer currently generating more than 1.5 billion dollars in revenue (Elzinga, 1971, p. 210) (U.S. Brewers Association, 1970, p. 110).

In what follows, we first summarize available knowledge on the demand for beer. Then we discuss the methodology and data employed in the present study. Finally, we present our findings and their implications.

II Previous Studies

William Niskanen (1962) analyzed the markets for alcoholic beverages with aggregate time series data for the 22 years 1934–1941 and 1947–1960. Wholesale price indexes (including taxes) for spirits and wine were prepared specially for his study from data provided by the Washington State Liquor Control Board. The beer price indexes were derived from a (now discontinued) Census series by Niskanen on total expenditures for beer (1962, p. 41). The results of his study, as they apply to the demand for beer, were that (1962, pp. 61–62): (1) the price elasticity of beer was about −0.7; (2) the income elasticity of beer was about −0.4; (3) spirits and beer were weak substitutes while the relations between the beer and wine markets were highly unstable.

Received for publication September 24, 1971. Accepted for publication November 17, 1971.

* This paper has benefitted considerably from helpful comments and suggestions by Ann Horowitz, Bennett T. McCallum, William Niskanen, and Eldon Reiling. Any remaining errors are the responsibility of the authors.

Ira and Ann Horowitz (1965), as part of their overall study of the beer industry, estimated the price and income elasticity of demand for beer with combined cross-section and time series data. Lacking specific data on beer prices, they used state excise tax levels as proxies. They found a weak, negative correlation between beer consumption and excise taxes on beer for 9 of the 13 years (1949–1961) studied. Their estimates of income elasticity were uniformly positive, but not significantly different from zero after 1956.

III The Present Study

(A) *Sample Data*

The price indexes used in this study are based primarily on the FOB mill prices of "Blatz Pilsner" and "Pabst Blue Ribbon" beers for 48 states and the District of Columbia for the years 1956–1959.[1] In raw form these price data consisted of FOB mill prices for cases of twenty-four 12-ounce returnable bottles, exclusive of state excise taxes and bottle deposits. We made the following adjustments:

1) Where prices changed during the year, we computed an average price, weighted in terms of the relative number of months the new price was in effect.

2) States vary enormously in terms of consumption of packaged and draft beer, e.g., in Alabama in 1956–1959 virtually all beer consumed was packaged beer; while in Wisconsin draught beer comprised some 40 per cent of consumption. Niskanen calculated from 1947, 1954 and 1958 Census of Manufactures data that the average wholesale value of packaged beer, exclusive of all excise taxes, was about 1.8 times the average value of draught beer

[1] These data became a matter of public record as a result of the Department of Justice suit against the Pabst-Blatz merger of 1958. See *U.S. v. Pabst Brewing Co.*, 233 F. Supp. 475 (1964); 384 U.S. 546 (1966); 296 F. Supp. 994 (1969). These price data are available as Appendix B from the authors on request.

Decision Making in the Private Sector

in each year (Niskanen, 1960, p. 12). We used this relation to calculate approximate FOB prices (in case equivalents) for draught beer. After adding appropriate federal and state excise taxes [2] to both the packaged and draught FOB prices, we computed for each state a weighted average price for each brand of beer, the weights then consisting of the relative proportions of packaged and draught beer consumed in the various states (U.S. Brewers Association).

3) These first three adjustments produced approximate retail prices for each of the two brands of beer. Our price index was then calculated as a simple average of these two brand prices.[3]

4) Data on transport rates from Milwaukee for 1957 only were used in conjunction with the 1957 Blatz price data to estimate the impact of excluding transport rates from other years. These and other data on distances show this source of bias to be relatively minor (see appendix A).[4]

5) A final insoluble problem was lack of reliable data on retail markups. Fortunately, in view of our results (see section IV below), this defect causes modest concern.[5]

6) As a final adjustment, the price indexes were expressed in real terms by means of the Bureau of Labor Statistics Consumer Price Index for 1956–1959.

Data on quantity (U.S. Brewers Association (USBA)), consisted of apparent consumption (in cases) per adult. Estimates of the *adult* population in each state consisted of interpolated Census data (1950, 1960). Estimates of state *per capita* income, also expressed in real terms, were derived from a special Census estimate (1966).

(B) *Methodological Issues and Data Problems*

Two potential difficulties confront our attempt to estimate demand elasticities for beer. The first is the standard identification problem; the second results from our use of individual brand prices.

The first problem appears inconsequential. The period 1956–1959 was one of excess capacity in the beer industry.[6] Hence, the assumption of perfectly elastic supply appears appropriate.

The second problem appears almost as minor. To begin with, the brand structure of prices in the beer industry is (or at least was) relatively stable:

"Anheuser-Busch once conducted a survey involving 113,305 price comparisons in 78 areas. In over 100,000 comparisons, a differential of 5 cents per can or per 12-ounce bottle existed between Budweiser and the popular priced beers. In over 90 per cent of the comparisons a 10 cent differential existed over local beers" (Elzinga, 1971, p. 85).

In addition, the nationwide market shares of Pabst and Blatz were relatively stable during 1956–1959, as were the shares of premium, popular, and local beers in three states during 1957–1960.[7] Finally, the prices of Pabst and Blatz can be considered representative of premium and popular priced beers, respectively. Unfortunately, price data for local beers are unavailable.

Ideally, of course, we should like to use a weighted index of prices, with the weights corresponding to the relative market shares of premium, popular, and local beers in the various states. Fortunately, however, our lack of data on prices of local beers and relative market shares does not seriously distort our price elasticity estimates.[8]

(C) *Procedure*

Our mode of analysis consisted of ordinary least squares with, at least initially, all variables expressed in logarithmic form, as in

$$\ln Q_{it} = b_0 + b_1 \ln P_{it} + b_2 \ln Y_{it} \qquad (1)$$

where

Q_i = apparent consumption (in cases) of beer *per adult* in i^{th} state in year t

P_i = real price of case of beer in i^{th} state in year t

---

[2] Four states had significant local excise taxation of beer and hence were excluded from the sample. These four states were Alabama, Georgia, Louisiana and Tennessee.

[3] The issue of a weighted average is discussed in part B below.

[4] Appendix A is available on request from the authors. Transportation rate data were kindly provided by Mr. Norman A. Domrose, General Traffic Manager of the Pabst Brewing Company. We are much indebted to Mr. Domrose for his assistance.

[5] The general impact of this omission will be that: (a) our estimate of income elasticity will tend to be low or biased toward zero; (b) our estimate of price elasticity will also understate, for a wide variety of cases, the true elasticity. See Foote, Richard J. *Analytical Tools for Studying Demand and Price Structures*. Agricultural Handbook No. 146, U.S. Department of Agriculture. (Washington: U.S. Government Printing Office, Aug., 1958), pp. 104–105.

[6] During 1956–1959, United States breweries, on the average, operated at about 64 per cent of capacity. Sources: Research Company of America, *Brewing Industry Survey* and U.S. Brewers Association, *Brewers Almanac* (both annual).

[7] For Blatz, the correlations between market share in 1956 and market shares in 1957–1959 were 0.97, 0.87, and 0.81, respectively; for Pabst, the corresponding correlations were 0.99, 0.95, and 0.90, respectively.

For the three-state area comprised of Illinois, Michigan, and Wisconsin, the following market shares prevailed during 1957–1960.

Year	Premium Beers	Popular Priced Beers	Local Beers
1957	27.86	51.80	20.34
1958	28.54	50.13	21.33
1959	29.05	51.02	19.93
1960	29.51	50.22	20.27

Source: *U.S. vs. Pabst Brewing Co., op. cit.*, JX 91–98.

[8] The use of an unweighted average and the lack of price data for local beers tends to impart a small upward bias to our price index. However, experimentation with the price index defined as the price of Pabst (or Blatz) alone showed that our estimates would not be drastically altered.

Y_i = real, *per capita* income in i^{th} state in year t
i = 1, 2, . . . , 45
t = 1, 2, 3, 4

Estimates of the coefficients of equation (1) were made for each of the years 1956–1959 individually ($n = 45$) and for a combined sample consisting of data for the entire period ($n = 180$). A test for overall homogeneity indicated that all four cross-sections could be regarded as coming from the same population and hence only estimates for the entire period are presented.[9]

IV Results

As indicated in equation (1), our initial estimates presumed constant price and income elasticities. The estimates obtained are presented in table 1 (line 1).

TABLE 1. — ESTIMATES OF PRICE AND INCOME ELASTICITY [a] OF BEER BASED ON SAMPLE EXCLUDING STATES WITH SUBSTANTIAL LOCAL EXCISE TAXATION OF BEER [b] ($n = 180$)

	b_0	b_1	b_2	b_3[c]	b_4	$\bar{R}^2$
(1)	−2.935	−1.128	0.926			.666
(2)	4.823	−0.992		0.942		.687
(3)	3.539	−0.889		0.430[d]	0.174[d]	.759

Entry identification:

b_0 = intercept
b_1 = price elasticity
b_2 = (constant) income elasticity
b_3 = (median) income elasticity
b_4 = elasticity of beer consumption with respect to national origin.

[a] Unless otherwise indicated, all coefficients are significantly different from zero at the 0.01 level or better; however, unless otherwise indicated, none of the coefficients are significantly different from unity at the 0.10 level or better.
[b] These states were Alabama, Georgia, Louisiana, and Tennessee.
[c] The income elasticities in this column were calculated at the income level prevailing in the median income state.
[d] Significantly different from unity at 0.01 level.

[9] The test for overall homogeneity is:

$$F = \frac{[S_d^2 - \sum_t S_{dt}^2]/(T-1)(K+1)}{\sum_t S_{dt}^2/[N - T(K+1)]}$$

where
S_d^2 = residual sums of squares from grand regression ($n = 180$)
S_{dt}^2 = residual sums of squares from cross-section regression t (t = 1956, 57, 58, 59) ($n = 45$)
T = number of years (sub-samples)
K = number of independent variables.

For our sample

With respect to price elasticity, our estimate of unity plus accords approximately with those of Niskanen in that neither Niskanen's estimates nor ours differed significantly from unity. The estimate of income elasticity was more surprising inasmuch as the Horowitz' found beer consumption to be unrelated to income while Niskanen found beer to be an inferior good. Experimentation with subsamples of high and low income states [10] demonstrated a tendency for the income elasticity of beer to vary inversely with the level of income.

Accordingly, we reformulated equation (1) to read: [11]

$$\ln Q_{it} = b_0 + b_1 \ln P_{it} - b_3(1/Y_{it}). \quad (2)$$

The results of fitting equation (2) to our data are contained in table 1 (line 2). The estimate of income elasticity presented is calculated at the median level of real, *per capita* income.

Our next step consisted of adding as independent variables indexes of spirits and wine prices.[12] Unfortunately, these attempts were unsuccessful.[13] On the other hand, we were able to account, at least in part, for differences in taste. On the presumption that immigrants were more prone to beer drinking than native Anglo-Saxons, we introduced as a proxy variable the per cent of each state's population that was foreign born. The results are presented in table 1 (line 3).

Thus, our final estimates of price and income elasticity for beer are −0.9 and 0.4, respectively. In addition, we estimate the beer drinking capacity

---

$$F = \frac{[7.715 - 7.309]/9}{(7.309)/168} = 1.025$$

which is not statistically significant at the 0.05 level.

[10] The states were classified as high or low income according to whether or not their *per capita* income for 1956–1959 was above or below that for the *median* state.

[11] The income elasticity for equation (2) is

$$I_E = e^{b_0 - b_3/Y} \cdot \frac{b_3}{QY}$$

$$= \frac{b_3}{Y} \text{ since } Q = \frac{e^{b_0 - b_3}}{Y}$$

$$= 2 \text{ when } Y = \frac{b_3}{2}.$$

Hence, income elasticity varies inversely with income and asymptotically approaches zero as income increases.

[12] Our initial step consisted of using excise taxes on spirits and wine as proxies for price. This procedure produced cross elasticity estimates of zero for both spirits and wine. Our second attempt consisted of using the retail price of Seagram's 7 Crown (fifth) as an index of retail prices in general (Simon, 1966).

[13] The estimates of cross elasticity between beer consumption and the price of spirits were statistically significant, but negative. These results persisted despite use of subsamples which excluded dry, moonshine and transient liquor traffic states. We rejected these results on the grounds that beer and spirits were unlikely complements. Nonetheless, these results, insofar as they applied to the estimates of price and income elasticity for beer, were roughly in accord with those presented in table 1.

of the United States as a little more than two cans (12 ounces) per adult per day.[14]

V Concluding Remarks

Although lack of price data on beer for the past decade makes prediction impossible, we note that from 1962 to 1969 per adult beer consumption increased by 16 per cent (USBA, 1970, p. 59) while real, *per capita* income rose by 27 per cent. Assuming stable real prices for beer, the implied income elasticity is 0.59. Average *per capita* income (1958 dollars) during 1962–1969 was approximately $2,250. At this level we estimate income elasticity as 0.37. Since average state taxes on beer increased about 7 per cent in real terms during 1962–1969 (USBA, 1970, p. 105), our estimate appears sufficiently close to warrant confidence in its reliability.

Regarding implications for the future, it appears that the beer industry can anticipate moderate increases in consumption, assuming the price of beer remains relatively stable. Moreover, it further appears that excise taxes on beer could be reduced considerably with only modest losses in tax revenues. The desirability of such reductions might be questioned on noneconomic grounds; however, there appears little doubt that beer excise taxes are regressive.

[14] Ignoring price effects, the drinking capacity of the United States is that level of consumption which would prevail at infinitely high levels of income. In our formulation this is e^{b_0} cases per adult per year or, as noted, approximately two cans per adult per day.

REFERENCES

Elzinga, K. G., "The Beer Industry," in Walter Adams (ed.) *The Structure of American Industry*. 1971.

Gavin-Jobson Associates. *Liquor Handbook* (New York: Gavin-Jobson Associates, Inc.) (annual).

Horowitz, I. and R. Ann, "Firms in a Declining Market: The Brewing Case," *Journal of Industrial Economics*, 13 (Mar., 1965), 129–153.

Nerlove, M. and W. Addison, "Statistical Estimation of Long Run Elasticities of Supply and Demand," *Journal of Farm Economics*, XL (Nov., 1958), 861–880.

Niskanen, W. A., "Taxation and the Demand for Alcoholic Beverages" (Santa Monica: The Rand Corporation, Jan., 1960).

———, "The Demand for Alcoholic Beverages," Unpublished doctoral dissertation, University of Chicago, 1962.

Simon, J. L., "The Price Elasticity of Liquor in the U.S. and a Simple Method of Determination," *Econometrica*, 34 (Jan., 1966) 193–205.

Tax Foundation, Inc. *Facts and Figures* (New York: The Tax Foundation, Inc.) (biennial).

U.S. Brewers Association, *Brewers Almanac* (Washington, D.C.: U.S.B.A. (annual).

U.S. Bureau of the Census. *Long Term Economic Growth*, 1860–1965 (Washington: U.S. Government Printing Office) (Oct. 1966), 212–217.

U.S. Bureau of the Census. *Census of Population, Vol. I, Parts 1–53* (table 16). (Washington: U.S. Government Printing Office), 1950 and 1960.

Internal Revenue Service. *Statistics Relating to the Alcohol and Tobacco Industries*. Publication No. 67 (1960) (table 90, p. 77).

READING
5 THE ANALYSIS OF ECONOMIC INDICATORS
Geoffrey H. Moore

Economic indicators are specific measures such as production, prices, incomes, employment and investment. Subtle relations among them must be perceived if they are to be used to predict economic developments.

Business cycles, large and small, appear to be a continuing feature of the economic landscape. A turn up or down in the economy is clearly an event of major social significance. Considerable interest therefore attaches to the means whereby an economic turn can be forecast and its extent can be estimated. That is the role of economic indicators, which rest on the numerous measurements of the pulse of the economy made by Government agencies, private organizations and individual economists. The analysis of economic indicators (a subject in which my colleagues and I at the National Bureau of Economic Research have been much interested) is a well-developed technique for ascertaining what the many pulse readings are saying about the state of the economy.

Economic indicators are often likened to a barometer because they register some significant aspect of the performance of the economy, are sensitive to changes in the economic climate and may portend further changes. A barometer, however, measures only one characteristic of the atmosphere. Moreover, the barometer itself does not cause a change in the weather. Hence it is frequently in a disparaging sense that the term barometer is applied to an economic indicator; the implication is that the indicator is only a barometer, having no real causal significance and covering only a small part of what one should know about economic change.

Such characterizations may apply to many individual economic indicators, but they do not apply to indicators as a class. Economic indicators have come to embrace virtually all the quantitative measures of economic change that are continuously available. One can find daily, weekly, monthly and quarterly indicators; they measure production, prices, incomes, employment, investment, inventories, sales and so on, and they record plans, commitments and anticipations as well as recent transactions. Some of the indicators, such as the unemployment rate or the consumer price index, are calculated by the Federal Government on the basis of elaborate sampling surveys conducted each month. Others, such as the indexes of stock-market prices and the surveys by purchasing agents of prices, orders and inventories, are constructed by private organizations on the basis of information they collect or obtain as a by-product.

As a result the economist or businessman interested in forecasting change is faced, like the weather forecaster, with a mass of factual information that pours in constantly. He must assess in some systematic way what the information says about the present and the future. The technique of indicator analysis embraces various systematic ways of looking at this information with a view to discerning significant developments in the business cycle.

One of the earliest systems of the kind, which was devised shortly before World War I, came to be known as the Harvard *ABC* curves. The *A* curve was an index representing speculation, more specifically stock prices. The *B* curve represented business activity, measured by the dollar volume of checks drawn on bank deposits. The *C* curve represented the money market, measured by the rate of interest on short-term commercial loans. Historical studies, particularly those carried out by Warren Persons of Harvard University, showed that these three curves typically moved in sequence: stock prices first, bank debits next and interest rates last, with the lagging turns in interest rates preceding the opposite turns in stock prices. The economic logic of the sequence was that tight money and high interest rates led to a decline in business prospects and a drop in stock prices, which led to cutbacks in investment and a recession in business. The recession in turn led to easier money and lower interest rates, which eventually improved business prospects, lifted stock prices and generated a new expansion of economic activity.

The system came to grief in the Great Depression of 1929 because the interpreters of the curves took too optimistic a view and failed to foresee the debacle. Economists generally regard the episode as one of the great forecasting failures of all time. Curiously, however, the timing of the sequence of events on which the system was originally based has in large measure persisted. This is not to say, however, that the *ABC* curves would still suffice if they were revived; since 1929 much more comprehensive systems of indicators have been developed, and the empirical and theoretical base on which they stand has been far more thoroughly studied, documented and tested.

The sharp recession of 1937–1938, which occurred before the economy had fully recovered from the Great Depression, helped to spur that development. In the fall of 1937 Henry Morgenthau, Jr., the Secretary of the Treasury, asked the National Bureau of Economic Research (which is a private, nonprofit research agency) to devise a system of indicators that would signal when the recession was nearing an end. At that time the quantitative analysis of economic performance in the U.S. did not approach today's standards. The Government's national income and product accounts,

31

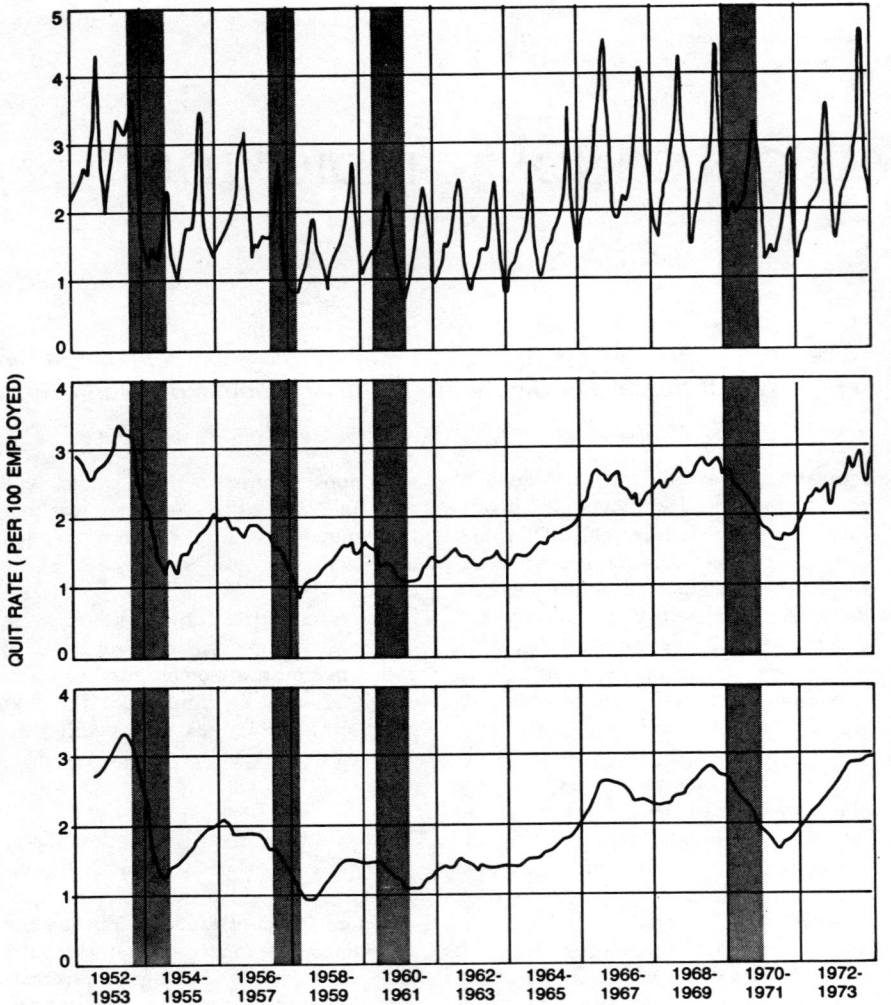

CONSTRUCTION OF INDICATOR involves the removal of factors that are unrelated to the business cycle. Here the indicator is the quit rate, meaning the number of people per 100 employed who voluntarily leave their jobs. At top is the curve reflecting the raw data, with shaded areas showing four periods of recession. Below it is the seasonally adjusted curve. Bottom curve shows the cyclical movement and the long-term trend of the quit rate.

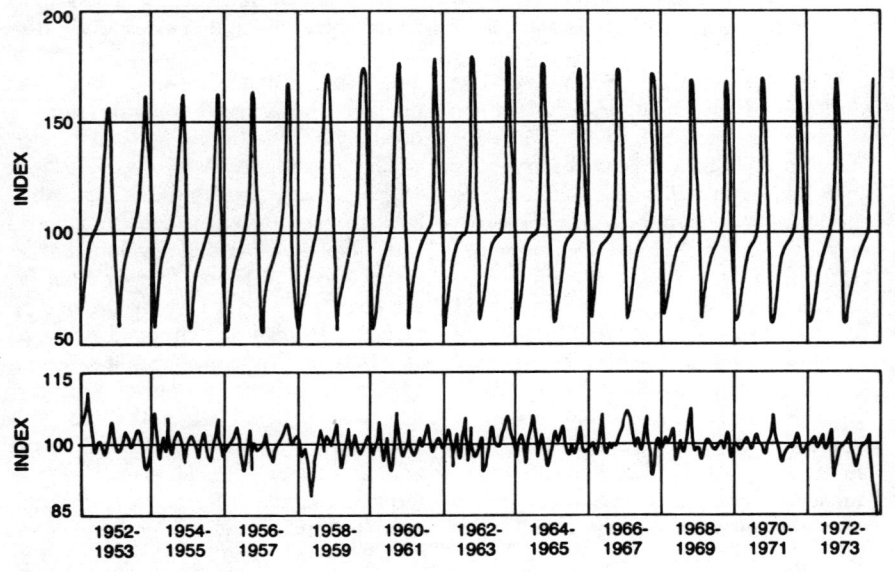

ELEMENTS REMOVED from the quit-rate curve are a seasonal component (*top*) and an irregular component (*bottom*), which includes such factors as strikes and errors in sampling.

which form the foundation of much modern economic analysis, were just being established. Other vital economic statistics, including unemployment rates, were being developed or refined by public agencies trying to provide information that would be useful in fighting the depression. Few statistical series were issued in seasonally adjusted form, as they are now. Comprehensive econometric models (systems of equations expressing quantitative relations among economic variables), which are widely employed now to forecast the economy and to evaluate economic policies, were virtually unknown then.

Under the leadership of Wesley C. Mitchell and Arthur F. Burns the National Bureau of Economic Research had since the 1920's assembled and analyzed a vast amount of monthly, quarterly and annual data on prices, employment, production and other factors as part of a major research effort aimed at gaining a better understanding of business cycles. This project enabled Mitchell and Burns to select a number of series that, on the basis of past performance and of relevance in the business cycle, promised to be fairly reliable indicators of business revival. The list was given to the Treasury Department late in 1937 in response to Morgenthau's request and was published in May, 1938. Thus originated the system of leading, coincident and lagging indicators widely employed today in analyzing the economic situation, determining what factors are favorable or unfavorable and forecasting short-term developments.

Since 1938 the availability, the study and the use of economic indicators have been greatly expanded under the leadership of the National Bureau of Economic Research, the U.S. Bureau of the Census and other public and private agencies. The list of indicators assembled in 1937 was revised in 1950, 1960 and 1966 to take account of the availability of new economic series, new research findings and changes in the structure of the economy. A new evaluation is currently in progress under the auspices of the U.S. Department of Commerce. With each revision the performance of the indicators both before and after the date of their selection has been carefully examined and exposed to public scrutiny.

In 1957 Raymond J. Saulnier, who was then chairman of the President's

Demand and Forecasting

Council of Economic Advisers, asked the Bureau of the Census to develop methods whereby the appraisal of current business fluctuations could take advantage of the large-scale electronic data processing that was becoming available at the time, with the results to be issued in a monthly report. Experimental work done over the next few years under the leadership of Julius Shiskin, who was the chief economic statistician of the Bureau of the Census, resulted (in 1961) in the publication by the Department of Commerce of *Business Cycle Developments*. (It is now called *Business Conditions Digest*; under both names economists have referred to it as *BCD*, and those initials appear on its cover in larger type than the full name does.) This monthly publication has greatly increased the accessibility of current indicator data and of various statistical devices that aid in their interpretation. As a result the analysis of the indicators has become a major tool of economic forecasting among the economists whose interest is in the current and future performance of the economy.

As I have noted, the analysis of economic indicators rests on an empirical footing and a theoretical one. Both the selection of particular indicators and the emphasis given to them have been guided by what is understood of the causes of business cycles. Obviously one would wish to examine recent changes in any economic process that is believed to play a significant role in any widely accepted explanation of cyclical fluctuations.

Many different explanations have been advanced for these fluctuations. Some of them lay primary stress on the swings in investment in inventory and fixed capital that both determine and are determined by movements in final demand. Others assign a central role to the supply of money and credit or to Government spending and tax policies or to relations among prices, costs and profits.

All these factors undoubtedly influence the course of business activity. Some of them may be more important at a given time than others. No consensus exists, however, on which is the most important or even on how they all interact. Hence it is prudent to work with a variety of indicators representing a broad range of influences. Ready access to a wide range of indicator data enables one to test competing or complementary hypotheses about current economic fluctuations.

With this principle in mind the National Bureau of Economic Research has classified economic activities into a few broad categories of closely related processes that are significant from the business-cycle point of view. Indicators have been selected from each group. The principal categories now included in *Business Conditions Digest* are employment and unemployment; production, income, consumption and trade; fixed capital investment; inventories and inventory investment; prices, costs and

ECONOMIC PROCESS	RELATION TO BUSINESS CYCLE			
	LEADING	ROUGHLY COINCIDENT	LAGGING	UNCLASSIFIED
Employment and unemployment	Average workweek and overtime Hiring and layoff rates New unemployment insurance claims	Job vacancies Total employment and unemployment	Long-duration unemployment	
Production, income, consumption and trade		Total production, income and sales		
Fixed capital investment	New investment commitments Formation of business enterprises	Backlog of investment commitments	Investment expenditures	
Inventories and inventory investment	Inventory investment and purchasing		Inventories	
Prices, costs and profits	Sensitive commodity prices Stock prices Profits and profit margins Cash flow	Wholesale price index for industrial commodities	Labor costs per unit of output	Consumer price index
Money and credit	Money and credit flows Credit delinquencies and business failures	Bank reserves Interest rates on money market	Outstanding debt Mortgage and bank-loan rates	
Foreign trade and payments				Imports, exports and export orders Balance of payments
Activities of Federal Government				Receipts and expenditures Defense orders, contracts and purchases

CLASSIFICATION OF INDICATORS is done in two ways. One is by major economic process, such as employment and unemployment. The other one is according to the relation the indicators have to turns in the business cycle. The leading, roughly coincident and lagging indicators shown in the table represent only a small portion of the many indicators that are normally classified in this way.

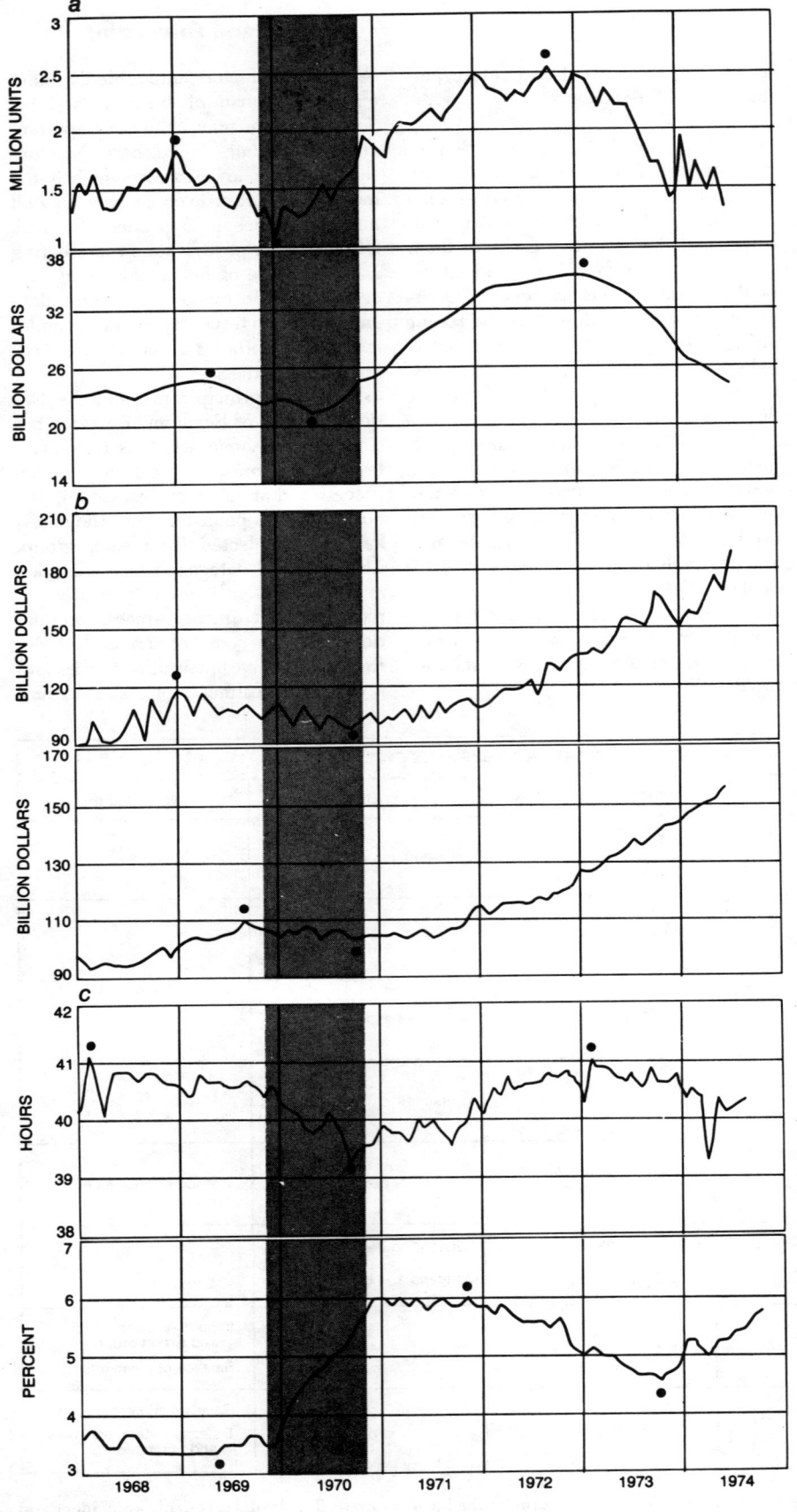

profits; money and credit; foreign trade and payments, and Federal Government activities.

The reader will note that these categories do not include all aspects of the economy. For example, statistics on agriculture, state and local government, population and wealth are omitted. Nevertheless, the categories do provide a framework of factors that enter into theories of the business cycle and are important in assessing the performance of the economy.

Within each category research on business cycles has uncovered statistical series that behave in a systematic way. These findings have provided a basis for selecting particular indicators and classifying them according to their characteristic cyclical behavior [see illustration on preceding page]. Two of the chief characteristics one looks for are the regularity with which the indicator conforms to business cycles and the consistency with which it leads or lags at turning points in the cycles. Other relevant considerations are the statistical adequacy of the data (since the statistical underpinning of an indicator has a bearing on how well the indicator represents the process it is supposed to reflect), the smoothness of the data (since highly erratic series are difficult to interpret at a given point in time) and the promptness with which the figures are published (since out-of-date figures have a limited bearing on the current situation).

Empirical measures of these characteristics have been drawn up for large numbers of indicators in the categories listed above. Such measures have been employed in the attempt to obtain data capable of conveying an adequate picture of the changes in the economy as it moves through stages of prosperity and recession. In addition the behavior of the indicators after they have been selected has been monitored closely. Many of the indicators have survived several successive evaluations. For example, the indexes of the average workweek, construction contracts and stock prices were on both the 1937 and 1966 lists of the National Bureau of Economic Research.

The same lists of indicators have also been tested by their performance in other countries, notably Canada, Japan and the United Kingdom. Every new recession or slowdown provides additional evidence against which the indicators can be assessed, as does every upturn.

RELATIONS AMONG INDICATORS are traced through the business-cycle contraction of 1969–1970. The three pairs of curves represent leading indicators (*black*) and the activities they led (*color*), namely housing starts and expenditures on residential structures (*a*), orders for plant and equipment and corresponding expenditures (*b*) and average workweek in manufacturing industries against unemployment rate (*c*). Dots show peaks and troughs.

Demand and Forecasting

All this examination and reexamination has accumulated a large amount of empirical evidence that demonstrates both the value of the indicators and their limitations.

A sampling of this evidence is contained in the accompanying illustrations. Let us consider the indicator called the quit rate, which measures the number of people in manufacturing industries (per 100 employed) who voluntarily leave their jobs [see *illustrations on page 18*]. The raw data are statistically decomposed in order to measure and eliminate regular seasonal variations and irregular movements. With factors that are unrelated to the business cycle thus removed, the indicator reveals the tendency for quits to diminish during a recession as new jobs become harder to find and to increase when more prosperous conditions return. The seasonally adjusted quit rate therefore reflects the view that workers have of the labor market and of economic prospects generally.

Most economic indicators today are available in seasonally adjusted form. Some of them are seldom reported in any other way. Examples of indicators that are invariably adjusted for seasonal factors include the gross national product, the unemployment rate and the index of industrial production.

The smoothing of irregular factors is less commonly practiced because the techniques are somewhat less routine. Certain statistical series, however, are subject to much wider irregular movements than others are because of differences in sampling error or in the effects of such factors as the weather and strikes. It is therefore useful in interpreting current changes to have a standard measure of the size of these irregular factors compared with the size of the movements reflecting long-term trends and the events of the business cycle. (In economic discussions these latter factors are often called trend-cycle movements.)

Two measures of this kind are provided for all the indicators carried in *Business Conditions Digest*. One shows how large the average monthly change in the irregular component is with respect to the average monthly change in the trend-cycle component. The other shows how many months must elapse on the average before the change in the trend-cycle component, which builds up over a period of time, exceeds the irregular component, which does not. For example, the measures show that monthly changes in housing starts are likely to be dominated by "noise," but that when these changes are measured over spans of four months, the trend-cycle "signal" becomes dominant. On the other hand, the index of industrial production is much less affected by noise, so that monthly movements are more significant.

The most important characteristic of an indicator from the point of view of forecasting is of course the evidence it provides concerning future changes in economic activity. Indicators differ in this respect for numerous reasons. Certain types, such as housing starts, contracts for construction and new orders for machinery and equipment, represent an early stage in the process of making decisions on investment. Since it takes time to build a house or a factory or a turbine, the actual production (or completion or shipping) usually lags behind the orders and contracts. The lag depends on, among other things, the volume of unfilled orders or contracts still to be completed; where goods are made for stock rather than to order there may be no lag because orders are filled as they are received.

Another kind of lead-lag relation exists between changes in the workweek on the one hand and employment on the other. In many enterprises employers can increase or decrease hours of work more quickly, more cheaply and with less of a commitment than they can hire or fire workers. Hence in most manufacturing industries the average length of the workweek usually begins to increase or decrease before a corresponding change in the level of employment. The workweek is therefore a leading indicator with respect to the unemployment rate.

Many bilateral relations of this kind have been traced. The matter obviously becomes more complex, however, when the relations are multilateral. Indexes of stock-market prices, for example, have exhibited a long-standing tendency to lead changes in business activity (the Harvard *ABC* curves relied in part on this tendency), but the explanation seems to require the interaction of movements in profits and in interest rates, and

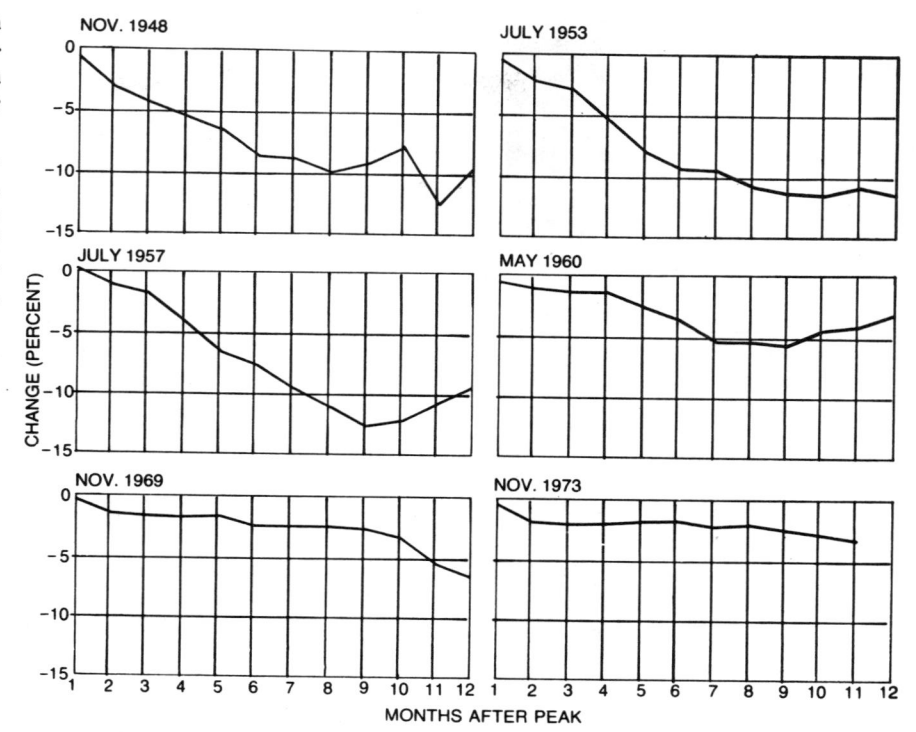

COINCIDENT INDICATORS are traced through six recessions, starting with the date of the business peak preceding the recession. Each curve represents the percentage change in the index of five indicators, namely industrial production, nonfarm employment, unemployment rate, personal income in constant dollars and total sales in constant dollars. Through last October the current decline most nearly resembled the ones in 1969–1970 and 1960–1961.

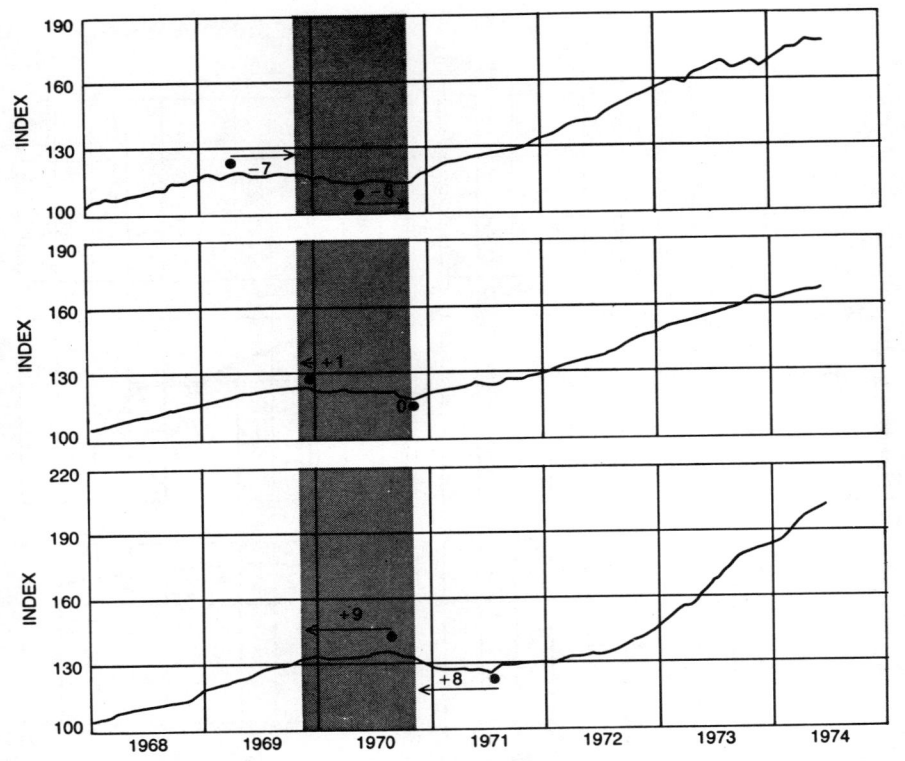

U.S. INDICATORS behaved differently in the recession of 1969–1970 according to whether they were leading (*top*), coincident (*middle*) or lagging indicators (*bottom*). Each curve represents an index of several indicators in its class. Negative numbers with arrows mean the curve was that number of months ahead of the corresponding peak or trough in the business cycle. Positive numbers mean the curve was that number of months behind the cycle.

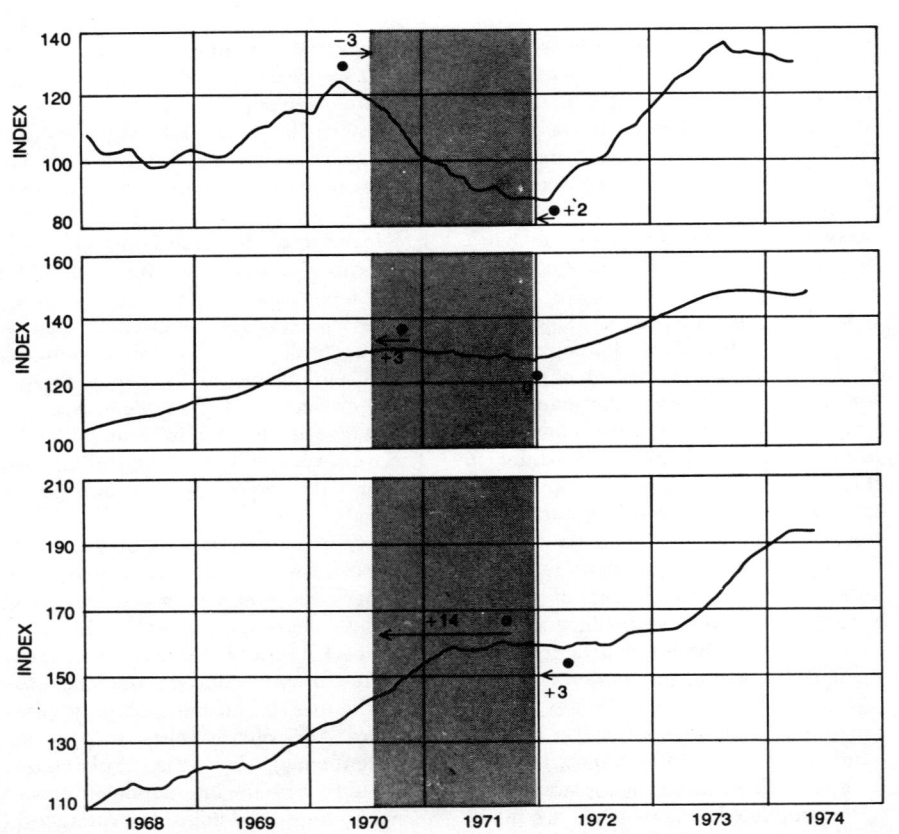

JAPANESE INDICATORS are portrayed for a recession that ran from July, 1970, to December, 1971. The method of presentation is the same as for the illustration at top of page.

other factors as well. A cyclical decline in profits often starts before a business expansion comes to an end; the proximate cause is usually a rapid rise in the costs of production. Interest rates also are likely to rise sharply. Both factors operate to reduce the attractiveness of common stocks and depress their prices, even though the volume of business activity is still rising. Near the end of a recession the opposite tendencies come into play and lift stock prices before business begins to improve.

One way to cut through such complexities instead of pursuing each bilateral or multilateral relation separately is to measure leads and lags against a common standard. For this purpose a chronology of business cycles has proved useful. The National Bureau of Economic Research has defined business cycles in such a way that peaks and troughs can be dated with reasonable objectivity. (Indeed, much of the dating procedure can now be carried out by computer.) Since the vast majority of indicators that are of interest show cyclical movements conforming to these general business cycles, the peaks and troughs in each indicator can be matched with those of the business cycle to determine characteristic leads and lags.

Following this plan, groups of indicator series that typically lead, coincide with or lag behind turns in the business cycle have been identified [*see top illustration at left*]. Summary indexes of these groups can be employed (as individual indicators can) to measure the relative severity of an economic downturn as it progresses from month to month. For example, indications of a slowdown in the U.S. economy began to accumulate during 1973. Early in 1974 it was possible to conclude that if a recession was under way, a reasonable choice for the date of the business peak from which it started was November, 1973. Percentage changes from then to successive months in 1973 and 1974 were calculated for a number of indicators month by month as new data became available and were compared with changes over corresponding intervals in earlier recessions, which had exhibited varying degrees of severity.

With such a monitoring scheme one could observe the relative severity of the current decline and draw certain inferences based on the fact that the rank-

Demand and Forecasting

ings among different recessions have usually not changed a great deal after the first few months. The figures show that the decline of 1974 was relatively sharp early in the year as the effect of the oil crisis began to be felt. According to the latest data available (for October) as of this writing, however, the decline in most indicators appeared moderate compared with the declines in earlier recessions over corresponding intervals. The major exceptions were the sharp declines in housing starts and in prices of common stocks, both of which reflected the sharp rise in interest rates and rapid inflation.

It is of course essential in any appraisal of the economic outlook to take into account actual and prospective policy actions by the Government. Such actions include tax reductions or increases, changes in required bank reserves, changes in military expenditures and the establishment of a program of public employment. They often do not fit readily into the framework of indicators, although their effects, together with other influences, may be registered promptly in orders, contracts, housing starts, stock prices and so on. Still, certain indicators do provide a nearly continuous reading on Government activities.

Government moves are often countercyclical. In a recession, for example, the Government can exert a stimulative effect on the economy by making bank deposits or currency more readily available or by spending more than tax revenues are bringing in. The impact of such measures is a matter of debate. Indeed, it is possible to argue from the figures that policy shifts by the Government have sometimes contributed, with a lag, to the cyclical movements in the economy that they were designed to offset.

The analysis of economic indicators is one way of assessing the behavior of the economy. Econometric models of the business-cycle process are another. Although the two techniques have developed along independent lines for many years, they have come together at a number of points. The mathematical equations that characterize econometric models can handle elegantly and systematically such matters as multilateral relations among indicators, the distinction between seasonal movement and other types of movement, the influence of changes in Government policy and the plausibility of alternative theoretical explanations of the cycle.

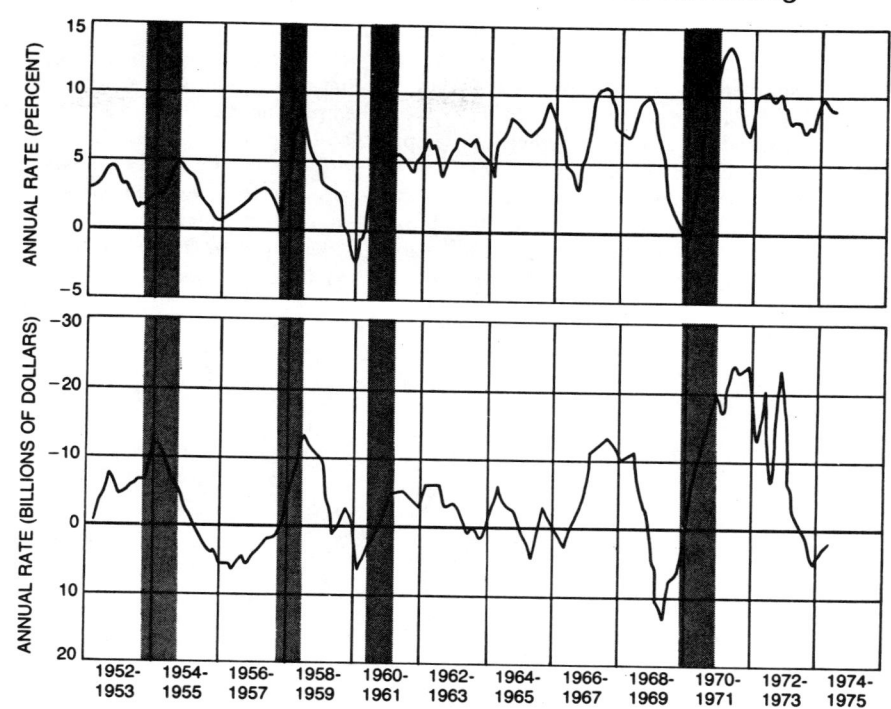

ROLE OF GOVERNMENT through four recessions is indicated by curves that portray rate of change in money supply (*top*) and Federal surplus or deficit (*bottom*). On bottom curve a rise indicates a shift toward smaller surplus or larger deficit, a fall the opposite. Behavior of curves in recessions indicates interaction of Government policy with business cycle.

The econometric models focus their explanatory power on such roughly coincident indicators as the gross national product, unemployment and the rate of inflation. Ofter they include such cycle-leading indicators as housing starts, the average workweek, stock prices and changes in business inventories, together with such lagging indicators as mortgage interest rates and investment in plant and equipment. Although the models have so far had a mixed record in representing and forecasting developments in the business cycle, with the result that the competition among alternative models is keen and changes in the specifications of each model are frequent, no user of indicators can afford to ignore the insights that econometric models bring to economic analysis. By the same token, people working with models can benefit from the empirical findings of indicator analysis and from the additional information that indicators often provide from outside the boundaries of a particular econometric model.

Economic indicators of all types are followed more widely in the U.S. than in most other countries. The growth of trade, travel and international finance, however, has increased the demand for promptly available statistics and readily accessible analytical records. Last year the National Bureau of Economic Research began a program of assembling and analyzing indicators for a dozen industrial countries.

Fortunately the indicator approach is sufficiently flexible to be adapted readily to situations where, as in many countries since World War II, economic recessions have taken the form of retardations in the growth of aggregate activity rather than absolute declines, and where such retardations may have been deliberately induced by government policies in order to cool off inflation or restore a deteriorating trade balance. Moreover, the approach is flexible enough to accommodate differences among countries in the types of indicator data that are available or are most revealing. For example, in Europe statistics on job vacancies are relied on more than in the U.S. and data on the international migration of workers are more significant because they have larger effects on the size of the work force.

Furthermore, since many economic

indicators are available in physical units (such as man-hours of employment or tonnage shipped) or can be expressed in constant prices, a system of indicators can be adapted to conditions where a high rate of inflation dominates the behavior of data that are expressed in current prices. Many countries have recently experienced such conditions. Physical indicators of demand, such as housing starts, hiring rates and orders for materials, can be expected to throw light not only on subsequent changes in output and employment but also on changes in prices and wages.

Our study is exploring these paths. Results already in hand for Canada, Japan, the United Kingdom and West Germany demonstrate the feasibility of the approach and its potential value in observing and appraising international fluctuations in economic growth rates and the accompanying trends in price levels, foreign trade, capital investment and employment. One can envision the evolution of a worldwide system of indicators, built on the plan originally developed for the U.S., to support the analysis of economic indicators on a global scale.

READING
6 HIGHER EDUCATION ENROLLMENT DEMAND

Thomas D. Hopkins*
BOWDOIN COLLEGE AND IRWIN MANAGEMENT COMPANY

The propensity to enroll in college varies markedly across state populations of high school graduates. During the 1963-64 academic year, for example, the percentage of a state's recent high school graduates enrolled somewhere in undergraduate programs ranged from a low of 26% (Maine) to a high of 48% (Arizona).

Recent efforts to explain such variation have focused on the influence of tuition and a variety of socio-economic variables on student demand for college enrollment. A major conclusion of most studies based on cross-section data is that higher tuition leads to lower total enrollment.[1] Support for this conclusion is provided by a time-series study by Robert Campbell and Barry Siegel.[2]

This focus on determinants of total enrollment, however, neglects an important question. College enrollment is not a homogeneous commodity. Changes in variables such as tuition may have a dual effect on enrollment—a substitution effect and a net discouragement effect. When tuition is increased at one type of college, some students may choose simply to enroll in a different type of college (substitution effect) while others may decide against enrollment altogether (net discouragement effect). This paper represents an effort to distinguish quantitatively these two enrollment effects. Enrollment demand functions are estimated which explain much of the variation both in the level of total enrollment and in the distribution of enrollees between public and private institutions. Furthermore, the paper explores the influence of three public policy variables: tuition, institutional location, and institutional educational expenditures per enrollee.

MODEL OF ENROLLMENT DEMAND

The decision to enroll in an institution of higher education (IHE) is treated here as a market phenomenon.[3] The potential enrollee is the buyer, and the IHE is the seller. The commodity is an academic year of instruction. Each recent high school graduate is regarded as a participant in a state-wide market for public enrollment and in a regional (multi-state)

---

*This paper is a revised portion of a dissertation submitted to Yale University. The author is indebted to Peter Mieszkowski, William D. Shipman, A. Myrick Freeman III, Paul G. Darling, and a referee for many helpful suggestions.

1. See studies by Richard Ostheimer; by Arthur Corazzini *et. al.*; and by Paul Feldman and Stephen Hoenack.

2. See also a related study by Harvey Galper and R. M. Dunn, Jr.

3. This study is based on cross-section state data for the 1963-64 academic year; these data and their sources are available from author upon request. This particular year was chosen because of the availability for that year of comprehensive student migration data (which are published at five-year intervals—similar data now are available also for 1968-69) and certain other necessary data and because the Vietnam War was a less disruptive influence on enrollment in the earlier year.

Decision Making in the Private Sector

market for private enrollment.[4] Each of the two enrollment alternatives open to the potential enrollee is characterized in terms of tuition, educational expenditures per enrollee, and proximity of IHE.

Public enrollment is distinguished from private enrollment for three reasons:

first, public IHE generally charge substantially lower tuition than do private IHE. In 1963-64, mean net tuition was $216 (for residents) at public IHE and $835 at private IHE (standard deviations: $72 and $159, respectively).

second, there is some reason to question whether students view public and private enrollment as essentially equivalent commodities. Indeed Feldman and Hoenack [p. 386] argue that:

". . . some students are willing to rank attendance at a private institution on the one hand, and not going to college (which can include deferred college attendance) on the other, both above public college attendance."

third, all public IHE located within a single state are controlled and financed, in large measure, by a single governing body; hence they constitute a natural unit for policy analysis. By contract, private IHE are considerably more autonomous.

For these reasons, total undergraduate enrollment is subdivided into two distinct commodities: public in-state enrollment and private enrollment (including out-of-state public enrollment).

It is assumed that non-market constraints (specifically, the Selective Service System and administrative rationing of admissions) have negligible influence in these enrollment markets. The military draft could have had two opposing influences on college enrollments during the year under investigation (1963-64). Probably some potential enrollees found themselves involuntarily inducted into the armed forces. On the other hand, some individuals probably did enroll in order to gain draft deferments. In the absence of evidence indicating the size and direction of any net influence attributable to these opposing forces, it is assumed that such net influence is negligible. Hence, every recent high school graduate is regarded as a potential enrollee.[5]

With respect to the other such constraint (the admissions process), it is assumed that every recent high school graduate can find some in-state public (or in-region private) institution which will accept him, if he wants

---

4. All institutions are included which (a) offer regular programs that provide credit toward undergraduate academic degrees and (b) are recognized universities, liberal arts colleges, teachers colleges, four-year technological schools, and two-year junior (community) colleges. The market area definitions used here are based on student migration data. The U.S. has been divided here into seven regions in such manner that intra-regional (inter-regional) student migration to private IHE is considerable (small). Further details available in Appendix from author upon request.

5. This position differs from that taken by Campbell and Siegel. Since persons serving in the armed forces cannot simultaneously attend college, Campbell and Siegel exclude such individuals from their measure of potential enrollees and use this measure in estimating enrollment demand functions. This is equivalent to arguing that all young high school graduates who are in the service were inducted involuntarily. Campbell and Siegel neglect the fact that some potential college enrollees voluntarily prefer the armed forces to college, just as others prefer civilian employment to college. Their approach constitutes an over-adjustment for the constraining influence the military has on college enrollment, coupled with no adjustment for the stimulative influence that military draft deferments have on college enrollment.

and can afford to enroll.[6] Administrative rationing very likely does influence the distribution of students among individual public and private IHE; it is less likely that administrative rationing effectively denies any high school graduate access either to all public in-state IHE or to all regional private IHE.

Each eligible individual chooses the single most appealing alternative—public enrollment, private enrollment, or non-enrollment (including immediate employment)—based on his evaluation of their relative benefits and costs. The enrollment demand functions are estimated by regressing state enrollment ratios on explanatory variables which describe characteristics of the eligible individuals residing within a given state and the alternatives open to these individuals. The enrollment ratios used as dependent variables are:

$$(N_1/R) : \frac{\text{in-state public enrollment of residents}}{\text{eligible residents}}$$

$$(N_2/R) : \frac{\text{private enrollment of residents}}{\text{eligible residents}}$$

$$(N_1 + N_2)/R : \frac{\text{eligible residents minus non-enrollees}}{\text{eligible residents}}$$

"Eligible residents" is defined as the total number of high school diplomas granted by all private and public secondary schools located within a given state, during the four academic years immediately preceding the fall of 1963, adjusted for inter-state migration.

"In-state public enrollment of residents" is defined as total full-time-equivalent undergraduate enrollment by residents of a state in all public IHE located within that state.[7]

"Private enrollment of residents" is defined as total full-time-equivalent enrollment by residents of a state in all other IHE (in-state private, out-of-state private, and out-of-state public).[8]

The measure of those who choose employment and other non-enrollment pursuits is defined residually by the expression:

$$1 - [(N_1 + N_2)/R]$$

---

6. Some empirical justification for this assumption is provided by Feldman and Hoenack (p. 381). For supporting views, see Blaug (p. 171), Ostheimer (pp. 103-106), and Corazzini. To allow for the possibility that somes states do have severe IHE capacity constraints which could bias the demand estimations, regressions were run on subsets of states having relatively little student out-migration (taken to indicate absence of such constraints); the results did not differ substantially, so this possibility was rejected.

7. The number of part-time students is converted into an equivalent number of full-time students, using an assumption that the average part-time undergraduate carries two-sevenths of a full academic load. See Mushkin and McLoone, p. 82.

8. If a student chooses to enroll in an out-of-state public IHE (only 6.8% of college enrollees did so in 1963), he is numbered among the private enrollees in this study. The rationale is that (a) the higher non-resident tuition and other costs (such as transportation) associated with out-of-state enrollment, and (b) the fact that such enrollment is not subject to control by the same governmental unit, make it reasonable to exclude out-of-state public enrollment from the public enrollment category.

Decision Making in the Private Sector

Explanatory variables: enrollment benefits[9]

B: index of lifetime income benefit—specifically, the absolute difference between average annual incomes of college and high school graduates; expected to bear positively on enrollment.

E: family education—per cent of families with children under 18 in 1959 whose head had completed at least one year of college; expected to bear positively on enrollment, as an influence on student assessment of enrollment benefits.

A: academic achievement—per cent failing Selective Service mental test; expected to bear negatively on enrollment, as influence on student assessment of enrollment benefits.

Q_1: public expenditure per enrollee—total educational expenditures divided by total enrollment, all in-state public IHE; expected to bear positively on public enrollment.[10]

Q_2: private expenditure per enrollee—total educational expenditures divided by total enrollment, all private IHE located within the given region; expected to bear positively on private enrollment.[10]

Y_s: family affluence—per cent of families with children under 18 in 1959 whose income exceeded $10,000; expected to bear positively on private enrollment, as an influence on student preference of private over public enrollment.

C: religion—per cent Catholics in the total population; expected to bear positively on private enrollment as an influence on attractiveness of Catholic IHE.

Explanatory variables: enrollment costs

W_1: opportunity costs (foregone earnings)—average annual income of high school graduates; expected to bear negatively on enrollment.

Y: ability to finance education costs—family income—median real income of families with children under 18 in 1959; expected to bear positively on enrollment.

T_1: net public tuition per enrollee (weighted average based on charges at all public IHE in a given state, using undergraduate enrollments as weights, less the state's mean scholarship aid); expected to bear negatively on public enrollment.[11]

L_1: proximity of public institutions to eligibles—$L_1 = \sum_{i=1}^{n} \sqrt{e_i p_1}$, where e_i is per cent of total full-time-equivalent undergraduate enrollment accounted for by the i-th institution (or group of institutions located within 15 miles of each other), and p_i is per cent of total 1960 popu-

---

9. The paucity of cross-section data by state, as well as collinearity problems, severely limits the choice of explanatory variables.

10. Further detail in Appendix available from author. Perhaps the most obvious defect of this measure is that it is one of input rather than of output; hence, it does not differentiate changes attributable to more efficient operation from those due to better instruction. Yet the nature of the output is not well-defined, either conceptually or empirically, other than in terms of numbers of students.

11. One additional important assumption of this analysis should be made explicit. Within each market, tuition is held to be a pre-determined variable. This can be stated equivalently: supply is infinitely elastic with respect to tuition, in any given market. The interpretation of the regression results as structural demand equations rests on this assumption, which also is implicit in previous research into enrollment determinants.

Demand and Forecasting

lation located within a 30-mile radius of the i-th institution; expected to bear positively on public enrollment.

T_2: net private tuition per enrollee (weighted average based on charges at all private IHE in a given region, using undergraduate enrollments as weight, net of scholarship aid); expected to bear negatively on private enrollment.[11]

L_2: proximity of private institutions to eligibles—ratio of [per cent of U.S. private enrollment located in region i] to [per cent of U.S. eligibles residing in region i], where $i = 1, 2, \ldots, 7$, and each state takes on one of these seven values, depending on its location; expected to bear positively on private enrollment.

REGRESSION RESULTS

All three dependent variables are regressed separately on the same set (subsets) of explanatory variables. This permits conclusions to be drawn about the influence each variable has on whether or not an eligible will attend college, and whether he will select a public or private college. The most instructive results are provided by the following set of estimated equations, which are elaborated in Table 1. More complete results are reported in Table 2. Forty-nine observations are used in estimating each equation.

Public Enrollment Demand

$$(N_1/R) = -.000306(T_1) + .000066(T_2) - .141(L_2)$$
$$(.000095) \quad (.000076) \quad (.035)$$

$$-.720(Y_s) + .767(E) + .0625(L_1) + .261 \qquad R^2 = .73$$
$$(.216) \quad (.212) \quad (.0697) \qquad\qquad s(u) = .043$$

Private Enrollment Demand

$$(N_2/R) = +.000135(T_1) - .000137(T_2) + .138(L_2)$$
$$(.000081) \quad (.000065) \quad (.030)$$

$$+.804(Y_s) + .007(E) - .0579(L_1) + .042 \qquad R^2 = .63$$
$$(.184) \quad (.180) \quad (.0593) \qquad\qquad s(u) = .037$$

Total Enrollment Demand

$$(N_1 + N_2)/R = -.000171(T_1) - .000072(T_2) - .003(L_2)$$
$$(.000077) \quad (.000062) \quad (.029)$$

$$+.085(Y_s) + .775(E) + .0045(L_1) + .303 \qquad R^2 = .67$$
$$(.176) \quad (.172) \quad (.0567) \qquad\qquad s(u) = .035$$

Demand for public enrollment appears to be influenced strongly by four factors:[12]

---

12. Conclusions drawn here from regression estimates are guided by two criteria:
   a) the estimated coefficient should have a small enough standard error to yield a t-ratio significant at the 5% level or better; there being 42 degrees of freedom, the t-ratio should exceed 2.0;
   b) an absolute change by one standard deviation in an explanatory variable should be associated with an absolute change of at least .01 in the value of the enrollment ratio.

   Criterion (b) reflects an interest in the enrollment response to changes in explanatory variables which are substantial, but which are well within the range of observed variation.

Decision Making in the Private Sector

Table 1 — Main Regression Results

	Dependent variable change associated with a standard-deviation increase in explanatory variable			Mean	Standard Deviation
	(N_1/R)	(N_2/R)	$(N_1+N_2)/R$		
T_1 (public)	-.022**	+.010	-.012*	$216	$ 72
T_2 (private)	+.010	-.022*	-.011	$835	$159
L_2 (priv. Loc.)	-.052**	+.051**	-.001	.964	.370
Y_s (income)	-.032**	+.036**	+.004	.128	.045
E (educ.)	+.034**	+.000	+.034**	.205	.044
L_1 (pub. loc.)	+.007	-.007	+.001	.758	.116

** coefficient significant at one per cent level
* coefficient significant at five per cent level

(N_1/R)	(public enrollment ratio)	.227	.076
(N_2/R)	(private enrollment ratio)	.150	.056
$(N_1+N_2)/R$	(total enrollment ratio)	.377	

1) proximity of private IHE (greater availability of private IHE reduces public demand),
2) family educational attainment (if head of household had some college education, children are more likely to choose to enroll in public IHE),
3) high income incidence (if family income exceeds $10,000, children are less likely to choose to enroll in public IHE),
4) public tuition (higher tuition is associated with lower likelihood of enrollment in public IHE).

Demand for private enrollment appears to be influenced equally strongly by two of these factors—private proximity and high incomes. In addition, higher private tuition is associated with lower likelihood of enrollment in private IHE.

Total enrollment demand, which can be viewed as the converse of demand for non-enrollment pursuits (such as full-time employment), appears to be influenced strongly by two factors from the above list: family education, and public tuition. Eligibles from college-educated families are less likely to prefer employment to enrollment than are those from families whose head completed no college. In addition, any increase in public tuition increases the likelihood that the eligible will choose employment over any form of enrollment.

This suggests that private proximity (L_2) and high income (Y_s) primarily influence the type of college chosen by those who do want to enroll somewhere. The role of public proximity (L_1) may be analogous to that of (L_2), but its coefficient lacks statistical significance.[13] None of these

---

13. The lack of significant association between public enrollment and the index of public IHE location is an unexpected result. Intuitively it remains plausible to think that both transportation and living arrangements are less costly the shorter the distance between eligibles and IHE. Similarly, Mushkin [p. 231] reports:

"Report after report from the State study groups emphasizes that, if opportunities

Demand and Forecasting

three variables influence the choice between enrollment and employment (non-enrollment).

The two tuition variables (T_1 and T_2) appear to influence both the enrollment-employment choice and the public-private choice. An increase in public tuition appears to cause some eligibles to switch into private IHE, and some to avoid college altogether (the latter effect being the stronger). An increase in private tuition similarly seems to cause some to switch into public IHE, and some to avoid college altogether (about in equal numbers, though low t-ratios must limit the confidence placed in this result).[14] Relative magnitudes implied by these results are shown in Table 1. A $72 increase in public tuition (from its mean of $216 to $288 is associated with a drop in the percent of eligibles enrolled from its mean of 37.7% to 36.5%. The magnitude of this net discouragement effect is roughly similar to, although on the low side of, that predicted by previous studies.[15]

Given the above noted change in public tuition, the public enrollment measure would decline from 22.7% to 20.5%, while at the same time the private enrollment measure would rise from 15.0% to 16.0%. The implication is that tuition variation will have a substantially greater impact on public IHE enrollment levels than it will on the probability that any given eligible will fail to obtain a college education of some sort. The net discouragement effect of higher public tuition on total enrollment $\partial\left(\frac{N_1+N_2}{R}\right)/\partial T_1$ appears to be accompanied by a substitution effect $[-\partial(N_2/R)/\partial T_1]$ on the distribution of college enrollees between public and private IHE.[16]

The dependent variables are defined as proportions of a fixed number of eligible individuals, and the present model enables account to be taken of all these individuals. Estimation of the two separate enrollment demand functions (for public and private enrollment, respectively) can be validated against the estimation of a third function. This third function is demand for non-enrollment pursuits (or symmetrically, for total enrollment). The results of the two specific enrollment demand estimations cannot be relied upon unless the implied results for the third equation (which accounts for the residual group of eligibles) make good sense. This point has been emphasized in another context by Brainard and Tobin, but it has been

---

for college going are to be provided to the greatest number of young people, institutions of higher education must be distributed widely throughout the State."

While some support for this assertion is provided by Ostheimer, the present results suggest that the influence of public proximity on enrollment is slight. It should be noted that multi-collinearity is not a problem here, in that L_1 is not highly correlated with other explanatory variables. Measurement problems do exist, of course, in that L_1 is a very crude proxy for this dimension of costs.

14. This lends support to the view that some students prefer non-enrollment (including deferred enrollment) to public enrollment, when the price of private enrollment becomes excessive for them.

15. For example, Corazzini [pp. 39-40] estimates that a $100 increase in public four-year university tuition (from a mean of $290) would cause a decline in the (total) enrollment ratio in the amount of .0265 (from its mean of .4264), a 6.2% drop. The present estimates predict a somewhat smaller drop of 4.5%.

16. The substitution effect also can be expressed as the difference between $\partial(N_1/R)/\partial T_1$, the gross discouragement effect, and $\partial\left(\frac{N_1+N_2}{R}\right)/\partial T_1$, the net discouragement effect. While both of these latter two estimates are statistically significant, the estimate of the substitution effect lacks such significance. Nevertheless its magnitude and sign are plausible.

Decision Making in the Private Sector

overlooked in enrollment demand research. In the present model, simple addition of the coefficient estimates of any given variable appearing in the public and private demand equations provides a plausible estimate of that variable's coefficient in the implied third equation. Equally important, the statistical significance of the coefficients of the variables discussed above is generally satisfactory across all three equations. Hence the model can be used to account for the choices of all eligible individuals.

As is apparent from the estimations reported in Table 2, the following explanatory variables prove to have no clear effects on enrollment: income benefit (B), academic achievement (A), the expenditure per enrollee (Q_1 and Q_2), opportunity costs (W_1), family income level (Y), and religion (C).[17] There is a significant negative association between public expenditure (Q_1) and private enrollment, and between private expenditure (Q_2) and public enrollment, as expected. However the magnitudes of the coefficients are implausible, and their "adding-up" properties across equations are unsatisfactory. Hence these results are inconclusive.[18] The influence of opportunity costs (W_1) also remains unclear.[19]

CONCLUSIONS

College-eligible individuals are less likely to enroll in public IHE if:

1) private IHE are more geographically accessible,

2) their parents did not go to college,

3) their parents earn over $10,000 per year,

4) public tuition is higher.

Such individuals are less likely to enroll in private IHE if:

1) private IHE are less geographically accessible,

2) their parents earn less than $10,000 per year.

Institution location and family affluence, *cet. par.*, appear to influence the type of IHE chosen but not the enrollment/non-enrollment choice.[20] On the other hand, tuition and family education appear to have dual but distinct influences on whether and where to go to college. For example, for every ten students who drop out of college altogether when public tuition increases, another eight students will substitute private for public enrollment. Hence, enrollment fluctuations experienced by public IHE in response to changing public tuition levels will be substantially greater than

---

17. B and A are very crude proxy variables (for example, A reflects ability of non-high school graduates as well as that of college-eligible students). Collinearity between A and E (and in turn between E, Y_s, and Y) is also a problem. It should be noted that Corazzini and Feldman, using a different measure, found ability to be an influential variable.

18. Perhaps interstate differences in IHE efficiency distory what the expenditure variables measure.

19. Campbell and Siegel (p. 488) argue that student part-time employment possibilities call into question the usual treatment of foregon earnings. A variety of measures (generally wage and unemployment rates) have been tried by Corazzini (p. 39), Feldman and Hoenack (pp. 376, 388-89), and Hopkins (pp. 61-62), without much success.

20. This is not to argue that income level has no relationship with enrollment/non-enrollment. For to a considerable extent income is a function of past educational attainment, so that a better educated populace—which will send a higher proportion of their children to college—will at the same time be a higher income populace.

Table 2 – Regression Equation Estimates

	(N_1/R)	(N_2/R)	$(N_1+N_2)/R$	(N_1/R)	(N_2/R)	(N_1/R)	(N_2/R)	(N_1/R)	(N_1/R)	(N_1/R)	$(N_1+N_2)/R$	$(N_1+N_2)/R$	$(N_1+N_2)/R$
R^2	.738	.648	.671	.740	.655	.781	.701	.636	.534	.690	.68	.48	.69
B	-.0000249 (.0000193)	+.0000160 (.0000164)	-.0000898 (.00001600)			-.0000227 (.0000177)	+.0000113 (.0000143)						
E	+.655 (.250)	+.141 (.213)	+.796 (.207)	+.904 (.221)	-.0727 (.1870)	+1.02 (.28)	+.107 (.229)	+.365 (.159)		+.805 (.209)	+.830 (.124)		+.950 (.196)
A	-.0978 (.07040)	+.0380 (.0599)	+.0282 (.0584)			+.0910 (.0842)	+.00674 (.06800)						
Q_1				-.0000114 (.0000309)	-.0000395 (.0000262)	+.00000509 (.00003170)	-.0000604 (.0000255)						
Q_2				-.0001330 (.0000770)	+.0000814 (.0000648)	-.000176 (.000090)	+.0000520 (.0000724)						
Y_s	-.510 (.273)	+.675 (.233)	+.165 (.227)	-.804 (.219)	+.851 (.185)	-.989 (.290)	+.640 (.234)						
C						+.0979 (.0700)	-.0332 (.0564)						
W_1						+.0000142 (.0000192)	-.00000531 (.00001550)						
Y												+.00335 (.00092)	-.00091 (.00114)
T_1	-.000275 (.000100)	+.000120 (.000085)	-.000154 (.000083)	-.000340 (.000097)	+.000188 (.000082)	-.000281 (.000100)	+.000144 (.000081)	-.000305 (.000102)	-.000361 (.000115)	-.000309 (.000094)	-.0139* (.0048)	-.0271* (.0057)	-.0119* (.0055)
L_1	+.0974 (.0780)	-.0958 (.0664)	+.00153 (.06470)	+.0922 (.0794)	-.0686 (.0641)								
T_2	+.0000109 (.0000890)	-.0000838 (.0000757)	-.0000729 (.0000738)	+.000157 (.000092)	-.000178 (.000078)	+.000175 (.000118)	-.0000954 (.0000953)						
L_2	-.120 (.038)	+.123 (.033)	+.00215 (.03190)	-.099 (.037)	+.109 (.031)	-.109 (.045)	+.120 (.036)	-.117 (.020)	-.117 (.022)	-.104 (.019)			

*Single tuition measure reflecting both public and private IHE prices.

Decision Making in the Private Sector

the corresponding fluctuations in the number of eligibles who miss college altogether.

States in which relatively few high school graduates go on to college have several policy instruments with which they might alter the situation. Tuition policy would appear to be a more potent instrument than either of the two other instruments considered here—namely, educational quality and institutional location. Yet even with respect to tuition changes two points must be made:

a) tuition is a significant influence on enrollment, but it is less decisive than parental education, over which the state has very limited influence;

b) tuition has both a substitution and a net discouragement effect. Hence lower public tuition would cause some switching from private to public IHE, thereby reducing the desired effect of total enrollment.

Use of a policy instrument such as tuition can and should be evaluated with respect to cost as well as to effectiveness, of course. A state legislature would want some estimate of the budgetary impact of an enrollment-generating reduction in tuition. A rough idea of the net aggregate increase in costs to the state government due to a tuition reduction can be calculated as follows:

Assume (a) the level of public IHE expenditures per enrollee, Q_1, is to be held constant; and (b) tuition (T_1) and state aid (S) are the only sources of IHE revenues, so that $Q_1 = T_1 + S$.[21]

Then
$$C = [\Delta T_1][(N_1/R)(R)] + [\{\Delta(N_1/R)\}R][S+\Delta T_1]$$

where

C : net increase in aggregate state aid to public IHE

ΔT_1 : amount of reduction in public tuition per enrollee

(N_1/R) : ratio of (instate public enrollment of residents) to (eligible residents), prior to the proposed change

R : total number of eligible residents in the state

S : per enrollee level of state aid to public IHE (prior to proposed tuition reduction)

From the public enrollment demand equation (p. 6),

$$\partial(N_1/R)/\partial T_1 = -.000306.$$

Hence, at least approximately,

$$\Delta T_1 = \Delta(N_1/R)/(.000306).$$

For example, let us suppose the objective is to increase the enrollment ratio (N_1/R) by .010, and compute the resulting cost increment using representative data from a hypothetical state typical of those in the sample. Initial values of the variables: $R = 100,000$; $(N_1/R) = .227$; $T_1 = \$216$;

---

21. See Hopkins, ch. III, for evidence in support of this view.

$S = \$984$. Then a $33 reduction in tuition probably would be needed to increase public enrollment by roughly 1,000 students (increasing (N_1/R) from .227 to .237). Taken together, these changes would imply that the level of aggregate state aid to public IHE would need to be increased by roughly $1,770,000.

As noted earlier, of course, this additional enrollment would include students not previously enrolled in any college and also a substantial number of students who merely switch from private to public IHE.

These results carry with them the usual weaknesses inherent in generalizations based only on a single cross-section. Furthermore, additional research would be useful into possible interactions between the demand and supply sides of the enrollment market.[22] Nevertheless, the study does shed new light on the substantial interstate variation which continues in this nation in the higher education of our youth.

REFERENCES

1. M. Blaug, "An Economic Interpretation of the Private Demand for Education," *Economica*, May 1966, *NS 33*, 166-182.
2. W. C. Brainard and J. Tobin, "Pitfalls in Financial Model Building," *Amer. Econ. Review*, Proc. 1968, *58*, 99-122.
3. R. Campbell and B. N. Siegel, "Demand for Higher Education in the United States," *Amer. Econ. Review*, June 1967, *57*, 482-94.
4. A. J. Corazzini *et. al.*, *Higher Education in the Boston Metropolitan Area*, Boston 1969.
5. P. Feldman and S. A. Hoenack, "Private Demand for Higher Education in the U.S.," in U.S. Congress, Joint Economic Committee, *The Economics and Financing of Higher Education in the U.S.*, Compendium of Papers, 91st Cong., 1st sess., Washington 1969, 375-395.
6. H. Galper and R. M. Dunn, Jr., "A Short-Run Demand Function for Higher Education in the U.S.," *Jour. Pol. Econ.*, Sept. 1969, *77*, 765-777.
7. T. D. Hopkins, "The Provision of Higher Education: A Market Interpretation," unpublished doctoral dissertation, Yale Univ. 1971.
8. S. J. Mushkin, "State Financing of Higher Education," in U.S. Office of Education, *Economics of Higher Education*, Bull. 5, Washington 1962.
9. S. J. Mushkin and E. P. McLoone, *Public Spending for Higher Education in 1970*, Chicago 1965.
10. R. H. Ostheimer, *Student Charges and Financing Higher Education*, New York 1953.

22. See Hopkins, ch. IV.

CASE 7 THE DEMAND FOR ROSES

THE MARKET FOR ROSES

Roses have an almost universal identification with the act of sending flowers, and consequently, they are one of the major products that the retail florist sells either by itself or as part of floral arrangements. The wholesale cut flower supplier must therefore be able to supply roses to retail florists. However, a number of recent factors have affected the growth in demand for roses. First, there has been a general breakdown of "old country social customs" such as the tradition of always sending flowers for a funeral. Second, there has been a growth in demand for competing products, such as carnations, which live longer than roses. Likewise, there has been increased use by retailers of other flowers that are larger and require smaller quantities per arrangement. (Also, in this context, there has been accelerated growth in the demand for green plants. Green plant sales accounted for only 22 percent of the total sales for the floral industry in 1965, but had jumped to 42 percent by 1974, and are predicted to go to 50 percent by 1977.) Third, the costs of growing roses, particularly fuel and labor costs, have been increasing significantly.

DEVELOPING A DEMAND MODEL FOR ROSES

Mathews & Sons is a wholesale supplier of flowers to retail florists in the Detroit metropolitan area. This firm is concerned with developing a model that will aid in forecasting their rose sales (Q_t). Data on Mathew's rose sales over the past sixteen quarters was available from their monthly sales summaries. The variables that are thought to influence Mathew's rose sales included (1) their average wholesale price of roses, (2) their average wholesale price of carnations, (3) the average unemployment rate in the Detroit area, (4) the total number of "flower events" which, as defined here, means the total number of births, deaths, and marriages occuring during the quarter, (5) average weekly family disposable income, and (6) a "trend" variable. Price data for roses and carnations was available from Mathew's billing records; data on the unemployment rate in the Detroit area was available in the Michigan Manpower Review; information on births, deaths, and marriages occuring each quarter was obtained from the Michigan Department of Public Health; average family income data is available from the U.S. Department of Labor. The data on these variables is summarized in Table 1.

Questions for Discussion

1. Develop a linear demand model for Mathew's rose sales in terms of the six variables that are hypothesized to affect sales. From your knowledge of economic theory, develop a hypothesis concerning the sign (+ or —) for each of the explanatory variables (excluding the "trend" variable) in the demand model.
2. Using a multiple linear regression program, estimate the coefficients of the demand model for the data in Table 1.
3. Interpret each of the regression coefficients. Are the actual signs of the coefficients consistent with your hypothesized signs? Are the coefficients statistically significant?
4. What is the coefficient of determination for this model? Give an interpretation of its magnitude.
5. Calculate the price elasticity using the second quarter data for 1975. Give an economic interpretation of this figure.
6. Calculate the cross elasticity of demand using second quarter data for 1975. Give an economic interpretation of this figure.
7. In the demand model developed above we have ignored the competitive aspects of the metropolitan Detroit wholesale florist market. How might we go about incorporating this factor into the demand model?
8. What problem(s) could arise in developing a demand model using *quarterly* data?
9. How does the possible presence of autocorrelation and multicollinearity in the data affect our interpretation of the results?
10. What are some of the shortcomings of using this model to forecast Mathew's future rose sales?

Demand and Forecasting

Table 1 Raw Data for Rose Demand Study

(1) Quarter	(2) Year	(3) Quantity of Roses Sold (Dozen) Q_t	(4) Average Wholesale Price of Roses ($/Doz) P_t	(5) Average Wholesale Price of Carnations ($/doz) C_t	(6) Average Unemployment Rate (%) U_t	(7) Births (B)	(8) Deaths (D)	(9) Marriages (M)	(10) Total "Flower Events" (B+D+M) E_t	(11) Average Weekly Family Disposable Income ($/week) Y_t	(12) Trend T
3	71	11484	2.26	3.49	8.8	19284	8819	11919	40022	158.11	1
4	71	9348	2.54	2.85	7.1	18062	9334	9600	36996	173.36	2
1	72	8429	3.07	4.06	8.1	17207	9828	7000	34035	165.26	3
2	72	10079	2.91	3.64	9.0	16771	8900	10926	36597	172.92	4
3	72	9240	2.73	3.21	8.6	17118	9008	11958	38084	178.46	5
4	72	8862	2.77	3.66	6.3	16533	9217	9454	35204	198.62	6
1	73	6216	3.59	3.76	6.2	16160	9570	7381	33111	186.28	7
2	73	8253	3.23	3.49	7.0	16059	8931	11257	36247	188.98	8
3	73	8038	2.60	3.13	7.1	16844	9165	11666	37675	180.49	9
4	73	7476	2.89	3.20	5.4	15518	9165	9431	34114	183.33	10
1	74	5911	3.77	3.65	8.8	14819	8983	6475	30277	181.87	11
2	74	7950	3.64	3.60	9.1	15033	8924	10664	34621	185.00	12
3	74	6134	2.82	2.94	9.4	16178	8618	11140	35936	184.00	13
4	74	5868	2.96	3.12	9.9	15190	9956	9005	34151	188.20	14
1	75	3160	4.24	3.58	15.7	14455	9057	6455	29967	175.67	15
2	75	5872	3.69	3.53	15.9	14769	8324	10814	33907	188.00	16

CASE 8 A DEMAND STUDY OF BUS RIDERSHIP IN THE CITY OF DETROIT

BACKGROUND

The automobile has been the focal point of Detroit's economy, and, consequently, the "motor capital of the world" has paid little attention in past years to the need for public transportation. The only type of public transportation available in Detroit is the bus service offered through the City of Detroit's Department of Transportation (formerly the DSR—Department of Streets and Railways), which has been experiencing difficulties in recent years. Service has been cut, funding reduced, and bus maintenance neglected. These problems have been caused by a number of factors including a reduction in ridership, economic problems of the city itself, and attitudes toward the need and use of bus service. Recently, however, the need for mass transportation in the city has received increased attention in light of the energy shortage and economic recession.

FACTORS AFFECTING BUS RIDERSHIP

The objectives in this case are to analyze the factors that affect the demand for bus service in Detroit and to develop a model that could be used in forecasting future demand. Demand for bus service is represented by annual bus ridership (Q_t), which, defined here, means the number of fare-paying passengers. It has also been estimated that approximately 10,000 senior citizens in Detroit ride the buses free each year. The Department of Transportation is primarily interested in estimating demand based on revenue passengers, since these are the people who keep the system operating on a financially sound basis. Therefore, nonrevenue generating passengers are not incorporated into the bus ridership variable.

Bus ridership is hypothesized to be a function of the following measurable variables: the price charged, population, per capita income, advertising and promotional expenditures, the price of substitute transportation services, and a "trend" factor.

Price Charged (P_t) In this study, price is measured by the base fare per ride and excludes the cost of transfers and quantity discounts offered on weekly or monthly bus passes. Economic theory suggests that there should be an inverse relation between the fare charged and bus ridership.

Population (N_t) Bus ridership should vary directly over time with the population of the City of Detroit.

Per Capita Income (Y_t) One could hypothesize that there should be an inverse relationship between bus ridership and income. The more income that a person has, the greater will be the likelihood of that person owning an automobile and hence the less likely that the person will use bus transportation.

Advertising and Promotional Expenditures (A_t) The greater the advertising and promotional expenses, the more people are encouraged to use the bus system. Advertising and promotional expenditures include all outlays for literature, hand-outs, billboards, radio, and television. Not included are barter arrangements in which the Department of Transportation gives advertising space on its buses to radio and television stations in exchange for their airing commercial messages which promote bus ridership.

Price of Substitute Transportation Services (C_t) The automobile is the most widely used substitute for bus transportation. One would normally expect bus ridership to vary directly with the cost of operating an automobile since a lower (higher) average annual operating cost makes it more (less) attractive to substitute automobile transportation for bus ridership.

Trend Factor (T) A "trend" variable is incorporated into the analysis to account for any underlying long-term growth (or decline) effects that are not represented by the other explanatory variables.

DATA

Data on the variables described above for the years 1962 to 1974 are shown in Table 1. Detroit's Department of Transportation provided data on bus ridership, fares, and advertising expenditures; the City of Detroit Municipal Library provided the data on the

Demand and Forecasting

Table 1 Raw Data for Bus Ridership Study

(1) Year	(2) Bus Ridership (millions of passengers)	(3) Fare ($)	(4) Population (thousands)	(5) Per Capita Income ($)	(6) Advertising and Promotion Expenditures ($)	(7) Automobile Operating Costs ($ per yr.)	(8) Trend
t	Q_t	P_t	N_t	Y_t	A_t	C_t	T
1962	117.020	.25	1645	2860.	9790.	1100.	1
1963	114.860	.25	1627	2980.	9827.	1100.	2
1964	112.560	.25	1620	3120.	9894.	1180.	3
1965	115.050	.25	1615	3330.	9812.	1180.	4
1966	122.800	.25	1640	3530.	10713.	1250.	5
1967	130.720	.25	1620	3660.	11657.	1250.	6
1968	126.650	.30	1570	4020.	11905.	1289.	7
1969	121.020	.30	1500	4343.	13165.	1289.	8
1970	115.200	.40	1511	4454.	14579.	1289.	9
1971	103.180	.40	1467	4768.	13146.	1550.	10
1972	94.344	.40	1438	5317.	15283.	1550.	11
1973	91.006	.40	1396	6071.	22318.	1550.	12
1974	85.460	.40	1362	6123.	16673.	1640.	13

population and per capita income; and the American Automobile Association's publication entitled "Your Driving Costs" contained estimates of the average annual operating costs of an automobile over the 13 year period.

In doing multiple regression analysis using economic time series data such as those in Table 1, the presence of autocorrelation and multicollinearity can cause problems in interpreting the results.

Questions for Discussion

1. What is the dependent variable in this demand study?
2. What are the independent variables?
3. Develop a linear demand model for bus service in terms of the variables that are hypothesized to affect bus ridership.
4. What are the hypothesized signs (+ or —) of the coefficients of each of the explanatory variables in the demand model?
5. Using any multiple linear regression program available on a computer to which you have access, estimate the coefficients of the demand model for the data given in Table 1.
6. Give an interpretation to each of the regression coefficients. Are the actual signs of the coefficients consistent with the hypothesized signs? Are the coefficients statistically significant?
7. What is the value of the coefficient of determination? Give an interpretation of its magnitude.
8. Calculate the price elasticity using 1974 data. Give an economic interpretation of this figure.
9. Calculate the income elasticity using 1974 data. Give an economic interpretation of this number.
10. The effects of inflation were ignored in estimating the demand equation. How might one go about incorporating into the analysis the effect of changes in the purchasing power of the dollar over this time period (1962-74)?
11. What problems in interpreting the results will arise if autocorrelation and multicollinearity are present in the data?

EXERCISES
9

9-1. Given the following demand function:

Price P ($)	Quantity Q_D (units)	Arc Elasticity E_D	Total Revenue ($)	Marginal Revenue ($)
12	30			
11	40	—	—	—
10	50	—	—	—
9	60	—	—	—
8	70	—	—	—
7	80	—	—	—
6	90	—	—	—
5	100	—	—	—
4	110	—	—	—

a. Compute the associated arc elasticity, total revenue and marginal revenue values.

b. On separate graphs, plot the demand function, total revenue functions, and marginal revenue function.

9-2. The Stopdecay Company sells an electric toothbrush for $25.00. Their sales have averaged 8,000 units per month over the last year. Recently, their closest competitor, Decayfighter, reduced the price of their electric toothbrush from $35.00 to $30.00. As a result, Stopdecay's sales declined by 1,500 units per month.

a. What is the arc cross elasticity of demand between Stopdecay's toothbrush and Decayfighter's toothbrush? What does this indicate about the relationship between the two products?

b. If Stopdecay knows that the arc price elasticity of demand for its toothbrush is —1.5, what price would Stopdecay have to charge in order to sell the same number of units as it did before the Decayfighter price cut? Assume that Decayfighter holds the price of its toothbrush constant at $30.00.

c. What is Stopdecay's average monthly total revenue from the sale of electric toothbrushes before and after the price change determined in b.?

d. Is the result in c. necessarily desirable? What other factors would have to be taken into consideration?

9-3. The demand for renting motor boats in a resort town has been estimated to be $Q_D = 5000 - 50P$ where Q_D is the quantity of boats demanded (boat-hours) and P is the average price per hour to rent a motor boat. If this relationship holds true in the future:

a. How many motor boats will be demanded at a rental price of $10, $20, and $30 per hour?

b. What is the *arc* price elasticity of demand between $10 and $20? Between $20 and $30?

c. What is the *point* price elasticity of demand at $10, $20, and $30?

Demand and Forecasting

d. If the number of boat rental hours was 4,250 last year, what would you expect the average rental rate per hour to have been?

9-4. The following table gives hypothetical data for the weekly purchase of sirloin steak by a college fraternity house. Compute all meaningful arc elasticity coefficients (price, cross, and income). Remember that the effects of the other factors must be held constant when computing any of the above elasticities.

Week	Price per Pound of Steak	Quantity of Steak Purchased (pound)	Income (Member Dues)	Price per Pound of Hamburger
1	$1.50	100	$500	$ .90
2	1.60	95	500	.90
3	1.60	100	550	.90
4	1.60	105	550	.95
5	1.50	115	550	.95
6	1.50	105	550	.90
7	1.50	100	500	.90
8	1.65	90	500	.90
9	1.65	110	500	1.00
10	1.65	90	400	1.00

9-5. The Reliable Aircraft Company manufactures small, pleasure-use aircraft. Based on past experience, sales volume appears to be affected by changes in the price of the planes and by the state of the economy as measured by consumers' disposable personal incomes. The following data pertaining to Reliable's aircraft sales and selling prices, and consumers' personal income were collected:

Year	Aircraft Sales	Average Price	Disposable Personal Income (in constant 1958 dollars— billions)
1973	525	$7200	$610
1974	450	8000	610
1975	400	8000	590

a. Estimate the arc price elasticity of demand using the 1973 and 1974 data.
b. Estimate the arc income elasticity of demand using the 1974 and 1975 data.
c. Assume that these estimates are expected to remain stable during 1976. Forecast 1976 sales for Reliable assuming that their aircraft prices remain constant at 1975 levels and that disposable personal income will increase by $40 (billion). Also assume the arc income elasticity computed in b. above is the best available estimate of income elasticity.
d. Forecast 1976 sales for Reliable given that their aircraft prices increase by $500 from 1975 levels and that disposable personal income will increase by $40 (billion). Assume that the price and income effects are *additive* and that the arc income and price elasticities computed in a. and b. above are the best available estimates of these elasticities to be used in making the forecast.

9-6. The Sure-Fire Spark Plug Co. performed a regression analysis to

Decision Making in the Private Sector

determine the demand for its spark plugs in the "aftermarket" (i.e., replacement) and obtained the following results:

$$Q_D = 1060 - 2.86\,P + 36.3\,A + 2.3\,N - .172\,Y$$

where

Q_D = quantity demanded (millions of units)
P = price index of automobile replacement parts (1967 — 69 = 100)
A = advertising expenditures (millions of dollars)
N = numbers of used cars registered (millions of vehicles)
Y = per capita disposable income (dollars)

a. Economists estimate that for next year P = 125, N = 98.5, and Y = $3,300. If the company wishes to sell 450 (million) spark plugs next year, how much should it spend on advertising?
b. For the information given (and computed) in part a., compute the point elasticity of demand with respect to advertising.
c. Using the answer obtained in part b., predict the effect on quantity of spark plugs demanded of a 5 percent cutback in Sure-Fire's advertising budget for next year.

9-7. Bell Greenhouses has estimated its monthly demand for potting soil to be the following:

$$N = 400 + 4X$$

where

N = monthly demand for bags of potting soil
X = time periods in months (March 1974 = 0)

Assume that this trend factor is expected to remain stable in the foreseeable future. The following table contains the monthly seasonal adjustment factors, which have been estimated using actual sales data from the past five years:

Month	Adjustment Factor
March	+ 2%
June	+ 15%
August	+ 10%
December	— 12%

a. Forecast Bell Greenhouses' demand for potting soil in March, June, August, and December 1976.
b. If the following table shows the forecasted and actual potting soil sales by Bell Greenhouses for April in each of the past five years, determine the seasonal adjustment factor to be used in making an April 1976 forecast.

Year	Forecast	Actual
1975	500	515
1974	452	438
1973	404	420
1972	356	370
1971	308	305

9-8. The manager of the Midwestern University Book Store is attempting to forecast next year's demand for "Whizzo," a mini, wrist-watch size calculator. She hypothesizes that the number of units sold (S) in any

Demand and Forecasting

period should be directly proportional to the engineering enrollment at the university in hundreds of students (E), average professors' salaries at the university in thousands of dollars (I), and inversely proportional to the price of these calculators (P) and expresses the relationship in the following form:

$$S = k \frac{EI}{P}$$

a. Estimate k given the following data from the previous year: S = 150 units, E = 25 (hundred) students, I = $18 (thousand) and P = $200.
b. Use the equation in a. to forecast next year's calculator sales assuming that the price of the calculators declines to $150 and that the other variables remain unchanged.
c. Use the equation in a. to forecast next year's calculator sales assuming that the price declines to $150, engineering enrollment increases by 10 percent to 27.5, and average professor's salaries increase by 5 percent to $18.9.
d. What other factors might the manager want to consider in analyzing the demand for Whizzo calculators?

9-9. General Cereals is using a regression model to estimate the demand for Tweetie Sweeties, a whistle-shaped, sugar-coated breakfast cereal for children. The following (multiplicative) demand function is being used:

$$Q_D = 6{,}280\, P^{-2.15}\, A^{1.05}\, N^{3.70}$$

where

Q_D = quantity demanded, in 10 oz. boxes
P = price per box, in dollars
A = advertising expenditures on daytime television, in dollars
N = proportion of the population under 12 years old

a. What is the point price elasticity of demand for Tweetie Sweeties?
b. What is the advertising elasticity of demand?
c. What interpretation would you give to the exponent of N?

Chapter 4 Production and Cost Analysis

READING
10 STATISTICAL COST ANALYSIS
William A. Longbrake*

Statistical techniques provide information useful in making many types of business decisions. For several reasons, however, statistical analysis is seldom used in analyzing production and other costs. Standard costing procedures, such as time and motion studies and direct costing procedures based on past experience and modified by anticipated changes, are sufficient in many decision-making situations.

Data limitations frequently hinder the employment of statistical analysis. To use it, data concerning costs, output, and product characteristics must exist for a sufficient number of time periods in one business firm or, alternatively, these data must be available for one time period for several firms producing essentially the same product. Another impediment is the general lack of knowledge about statistical cost analysis.

This article will demonstrate the use of statistical analysis for product costing, incremental costing, and cost forecasting. While the illustrations are developed specifically for use by commercial banks in making decisions about demand deposit operations, the basic techniques could be modified for cost analysis of products in other industries or products of a single firm.

Detailed cost accounting and production data exist for a sample of nearly 1,000 banks that have voluntarily participated in the Federal Reserve Banks' Functional Cost Analysis (FCA) program. Development of uniform accounting classifications and methods of allocating costs by the FCA has enabled participating banks to compare their performance with the average performance of similarly-sized banks. As a result, the accuracy and consistency of FCA data is excellent. Hence, the data afford a good basis for demonstrating the uses of statistical analysis.

Methodology

Before statistical analysis can take place, it is necessary to construct a cost function that describes accurately all relevant factors. First, cost categories must be defined. For example, three types of costs are incurred in providing services to demand deposit customers—fixed maintenance costs, variable maintenance costs, and transactions costs. Fixed maintenance costs arise from routine operations performed on a regular basis for every account, e.g., carrying a master record of an account on a ledger card and preparing and sending monthly statements. Variable maintenance costs, such as FDIC insurance and "free" services, vary with the size of an account. Transactions costs vary directly with the volume of transactions.

Second, measurable variables must be found that explain variations in each general cost category.

Third, other factors that may indirectly influence the costs of providing demand deposit services should be identified, and variables should be defined that

---
*Dr. Longbrake is a Financial Economist with the Federal Deposit Insurance Corporation. He has published articles in the *Journal of Finance*, the *Journal of Bank Research*, the *Quarterly Review of Economics and Business*, and the *Journal of Money, Credit and Banking*.

Production and Cost Analysis

explain their effects. For example, to the extent that common production costs exist and cannot be allocated precisely, the level of time deposit operations may have an influence on demand deposit costs. Other factors arise when the cost behavior of several firms is being analyzed. For instance, legal organizational form—unit, branch, or holding company affiliate—may influence the organization of demand deposit operations and, therefore, influence operating costs as well. In addition, wage rates prevailing in local labor markets will have an important effect on demand deposit costs because of the large amount of labor required.

It may be impossible to determine the separate effects of each of these factors because of their complex interrelationships. Moreover, if the volume of output affects the unit cost related to any one of these factors, the accountant's use of standard costs may overlook important variations, that occur with changes in the level of output. Thus, a cost function may be a useful alternative to ordinary accounting practices.

Bell and Murphy [1] and Longbrake [2] have demonstrated that a log-linear cost function of the type defined in the following equation is appropriate for commercial banks and explains most of the variation in demand deposit operating costs among banks:

$$\log C = \log H + \delta_1 \log N + \delta_2 \log S + \psi_1 \log T_1 +$$
$$\psi_2 \log T_2 + \psi_3 \log T_3 + \psi_4 \log T_4 +$$
$$\psi_5 \log T_5 + \psi_6 \log T_6 + \alpha_1 \log B +$$
$$\alpha_2 \log M + \alpha_3 \log w + \alpha_4 \log I,$$

where C is total *direct* operating costs allocated by a bank to the demand deposit function. A glossary of the symbols in the equation appears in the inset. The reader is asked to peruse them before proceeding, and refer to them as necessary in company with the following exposition.

Glossary of Symbols

C	=	total *direct* operating costs allocated by a bank to the demand deposit function
log H	=	cost function constant
N	=	average number of accounts per banking office
S	=	average dollar size of a demand deposit account
T_1	=	average number of home debits (items posted to the debit column in the ledger for each account) per account
T_2	=	average number of deposits per account
T_3	=	average number of transit checks (checks written on banks other than the home bank) deposited per account
T_4	=	average number of official checks issued per account
T_5	=	average number of checks cashed per account
T_6	=	average number of transit checks cashed per account
B	=	number of offices operated by a bank
M	=	ratio of the number of regular checking accounts to the sum of both regular and special accounts
w	=	average annual wage rate per demand deposit employee
I	=	ratio of the dollar volume of demand deposits to the dollar volume of demand and time deposits, measures the effects of time deposit production activities on demand deposit costs
$\delta_i, \psi_i, \alpha_i$		indicate that percentage change in total cost that occurs when a particular variables changes by 1 percent, given that all other variables remain unchanged.

Coefficients of the variables in the cost equation shown above—δ_i, ψ_i, and α_i—indicate that percentage change in total cost occurring when a particular variable changes by 1%, with all other variables unchanged. The effect on costs of the addition of a new account with characteristics *identical* to the existing "average" account is measured by the coefficient of log N. The indicated percentage change in costs will include additional fixed maintenance, variable maintenance, and transactions costs. The percentage change in costs caused by an increase in the average size of account S will indicate primarily increases in variable maintenance costs associated with account size. The percentage change in costs caused by an increase in T_1 will show the change in transactions costs due to a large number of home debits per account. Changes in the other transactions variables can be interpreted in a similar fashion.

If a regular account is substituted for a special account, the coefficient of log M will indicate whether costs increase or decrease. The change in costs may result from differences in either fixed maintenance, variable maintenance, or transactions costs for two accounts which are identical in all respects except that one is a special account and the other is a regular account. The coefficient of log w indicates the percentage change in costs which occurs when the wage rate changes. Differences in local wage rates or differences in the mix of personnel engaged in demand deposit operations could cause differences in total costs. Therefore, the effects of maintenance, transactions, and other factors on demand deposit costs are contained within the cost function. Although the cost of a specific demand deposit production operation may not be identifiable, the statistical cost function can be used to determine the costs which occur for a given set of production relationships.

Data for estimating the coefficients of the cost equation shown above were obtained from 964 banks that participated in the 1971 FCA program. These banks ranged in size from $5 million to $6 billion in total deposits. Regression analysis was used to estimate the coefficients; the results are presented in Exhibit 1. These results will serve as a base for developing illustrations of product costing, incremental costing, and cost forecasting below.

Product Costing

Accountants generally recognize two methods of product costing — job order costing and process costing. In job order costing, each job is an accounting unit to which material, labor, and other costs are assigned. However, in process costing, attention centers on total costs incurred by a department for a given time period in relation to the units processed. Dividing total costs by the quantity of units produced gives the average unit cost. Process costing is usually more appropriate for mass production.

Statistical analysis of costs is more applicable in process than in job order costing. Costs are accumulated over a period of time for a specific department, and data concerning production activities in the department are collected for the same time period. However, rather than employing traditional accounting methods to ascertain average unit costs, average unit costs are estimated through a statistical analysis of the cost-output relationship as defined in a cost function. Traditional accounting methods must assume a rather uncomplicated relationship between output and costs (or various categories of costs); however, if complex interrelationships prevail among the various factors influencing total costs, statistical methods may be more appropriate. It must be remembered that data are required for several time periods or for several firms producing essentially the same product before statistical analysis is feasible. Traditional accounting methods do not have such a requirement.

In many respects, servicing demand deposits in a bank is similar to a continuous production process in manufacturing and thus will serve as a good general illustration. Tellers perform several operations including counting cash, verifying deposit amounts, and issuing receipts. The proof department sorts checks by type and identifies questionable checks. The bookkeeping department posts deposits and

Exhibit 1. Regression Results for the 1971 Demand Deposit Cost Function*

$$\log C = -1.7345 + .9503 \log N + .3936 \log S + .0467 \log T_1$$
$$(.1792) \quad (.0127) \quad (.0248) \quad (.0268)$$

$$+ .1427 \log T_2 + .0742 \log T_3 + .0583 \log T_4 +$$
$$(.0348) \quad (.0126) \quad (.0111)$$

$$+ .0183 \log T_5 - .0046 \log T_6 + 1.0150 \log B +$$
$$(.0105) \quad (.0124) \quad (.0092)$$

$$- .0626 \log M + .4312 \log w + .0113 \log I$$
$$(.0251) \quad (.0470) \quad (.0311)$$

$\bar{R} = .9630$
Standard Error of Estimate $= .0998$
F-Ratio $= 2087.5$

*Numbers in parentheses are standard errors of the regression coefficients.

Production and Cost Analysis

checks to appropriate accounts. Furthermore, many other activities, in addition to those mentioned above, occur on a regular and continuing basis.

Two kinds of demand deposit accounts—regular and special—customarily exist in most banks. Special accounts have no minimum balance requirement whereas regular accounts do. As a result of the no minimum balance feature, special accounts tend to be held by individuals rather than businesses and they tend to be less active and have smaller average balances than regular accounts. Thus, regular and special accounts are distinct products; however, production operations for both always occur simultaneously. Consequently, the cost of servicing each type of account is not easily separable.

In Exhibit 2, it is shown how the total and average cost per $100 of an average regular and an average special account can be determined from the results of the statistical analysis shown in Exhibit 1. For convenience, values of the various account characteristics and bank characteristics have been selected that are approximately equal to the sample geometric means of these characteristics. In the cost computations for regular accounts, it is assumed that no special accounts exist. However, in the cost computations for special accounts, it is assumed that 1% of the accounts are regular. This assumption is required because the log of the mix variable (M) is undefined when there are no regular accounts.

The average regular account in Exhibit 2 is more than twice as costly to service as the average special account. However, the average regular account is only 29% as costly per *dollar* of deposits as the average special account. Product costs developed in this way can be used to develop pricing policy. In the case of banks, this kind of information is useful in establishing service charge schedules. It should be noted that the average unit cost of an account need not be the same for each set of account characteristic and bank characteristic variables. Any bank which knows its values for the variables in Exhibit 2 may determine its average unit costs by following the demonstrated computational procedure.

This method of product costing would be useful in any business enterprise that produces more than one product on a regular and continuing basis using essentially the same types of resources. For example, different types of telephone service—private, party, or commercial—could be costed using the methods described above. Other possible applications might

Exhibit 2. Computation of Average Unit Costs for Regular and Special Checking Accounts

		Regular account				Special account		
		(1) Value	(2) Log of value	(3) Cost function coefficient	(4) Product of columns 2 and 3	(5) Value	(6) Log of value	(7) Product of columns 3 and 6
Characteristics of average account								
S	Account size	$2,100	3.32222	.3936	1.30763	$ 300	2.47712	.97499
T_1	Home debits/accounts	230	2.36173	.0467	.11029	100	2.00000	.09340
T_2	Deposits/accounts	40	1.60206	.1427	.22861	25	1.39794	.19949
T_3	Transit checks deposited/accounts	180	2.25527	.0742	.16734	20	1.30103	.09654
T_4	Official checks/accounts	3	.47712	.0583	.02782	2	.30103	.01755
T_5	Checks cashed/accounts	30	1.47712	.0183	.02703	30	1.47712	.02703
T_6	Transit checks cashed/accounts	14	1.14613	−.0046	−.00527	16	1.20412	−.00554
Bank characteristics								
$\bar{N}$	Number of accounts	3,250	3.51188	.9503	3.33734	3,250	3.51188	3.33734
B	Number of offices	3	.47712	1.0150	.48428	3	.47712	.48428
M	Regular accounts/all accounts	100%	.00000	−.0626	.00000	1%	−2.00000	.12520
w	Annual wage rate	$5,700	3.75587	.4312	1.61953	$5,700	3.75587	1.61953
I	Demand deposits/total deposits	40%	−.39794	.0113	−.00450	40%	−.39794	−.00450
H	Cost function constant				−1.73447			−1.73447
Total cost	(log)				5.53860			5.23084
	(antilog)				$345,623.00			$170,054.00
Average cost per account					$ 35.45			$ 17.44
Average cost per $100					$ 1.69			$ 5.81

include the manufacture of canned and processed foods, book publishing, manufacture of apparel, manufacture of consumer durable goods such as automobiles, refrigerators, television sets, appliances, lawn mowers, and so on.

Incremental Costing

Incremental or differential costs are the increases or decreases in total costs, or the changes in specific elements of cost, that result from some variation in operations. An incremental costing approach to decision making is important when certain costs are fixed and, as such, are not influenced by changes in operations. Ordinarily such a situation occurs in the short run when scale of operations cannot be changed. When the decision is whether or not to accept another order or expand output from a given level, and certain costs are fixed or are relatively inflexible, use of standard costs or average unit costs may lead to the wrong decision. This could happen because the incremental cost of the additional output may differ from the change in total costs indicated by multiplying the additional output by the average unit cost.

Situations in which an incremental cost approach to decision making may be appropriate include: taking on new orders; increasing, decreasing or eliminating production of certain products; replacing old equipment with new; and so forth. In commercial banks, it may be useful to know the incremental costs of a new demand deposit account, especially if it is tied to a loan arrangement, so that an appropriate pricing strategy can be developed. Incremental costs can also be developed for specific types of demand deposit accounts that differ in various respects from the average account.

The usual accounting approach to differential costing is to identify variable and fixed costs. Then, in a particular situation the affected variable costs can be used to determine the differential cost. However, if variable costs cannot be determined easily or, if variable costs do not remain constant per unit of output at various levels of output, the usual accounting techniques may prove to be insufficient.

Statistical cost analysis may improve the accuracy of incremental cost determination in such circumstances because estimates of incremental (marginal) costs can be derived directly from the cost function for every variation in the basic product that might exist. For example, incremental costs can be determined for each type of transaction that is identified in the demand deposit cost function. Thus, the incremental cost of one additional home debit per account is the change in total cost, C, which results from an increase in home debits per account, T_1, while all other variables in the cost equation shown above remain unchanged. This incremental cost is computed by taking the partial derivative of total cost, C, with respect to home debits per account, T_1. In the present instance, the incremental cost of one additional home debit per account is equal to the cost function coefficient of T_1 (ψ_1) times total cost (C) divided by T_1. Thus, the incremental cost of an additional home debit per regular demand account is computed in column 3 of Exhibit 3 by multiplying the appropriate cost function coefficient in column 1 (.0467) by total cost ($345,623) and then dividing by the number of home debits per regular account (230). Incremental cost per unit, shown in column 4, is obtained by dividing the incremental cost figure in column 3 by the number of regular accounts (9,750). Incremental costs for other variations in the product are calculated in a similar fashion and the results are shown in Exhibit 3.

The incremental cost of an additional regular demand deposit account that is *identical* to the average regular account is $33.69. This is less than the average unit cost of $35.45 for an existing regular account as indicated in Exhibit 2. However, the incremental cost of an additional special account is slightly larger than the average unit cost of a special account. Thus, increases in the number of regular accounts would reduce average unit cost, but increases in the number of special checking accounts would increase average unit cost. To the extent that unutilized capacity exists, management may wish to promote regular rather than special accounts.

An additional dollar in a special account is more than three times as costly to service as an additional dollar in a regular account. This indicates that the cost of providing extra services to small special checking accounts is greater per dollar than the cost of providing additional services to large regular checking accounts. This also implies that the incremental cost associated with an additional dollar of deposits most likely depends on the size of the deposit, i.e., fixed account maintenance costs can be spread over more dollars in large accounts. Home debits are associated with highly routinized operations which may explain why there is little difference in the incremental costs of home debits in regular and special checking accounts. With the exception of transit checks deposited, incremental costs of changes in other account characteristics are greater for regular accounts than they are for special accounts. There are only one-ninth as many transit checks deposited

Production and Cost Analysis

annually in special accounts as in regular accounts. The difference in incremental costs for transit checks deposited in regular and special accounts may occur if the cost of handling the first few transit checks is high while the cost of handling each additional transit check declines.

Suppose management wishes to know the cost of a specific regular checking account that differs in identifiable ways from the average regular account. Incremental cost analysis can be used to help determine the cost of this *example* regular account. Characteristics of the example regular account to be costed are shown in column 1 of Exhibit 4 and characteristics of the average regular account are contained in column 2. Column 3 is the difference of the first two columns. The incremental cost in column 5 is the product of the figure in column 3 and the incremental cost per item in column 4, which was computed in Exhibit 3.

Although the cost of the example regular account in Exhibit 4 is considerably greater than the cost of the average regular account, the cost per $100 is lower because of the larger balance. This result suggests that service charge rates should be based on account size and the number of various types of transactions. Knowledge of incremental costs can be used to establish variable rate service charge schedules which reflect the actual cost incurred in servicing a particular account more accurately than using average unit costs or some kind of standard costing procedure.

Such an approach to pricing may be useful in nonfinancial firms that produce a product or service capable of being differentiated or varied in several ways. For example, the incremental costing method may be useful in establishing the cost of selling particular types of merchandise in retailing firms or in determining the cost of handling particular types of customer credit accounts.

Cost Forecasting

When management contemplates or expects some change in operations at a future date, it is important to forecast the effects of this change on costs. The use of statistical analysis in forecasting, especially for forecasting sales, is well established. However, cost forecasts ordinarily are based on a nonstatistical evaluation of the production facilities, equipment, labor, and materials required to produce enough to meet the sales forecast. When statistical

Exhibit 3. Incremental Costs for Various Characteristics of Regular and Special Accounts

			Regular accounts			Special accounts		
		(1) Cost function coefficient	(2) Value	(3) Incremental cost	(4) Incremental cost per unit*	(5) Value	(6) Incremental cost	(7) Incremental cost per unit*
Characteristics								
N^{**}	Account	$\delta_1=$ .9503	9,750	$ 33.69	$33.6867	9,750	$ 17.67	$17.6664
S	Account size	$\delta_2=$ .3936	$ 2,100	64.78	.0066	$ 300	223.11	.0229
T_1	Home debits/accounts	$\psi_1=$ .0467	230	70.18	.0072	100	79.42	.0081
T_2	Deposits/accounts	$\psi_2=$ .1427	40	1,233.01	.1265	25	970.67	.0996
T_3	Transit checks deposited/accounts	$\psi_3=$ .0742	180	142.47	.0146	20	630.90	.0647
T_4	Official checks/accounts	$\psi_4=$ .0583	3	6,716.61	.6889	2	4,957.07	.5084
$(T_5-T_6)^{***}$	Nontransit checks cashed/accounts	$\psi_5=$ .0183	16	210.83	.0216	14	103.73	.0106
T_6	Transit checks cashed/accounts	$\psi_6=-.0046$ $\alpha_2=-.0626$	14	97.27	.0100	16	54.84	.0056
C	Total Costs		$345,623			$170,054		

*Incremental cost per unit is determined by dividing incremental cost by 9,750 accounts.

**The number of accounts variable (N) includes both regular and special accounts. However, the mix variable also contains both regular and special accounts. Let $N = (N_R + N_S)/B$ and $M = N_R/(N_R + N_S)$. Then, the incremental cost of another regular account = $(\delta_1 - \alpha_2)[C/N_R + N_S] + \alpha_2(C/N_R)$. The incremental cost of another special account = $(\delta_1 - \alpha_2)[C/N_R + N_S]$.

***Nontransit checks cashed per account equals $(T_5 - T_6)$ while transit checks cashed equals T_6. The sum of these two categories is total checks cashed (T_5). The incremental cost of nontransit checks cashed = $\psi_5(C/T_5)$. The incremental cost of transit checks cashed = $\psi_5(C/A_5) + \psi_6(C/T_6)$.

Decision Making in the Private Sector

Exhibit 4. Computation of the Cost of a Regular Checking Account which Differs from the Average Regular Checking Account

Characteristics		(1) Value example account	(2) Value average account	(3) Difference (1)−(2)	(4) Incremental cost per item	(5) Change in average cost per account
S	Account size	$5,000	$2,100	2,900	.0066	$19.14
T_1	Home debits/account	400	230	170	.0072	1.22
T_2	Deposits/account	50	40	10	.1265	1.26
T_3	Transit checks deposited/account	300	180	120	.0146	1.75
T_4	Official checks/account	5	3	2	.6889	1.38
(T_5-T_6)	Nontransit checks cashed/account	20	16	4	.0216	.09
T_6	Transit checks cashed/account	20	14	6	.0100	.04
Total						$24.88
Cost of Average Regular Account						+35.45
Cost of Example Regular Account						$60.33
Cost Per $100 of the Example Regular Account						$ 1.21

methods are used to forecast costs, it usually involves either a simple regression analysis of volume and cost or, in rare cases, a multiple regression analysis.

The principal danger inherent in statistical cost forecasting is that future behavior may differ substantially from past cost behavior, thus making forecasts unreliable. Changes in plant and equipment, materials, products, production techniques, personnel, internal organization, prices paid for materials and labor, and many other factors will tend to impair the reliability of statistical cost forecasts. Nevertheless, in some circumstances statistical cost forecasting may provide helpful information. For example, if prices of materials and labor have varied in the past, this information can be included in the statistical cost function. Then, the effect of expected future changes in these prices on costs can be determined. In a firm that operates several plants or branches, all producing and selling the same product, statistical cost analysis may prove useful in forecasting the costs of *operating* a new plant or branch. Statistical analysis is not as likely to be useful in determining the cost of constructing a new plant. Several illustrations of cost forecasting are given below.

Turning to the banking example, suppose a branch bank is operating three offices with an average of 3,250 demand deposit accounts per office. It is considering opening a new office that it expects to be able to attract 3,250 new demand deposit accounts having characteristics essentially similar to those of existing demand deposits. Management is concerned about the effect of this expansion on its costs of operation for demand deposits. The change in costs can be forecast by making appropriate changes in the statistical cost function shown in the cost equation above:

$$\log C_1 = \log C_0 + \alpha_1 (\log B_1 - \log B_0)$$

$$= 5.53860 + 1.0150 (.60206 - .47712)$$

$$= 5.53860 + .12681$$

$$= 5.66541.$$

Total costs are $345,623 before the addition of the new branch and will be $462,820 afterwards, an increase of $117,197. Average unit cost before expansion is $35.45, but after expansion it will be $35.60. The $.15 increase in average unit cost reflects added costs of coordination associated with the operation of the new branch.

Suppose that this branch bank is not considering opening a new branch but expects the number of demand deposits handled by each branch to increase from 3,250 to 4,333. The change in costs that occurs when 1,083 new demand accounts are added to each of the three existing branches can be computed in the same manner as described above: 5.53860 + .9503(3.63682 − 3.51188) = 5.65733. Total costs will be $454,289 and average cost per account will be $34.95, a decline of $.50 per account. In both of the cost forecasting examples given here, there will be 13,000 accounts and

$27.3 million in deposits (assuming that average account size is $2,100). In one example, though, there are four offices while in the other there are only three. Having one more branch for the same number of accounts and the same amount of deposits causes a difference of $7,531 or nearly 2% in total operating costs.

Management can also forecast the effect of an increase in the average annual wage paid per employee. Suppose management expects wages to rise by 10% from $5,700 to $6,270. Total costs will be: 5.53860 + .4312 (3.79727 − 3.75587) = 5.55645 or $360,125. Average unit costs will be $36.94, an increase of $1.49 per account.

The effects of other anticipated changes, in addition to those illustrated above, can be determined in the same way. In fact, the effects of all expected changes on total costs can be forecast simultaneously.

Any business firm able to construct its own cost function can use it to forecast the effects of changes in any or all of its variables. This procedure is legitimate so long as there is no significant change in the production-cost relationship.

Concluding Remarks

These uses of statistical cost analysis were demonstrated for commercial banks. However, any business enterprise which produces its products on a relatively regular and continuing basis and which maintains detailed records about output, resource prices, product characteristics, and costs can construct its own statistical cost function and use it for product costing, incremental costing, or cost forecasting. Thus, a host of business enterprises have the potential to use some kind of management oriented statistical cost analysis.

If the production-cost relationship is more complex than that presumed in break-even analysis or variable budgeting, statistical cost analysis may provide useful supplemental information that these more conventional cost accounting techniques are incapable of providing. It is not suggested that information derived from employing statistical techniques should supplant other types of information; rather, it is urged that statistical cost information be used in conjunction with other cost accounting information to help *improve* decision making.

REFERENCES

1. Frederick W. Bell and Neil B. Murphy, *Costs in Commercial Banking: A Quantitative Analysis of Bank Behavior and Its Relation to Bank Regulation,* Research Report No. 41, Federal Reserve Bank of Boston, April, 1968.

2. William A. Longbrake, "Productive Efficiency in Commercial Banking: The Impact of Bank Organization Structure and Bank Size on the Cost of Demand Deposit Services," Federal Deposit Insurance Corporation, Working Paper No. 72-10.

READING
11 ECONOMIES OF SCALE IN HIGH SCHOOL OPERATION*

John Riew

IN THE school year 1963–1964, according to the National Education Association, the total expenditures to educate 41.7 million pupils of the Nation's public schools exceeded 21 billion dollars. This expenditure figure shows a significant increase from 15.6 billion dollars in 1959–1960 and 5.8 billion dollars in 1949–1950 which were spent, respectively, for 34.2 million and 24.1 million pupils. In view of the magnitude of the resources involved and the rapid growth of their amounts, inquiry into scale economies in public education has not received adequate treatment by researchers.

The main reasons for this seem to be (1) the difficulty of determining the quality of various schools, and (2) varying opinions regarding the importance of the implications of such a study. The cost per pupil may reflect differences in the quality of education among schools, unless this quality differential is somehow taken into account. Then, if a study indicates an economic advantage for large size schools, there is a question of how this fact should affect policy decisions when there are other factors to be considered.

The United States Office of Education, for many years, has been making surveys of public school costs in cities of varying sizes. Their results in general show higher per-pupil costs for schools in larger cities. In the year 1958–1959, the cost per pupil in cities with a population of less than 10,000 was 312 dollars. The cost in cities with populations ranging from 10,000 to 24,999 was 305 dollars. In cities with populations from 25,000 to 99,999, it was 321 dollars, and in cities of over 100,000 people, 361 dollars.[1] In 1939–1940, the equivalent figures were 80 dollars, 87 dollars, 102 dollars and 127 dollars, respectively.[2]

The surveys obviously were not intended for analysis of economies of scale in school operation. Although large schools are typically in large cities and small ones in smaller cities, city population is hardly a suitable index of school size. Also these surveys do not account for differences in the quality of schools among size classes.

The first serious inquiry on the subject was made recently by Werner Z. Hirsch.[3] In his analysis, which employs multiple correlation and regression techniques and uses an elaborate device to distinguish quality differences among schools, he finds no significant economies of scale. He thus concludes that consolidation is unlikely to solve the fiscal problems of public schools. Hirsch uses a school district as the unit of observation. A study based on school districts undoubtedly has its merits, but schools, by and large, operate independently within a district. Thus, a more meaningful analysis of the size-cost relation, as Hirsch also implies, should be based on *individual schools*. Of the 27 St. Louis public school systems included in his study, all but six had enrollments of more than 1,500. To test the validity of a conjecture that significant scale economies exist over a relatively low size-range into which the nation's great majority of schools fall,[4] we need a sample with a larger number of smaller units.

Schmandt and Stephens, in a rank order

---

* I am indebted for many valuable suggestions to Professors Martin Bronfenbrenner, Harold M. Groves, Werner Z. Hirsch, Thomas Iwand, and Peter O. Steiner. The assistance from the Social Systems Research Institute of the University of Wisconsin is also gratefully acknowledged.

[1] Gerald Kahn, *Current Expenditures Per Pupil in Public School Systems, 1958–59* (Washington, D.C.: U.S. Office of Education, Circular No. 645, Government Printing Office, 1961), 6.

[2] Lester B. Herlihy and Walter S. Deffenbaugh, *Statistics of City School Systems, 1939–40 and 1941–42* (Washington, D.C.: U.S. Office of Education, Government Printing Office, 1945), 15. (For this earlier year, the second and the third size classes were divided at 30,000 instead of 25,000.)

[3] See Werner Z. Hirsch, "Expenditure Implications of Metropolitan Growth and Consolidation," this REVIEW, XLI (Aug. 1959), 232–240 (especially 239–240); and "Determinants of Public Education Expenditures," *National Tax Journal*, XIII (March 1960) 29–40.

[4] Of 37,019 public school districts that existed in the United States in 1961–1962, 84.2 per cent had enrollments of less than 1,200 and 75.7 per cent had less than 600. United

correlation analysis, offer the conclusion that there is a significant negative relation between school size and per pupil current expenditures.[5] They too attempt to consider quality variation among schools, but for the measure of quality they use the number of subfunctions performed in each school. As the authors admit, this fails to differentiate the quality of each subfunction and gives equal weight to all such functions. Their study was based on 18 "school district areas" of Milwaukee County, the district areas again taken as the basis of analysis.[6]

In these previous studies,[7] elementary and secondary schools are combined into individual units. Elementary schools operate differently from secondary schools. Most important, the secondary schools call for a higher degree of specialization in the teaching staff and for more facilities than do the elementary schools. Thus, these two levels of public schools should be considered as two distinct industries, and a joint treatment results in mixing two possibly dissimilar tendencies.

The Approach and the Data

The present study, in analyzing the relationship between school size and cost, concentrates on public high school systems and approaches the subject on the basis of individual schools rather than school districts. This study deals exclusively with the senior high schools, comprising grades nine to 12 and ten to 12. Junior high and combined high schools of grades seven to 12 were not included because of the probable cost variation associated with the differences in organization.

States Office of Education, *Digest of Educational Statistics* (Washington, D.C.: U.S. Government Printing Office, 1963), 29.

[5] Henry J. Schmandt and G. Ross Stephens, "Measuring Municipal Output," *National Tax Journal*, III (Dec. 1960), 369–375.

[6] Of the 18 school district areas, only 13 provide both elementary and secondary schools. Each of the remaining five is a combination of an elementary district and the secondary district to which they send their pupils. Thus, all 18 units are made to cover grades one to 12 or kindergarten to 12 for the sake of comparability, but when some units are a multiple of districts while the others are single districts the meaning of the analysis becomes more doubtful.

[7] There is also a recent study by the Committee for Economic Development which stresses the advantage of a larger school system. It suggests that educational advantages continue to accrue until a combined school system (kindergarten to 12 or one to 12 years) has "perhaps 25,000 students" and that there are financial advantages of many kinds in even larger units. The Committee for Economic Development, *Paying for Better Public Schools* (New York, Dec. 1959), 64.

Production and Cost Analysis

Wisconsin high schools were chosen as the object of the study because the state offers unusually good sources of information for the purpose. In Wisconsin, the State Department of Public Instruction, actively committed to aid for public education, secures quite a thorough annual report from each school district. The report contains a school census and detailed information on revenues and expenditures for all elementary schools and for all high schools in the district separately. However, neither the annual report nor the district files give separate accounts for individual schools. Thus, for this study, districts were selected which had only one high school. Many larger schools are in larger school districts and eliminating these districts which have more than one high school reduces the number of large schools in the sample. There is, however, a sufficient number of districts with one high school of larger size for the purposes of this study.

All told, there were 430 public senior high schools in the state in 1960–1961. We observe in table 1 that more than half of these schools had an enrollment of less than 300 and only about one-quarter had an enrollment of more than 500.

TABLE 1. — DISTRIBUTION BY ENROLLMENT — WISCONSIN PUBLIC HIGH SCHOOLS 1960–1961

Pupils in Average Daily Attendance	Number of Schools
200 or less	134
201–300	93
301–500	86
500 or more	117
Total	430

SOURCE: Wisconsin Department of Public Instruction, *The Summary of High School Preliminary Reports* (1960–1961).

Undoubtedly, educational programs and qualities among these schools vary and it will be futile to attempt an inquiry into size-cost relations without taking into account these variations.

As a partial measure of quality for this analysis, a step was first taken to select only those schools which were accredited by the North-Central Association. In 1960–1961, there were 152 accredited public high schools, of which 142 encompassed grades nine to 12 or ten to 12. The elimination of districts with more than one high school reduced the sample size by 26. To further narrow differences in standards, schools which appeared to rank considerably above the majority were excluded. This was done by eliminating schools where the 1960–

Decision Making in the Private Sector

1961 average teacher salary exceeded $6,500. This produced an additional loss of seven schools (several schools paying high teacher salaries were already excluded when large districts with two or more high schools were left out).[8]

We have, thus, 109 schools (92 four-year and 17 three-year high schools) which survived the tests of accreditation and "non-exceptionality" and are by and large comparable in organization. In setting a floor based on the judgment of the North-Central Association and arbitrarily setting a ceiling based on average teacher salary, the intent was to reduce variations in the standard of schools and analyze the size-cost relation with minimum interference from these variations.

In table 2, schools are grouped by size, and average per pupil expenditures are related to various size classes. Additional information is then provided for respective size classes concerning (1) average teacher's salary, (2) ratio of teachers holding a master's degree, (3) average years of teacher experiences, (4) average pupil-teacher ratio, (5) number of credit units offered, and (6) average number of courses taught by a teacher. The first three are assumed to reflect teacher qualifications, the fourth class size, the fifth breadth of school programs, and the last the degree of specialization in instruction. While the foregoing aspects are not all that may be relevant in judging a school they do constitute important ingredients of school qualities.[9] The size-cost relation, then, can be observed along with those measures which indicate the nature and direction of quality biases that may be associated with size.

The expenditure figures in table 2 relate to operational items only; neither capital outlays nor debt services are included. Of the operational expenditures, those for transportation, auxiliary services, and other minor items are excluded. The per pupil costs of transportation often vary more with population density, and the distance a school bus has to travel, than with the size of a school, which may or may not reflect population density. As for auxiliary services, which include school lunch, pupil recreation and health programs, a comparison of costs is

[8] There is no great significance to this particular figure. It was observed that $6,000 was not very far above average salaries for the majority and using that figure would have eliminated too many schools. On the other hand, $7,000 was too far up in the salary scale. The mean of the average salaries for the 109 schools was $5,662. Teacher salaries alone certainly cannot be an adequate measure of the standard of a school. It was assumed, however, that salaries are in general significantly associated with the quality of teachers and often even with other provisions offered in a school.

[9] These are largely input measures. An ideal approach to the measurement of school quality would be to consider *output* rather than *input* inasmuch as our prime concern in education is not with what we invest in schools but with what we get out of them. However, unavailability of output measures (not to mention difficulties in agreeing upon output substances) and variation in intelligence and socio-economic background among pupils make such a project extremely difficult.

TABLE 2. — AVERAGES OF OPERATING EXPENDITURES AND CHARACTERISTICS OF TEACHERS IN 109 ACCREDITED HIGH SCHOOLS OF WISCONSIN GROUPED BY SIZE, 1960–1961

Number of Schools	Pupils in Average Daily Attendance	Operating[a] Expenditure Per Pupil	Average Teacher's Salary	Percentage Teachers Holding Master's Degree	Average[b] Years Taught	Pupil-[c] Teacher Ratio	Credit[d] Units Offered	Average[e] Course Load Per Teacher
6	143–200	$531.9	$5,305	18.1	6.3	17.3	34.7	3.8
12	201–300	480.8	5,187	15.1	6.1	18.2	36.9	2.9
19	301–400	446.3	5,265	18.8	6.3	20.0	39.6	2.5
17	401–500	426.9	5,401	18.5	7.4	20.9	44.0	2.3
14	501–600	442.6	5,574	23.5	7.5	20.7	46.5	1.9
13	601–700	413.1	5,411	22.5	6.8	20.9	45.3	1.7
9	701–900	374.3	5,543	22.3	7.1	24.1	46.4	1.8
6	901–1100	433.2	5,939	34.0	7.3	21.4	57.7	1.6
6	1101–1600	407.3	5,976	36.5	11.9	24.4	63.4	1.6
7	1601–2400	405.6	6,230	54.5	11.2	24.2	80.3	1.6

SOURCES: For information on accreditation, *The North Central Association Quarterly*, XXXVI (Summer 1961), 123–127; For teacher degrees, credit units number of pupils and number of teachers, Wisconsin Department of Public Instruction, *High School Preliminary Report* (1960–1961); for operating expenditures, teacher's salaries, and years of teacher experience, Wisconsin Education Association, *Expenditures Per Pupil in City Schools* (1960–1961), *Expenditures Per Pupil in Village Schools*, (1960–1961), *Salaries in City Schools* (1960–1961), and *Salaries in Schools Under Supervising Principals* (1960–1961). (The data in these Wisconsin Education Association bulletins are abstracted mostly from the Annual Report of School District and High School Preliminary Report to the State Superintendent of Public Instruction.)

[a] The figures represent the sum of current operating expenditures on administration, teacher's salaries, other instruction, operation, and maintenance. Expenditures on transportation, auxiliary services (school lunch, pupil recreation and health programs) and other minor items are not included.

[b] The mean of median years taught in individual schools within each size-class. (For other variables, the average was the mean of mean values for individual schools in each size-class.)

[c] Number of pupils in average daily attendance divided by number of teachers, the latter being the full-time equivalent of staff members devoted to teaching only.

[d] A two-semester course meeting five times weekly is counted as one credit unit. For smaller schools, the number of credit units relate to a two-year program because in these schools some courses are offered only in alternate years.

[e] Total credit units divided by number of teachers. In determining the number of teachers, multiple counting is avoided. If, for instance, because of large enrollment, several teachers teach the same course, they are counted as one. When a teacher devotes part of his time, say two-fifths, for a course taught by others, only that fraction is subtracted.

made difficult because some schools, especially larger ones, do not have lunch programs.

Thus, included in our analysis are outlays for *administration, teacher's salaries, other instruction* (salaries for clerical assistants to the teaching staff, text books, library books, and other instructional supplies), *operation* (salaries and wages of the custodial staff, fuel, utilities, etc.), and *maintenance* (staff salary, supplies, and contract services related to property maintenance). For high schools of Wisconsin as a whole, these items in 1960–1961 comprised 92.1 per cent of total operating expenditures (the total excluding costs of transportation) and 63.0 per cent of all school expenditures.[10]

Table 2 provides a fairly comprehensive picture and may be considered highly informative. We shall first examine the table and then, for further insights, we shall turn to a more rigorous statistical analysis.

Findings and Evaluations

1) The per-pupil expenditures decline fairly steadily from $531 to $374 as enrollment rises from less than 200 to 701–900. Within the above range of enrollment, (a) smaller schools have lower average pupil-teacher ratios, (b) larger schools, on the other hand, have relatively more teachers with advanced degrees on their faculty, and, more important perhaps, (c) larger schools offer a broader curriculum and more specialized instruction.[11] The number of credit units, an indication of the breadth of curriculum (see note d to table 2), ranges from 34.7 for schools with less than 200 pupils to 46.4 for those with 701–900 pupils. The average number of courses taught per teacher varies from 3.8 for the smallest schools to 1.8 for those with 701–900 pupils.[12]

2) The per pupil expenditures, after a fairly consistent fall, rise from $374 to $433 as enrollment increases from 701–900 to the next size-class of 901–1,100. However, this rise in expenditures accompanies a notable rise in the proportion of teachers with a master's degree and a considerable broadening of the school curriculum. It appears that, with enrollment in the vicinity of one thousand, the demand for advanced courses and for teachers with advanced training rises and becomes more effective.[13]

3) As enrollment rises from 901–1,100 to 1,101–1,600, the per pupil expenditures fall again, from $433 to $407. Then, with a further increase to 1,601–2,400, the expenditures remain stable while the ratio of master's degrees in the faculty and the number of credit units continue to rise.

The average pupil-teacher ratio varies rather moderately from 17 to one for schools with less than 200 pupils, 20 to one for those with 301–700 pupils, and about 24 to one for most of the larger schools. The pupil-teacher ratios for schools observed here are all relatively low and differences in pupil-teacher ratios do not seem crucial (none of the individual schools included in the present study had an average ratio of more than 27 to one).

The significance of the pupil-teacher ratio has been challenged for some time and more so recently. Past studies of class-size provide little evidence that large classes materially affect the academic efficiency of the class. After reviewing a great number of class-size studies conducted in the past, Otto and von Bergersrode conclude that "... mere size of class has little significant influence on educational efficiency as measured by achievement in the academic subjects ...," and that "... although experimental evidence does not provide a clear-cut answer to the class-size issue, the general trend of the evidence places the burden of proof squarely upon the proponents of small classes."[14]

Within the range of enrollment of less than

---

[10] All school expenditures include both operational and capital outlays, but not debt services, since including the latter would be a double counting for loan-financed capital outlays. The percentage figures are computed from the data available in the *1960–61 Summary of Annual Reports of School Districts* (Wisconsin Department of Public Instruction), 9–10.

[11] James B. Conant, in his noted study of American high schools, emphasizes the need for more diversified high school programs. He strongly recommends that students be provided with adequate elective programs in mathematics, languages, science, English, and social studies and that a seven- or eight-period school day be organized to allow students more flexiblity in taking these courses. See James B. Conant, *The American High School Today* (McGraw-Hill 1959), 41–76.

[12] As was noted in table 2, the number of credit units for smaller schools was related to programs covering a two-year period. In these schools, some courses are offered only in alternate years. To the extent that these two-year arrangements limit the alternatives available for pupils, comparison of the figures shown here does not fully account for their differences.

[13] The fall in pupil-teacher ratio from 24.1 to one to 21.4 to one suggests also that a rise in enrollment at this level introduces more advanced courses where class sizes are typically small until a further increase in enrollment gives the teachers a fuller load.

[14] Henry J. Otto and Fred von Bergersrode, "Class Size," in Walter S. Monroe, ed., *Encyclopedia of Educational Research*, (New York: Macmillan, 1950), 212–216. (The authors, however, feel that for elementary schools smaller classes are still preferable to larger classes.) See also John I. Goodland, "Room to Live and Learn: Class Size and Room Space as Factors in the Learning-Teaching Process," *Childhood Education*, 30 (Apr. 1954), 355–361; and Herbert F. Spitzer, "Class Size and Pupil Achievement in Elementary Schools," *The Elementary School Journal*, 55 (Oct. 1954), 82–86.

Decision Making in the Private Sector

200 to 701–900, then, advantages of a larger school may be considered overwhelming. A larger school not only spends considerably less per pupil but has decisive advantages in curriculum and in teacher specialization.

Whether schools with an enrollment of more than 701–900 provide additional economies depends on one's appraisal of the cost differential as against the differences in what the schools offer. With enrollment of 1,101–1,600 or 1,601–2,400, the per pupil expenditures are $407 or $406 as compared with $374 for schools with 701–900 pupils. However, these larger schools distinguish themselves with broader curricula (63.4 or 80.3 credit units against 46.4), higher proportions of faculty holding advanced degrees (36.5 or 54.5 per cent against 22.3) and teachers with more experience (11.9 or 11.3 years against 7.1). If one believes these improvements in standards more than compensate for the differences in expenditures this then may be construed as an economy.

One may make an evaluation by direct examination of table 2 which provides comprehensive information on the subject. Judging school qualities involves subjective values. Given the size, the cost, and variables that are considered relevant to school qualities, one could make his own appraisal and final judgment.

Nevertheless, this approach leaves some important questions unanswered. If, for instance, we agree that there are economies of scale and that cost per pupil decreases with an increase in the size of enrollment, we would want to have estimations on such decreases in cost and on their statistical significance. It should be noted also that the figures shown in our table are average values for each size class and tend to conceal variations within classes.

In the estimation of possible cost savings, we seek to isolate the influence of size upon cost. For this we would need to consider other factors which are expected to affect the cost. Presumably, the most important of such factors is school quality. Regardless of the method of analysis, we must make certain assumptions as to what constitute school qualities and our conclusions necessarily must be evaluated with reference to the manner in which qualities are taken into account. Besides quality differences, there are other conditions to account for variations in input requirements and thus in average costs among schools.

The method employed here to approximate the net relationship between school size and per pupil cost is least-squares multiple regression analysis. The analysis is based on the 109 selected high schools which are included in table 2. Using largely the factors already introduced in the table, our regression equation includes the following variables:

X_1 — Operating expenditures per pupil in average daily attendance.

X_2 — Enrollment (number of pupils in average daily attendance).

X_3 — Average teacher's salary.

X_4 — Number of credit units offered (a two-semester course meeting five times a week is counted as one unit).

X_5 — Average number of courses taught per teacher.

X_6 — Change in enrollment between 1957 and 1960 (the 1960 enrollment is taken as a percentage of the 1957 enrollment).

X_7 — Percentage of classrooms built after 1950.

Used here as our quality variables are average teacher's salary (X_3), number of credit units offered (X_4), and average number of courses taught per teacher (X_5), which may be considered to represent, respectively, teacher qualifications, the breadth of curriculum, and the degree of specialization in instruction. The pupil-teacher ratio is left out in view of the controversies as to how the ratio is associated with classroom efficiency and of the fact that the pupil-teacher ratios observed in the present study are all relatively low. A preliminary result, furthermore, indicated high correlation between average teacher's salary and teacher status with respect to degree and experience; thus, these two were also eliminated.[15]

Changes in enrollment over a period of a few years (X_6) may indicate the pace at which demand for school services changed and thus possibly reflect some lagging adjustments in cost. The last variable, the proportion of new classrooms (X_7) was included because costs of mainte-

[15] Of a number of conceivable variables, the teacher's salary seems preferable as an indicator of teacher qualifications, even to the composite of academic degree and experience. Two persons with the same degree and years of experience can be rated differently as teachers and such differences are likely to be reflected in their salaries. It may be argued that living costs are higher in larger cities where there are more larger schools and a part of the salary differential between large and small schools may be considered a corrective of local price variation. Most of the schools included here, however, are in places of less than 50,000 in population, and price variation, if any, cannot be significant.

nance and operation may vary by the ages of school properties.

In this statistical test, we assume a parabolic relationship between per pupil cost and enrollment. The relations between the cost and the other independent variables were all assumed to be linear. The following results are then obtained:

$$X_1 = 10.31 - \underline{.402X_2} + \underline{.00012X_2{}^2} + \underline{.107X_3}$$
$$\quad\quad\quad\quad (.063) \quad\quad (.000023) \quad\quad (.013)$$
$$+ .985X_4 - 15.62X_5$$
$$\quad (.640) \quad\quad (11.95)$$
$$+ \underline{.613X_6} - .102X_7$$
$$\quad (.189) \quad\quad (.109) \quad .$$

The figures in parentheses are standard errors of the net regression and the statistically significant coefficients (at a probability level of .01) are underlined. The coefficient of multiple determination adjusted for degrees of freedom lost, R^{*2}, is .557 and is highly significant at a probability level of .01.

Thus, about 56 per cent of the variation in average per pupil operating expenditures among the 109 high schools in 1960–1961 was accounted for by the six independent variables of which average teacher's salary, enrollment, and changes in enrollment were statistically significant.[16] The partial correlation coefficients of these variables are:

$$r_{12.2^2 34567} = .539,$$
$$r_{12^2 .234567} = .465,$$
$$r_{13.2^2 4567} = .648, \text{ and}$$
$$r_{16.2^2 3457} = .307.$$

When school enrollment (variables X_2 and $X_2{}^2$) is eliminated from our multiple regression analysis, R^{*2} is reduced from .557 to .374. Holding constant the effects of changes in the other five variables, then, 18.3 per cent of the variation in per pupil operating expenditures is explainable in terms of variation in enrollment.

Our regression equation suggests, further, that an enrollment increase of one pupil, holding the other variables constant, lowers average per pupil operating expenditures by $[40.2 - 2(.012X_2)]$ cents at X_2 level of enrollment until X_2 finally reaches 1,675.[17] Thus, a school with an enrollment of 200, for instance, if it behaves in "average fashion," will reduce its per pupil operating expenditures 35.4 cents by having one more pupil. For a school with 500 pupils, adding one pupil would reduce per pupil expenditures by 28.2 cents and for one with 1,000 pupils, by 15.8 cents. Increase in the enrollment of a school from 200 to 500, the other independent variables held constant, would thus mean a saving of $95.45 in average per pupil operating expenditures.[18] With an increase in enrollment of from 500 to 1,000 the expected saving in per pupil expenditures would be $111.00 and from 1,000 to 1,675 the expected saving would be $54.67.

These figures of course provide only approximations and are subject to error limitations. However, if we are concerned with an "average" school and our assumptions on school qualities are acceptable, they may be considered as meaningful estimates.[19] That the coefficient of X_6 (the change in enrollment) is significantly positive may deserve some attention. It suggests that under conditions of rapid expansion, the school operates on a short-run cost curve above the level that is achievable under a full long-run adjustment to increased enrollment levels.

A larger school may mean an added transportation cost, especially in a thinly populated area. This additional cost (and perhaps the nonmonetary costs of fatigue, time, parental concern, etc.) would have to be subtracted from the "saving" referred to above. This point, however, should not be overly stressed. There are indications that in the great majority of instances a small enrollment is simply a reflection of a small size of the school district rather than population sparsity. "In only 19 states," a

---

[16] Obviously, some of the unexplained portion of the variation in average per pupil expenditures is attributable to other causal forces not included in the analysis and perhaps, to some degree, to deficiencies of the variables included. Our assumption of linear functional relationships (between per pupil cost and variables other than size) and possible errors and arbitrariness in the reporting of data would undoubtedly have some effects also.

[17] From our regression equation,
$$\frac{\partial X_1}{\partial X_2} = -.402 + 2(.00012X_2). \text{ Thus, when } \frac{\partial X_1}{\partial X_2} = 0$$
$$X_2 = \frac{.402}{.00024} = 1,675.$$

[18] From our equation, the change in the average per pupil operating expenditures (X_1) to result from the change in enrollment (X_2) from 200 to 500 would be:
$$\Delta X_1 = [-.402(500) + .00012(500^2)]$$
$$\quad\quad - [-.402(200) + .00012(200^2)]$$
$$\quad\quad = -95.40.$$

[19] The concept of returns to scale deals with a given technology. Thus, in using the present analysis as the basis for future projection, we must assume that the educational methods and policies remain largely unchanged.

Decision Making in the Private Sector

C.E.D. study points out, "... is the average geographic area covered by a school system as much as 225 square miles — equivalent to an area 15 miles square. In 21 states it is less than 49 square miles."[20]

A recent study conducted by the Wisconsin Department of Public Instruction reveals, furthermore, that differences in average transportation costs between rural and urban areas and between districts covering large areas and those covering small areas are considerably less than commonly believed. In the 1961–1962 academic year, the average of per pupil transportation expenditures in the most thickly populated counties of Milwaukee, Racine, Kenosha, and Winnebago (each with population density of more than 200 per square mile) was $54.16 as compared with $65.10 for the most thinly populated counties of Sawyer, Bayfield, Florence, and Forest (each with the density of less than ten per square mile) where school districts are much larger in area.[21] This may in part be accounted for by differences in service qualities. The better explanation, however, is that in school transportation the fixed costs (depreciation, driver salary, insurance, garage rental, etc.) comprise such an important part that differences in the mileage of operation, in many cases, affect the total transportation cost much less than is often anticipated.[22]

---

[20] The Committee for Economic Development, *op. cit.*, 6.

[21] Wisconsin Department of Public Instruction, *Transportation Facts 1962–63* (Madison, Wisconsin, March 1963). The figures are computed from the data available on pages 12–13.

[22] *Ibid.*, 11. The study presents the following illustration of a typical contract for a bus with a daily mileage of 60 miles:

Fixed charge per day for:	Depreciation	$ 4.50
	Driver Salary	6.25
	Insurance	.50
	Garage Rental	.75
		$12.00
Variable charge per bus mile for gas, oil, grease, repairs, maintenance, etc. 10¢ (per mile) × 60		$ 6.00
Total charge per day		$18.00

In the present analysis capital outlays are excluded as they generally fluctuate widely over time. When they are taken into account, greater variation in per pupil costs among size groups may be expected. Physical education programs and a library, for instance, require many provisions which a school of any size should not lack. For a satisfactory high school program, various equipment and provisions for science laboratories, language, music, and vocational training are basic and essential. For these items, smaller schools bear larger overhead costs. As general standards of high schools continue to improve with increasing investment in capital items, the issue will become even more important.

Conclusion

Differentiating educational qualities among individual schools is a difficult task, but based on what may be considered as reasonable assumptions, the study of Wisconsin high schools suggests that economies of scale at this level of public education are very significant.

Taking the high schools as a whole, capital outlays in recent years comprised roughly a quarter of the total expenditures. Their inclusion in the analysis would most likely have strengthened the present conclusion. This would have increased cost variation among schools, the higher overhead costs being expected to fall on smaller schools.

A sample with a larger number of schools, especially of the upper size classes, and with its size range extended beyond the present limit of 2,400 pupils would have been more informative. The virtue of "that little red schoolhouse" may be of more than an emotional nature. But whatever the merits, they ought to be considered negotiable. When better informed of the opportunity costs, one may wish to reexamine his traditional preference.

READING 12 THE IMPACT OF EXPERIENCE ON KIBBUTZ FARMING

Haim Barkai and David Levhari*

I Introduction

IT is an accepted proposition that there is a positive association between efficiency and experience in production. Yet, until quite recently, only industrial engineers tried to estimate and evaluate the contribution of experience to productivity, while economists have on the whole neglected this aspect of production. The growing interest in growth and the search for factors which can help to explain quantitatively the growth of production over and above the growth of the conventionally identified inputs have led economists to reconsider the problem. Arrow's pioneering article on the subject suggested that "learning," which may be identified with cumulated experience, contributes to the growth of productivity.[1] In contrast to the engineer's approach, which usually concentrates on the effect of experience on efficiency in specific processes, the economist's approach is more general. Learning is not exclusively attributed to the individuals who make up a firm's labor force or to specific processes, though both are considered to be integral elements of the process. Rather, it is ascribed to the production unit as a multidimensional entity. It is therefore the *modus operandi* of the firm in each of its many facets — entrepreneurial ability, technical expertise, the know-how of its labor force, layout, buying and selling, human relations, lines of command, all of them subject to continuous change — which is the best testing ground of the empirical significance of the learning hypothesis.

Since the acquisition of experience requires time, time or a proxy for it, such as cumulated investment and cumulated output, must obviously appear as an explicit variable in an empirical test of the hypothesis. Production-function analysis based on time series is therefore an obvious way of studying the quantitative effect of learning. Arrow's reference to the Swedish Horndal firm is a case in point.[2]

However, it is only rarely possible to find a similar example. This means that although empirical testing of the learning hypothesis can be carried out on the basis of time-series data,[3] it strains the theoretical framework of the analysis. The use of cross-section data in estimating the contribution of experience to productivity is therefore an obvious alternative. Since the input and output figures necessarily refer to different firms, this way of tackling the problem is also constrained by the necessity of assuming that, except for random differences, the technologies applied by the firms concerned are identical.

The requirement of intra-firm technological identity, or to put it more mildly, the similarity-of-technology condition, can, in practice, be approximated under certain conditions. For example, a good approximation to the identical technology constraint can be obtained within a narrowly defined branch and for a group of firms located in a relatively small area, which maintain strong personal contact between managements so as to facilitate the inter-firm flow of information and whose labor forces are similar in background, attitude, and know-how. If the firms in such a group differ in their ac-

---

Received for publication December 6, 1971. Revision accepted for publication July 10, 1972.

* This article makes use of data prepared for a comprehensive study on the Israeli kibbutz economy currently in preparation at the Falk Institute for Economic Research in Israel, and financed by the Falk Institute and the Twentieth Century Fund.

The authors are indebted to Yoram Levin for his help in the preparation of the quantitative skeleton of this article.

[1] See Kenneth J. Arrow (1962), pp. 155–174.

[2] Production methods in this firm do not appear to have changed for about 15 years; productivity, however, increased continuously.

[3] Shifts in the production function cannot be ruled out if the period studied is long. For shorter periods, for which this objection may have less force, the number of observations may be too small to allow for statistically significant results.

quired "experiences," and if these differences can be easily measured in terms of simple units, such a group may be a satisfactory testing ground for the learning hypothesis.

These conditions obtain in the case of kibbutzim in Israel. They form a tightly organized group of collectives, relatively homogeneous in manpower, which has established efficient mechanisms of communication and dissemination of knowledge. Furthermore, kibbutzim are located within a small geographical area by European, not to mention American, standards. Thus, the presumption that the about 200 kibbutzim apply very similar technologies in their farming activities is evidently a satisfactory working hypothesis.

They differ, however, in age — the oldest kibbutzim were established in the early 1920's and the youngest in the 1950's and 1960's. Since the age of each settlement is known, it can be used as an explicit variable in a cross-sectional production function analysis as a proxy for experience. The value of its coefficient would accordingly yield an estimate of the contribution of experience to productivity.

The choice of age of settlement as a proxy for experience may raise some objections. The age of a settlement is not unambiguously related to the (average) length of time during which the labor force was at work on the kibbutz "premises." The average number of years for which the average member of a kibbutz has belonged to its labor force is not necessarily proportional to the age of the settlement because of significant migration — inflows and outflows into each settlement. In extreme cases it is even possible that this average might be lower for an older kibbutz than for a younger one. This may suggest that the age of a kibbutz is not the most appropriate measure for experience.

This objection, however, restricts implicitly the significance of the learning process. It identifies it with the acquisition of experience by the labor force, which, though important, is only one facet of the much wider concept signified by the term experience. Our interpretation of experience, which we believe is the accepted approach, attributes a much broader significance to the concept. It refers to the process by which the firm as an entity, and not merely the several factors involved in production, increases its stock of know-how. Running a firm involves juggling the many factors and components which among them determine the input structure, the output mix, selling and financing techniques, internal factor mobility, and all these may be expected to improve in the course of time, so that the use of an aggregative measure for experience is evidently preferable. The age of a settlement which measures the impact of time on the kibbutz as a social and economic organism, is therefore *prima facie* a good proxy for a quantitative measure of experience. Since we use age and not cumulated investment as the proxy for learning, the restriction involved in assuming that learning and technical change are embodied in new capital goods, and other constraints which follow from this assumption, or the assumptions involved in using cumulated output as a proxy for experience, do not obtain in this case. This, of course, means that our variant of the learning hypothesis model is more general.

The nature of kibbutz production data allows the application of the most simple model for estimation — a single-equation model — for the purpose of testing this theory without coming to grief over the problem of simultaneity. Ever since the publication of the classical paper by Marschak and Andrews on the subject it has been accepted that when output is specified as a function of inputs which appear as independent variables in the formulation of the production function, a further, implicit, assumption is involved in every case in which the production function is not estimated within the context of a more comprehensive model.[4] The implicit assumption of a single-equation model is that the inputs involved are completely exogenous. However, if firms try to maximize profits, which is the conventional assumption in this kind of analysis, this is evidently not the case. Thus, the values of production coefficients estimated by regressing a measure of output or relevant measures of input, are inevitably biased.

The great advantage of the kibbutz data is that the simultaneity problem is, in practice, of minor relevance since the values of some of the major inputs are exogenously determined. Because of ideological considerations, which bar the hiring of labor, the kibbutz labor force, particularly in farming, is almost entirely composed of people who belong to the kibbutz. This means that wages are, at most, an indirect determinant of the supply of kibbutz labor. In

[4] See J. Marschak and W. H. Andrews (1944).

the long run the kibbutz labor force does vary in response to changes in population. Yet the size of kibbutz population and hence of the labor force is to a great extent determined by noneconomic motives. And in any case, it is per capita income rather than wages which is probably the major economic determinant of population and hence of the supply of labor. In other words, labor in the kibbutz production sector and in kibbutz farming is to a great extent a predetermined variable.

This applies to land, too, though not to irrigated land, since the size of the land endowment is practically always determined at the time of settlement.[5] The size of the capital stock is, however, constrained by neither ideological considerations nor institutional factors. Here too, the initial endowment (which is a capital grant) and then loans at heavily subsidized interest rates are the dominant determinants of the size of the capital stock in younger settlements and are still a major determinant of its size in the older ones. Furthermore, the size of the stock changes slowly over time. This, of course, suggests that factor simultaneity is, in this case too, less of a problem than usual.

Since inputs are predetermined to such an extent, the simultaneity issue is undoubtedly of minor consequence. The kibbutz data therefore offer a unique opportunity to estimate production functions under almost laboratory conditions, and hence to use the simplest models for this purpose.

II The data

The data on kibbutz farming consist of figures on output, gross (and net) product, labor input, capital stock by type of asset, and land classified as irrigated and dry. These figures, which are available for each of the roughly 200 kibbutzim for each of the years 1954–1965, have been compiled from the annual financial reports of the kibbutzim.[6]

Output (sales) is measured in constant 1958

[5] Kibbutzim pay a nominal rent for the land and, in practice, can neither buy nor rent additional land, though this is permitted by law and kibbutz ideology. The leasing of their own land to others is, on the other hand, barred by both ideology and contract.

[6] The very detailed data available by settlement are collected and processed as a matter of accounting, routine for internal use, it is simply impossible to run a kibbutz without such a comprehensive and detailed system of economic and financial information. Hence the relative accuracy and reliability of the figures.

Production and Cost Analysis

IL. Gross and net product are estimated from the product side on the basis of data on output and the cost of raw materials. The labor figures, which are from the daily records on work allocation, measure labor input in terms of days actually worked and are fully adjusted for part-time employment. Data on land, irrigated and dry, are in dunams (one dunam is 1,000 square metres).

The stock of physical capital is a perpetual inventory estimate. The detailed classification by type of asset allowed for a breakdown into two categories convenient for our purpose. The first consists of assets which are complementary to irrigated land — orchards and irrigation fixtures and equipment; the second consists of all the other assets which make up the capital stock.

Since 1954 was the benchmark for the capital stock estimates and these are based on gross investment series which go back for two decades and sometimes more, the statistical quality of the series is necessarily better for the later years of the 1954–1965 period. Their quality kept improving through time.[7]

III The Models and the Estimates

A Cobb-Douglas production function which involves labor, total capital stock, and age of settlement is the basic form of the single-equation model used to study the effect of experience on kibbutz farm production. The age of settlements (in years) is identified as the proxy for experience; gross capital stock measured in constant (1958) IL and labor measured in man-years are specified as the conventional inputs. Gross farm product in 1958 IL serves as the measure of production. Thus, writing Y for gross product, L and K for capital and labor respectively, and t for age of settlements, we have

$$Y = AL^\alpha K^\beta e^{\lambda t}. \qquad (1)$$

Accordingly, α and β are the elasticity of production for labor and capital, respectively, λ is the rate of change of productivity, and A is a constant.

This aggregative form of the function, which identifies two of the conventional inputs only, ignores land, which is *prima facie* a relevant factor in farming, altogether. We have there-

[7] A description of the technique of estimation and detailed investment and capital stock data for kibbutzim is given in Barkai (1969).

75

Decision Making in the Private Sector

fore specified an alternative model in which land is an explicit variable. This variant of a Cobb-Douglas production function specifies irrigated land as one of the conventional triad of inputs — land, labor and capital stock. The latter is redefined to exclude the components which are directly related to irrigation component of the capital stock. Thus, if C stands for capital stock excluding the irrigation component, and S for the input of irrigated land, the function has the form [8]

$$Y = AL^{\alpha}C^{\beta}S^{\gamma}e^{\lambda t}. \qquad (2)$$

This formulation involves three production elasticities — α, β, and γ, for labor (adjusted), capital stock, and irrigated land, respectively.[9]

Estimates of production elasticities and of the "experience" coefficient derived by fitting the Cobb-Douglas production functions specified above to the cross-section data for the 1954–1965 interval are presented in tables 1 and 2.

Inspection of the entries in table 1 shows that production responds to scale and that barring two estimates for labor (in 1955 and 1960) the production elasticities of labor and capital are of reasonable orders of magnitude. This impression is strengthened when the implied marginal productivities are compared to exogenous wage and interest rate data. The standard errors of the production elasticities of labor and capital suggest that the elasticities are significant. The coefficients of determination, of 0.71 and over, for the period 1956–1965, indicate that the explanatory power of the hypothesis is satisfactory in terms of accepted criteria.[10]

Consider now the values of λ, which repre-

TABLE 1. — PRODUCTION ELASTICITIES AND THE EXPERIENCE COEFFICIENT

Model (1): $Y = AL^{\alpha}K^{\beta}e^{\lambda t}$

	α	β	λ	R^2	Returns to scale $\alpha + \beta$
1954	0.937 (0.108)	0.151 (0.116)	0.0114 (0.0046)	0.557	1.088
1955	1.056 (0.076)	0.253 (0.081)	0.0640 (0.0029)	0.489	1.309
1956	0.860 (0.070)	0.330 (0.080)	0.0065 (0.0027)	0.748	1.190
1957	0.839 (0.062)	0.329 (0.073)	0.0069 (0.0022)	0.799	1.168
1958	0.914 (0.060)	0.341 (0.071)	0.0069 (0.0021)	0.822	1.255
1959	0.888 (0.065)	0.294 (0.080)	0.0021 (0.0023)	0.779	1.182
1960	1.034 (0.067)	0.240 (0.083)	−0.0030 (0.0022)	0.806	1.277
1961	0.815 (0.078)	0.296 (0.088)	0.0031 (0.0024)	0.741	1.111
1962	0.791 (0.073)	0.294 (0.090)	0.0026 (0.0023)	0.744	1.085
1963	0.717 (0.070)	0.391 (0.086)	0.0049 (0.0021)	0.768	1.108
1964	0.912 (0.081)	0.170 (0.089)	−0.0001 (0.0023)	0.708	1.082
1965	0.703 (0.076)	0.548 (0.042)	0.0046 (0.0023)	0.858	1.251

sent the contribution of experience to production. In all but two years of the period, λ has the "right" sign. In the two years in which it is negative the coefficient is either not significant (1960) or very small and not significant (1964).[11] The coefficients for the years up to 1958, all of which are statistically significant, suggest that productivity gains due to experience were of the order of 0.6 per cent annually. In the 1960's there are only two statistically significant values of λ. These indicate, however, that the impact of experience of productivity, about 0.45 per cent annually, has probably been falling.

The coefficients derived from the second formulation yield similar results. The production elasticities and implied marginal productivities of the three inputs — labor ("dry"), capital stock and irrigated land — are significant and reasonable by accepted criteria. The coefficients of determination vary in the 0.75–0.85 range and are on the whole higher than in

---

[8] The components here excluded from the capital stock C represent the value of land improvement, irrigation fixtures, and orchards, which are evidently part and parcel of what is meant by irrigated land. They are excluded from the capital stock figures to prevent double counting.

[9] The exclusion of dry land as a separate factor of production from the two models is an apparent deficiency. But in a semi-arid area the contribution of dry land to production is small in the first place. This is even more so in the case of a highly modern farm sector in which the production of field crops is a minor item and which therefore requires a rather small acreage. Experimentation with production functions which included dry land yielded coefficients for the contribution of dry land which were low and not significant. Since the more detailed form of the function did not improve the explanatory power of the hypothesis, we preferred to drop it altogether.

[10] The relatively low coefficients of determination for the 1954 and 1955 estimates suggest that the results for these years are weaker. This is probably due to the significantly worse quality of the capital stock estimates for these years.

[11] The 1960 value of the production elasticities suggests that despite the high value of R^2 the significance of the estimate is problematic. This is presumably due to the severe drought which affected farming in different parts of the country differently.

TABLE 2.—PRODUCTION ELASTICITIES AND THE EXPERIENCE COEFFICIENT

Model (2): $Y = AL^\alpha C^\beta S^\gamma e^{\lambda t}$

	α	β	γ	λ	R^2	Returns to scale $\alpha + \beta + \gamma$
1954	0.853 (0.113)	0.132 (0.105)	0.119 (0.058)	0.0101 (0.0046)	0.567	1.104
1955	0.956 (0.081)	0.181 (0.077)	0.137 (0.038)	0.0064 (0.0029)	0.797	1.274
1956	0.798 (0.074)	0.243 (0.081)	0.132 (0.036)	0.0063 (0.0028)	0.759	1.173
1957	0.805 (0.063)	0.326 (0.071)	0.065 (0.035)	0.0059 (0.0021)	0.806	1.196
1958	0.858 (0.067)	0.244 (0.071)	0.108 (0.037)	0.0065 (0.0021)	0.823	1.210
1959	0.768 (0.069)	0.315 (0.076)	0.122 (0.036)	0.0020 (0.0022)	0.798	1.205
1960	0.949 (0.073)	0.289 (0.080)	0.074 (0.041)	−0.0028 (0.0022)	0.815	1.312
1961	0.736 (0.078)	0.265 (0.086)	0.123 (0.044)	0.0029 (0.0023)	0.754	1.124
1962	0.711 (0.074)	0.303 (0.083)	0.088 (0.044)	0.0027 (0.0022)	0.756	1.102
1963	0.643 (0.070)	0.352 (0.081)	0.133 (0.044)	0.0047 (0.0021)	0.783	1.128
1964	0.811 (0.082)	0.252 (0.085)	0.054 (0.039)	0.0036 (0.0022)	0.721	1.117
1965	0.638 (0.081)	0.581 (0.045)	0.067 (0.045)	0.0041 (0.0023)	0.862	1.286

model (1), so that we may say that the three conventional inputs and time, the proxy for experience, do satisfactorily explain the inter-settlement variance of gross product.

The value of λ, which indicates the annual contribution of experience to production, is of the same order of magnitude as in the first model. In the 1950's it contributed to the growth of farm product at an annual rate of 0.60–0.65 per cent. The estimates for the 1960's yield significant results for a longer period than in model (1). The 1963–1965 λ values range from 0.36 to 0.41 per cent, underlining the impression gathered from model (1) that the contribution of experience to production has been declining. In other words, the significantly lower λ's for the 1960's suggest that experience may have diminishing returns.[12]

Diminishing returns to experience are obviously consistent with the first principles of production theory. To find out whether it ap-

[12] The average age of kibbutzim has risen rapidly in the last two decades — it was 14 years in 1955 and 24 in 1965. This "aging" of the kibbutz movement thus explains the falling relevance of experience to production. It means that the learning process is rapid at the beginning when experience is scarce, and inevitably slows down when, with time, it becomes less so.

plies in this case, we have formulated a second group of models which allow a closer test of the hypothesis. This required a reformulation of the proxy for experience. The production function with two measured inputs was specified as

$$Y = AL^\alpha K^\beta e^{\lambda t + \mu t^2}. \qquad (3)$$

The proxy for experience in (3) involves two coefficients, λ and μ. Since the rate of change of product in response to experience is $(\lambda + 2\mu t)$, according to this formulation a negative μ derived from a regression of Y on L, K, and t indicates that the contribution of experience to production diminishes with time.

The same form of the experience proxy has been similarly put into the alternative model with irrigated land as a separate factor of production. Model (4) is accordingly specified as

$$Y = AL^\alpha C^\beta S^\gamma e^{\lambda t + \mu t^2}. \qquad (4)$$

The estimates of the production elasticities and of the contribution of experience to production are presented in tables 3 and 4.

The entries in the two tables suggest that production elasticities of labor and capital in the case of model (3), and of these two variables and irrigated land, in the case of model (4), are reasonable. The contribution of experience to production was found to be positive in all years, with the exception of 1954 and 1960 in model (3) and 1960 in model (4).[13] The response of product to experience in terms of the annual rate of change, here represented by $(\lambda + 2\mu t)$, shows more year-to-year fluctuations than in the estimates derived from models (1) and (2). Their statistical quality is also lower.[14] Yet, though less systematic than the two previous variants the estimates do indicate that experience could explain an annual growth of farm product of about 0.7 per cent and more in the later 1950's and that by the middle 1960's its contribution was significantly lower.

The estimates of μ which were the raison d'être of this exercise, are consistently negative. This does suggest that returns to experience do diminish as is usually the case for the more

[13] The two years are problematic in our context. The second was a year of differential drought, and the first is the benchmark for our capital stock estimates. Note further that the estimate for the rate of change of product in response to experience (in each of the years) in this case involved specification of a relevant t. The obvious choice for this purpose was the mean age of kibbutzim in each year.

[14] The number of years in which λ is not statistically significant is greater than in the estimates for models (1) and (2).

Decision Making in the Private Sector

TABLE 3. — PRODUCTION ELASTICITIES AND THE EXPERIENCE COEFFICIENTS

Model (3): $Y = AL^{\alpha}K^{\beta}e^{\lambda t + \mu t^2}$

	α	β	λ	μ	$\lambda + 2\mu t$	R^2	Returns to scale $\alpha + \beta$	Mean age of settlements (years)
1954	0.873 (0.112)	0.381 (0.063)	0.0300 (0.0132)	—0.0005 (0.0132)	0.0173	0.763	1.254	12.7
1955	0.103 (0.076)	0.351 (0.037)	0.0199 (0.0009)	—0.00034 (0.0002)	0.0104	0.920	1.378	14.0
1956	0.831 (0.073)	0.422 (0.048)	0.0179 (0.0089)	—0.00029 (0.00019)	0.0087	0.836	1.253	15.0
1957	0.834 (0.064)	0.284 (0.076)	0.0188 (0.0074)	—0.00027 (0.00016)	0.0101	0.790	1.118	16.2
1958	0.925 (0.057)	0.331 (0.069)	0.0100 (0.0070)	—0.00009 (0.00014)	0.0069	0.836	1.256	17.2
1959	0.830 (0.064)	0.477 (0.030)	0.0067 (0.0084)	—0.0009 (0.00016)	—0.0257	0.910	1.307	18.0
1960	1.044 (0.068)	0.199 (0.088)	0.0050 (0.0083)	—0.00017 (0.00016)	—0.0015	0.797	1.243	19.2
1961	0.819 (0.080)	0.295 (0.094)	0.0097 (0.0090)	—0.00014 (0.00016)	0.0040	0.735	1.114	20.2
1962	0.771 (0.072)	0.216 (0.088)	0.0162 (0.0086)	—0.00024 (0.00015)	0.0061	0.727	0.987	21.1
1963	0.721 (0.069)	0.286 (0.088)	0.0132 (0.0087)	—0.00014 (0.00015)	0.0070	0.750	1.007	22.2
1964	0.924 (0.083)	0.091 (0.097)	0.0064 (0.0097)	—0.00011 (0.00016)	0.0013	0.691	1.015	23.2
1965	0.816 (0.087)	0.269 (0.105)	0.0112 (0.0104)	—0.00013 (0.00017)	0.0049	0.682	1.085	24.3

conventional inputs. Since almost none of the estimated values of μ [in models (3) and (4)] are significant at the 95 per cent level,[15] it cannot be maintained that each equation proves that learning, in our sense of the term, is subject to diminishing returns. Yet on the basis of the entire body of the data, it may be claimed that the hypothesis of diminishing returns to experience may be accepted.

Tables 1 through 4 indicate that the estimated production elasticities add up to more than unity in almost all the years in the 1954–1965 period. In some years the sum of the elasticities is as high as 1.35, and there is only a single instance of a sum less than unity. This, of course, suggests that farm production in kibbutzim is subject to considerable returns to scale. It also means that the size of the farming unit as it was in our period was too small to exhaust these returns to scale.

An alternative hypothesis could attribute these results, and particularly the higher values of the sum of elasticities, which for some years imply returns to scale of 30 per cent and more to inter-kibbutz differences which have not been explicitly identified in models (1) and (2), (3) and (4). A possible source of inter-kibbutz differences is differences in organizational and managerial ability and in the quality of the labor force. That such differences do exist is common knowledge, though their quantitative significance is obscure. A model which explicitly identifies inter-settlement differences may therefore give better estimates of production elasticities and also of the contribution of experience to production.

The data at our disposal, which give inputs and outputs for each settlement over a period of 11 years, make it possible to study the effect of experience on production quantitatively, within the context of a model which specifies explicitly such inter-settlement differences. This could be done by applying conventional techniques of interrelated cross-sectional and time-series analysis. Thus, writing Y_{it} for the product of the ith settlement in year t, A_i for the settlement productivity coefficient, and Z_t for the year effect, we have estimated the two functions

$$Y_{it} = A_o A_i Z_t L^{\alpha}_{it} K^{\beta}_{it} e^{\lambda t} \qquad (5)$$

and

$$Y_{it} = A_o A_i Z_t L^{\alpha}_{it} K^{\beta}_{it} e^{\lambda t + \mu t^2}. \qquad (6)$$

---

[15] The exceptions are the estimates for 1955 in model (3) and 1954 and 1955 in model (4).

Production and Cost Analysis

Table 4. — Production Elasticities and the Experience Coefficients

Model (4): $Y = AL^a C^\beta S^\gamma e^{\lambda t + \mu t^2}$

	a	β	γ	λ	μ	$\lambda + 2\mu t$	R^2	Returns to scale $a + \beta + \gamma$
1954	0.828 (0.117)	0.405 (0.065)	0.104 (0.059)	0.0253 (0.0133)	−0.00047 (0.00030)	0.0134 (0.00631)	0.768	1.337
1955	0.965 (0.083)	0.366 (0.039)	0.118 (0.039)	0.0160 (0.0087)	−0.00029 (0.00020)	0.0078 (0.00396)	0.921	1.449
1956	0.780 (0.076)	0.407 (0.050)	0.123 (0.037)	0.0152 (0.0089)	−0.00026 (0.00019)	0.0077 (0.00383)	0.839	1.310
1957	0.790 (0.066)	0.295 (0.073)	0.063 (0.036)	0.0185 (0.0073)	−0.00028 (0.00015)	0.0094 (0.00297)	0.798	1.148
1958	0.870 (0.063)	0.246 (0.069)	0.096 (0.035)	0.0104 (0.0069)	−0.00010 (0.00014)	0.0070 (0.00272)	0.837	1.212
1959	0.727 (.070)	0.519 (0.037)	0.109 (0.037)	0.0056 (0.0081)	−0.00009 (0.00016)	0.0024 (0.00362)	0.917	1.355
1960	0.948 (0.074)	0.259 (0.085)	0.078 (0.042)	0.0041 (0.0081)	−0.00014 (0.00015)	0.0013 (0.00298)	0.807	1.285
1961	0.735 (0.079)	0.276 (0.092)	0.123 (0.045)	0.0081 (0.0088)	−0.00011 (0.00016)	0.0036 (0.00314)	0.751	1.134
1962	0.690 (0.074)	0.212 (0.088)	0.101 (0.044)	0.0148 (0.0085)	−0.00021 (0.00015)	0.0060 (0.00287)	0.740	1.003
1963	0.646 (0.069)	0.233 (0.085)	0.149 (0.043)	0.0106 (0.0084)	−0.00010 (0.00014)	0.0061 (0.00266)	0.767	1.028
1964	0.812 (0.084)	0.192 (0.096)	0.059 (0.039)	0.0043 (0.0096)	−0.00007 (0.00016)	0.0011 (0.00297)	0.702	1.063
1965	0.732 (0.087)	0.316 (0.100)	0.078 (0.045)	0.0077 (0.0103)	−0.00008 (0.00016)	0.0043 (0.00338)	0.696	1.126

For each of these two we have also run regressions for the corresponding formulations, designated by (5′) and (6′), which specify irrigated land as a separate factor of production. The estimated production elasticities and experience coefficients are presented in table 5.

The elimination of the year effect, which even in Israeli farming, so much dependent on irrigation, is still important, and the settlement effect, yields estimates of the coefficients of what might be called a "representative" production function. In a sense, it describes the relationship of inputs to output for the "representative" kibbutz in a "representative" year within the period to which the data apply. Though conceptually meaningful, both the representative kibbutz and the representative year are evidently statistical artifacts.

The model (5) column shows production elasticities of about 0.5 for labor and about 0.6 for capital. They add up to 1.1, which suggests that on the whole returns to scale were increasing but less so than one might gather from the cross-section data presented in tables 1 and 3. The estimated coefficients of the alternative formulation which allow for an explicit

Table 5. — Production Elasticities and the Experience Coefficients

Models (5) and (6)[a]

	Model			
	(5)	(6)	(5′)	(6′)
a	0.498 (0.032)	0.463 (0.031)	0.515 (0.032)	0.495 (0.032)
β_k	0.606 (0.184)	0.585 (0.182)	—	—
β_c	—	—	0.601 (0.019)	0.579 (0.020)
γ	—	—	0.100 (0.017)	0.082 (0.017)
λ	0.00443 (0.00357)	0.03158 (0.00464)	0.00628 (0.00362)	0.03039 (0.00480)
μ	—	−0.00060 (0.00007)	—	−0.00053 (0.00007)
$\lambda + 2\mu t$	—	0.00925	—	0.01067
R^2	0.934	0.937	0.932	0.934
$(a + \beta)$	1.104	1.048		
$(a + \beta + \gamma)$			1.216	1.156

[a] The functions are:
(5) $Y_{it} = A_0 A_i Z_t L^a K^\beta e^{\lambda \nu}$
(6) $Y_{it} = A_0 A_i Z_t L^a K^\beta e^{\lambda \nu + \mu \nu^2}$
(5′) $Y_{it} = A_0 A_i Z_t L^a C^\beta S^\gamma e^{\lambda \nu}$
(6′) $Y_{it} = A_0 A_i Z_t L^a C^\beta S^\gamma e^{\lambda \nu + \lambda \nu^2}$

test of the diminishing returns hypothesis [model (6)], however, also indicate that returns to scale were increasing, though at a lower rate.

Both models show that experience increased production by an annual 0.4–0.6 per cent. The negative sign of μ, which in this model is statistically significant at the 1 per cent level, suggests that the hypothesis of diminishing returns to experience may be accepted. The two corresponding forms (5′) and (6′), which suggest a somewhat stronger scale effect, yield correspondingly higher values for the experience variables. At 0.62 per cent annually for (5′) and about 1 per cent annually for (6′), they do support the results derived from the previous regressions.

These results suggest that the learning hypothesis cannot be rejected. In our specific context, they evidently warrant the stronger statement that experience has contributed significantly to the growth of productivity in kibbutz farming, although this contribution was probably diminishing over time.[16]

REFERENCES

Arrow, K. J., "The Economic Implications of Learning by Doing," *Review of Economic Studies*, XXIX (1962), 155–174.

Barkai, H., *Capital Stock in Kibbutzim 1936–1965* (Research Paper no. 24; Jerusalem, Falk Institute, 1969; Hebrew).

Kaldor, N., "Comment," *Review of Economic Studies* XXIX (1962).

Marschak, J., and W. H. Andrews, "Random Simultaneous Equations and the Theory of Production," *Econometrica* (1944), 143–205.

[16] Let us repeat that our measure of experience, which is "time," has a different significance from that of Arrow's cumulated investment, which according to his model is the only agent of experience-induced technical change. Note further that our measure does in a sense take into consideration one of Kaldor's points in his comment on Arrow's article (Arrow, 1962) — "that learning takes time."

CASE

13 BREAK-EVEN ANALYSIS FOR LOCKHEED'S TRI-STAR: A CASE ON APPLICATION OF FINANCIAL TECHNIQUES*

One of the more controversial issues during the 1971 Congressional hearings over emergency loan-guarantee legislation was the economic merit of Lockheed's L-1011 Tri-Star program.[1] In those hearings, Lockheed sought a federal guarantee for $250 million of additional bank credit required for the completion of the Tri-Star program. The loan guarantee was designed to help Lockheed over the severe liquidity crisis that followed the Defense Department's refusal to absorb all of the cost overruns Lockheed had experienced on a number of military contracts.

Representatives for Lockheed insisted that the Tri-Star program was basically sound and in jeopardy only because of the independently generated liquidity crisis. The opponents to the guarantee, on the other hand, argued that the program had been economically unsound from the outset and was doomed to financial failure whether or not the loan guarantee was granted.

The debate on this issue proceeded almost entirely on the basis of estimated "break-even" sales. In his testimony before Congress, Lockheed's chief executive asserted that this break-even point would be reached at sales between 195 and 205 aircraft. Although at the time of the hearings Lockheed had placed only 103 firm orders and 75 optional orders, management was confident that sales would eventually reach or exceed the predicted break-even point and that the project would thereby become a "commercially viable endeavor."

*This is based upon a paper entitled, "Break-Even Analysis for Lockheed's Tri-Star: An Application of Financial Theory," by U. E. Reinhardt, published in *The Journal of Finance*, Vol. XXVIII, No. 4, pp. 821-838, Sept. 1973. Adaption to case form by George W. Trivoli.

[1] The L-1011 Tri-Star Airbus is a wide-bodied commercial jet aircraft capable of carrying between 260 and 400 passengers (depending on interior design). The original design of the aircraft was optimized for medium range intracontinental traffic, although a long range intercontinental version may eventually be developed as well. The L-1011 is directly competitive with McDonnel Douglas' intermediate range DC-10 trijet and with the A-300B airbus developed by a European consortium. In the longer range versions the trijets also compete with modified versions of Boeing's 747.

One infers from the context of the debate that Lockheed defined the break-even point as that level of sales at which cumulative revenues just cover the algebraic sum of all development and production costs associated with the Tri-Star. Oddly enough, no one during the hearings took Lockheed to task for excluding from this definition one of the more significant costs of producing new aircraft: the opportunity cost of the enormous financial resources that must be committed to the development of the requisite technology and to the construction of appropriate production facilities. There is evidence that, for the Tri-Star, these outlays may have amounted to as much as $1 billion, much of which is likely to remain committed to the project for the better part of a decade. To overlook the opportunity cost of such funds is clearly a major error.

THE BASIC ANALYTIC FRAMEWORK

It is widely agreed among students of corporate finance that, for practical purposes, the most appropriate evaluation criterion for a corporate investment project is the net present value of that project.

$$NPV(k) = \int_0^T [R(t) - C(t)] \, e^{-\rho t} dt, \quad (1)$$

where $NPV(k)$ denotes the net present value of the project, discounted at the corporation's effective annual cost-of-capital rate, k; $R(t)$ and $C(t)$ denote the stream of cash revenues and cash outlays at time t; T is the investment horizon (the last period for which a cash flow is posited); and the continuously compounded discount rate ρ is equal to $\log_e(1 + k)$. For purposes of this analysis we assume that $t = 0$ falls somewhere into the spring of 1968 when Lockheed decided to go ahead with the Tri-Star program.

For a project consisting of the development, production, and sale of a new commercial aircraft, the revenue stream is composed of downpayments made by the airlines upon placing their orders and of payments upon delivery of the aircraft. The stream of

Decision Making in the Private Sector

cash outlays consists of three distinct though overlapping phases, namely;

1. The outlays associated with the Research, Development, Testing and Evaluation (RDTE) phase, covering the range of activities from the initial design stage to the evaluation of prototypes.
2. Outlays associated with the Initial Investment and Tooling phase, covering the construction of appropriate production facilities and the manufacture or procurement of the machine tools, assembly jigs, and so on, required during the production phase.
3. The costs of manufacture (or procurement) of components and their assembly into the airframe.

Hereafter, the costs associated with phases 1 and 2 will be referred to as the nonrecurring costs. Costs associated with phase 3 will be referred to as recurring, or production costs.

The Nonrecurring Costs of the Tri-Star Program In developing the L-1011 Tri-Star airbus, Lockheed has not had the benefit of significant spillovers from a similar military aircraft. The project has therefore required heavy outlays on research and development. For obvious reasons Lockheed itself has kept a tight lid on its Tri-Star cost data. It is possible, however, to piece together a fairly reliable cost estimate from bits of information revealed during the Congressional hearings in the financial press or in trade journals. These sources suggest rather consistently that the total nonrecurring outlays on the Tri-Star program have amounted to at least $800 million and probably to as much as $1 billion.

An analyst privy to Lockheed's internal records would, of course, be able to project the exact time path of the nonrecurring cost stream fairly accurately and construct an evaluation model accordingly. Such details are not available in the public record, and in the absence of better information, it is perhaps not unreasonable to approximate the sum of the phase 1 and phase 2 costs by a more or less even flow over the period beginning at time $t = 0$ and ending with the onset of the production phase at time $t = A$. In other words, we estimate the rate of RDTE and Initial Investment outlays at time t to be the following:

$$C_t = \frac{R + I}{A}, \text{ for } 0 < t < A, \qquad (2)$$

where R denotes the total RDTE costs associated with the project, I denotes the total initial outlay on production facilities and tooling, and A denotes the number of months elapsed between the beginning of a serious development effort at $t = 0$ and the onset of the production phase. In the light of the preceding comments, our analysis proceeds on the assumption $800 \text{ million} < R + I < \$1 \text{ billion}$.

The first delivery of a Tri-Star to an airline was made in April, 1972; however, it was about 6 months behind schedule (it should have been made sometime in the Fall of 1971). The slippage was caused primarily by an unforeseeable slippage in the development of the Tri-Star's Rolls Royce engines. It is therefore reasonable to suppose that Lockheed based its own calculations in 1968 on an assumed gestation period of not more than 42 months. The present analysis therefore proceeds on the assumption that parameter A in equation (2) is equal to 42.

Recurring Production Costs and the Learning Curve Past studies of aircraft production have led to the remarkable discovery that, for any given type of aircraft, the cumulative average (recurring) production cost per aircraft (excluding any amortization of nonrecurring costs) tends to decline by a more or less constant percentage between doubled quantities of production. Thus, if Q denotes any given number of aircraft produced and Y_Q the corresponding cumulative average production cost, then the average cost at an output level of 2Q tends to be γY_Q, where γ—the so-called learning coefficient—has a value less than unity and remains virtually constant over all empirically relevant values of Q. The assumption of a constant learning coefficient is almost always incorporated into cost models used by airframe manufacturers, and it is therefore most likely that Lockheed's break-even calculations for the Tri-Star are based on such an assumption as well.

The learning effect in aircraft assembly may be expressed mathematically by the formula

$$Y_Q = Y_1 Q^{-b}, \qquad (3)$$

where, in addition to the already familiar symbols, Y_1 denotes the first-unit cost and $b = -\log(\gamma)/\log(2)$. The parameters of this function can be estimated from cost data quoted in an article in Barron's. According to the article, presumably knowledgeable industry sources in 1971 estimated the cumulative average production cost per unit after the production of the 150th Tri-Star (i.e., Y_{150}) as $15.5 million. The corresponding figure for a volume of 300 Tri-Stars was estimated to be $12.0 million. If one makes the plausible assumption that these estimates were derived from a conventional learning curve such as equation (3), then the value of b is found to be equal to 0.369188 and the implied first-unit cost (Y_1) is found to be approximately $100 million. These parameter estimates are equivalent to a learning coefficient (γ)

of 77.4 percent, an estimate that is perfectly consistent with recent research on learning in aircraft production. Such research has indicated that, for complex modern aircraft, learning coefficients between 75 percent and 78 percent are typical.

If Q(t) denotes the total number of Tri-Stars that will have been produced by the end of period t, and $Y_{(Q)t}$ the corresponding cumulative average production cost, then, using equation (3), the cumulative total production cost at time t can be written as

$$TC(t) = Y_1 [Q(t)]^{(1-b)} \quad (4)$$

and the rate of production costs experienced at time t is given by

$$C(t) = (1-b) Y_1 [Q(t)]^{-b} \delta Q(t)/\delta t \quad (5)$$

According to testimony given before the House Committee on Banking and Currency, Lockheed's original production schedule called for the production of 220 Tri-Stars over a period beginning in late 1971 and ending in late 1977. This schedule is equivalent to an average production rate of three aircraft per month. Although the production rates foreseen in the original schedule do fluctuate somewhat from year to year, we shall find it analytically more convenient to posit a constant monthly production rate, N, for the entire program, so that Q(t) can be written as

$$Q(t) = (t - A) N \quad (6)$$

For the most part we shall base our calculations on a value of N = 3. But we shall experiment also with plausible alternative values for N.

The projected time path of recurring costs for the Tri Star program can now be expressed as

$$C(t) = (1-b) Y_1 (t-A)^{-b} N^{(1-b)}$$

where

A = 42,
b = .369188,
Y_1 = $100 million,
t > A

(7)

where t = A, it will be recalled, denotes the onset of the production phase. As will be indicated shortly, the average price the airlines were expected, in 1968, to pay for the Tri-Star (excluding any inflationary escalation) appears to have been somewhere between $15 and $16 million. Within that price range, we estimate a positive cash flow from the program after production of about the 50th aircraft. This estimate is virtually identical to that made public by Lockheed, whose chief executive testified before the Senate hearings that "a break-even point in terms of cash flow is reached at approximately the 50th aircraft in 1973. This cash break-even point compares production costs with sales price." Our recurring production cost estimates, therefore, appear to be fairly close to Lockheed's own forecast.

Lockheed's Cost-of-Capital Much has been written about the problem of estimating the value of the cost-of-capital rate, k, in practical applications. One's approach to the problem depends essentially on the goals that the firm is expected to pursue.

In a capitalist society it is normally assumed that, at any point in time, the management of a private corporation should conduct the affairs of the firm so as to maximize the wealth of existing shareholders. If this is the ultimate goal of corporate investment, then the appropriate cost-of-capital rate can be shown to be equal to

$$K = \sum_{j=1}^{j=n} (W_j k_j) \quad (8)$$

where k_j is the effective annual after-tax cost per dollar of the j-th source of funds and W_j is the proportion (measured at the aggregate market value of the underlying security) of the j-th source of funds in the long-run capital structure deemed optimal by the firm.

A review of Lockheed's historical record reveals that, under normal conditions, the firm tends to prefer a capital structure with about 30 percent debt and 70 percent equity. For a company in the rather unstable aerospace sector, this relationship is probably viewed as a prudent limit. At any rate, between the late 1950s and 1967 Lockheed has generally remained within this debt limit. Since 1968 the company's debt-to-equity ratio has, of course, risen enormously, and almost certainly against the company's wishes.

If one assumes that Lockheed's desired long-term capital structure consists of about 30 percent short- or long-term debt and 70 percent common stock and retained earnings (weighted at market values), then equation (8) can be restated as

$$k = .3k_d + .7k_e \quad (9)$$

where k_d denotes the average after-tax cost of debt and k_e the cost of equity capital.

In 1968, Lockheed probably faced an average after-tax cost of debt (k_d) between 4 percent and 5 percent. The effective rate would, of course, be higher if there were insufficient profits that could be shielded by

Decision Making in the Private Sector

interest expenses. In view of the likelihood of that circumstance, we may assume that k_d was equal to at least 5 percent.

It is more difficult to arrive at an estimate of the cost of equity capital, k_e. The theory of investors' behavior suggests that, if investors in the stock market, on average, believe that a firm's dividends per share will tend to grow at an average annual compound rate g over the long run, the firm's cost of equity capital can be approximated by the expression

$$k_e = \frac{D}{P} + g, \qquad (10)$$

where D denotes the dividends per share announced for the current period, and P is either the current market price per share (if k_e refers to the cost of retained earnings) or the net proceeds per share (after flotation costs) of a new common stock issue (if k_e refers to the cost of new equity capital).

Between 1957-61 and 1964-1968, Lockheed's cash earnings per share increased at an average annual compound rate of 19.1 percent. The corresponding growth rate for cash dividends per share was 22 percent. As late as April 1969, the *Value Line Investment Survey* forecast a future average annual growth rate in cash earnings per share of 6.5 percent. One might therefore set the growth rate, g, in equation (10) at 6 percent to 7 percent.

Lockheed's dividend yield (D/P) in 1968 was 4.2 percent. It had been close to 4 percent ever since the mid-1960s. If one takes into account the fact that, because of flotation costs, the ratio D/P for new equity is higher than the current dividend yield, then one is led to conclude that Lockheed's average cost of equity capital in 1968 must have been close to 12 percent.

Upon insertion of the estimated values of k_d and k_e into equation (9), Lockheed's overall cost-of-capital rate, k, prior to the acceptance of the Tri-Star project is found to be somewhere between 9 percent and 10 percent. In view of the enormous marginal business risk the Tri-Star project added to Lockheed's overall business risk, an argument can be made to apply a cost-of-capital rate of at least 10 percent, or possibly even higher, to the Tri-Star program.

Revenues from the Tri-Star Program The time profile of cash revenues from the Tri-Star program depends on the price the airlines pay for the aircraft, on the manner in which payment is made, and on the monthly rate, N, at which Lockheed produces and delivers the planes. For present purposes it is assumed that all customers pay the same price, although in fact there may be small price differences depending upon the interior layout ordered by individual airlines.

By mid-1971 Lockheed's customers had advanced about $260 million for future deliveries of the Tri-Star. One way of handling these down payments within a capital-budgeting framework would be to treat them as cash revenues received during the RDTE and Initial Investment phases and to deduct them from the non-recurring costs incurred during those phases. From an analytical standpoint this approach would certainly be sound. But without knowing the precise payment pattern it is difficult to implement that approach here.

An alternative approach, however, can be suggested. It is inconceivable that the airlines would commit funds of this magnitude without promise of a return either in the form of explicit interest charges or in the form of a discount off the price paid by customers who have not made any down payment. One may, therefore, treat the $260 million down payments as ordinary interest-bearing loans. The only distinguishing features of the loans are that they are granted by airlines rather than by banks, that some of the interest is paid in the form of a lower sales price rather than as periodic interest payments, and that the loans are repaid in kind (aircraft) rather than with cash. On this interpretation it is analytically acceptable to lump the down payments in with the rest of the firm's traditional sources of funds and to pretend that all cash revenues are earned as the aircraft are delivered to customers.

The original price of the Tri-Star is said to have been $14.7 million including the propulsion system of three engines. Subsequently, the price has been adjusted upward via escalator clauses in Lockheed's sales contracts. The average price is currently said to be between $15 and $16 million, although the price will undoubtedly rise further in step with inflationary increases in production costs. Price increases such as this will not affect future cash flows since they have an exact contemporaneous counterpart in costs. It is therefore legitimate to evaluate the Tri-Star program in terms of a constant base price envisaged in 1968. In line with that reasoning, the flow of revenues at time t may thus be defined as

$$R(t) = PN, \qquad \text{for } t > A \qquad (11)$$

A base value of P = $15.5 million is probably not far off the mark, though perhaps somewhat on the high side. The bulk of our analysis will be based on that value, although we shall evaluate the program also at other assumed values for P.

THE APPARENT PROFITABILITY (OR LACK OF IT) OF THE TRI-STAR PROGRAM

Estimated Net Present Values and Break-Even Sales: The 1968 Perspective Figure 1 presents estimated net present values of the Tri-Star program

Production and Cost Analysis

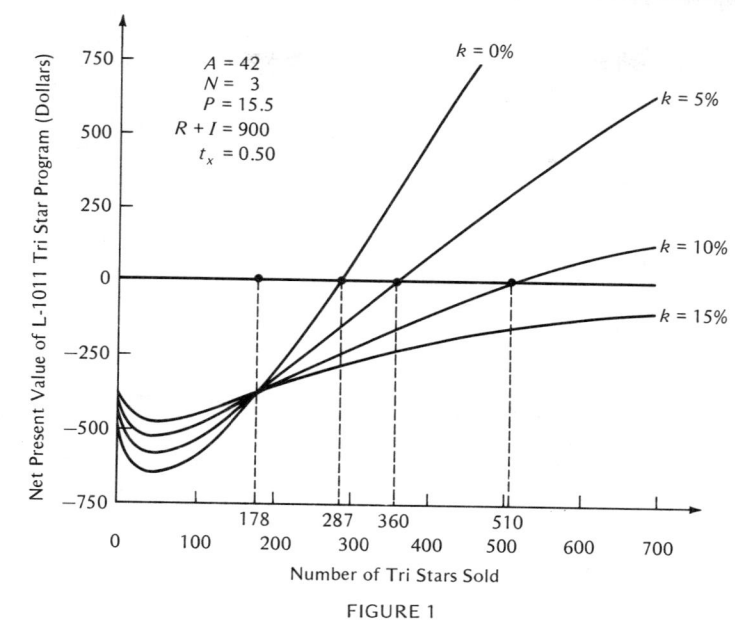

FIGURE 1

$A = 42$
$N = 3$
$P = 15.5$
$R + I = 900$
$t_x = 0.50$

at alternative sales levels and discount rates. The curves are drawn on the assumption that the total nonrecurring costs of the program (R + I) are $900 million, that the average price per aircraft (P) is $15.5 million, that an average of three aircraft per month are produced and sold (N), that the Development and Initial Investment phase (A) is 42 months, that Lockheed faces a 50 percent tax rate (t_x)[2], and that the Tri-Star program costs will always have positive income to shield. These assumptions are indicated in the upper left corner of the diagram.

The curve labeled "k = 0%" is a plot of net-present values at a zero cost-of-capital rate. At any given level of sales, the vertical distance between this line and the horizontal line labelled BE represents the projected profit (or loss) prior to deduction of any capital costs. Virtually the entire debate before Congress was based on this concept of "profits."

The curve labeled "k = 5%," "k = 10%," and "k = 15%" are similar to that labeled "k = 0%," but here the cost-of-capital has been explicitly taken into account.

Figure 1 is based on the assumption that Lockheed will produce and deliver the Tri-Stars at an average rate of three aircraft per month. The sensitivity of the break-even volume to the assumed delivery schedule is indicated in Figure 2. At cost-of-capital rates in excess of 5 percent, a speed-up in deliveries becomes increasingly beneficial. These benefits, however, accrue at a diminishing rate. Little appears to be gained by pushing deliveries beyond a rate of about six per month.

From the point of view of managerial decision making, Figure 3 is perhaps the most interesting constellation of program variables. The set of curves in that figure represents estimated break-even sales as a function of the sales price per Tri-Star. The lower curve of each pair of curves is based on assumed nonrecurring costs (R + I) of $800 million, the upper on $1 billion. The three pairs of curves are drawn on the assumption of a zero, 5 percent, and 10 percent cost-of-capital rate, respectively, as is indicated in the graph.

For a given level of nonrecurring costs and a given discount rate, any price-sales combination falling above the corresponding curve in Figure 3 yields a positive net present value for the Tri-Star program. Any price-sales combination falling below the curve, on the other hand, is associated with a negative net present value. Each of the curves may therefore be viewed as the break-even frontier corresponding to the assumed values of R + I and k.

The curves in Figure 3 may be superimposed on the demand schedule for Tri-Stars Lockheed appears to have faced in 1968. For the program to be economically viable, at least one point on that demand curve would have had to fall onto the relevant break-even frontier or, preferably, onto the positive side of that frontier.

Unfortunately, even the approximate shape of the demand curve perceived by Lockheed is unknown to outsiders, but we do know at least some points on the perceived and on the actual demand curves for the Tri-Star.

---

[2] In view of the possibility of loss carry forwards, from other projects, Lockheed's effective tax rates at various times in the future may be much lower than 50 percent. Changes in the assumed tax rates will alter the calculated net present value of the Tri-Star project but will not affect our break-even calculations.

Decision Making in the Private Sector

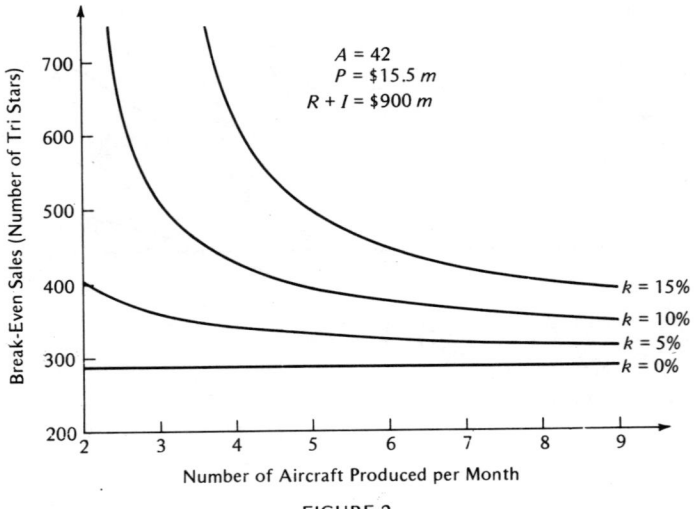

FIGURE 2

$A = 42$
$P = \$15.5\,m$
$R + I = \$900\,m$

(curves for $k = 15\%$, $k = 10\%$, $k = 5\%$, $k = 0\%$)

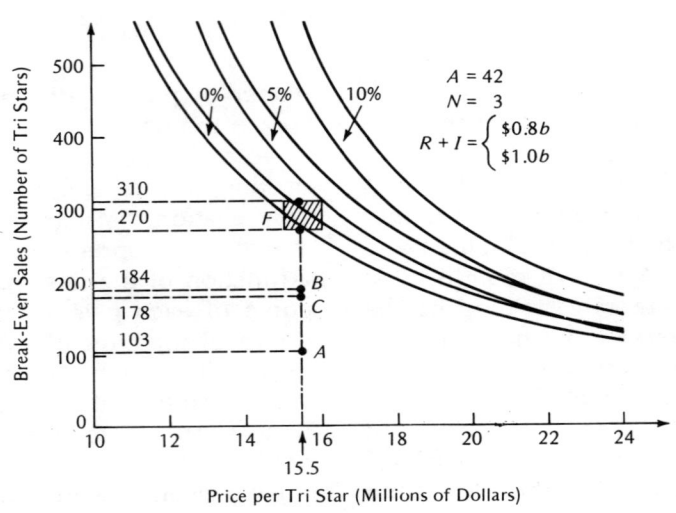

Break-Even Sales (Number of Tri Stars) vs. Number of Aircraft Produced per Month

FIGURE 3

$A = 42$
$N = 3$
$R + I = \begin{cases} \$0.8b \\ \$1.0b \end{cases}$

Break-Even Sales (Number of Tri Stars) vs. Price per Tri Star (Millions of Dollars)

Points: 310, 270 (F), 184 (B), 178 (C), 103 (A); curves at 0%, 5%, 10%; vertical at 15.5.

As indicated earlier, at the time of the Congressional hearings in mid-1971, Lockheed claimed to have orders for 178 Tri-Stars of which 103 were firm orders and seventy-five were so-called "second-buys" or options that are subject to cancellation by the customer. These orders were probably negotiated at prices (prior to inflationary escalation) in the neighborhood of $15.5 million. In Figure 3, the sales levels of 103 and 178 are indicated as points A and B. By the end of October 1972 total orders had increased only by eleven aircraft (117 firm and sixty-seven options). The total of 184 aircraft is shown as point C in Figure 3. All three sales levels lie very much below the break-even frontier, even if one posits only $800 million in nonrecurring costs and excludes capital costs from total program costs altogether.

In all fairness it must be acknowledged that, in 1968, Lockheed probably forecast sales in excess of 178 aircraft. From the testimony before Congress one gathers that Lockheed had originally hoped to capture 35 to 40 percent of a total free-world market of 775 wide-bodied airbuses of the medium range category for which the Tri-Star is designed. The forecast of 775 aircraft, however, was predicted on an assumed annual growth rate of 10 percent in air travel. In fact, air travel in recent years has not expanded at nearly this rate; it even declined somewhat during the period 1970-71. At the more realistic growth rate in air traffic of, say, 5 percent per annum the total demand for intermediate range airbuses during the next decade is estimated to be only 323 aircraft. Lockheed's original sales forecast therefore appears to have been unrealistically high.

But even if one accepts, for the sake of argument,

Production and Cost Analysis

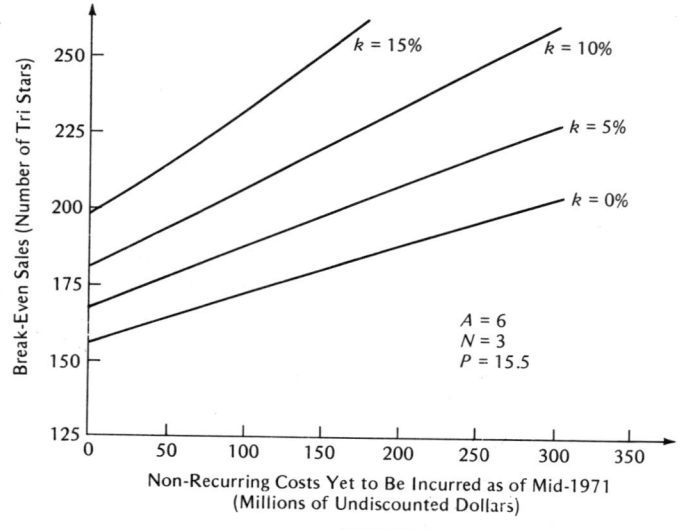

FIGURE 4

an assumed growth rate in air traffic of 10 percent per annum, it is clear that Lockheed expected to sell only between 270 and 310 of the 775 aircraft required under those traffic conditions. In Figure 3 the range of points encompassed by this forecast is shown as the shaded area labeled F. This set of figures also lies substantially below the $800 million 5 percent break-even frontier as would, in all probability, the entire band of demand schedules passing through area F.

Questions for Discussion

1. Calculate a "naive" break-even level of sales implicit in Lockheed's estimates and the author's cost model. Is the resulting break-even level of sales higher or lower than Lockheed's original forecast of sales of the Tri-Star?
2. Calculate estimated break-even sales levels for the three suggested cost-of-capital rates of 5 percent per annum, 10 percent and 15 percent. What is the effect of raising the cost of capital on the break-even level of sales?
3. Based upon the assumptions in the case and data supplied by Lockheed, was there a price-sales combination for the Tri-Star in 1968 at which the project could have been expected to generate a positive net present value? (*Assume* projected nonrecurring costs of $800 million, a cost-of-capital rate of 5 percent, and annual traffic growth of 10 percent per year—most favorable estimates).
4. Under what set of conditions would Lockheed's management have viewed the Tri-Star project as commercially attractive in 1968?
5. Review the Lockheed Tri-Star investment from the viewpoint of societal economic benefit, since the U.S. Congress decided to guarantee $250 million in additional bank credit to Lockheed for completion of the Tri-Star project. Are there lessons to be gained from this incident for future requests to Congress to guarantee or underwrite programs that more properly should be left to private markets? Under what conditions should the Federal Government enter into loan guarantees; to bail out defense contractors?

EXERCISES
14

14-1. Economists at General Industries have been examining operating costs at one of its parts manufacturing plants in an effort to determine if the plant is being operated efficiently. From weekly cost records, the economists developed the following cost-output information concerning the operation of the plant:
   a. AVC (average variable cost) at an output of 2,000 units per week is $7.50.
   b. At an output level of 5,000 units per week AFC (average fixed cost) is $3.00.
   c. TC (total cost) increases by $5,000 when output is increased from 2,000 to 3,000 units per week.
   d. TVC (total variable cost) at an output level of 4,000 units per week is $23,000.
   e. AVC (average variable cost) decreases by $.75 per unit when output is increased from 4,000 to 5,000 units per week.
   f. AFC plus AVC for 8,000 units per week is $7.50 per unit.
   g. ATC (average total cost) decreases by $.50 per unit when output is decreased from 8,000 to 7,000 units per week.
   h. TVC increases by $3,000 when output is increased from 5,000 to 6,000 units per week.
   i. TC decreases by $7,000 when output is decreased from 2,000 to 1,000 units per week.
   j. MC (marginal cost) is $16.00 per unit when output is increased from 8,000 to 9,000 units per week.

   Given the above information, complete the following cost schedule for the plant. Hint: Proceed sequentially through the above list, *filling in all the related entries before proceeding to the next item of information in the list.*

Output (Units per Week)	TFC	TVC	TC	AFC	AVC	ATC	MC
0	___	___	___	X	X	X	X
1,000	___	___	___	___	___	___	___
2,000	___	___	___	___	___	___	___
3,000	___	___	___	___	___	___	___
4,000	___	___	___	___	___	___	___
5,000	___	___	___	___	___	___	___
6,000	___	___	___	___	___	___	___
7,000	___	___	___	___	___	___	___
8,000	___	___	___	___	___	___	___
9,000	___	___	___	___	___	___	___

Dollars per Unit

14-2. The Shanghai Shipping Company has the following average variable cost function:

$$AVC = 4 - 2Q + Q^2/3$$

The average fixed cost at an output of 12 units is $12.

Production and Cost Analysis

a. What is Shanghai's total cost function?
b. Determine (using calculus techniques) the output level (Q) where the average variable cost function is minimized.
c. What is the value of the total cost and average variable cost functions at the output level determined in part b?
d. What is Shanghai's marginal cost function?
e. Determine the output level (Q) where the marginal cost function takes on its minimum value?
f. What is the value of the total cost, average variable cost, and marginal cost functions at the output level determined in part e.?

14-3. Araboco, a foreign-owned integrated oil company, has decided that U.S. service stations selling its products are to phase out their car repair activities and only pump gasoline. Araboco owns all of its service stations and leases them to individuals (usually mechanics) who manage and operate them. An economist for Araboco is attempting to determine the impact on the service station operators of the decision to phase out car repair activities. The economist develops the following information concerning a "typical" service station:

Monthly fixed costs	
Rent	$1,300
Utilities	250
Wages (excluding the operator)	1,400
Miscellaneous	150
Total Fixed Costs	$3,100
Variable costs	
Gasoline (per gallon)*	$ .53
Selling price (per gallon)	.61

*The station actually sells "regular" and "premium" gasoline. The cost per gallon (and selling price per gallon) represents an "average" cost (selling price) of the two grades of gasoline. The sales ratio of "regular" to "premium" is assumed to remain constant over time. Consequently, costs (and revenues) will vary only with the total number of gallons sold.

Answer the following questions assuming that the linear break-even model is an appropriate representation of the operation of a "typical" station:

a. What is the monthly break-even volume in gallons? In dollar sales?
b. Past studies have indicated that a "typical" independent operator earns an average total monthly profit of $2,000, consisting of $800 from repair work and the remainder from the sales of gasoline. How much gasoline does the "typical" operator sell per month?
c. Assuming that the operator wants to earn the same profit per month after phasing out the car repair activities, how much gasoline must the operator now sell per month?
d. Further analysis of the cost information above indicates that a saving of one attendant, or approximately $400 per month, would be realized from the phase-out of repair work. Again, assuming that the operator wants to earn the same total monthly profit as before the phase-out, how much gasoline must the operator sell per month?
e. In order to reduce the impact on the operators of phasing out

Decision Making in the Private Sector

the repair activities, one alternative under consideration by Araboco is to reduce by one cent per gallon the price that the operators must pay for the gasoline that they sell. How much gasoline per month must the operator now sell per month in order to earn the same total monthly profit as before the phase-out of repair work (Ignore the information in d.)?

14-4. The Blair Company has three assembly plants located in California, Georgia, and New Jersey. Currently, the company purchases a major subassembly, that becomes part of the final product, from an outside firm. Blair has decided to manufacture the subassemblies within the company and must now consider whether to rent one centrally located facility e.g., Missouri, where all the subassemblies would be manufactured or to rent three separate facilities, each located near one of the assembly plants, where each facility would manufacture only the subassemblies needed for the nearby assembly plant. A single, centrally located facility, with a production capacity of 18,000 units per year, would have fixed costs of $900,000 per year, and a variable cost of $250 per unit. Three separate decentralized facilities, with production capacities of 8,000, 6,000, and 4,000 units per year, would have fixed costs of $475,000, $425,000, and $400,000, respectively, and variable costs per unit of only $225 per unit due primarily to the reduction in shipping costs. The current production rates at the three assembly plants are 6,000, 4,500, and 3,000 units, respectively.
   a. Assuming that the current production rates are maintained at the three assembly plants, which alternative should management select?
   b. If demand for the final product were to increase to production capacity, which alternative would be more attractive?
   c. What additional information would be useful before making a decision?

14-5. The output (Q) of a certain production process is a function of two inputs (X and Y) and is given by the following relationship:

$$Q = \frac{1}{6} X^2 Y^2 - \frac{1}{3456} X^3 Y^3$$

Assume that input Y is fixed at 6 units.

   a. Determine the total product function (TP_X) for input X.
   b. Using the total product function in a., determine the marginal product function (MP_X) for input X.
   c. Using the total product function in a., determine the average product function (AP_X) for input X.
   d. Find the number of units of input X that maximizes the total production function (TP_X).
   e. Find the number of units of input X that maximizes the marginal production function (MP_X).
   f. Find the number of units of input X that maximizes the average product function (AP_X).
   g. Determine the boundaries for the three stages of production.

14-6. Suppose that the output of a certain coal mining operation, measured in tons/day, is a function of only two inputs—capital (C) and labor (L). Capital consists of the physical equipment used in the

Production and Cost Analysis

mining operation. Assume that the amount of capital employed can be represented by its horsepower rating. Labor consists of the crew size, or number of workers, used to operate the mining equipment. Based on past experience with the coal mining operation, the production schedule in the table below was developed. It shows the output (tons/day) that are obtained when the various combinations of capital and labor are employed in the mining operation.

	\multicolumn{8}{c}{Capital (C) — (Horsepower)}
Labor(L)—(Number of Workers)	1,000	2,000	3,000	4,000	5,000	6,000	7,000	8,000
1	2	5	10	17	27	28	27	22
2	3	10	27	40	48	48	73	63
3	7	27	48	73	92	93	92	83
4	10	48	73	92	97	100	99	92
5	27	72	92	100	102	103	104	100
6	48	92	100	104	105	106	106	104
7	73	97	104	105	107	108	108	107
8	84	100	103	105	107	109	109	109
9	92	99	101	105	107	109	110	110
10	89	93	98	104	106	108	110	111

Assume that the amount of capital employed in the mining operation is a fixed input equal to 3,000 horsepower and that labor is the variable input.

a. (i) Determine the total product, marginal product, and average product schedules for labor.
   (ii) Plot the total, marginal, and average product functions for labor.
   (iii) Determine the boundaries of the three stages of production.

Assume now that labor is a fixed input in the mining operation, being equal to four workers, and that capital is the variable input.

b. (i) Determine the total product, marginal product, and average product schedules for capital.
   (ii) Plot the total, marginal, and average product functions for capital.
   (iii) Determine the boundaries of the three stages of production.

14-7. Consider again the coal mining operation described in the previous problem. Assume that the amount of capital employed is a fixed input equal to 3,000 horsepower and that labor is the vairable input. Furthermore, assume that the per-unit costs of capital and labor are $ .10 and $60, respectively; that is, capital input costs $ .10 per horsepower per day and labor input costs $60 per worker per day.
   a. Compute the variable cost, fixed cost, and total cost schedules.
   b. Plot the cost functions in a. on one graph.
   c. Compute the average variable cost, average fixed cost, average total cost, and marginal cost schedules.
   d. Plot the cost functions in c. on one graph.

14-8. A study of the costs of electricity generation for a sample of fifty-six British firms in 1946-47 yielded the following long-run cost function:*

---
*Jack Johnston, *Statistical Cost Analysis* (New York: McGraw-Hill, 1960), Chapter 4.

Decision Making in the Private Sector

AVC = 1.24 + .0033Q + .0000029Q² — .000046QZ — .026Z + .00018Z²

where

AVC = average variable cost (that is, working costs of generation), measured in pence** per kilowatt-hour
Q = output, measured in millions of kilowatt-hours per year
Z = plant size, measured in thousands of kilowatts

a. Determine the long-run variable cost function for electricity generation.
b. Determine the long-run marginal cost function for electricity generation.
c. Holding plant size constant at 150 (thousand) kilowatts, determine the short-run average variable cost and marginal cost functions for electricity generation.
d. For a plant size equal to 150 (thousand) kilowatts, determine the output level that minimizes short-run average variable costs.
e. Determine the short-run average variable cost and marginal cost at the output level obtained in d.

**A pence was a British monetary unit, being equal to (at that time) two U.S. cents.

Chapter 5 Pricing

READING

15 PRICING BEHAVIOR OF LARGE FIRMS

J. Fred Weston*
UNIVERSITY OF CALIFORNIA, LOS ANGELES

Although many studies have been made, no consensus has been reached concerning the methods by which firms make pricing decisions. A controversy continues between full-cost or target pricing and the application of marginalist principles.[1] An unsatisfactory dichotomy (frequently separated by chapters in textbooks) is also found in the treatment of the goals and behavior of atomistic firms and oligopolists. The aim of this paper is to present new evidence that helps reconcile the conflicting approaches. A three-year study, during which extensive interviews were conducted with top managements concerning their capital resource allocation decisions, yielded fresh insights into the pricing process.[2] While my experiences confirmed the well-known weaknesses of the interview technique, the discussions enabled me to discern a process that: (1) explains why empirical work on the corporate pricing problem has led to conflicting views; (2) reconciles some apparent differences between decision-making in small and large firms; and (3) demonstrates that what appears to be irrational behavior in a static model is rational behavior in a dynamic world.

My plan is to begin by describing the pattern that emerged from the

---

*This paper draws on field studies supported by grants from the McKinsey Foundation to the UCLA Research Program in Competition and Business Policy for a study of Corporate Resource Allocation Policies. Helpful comments were received from R. M. Cyert, H. Demsetz, C. G. Krouse, N. H. Jacoby, M. E. Rubinstein, W. J. Vatter, O. E. Williamson and the Editor.

1. In a comprehensive survey of some 60 British and U.S. studies of price determination [38], Professor Silberston finds the evidence inconclusive with respect to full-cost or target pricing policy versus the application of marginal principles. Silberston appears to favor an emphasis on a full-cost approach in the initial procedures for assembling the cost information for pricing. In the processes of pricing over time, however, he recognizes important qualifications reflecting marginalist and behavioral qualifications. (See also Andrews [3], Langholm [21], and Robinson [35].) A recent econometric study by Eckstein and Fromm [14] also yielded mixed results. In summarizing the relative importance of cost and demand elements they state:

> ...While the different forms of the equations yield varying results on the relative importance of the competitive mechanism vis-a-vis oligopolistic pricing, there is pretty strong evidence that equations combining both mechanisms are superior to equations using either approach in isolation [14, p. 1171].

2. The companies interviewed include the following: A & P, Alcoa, American Can, Beckman Industries, Boeing, Borg-Warner, Douglas Aircraft, du Pont, Everest and Jennings, Fluor, Ford, General Electric, General Foods, General Motors, General Precision, Goodyear, Gulf Oil, Hughes Aircraft, IBM, International Harvester, Johns-Manville, Kennecott Copper, Kroger, Lear-Siegler, Litton, Lockheed, Mattel, National Cash Register, National Steel, North American Aviation, Northrup, Pabst Brewing, Purex, Radio Corporation of America, Revell, Reynolds Metals, Robertshaw

interviews. Next the formulation is tested by empirical studies. Finally, the analysis is used to provide a framework for explaining why other studies have often been misinterpreted. The core of the present reformulation lies in the nature of planning and control processes of firms; the key aspect of this perspective is that short-run decisions are made in the framework of longer-range planning. Thus, the underlying model for analysis is not the commonly-used static theory of the firm, but rather the theory of investment under uncertainty, with maximization of the present value of an earnings stream. Within the investment decision framework, adaptive learning by firms becomes a central feature of economic behavior, manifesting itself through the firm's use of (1) plans and standards of controls, (2) periodic review and analysis of divergences between planned and actual results, and (3) an information feedback system providing for revisions of plans, standards and policies.

In prior analysis of corporate pricing, a major source of confusion has resulted from the divergence between the time period covered in the questions posed and that of the economic model used to interpret the responses.[3] Although the Brookings [20] questionnaire began with four questions about policies over a twenty-five-year period and the Hall and Hitch [18] questions asked about behavior over a number of business fluctuations, the responses were analyzed with reference to "the common analysis of short-run equilibrium in terms of marginal cost and marginal revenue" [49, p. 124]. But businessmen, being much less myopic, must have made their responses to these surveys and interviews in the context of the firm's decision processes over the extended period of time suggested by the nature of the questions posed. As a consequence, the implications of reviews, decision revisions, and other adaptive behavior of firms which constitute elements of organizational decision processes, have been confounded in the pricing policy literature. These behavioral processes are evidence that firms do in fact develop strategies for "earning while learning" [27, p. 52]. The adaptive learning processes of business firms suggest a dynamic general equilibrium model of investment under uncertainty (for brief reference, DGU) as the appropriate framework for analysis of economic consequences. In contrast, similar information elicited in other previous surveys was analyzed with reference to a static partial equilibrium model of pricing under certainty (SPC). While business investment decisions are only beginning to be guided by formal dynamic models, the adaptive processes represent a heuristic dynamics.[4] Similarly, the trial-and-

---

Controls, Sears Roebuck, Standard Oil, Indiana, Standard Oil, N.J., Swift, Statham Instruments, Tridair Industries, U.S. Steel, Union Carbide, Whittaker, Xerox.

These include the 20 firms listed in [22] and 20 additional with similar characteristics (large firms in concentrated industries). Ten were small firms. Interviews with some firms were arranged by McKinsey & Co.; discussions with the others were facilitated by their participation in executive educational programs at UCLA.

3. One fundamental difference between the surveys in the Brookings Study and my own survey has important substantive implications and affected the nature of the responses. The Brookings Study surveyed sales departments and sales executives. My own survey began as a study of corporate resource allocation policy and so involved discussions with executives at corporate levels not responsible for specific management functions. From the standpoint of a specific functional area such as the sales department, operating standards or objectives become targets. From the standpoint of the corporate level, there is a continuous trade-off analysis between a wide range of variables. Pricing is only one and probably of relatively second-order importance in the hierarchy of operational standards and objectives employed by the firm.

4. The increasing importance of probabilistic economics has been emphasized by McCall [28].

error learning activities of business firms do not formally employ a general equilibrium framework, but neither are they restricted to the small number of variables of partial equilibrium analysis.

The two central themes of this paper are: (1) Business behavior superficially characterized as nonoptimizing by reference to an SPC model constitutes a strategic response to a DGU world. (2) The DGU model suggests revision of some of the inferences derived from deterministic models. Traditional price theory has employed static partial equilibrium analysis of output decisions in "price-taking" atomistic markets and of "price seeking" in imperfect markets. In the longer-run framework of investment decisions, additional variables with a wide range of values should enter the analysis. Forms of competition become numerous and complex. Therefore, collusion becomes more difficult and is not a simple function of the market shares of the largest firms. A related inference that atomistic market structures alone can guarantee maximal efficiency is derived from the assumptions of the SPC model. Firms in concentrated markets in a DGU model are subject to forces to achieve optimizing performance of the kind ascribed to competitive pressures.

I. MARKUP PRICING RULES

Previous surveys [18] [20] of pricing reported that instead of being guided by marginal principles, business firms used markup rules which reflected some degree of market control. The Hall and Hitch survey described full-cost pricing behavior, while the Brookings survey emphasized the predominance of target return-on-investment pricing. These two markup pricing rules are similar.[5] The full-cost pricing markup factor is applied to standard unit variable costs with overheads excluded. Target pricing is based on a fixed return on capital investment. If the ratio of investment to output is constant and if the full-cost markup base includes fixed costs, a constant relation between the percentage markup on total cost and the target rate of return on investment obtains.[6] Because the two concepts are similar and "target-return on investment was perhaps the most frequently mentioned of pricing goals" [22, p. 923], its implications will be pursued.

---

5. The two pricing rules can be expressed in the equation form used as a basis for econometric studies [14]

$$P_f = (1 + m)(ULC + UMC)$$
$$P_r = ULC + UMC + F/X + \pi K/X$$

where:

P_f = price per unit based on full-cost pricing formula

P_r = price per unit based on return-on-investment target pricing

ULC = unit labor cost

UMC = unit material cost

F = total fixed costs

X = quantity of units produced for the relevant planning horizon

K = investment (usually defined as total operating assets with depreciation added back)

m = profit markup when full-cost pricing is used

π = profit rate on investment, appropriately defined as earnings before interest and depreciation, when total assets are defined as above

6. Then $m = b\pi$ where b is some constant. The equivalence of the two methods can be illustrated by a numerical example. With a turnover of investment into total costs of 2 and a markup on total cost of 10 percent before taxes, the return on investment before taxes would be 20 percent.

Decision Making in the Private Sector

The target-return pricing literature is a collection of observations about limited aspects of firm behavior without a systematic theory of pricing. It fails to provide an explanation of why targets are formed, how their level is determined, or why or how targets are changed. Various advantages of target-return pricing for large firms have been set forth by other writers as its rationale: (1) "... target-return pricing makes for price stability, since standard costs change much less frequently than actual costs or short-run demand conditions" [13, p. 269]. (2) "... it is particularly suitable for price leadership" [14, p. 1165]. (3) Target pricing enables a firm to manage its profits. "The foregoing data, above all, make it clear that management's approach to pricing is based upon *planned* profits" [22, p. 938]. Thus, some writers on target-return pricing tend to view it not as a form of rule-of-thumb behavior, but rather as an effective instrument for achieving market control.

A basic source of confusion in these conflicting appraisals is that the survey responses were evaluated in terms of a static short-run partial equilibrium model of pricing, while the nature of the questionnaires and interviews elicited business responses based on a long-run time framework. The prevailing treatment of pricing in an SPC model is well known. An alternative investment model is now briefly summarized as the frame of reference formulation in a DGU model.[7]

II. AN ALTERNATIVE FRAMEWORK

Stimulated by the original work of Markowitz and Tobin, a capital-asset pricing model has been developed [24] [31] [37]. Under appropriate assumptions, a security valuation theorem is derived.

$$(1) \qquad E(R_j) = R_f + \lambda \, \text{Cov}(R_j, R_m)$$

where:

R_j (random variable) is the rate of return on security j

R_f is the rate of return on a risk-free security

R_m (random variable) is the rate of return on the market portfolio of risky securities

λ is a positive constant equal to $[E(R_m) - R_f]/\sigma_m^2$

σ_m^2 is the variance of market returns which standardizes the market risk premium

$\text{Cov}(R_j, R_m)$ is the covariance of the returns on security j with returns on the market

The intuitive logic of this theorem is that the return on a risky asset is composed of two elements. One is the risk-free return. The other is the market price of risk, λ, weighted by the asset's non-diversifiable risk measured by its covariance with fluctuations in the returns on the market.

The model can be used to indicate the influence of a firm's investment

---

7. McCall [28] has emphasized how probabilistic economics leads to formal models of increased diversity and richness as illustrated by his references to the work of Dhrymes, Mills, Tisdell, and Zabel. The present paper develops the implications of such uncertainty models for the behavior of firms. A dynamic general equilibrium model of investment under uncertainty is summarized to emphasize the framework within which adaptive decisions processes of firms are stimulated to optimum-seeking behavior.

decision on its share prices [19] [32] [33]. A rule based on the security valuation theorem expressed in equation (1) states that Firm j should accept an investment project only if

(2) $$E(R_{pj}) > R_f + \lambda \, \text{Cov}(R_{pj}, R_m)$$

where $E(R_{pj})$ is the rate of return on the project appropriately measured.

This decision rule provides for acceptance of the project only if its expected internal rate of return exceeds the appropriate risk-adjusted discount rate for the project. Figure 1 presents the framework. The market line shown in Figure 1 represents a risk-standardized marginal cost of capital appropriate to all firms and all projects. An individual investment project is described by its position in the risk-return space. For example, Project A and Project B have the same expected rate of return. However, the risk associated with Project B is greater than the risk associated with Project A. Thus Project A is an acceptable project, while Project B is not. When the firm accepts favorable projects, there will be an upward revision of the firm's share price which restores equilibrium in the financial markets by lowering $E(R_j)$. Since this theory of investment has been more fully developed elsewhere, this presentation will emphasize the more specific economic implications.

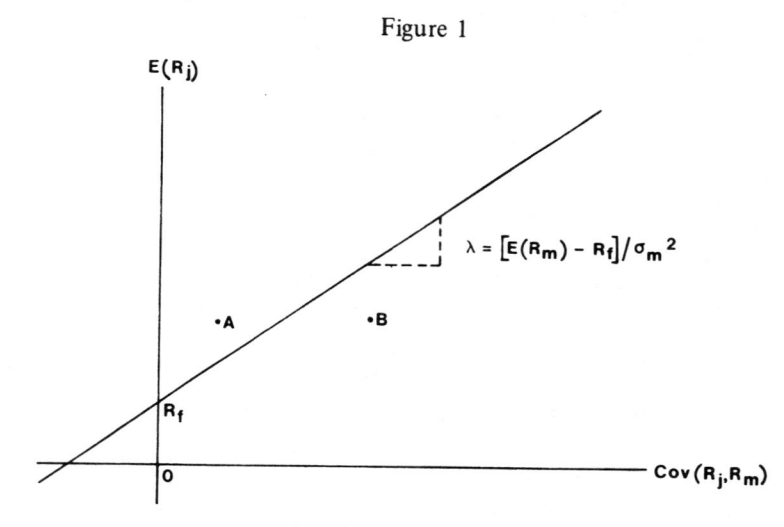

Figure 1

The relevant marginal analysis involves comparing the marginal efficiency of investment to the marginal cost of capital. But, more importantly, the marginal relationships are expressed in a risk-return analysis. In a DGU model the risk-return relationships, not point estimates of return, are the relevant decision variables. Furthermore, the long-run nature of the investment decision brings a wider range of variables into the analysis in order to estimate the characteristics of the probability distributions of returns and to select parameters for making decisions. The investment aspect of the decisions shifts the analysis to a broader time framework. The model constitutes a conceptual framework for understanding the implications of responses by businessmen to questions involving long-run resource allocation decisions under uncertainty.

III. PRICING IN A RESOURCE ALLOCATION PROCESS

With the improvement of information processing provided by the com-

Decision Making in the Private Sector

puter, the decision to commit or recommit corporate resources involves analysis of a wide variety of variables and, because of uncertainty, a repeated assessment of the decision [9] [10]. In this broad decision process, pricing performs a role, but a wide variety of other decision variables also enter the analysis. The familiar partial equilibrium *ceteris paribus* diagrams in textbook presentations give an unnecessarily narrow view of pricing decisions in both large and small firms. In the long-run framework it is not meaningful to hold other factors constant because of their interaction with pricing decisions.[8] Other groups of variables to be considered are: (1) product characteristic vectors; (2) relative price vectors in relation to product quality; (3) the nature of the sales or dealer organization vectors involved in marketing the product; (4) advertising and other promotional effort vectors; and (5) the quality of the financing and service organizations to support product sales and use.[9]

Broad environmental influences, combined with the constraints presented by existing products and firms in the market, lead the firm to develop adaptive policies with respect to product, quality, prices, sales methods, promotion efforts, service organization and financial facilities [9][10][30]. These decisions, in turn, have an influence on the quantity and type of fixed investments and on the level and behavior of other costs. Even on new products, constraints are set by the market, since new products substitute in some degree for older products. The price concept itself is extremely complex on durable goods for which maintenance costs and availability of repair and service facilities are important decision variables in the purchase. In addition, the stock of used durable goods represents a multiple of any given year's flow of new output. Hence there is continuous competition between the stock of used durable goods and those newly produced.[10]

Strategies are formulated to offer either breadth or specialization in a range of combinations of product characteristics. Iterated reviews of product quality characteristics, materials characteristics, production methods, and marketing methods seek the optimal product quality, cost levels and marketing attractiveness. Since administrative discretion is exercised in selecting among alternative combinations of choices under uncertainty involving pricing decisions in relation to the other variables, atomistic firms as well as firms in concentrated industries may be said to have price policies.

The decision process involves variables each of which represents vectors of numerous dimensions. In the effort to limit the costs of compiling and processing information, goals and tasks are "factored," and operational targets are employed at several levels of the firm. In the interviews, business executives emphasized four types of financial targets: (1) return on investment, (2) growth in sales or earnings per share, (3) check points

---

8. The theory of monopolistic competition in the Chamberlinian style is also subject to this criticism of treating inherently long-run adjustment processes within a partial equilibrium framework.

9. These variables are demand-increasing costs. Demsetz [11] has shown that the interaction of pricing with demand-increasing costs leads to competitive results.

10. An example is the strategy of Alfred Sloan in the early 1920's to aim to increase GM's share of the market at the expense of the Model T by seeking to make the two-year-old Chevrolet a more desirable object of purchase for the consumer than a new Model T Ford, both to sell at roughly the same price [39].

with regard to liquidity and solvency as measured by cash flows or leverage analysis, and (4) a favorable valuation relationship between the earnings of the company and the market price of its stock.

After the planning and budgeting decisions are made, managerial attention is focused on critical variables influencing the results of operations. As a consequence, statements of executives in interviews may be interpreted out of context.[11] For example, market share was said to be a goal which some firms substituted for profit maximization [22]. But instead of being a goal, market share is a managerial check point in the following adaptive process: An important factor in corporate resources allocation decisions is the potential sales volume for a product line. Given the industry potential, judgments are made about the probable share of the market or expected sales volume to provide a basis for capacity decisions. The size of the divergence of actual from expected returns will be a function of the divergence between the targeted and realized market share or total dollar value of sales. Thus, market share is likely to be regarded as an end in itself.[12] Targets or rules thus need to be distinguished from organization goals; targets are used to coordinate operating divisions in the achievement of corporate objectives.[13]

Because of change and uncertainty, emphasis was placed throughout the interview discussions on review and adjustment of decisions. The nature of satisficing behavior is also suggested by this learning process. Satisficing objectives represent check points in a firm's continuing effort to move toward higher levels of performance.[14] Thus whether rules and targets reflect nonoptimal behavior depends upon whether they are used inflexibly or whether they are employed as instruments in a dynamic information feedback process.

IV. ORGANIZATION PROCESSES AS VIEWED BY THE BEHAVIORAL THEORY OF THE FIRM

An alternative interpretation of the evidence on organizational proc-

---

11. Another illustration of misinterpretation of the statements of businessmen is represented by the 1924 article by Donaldson Brown, who had been Vice President of Finance at both du Pont and General Motors. This article has been widely quoted by economists as evidence of the use of target rate-of-return pricing by General Motors since the early 1920's. A key quotation from Brown [8] is the following:

> Thus it is apparent that the object of management is not necessarily the highest attainable *rate of return* on capital but rather the highest return consistent with attainable volume, care being exercised *to assure profit with each increment of volume that will at least equal the economic cost of additional capital required*. Therefore, the fundamental consideration is the economic cost of capital to the individual business.

This formulation cannot correctly be characterized as target return-on-investment pricing. Particularly inappropriate is its characterization as a kind of "noblesse oblige" approach to pricing in that a firm is satisfied with a just price and a just return, since providence enabled the firm to achieve a dominant position in the market (Lanzillotti [22]). Effective business strategy, the development of an efficient management organization, and a continued high level of efficiency are required to maintain a market position. Brown's statement represents a decision rule that an investment should not be undertaken unless its expected return exceeds the firm's relevant incremental cost of capital, taking the appropriate degree of risk into account [29].

12. It is in this framework that the sales maximization hypothesis of Baumol [5] should appropriately be viewed. The objective of sales maximization was expressed by businessmen on the assumption that investments had been committed and, therefore, sales maximization would result in favorable capacity utilization. Without special assumptions, sales maximization will not maximize share price.

13. In less effective management organizations, rules begin to take on a life of their own, and the formal processes begin to reflect some rigidities associated with the rules. These rigidities represent a pathological condition, not characteristic of companies with good performance records.

14. A formal development of the role of adaptive behavior in moving from various satisficing

Decision Making in the Private Sector

esses in the firm has been set forth in the behavioral theory of the firm [9]. Among the elements of the theory are observations on the divergence between organizational goals and individual goals. The firm is viewed as a coalition whose continuity is supported by organization slack, associated in some degree with imperfect competition. Shielded from the rigors of competition, organization slack is generated as a form of monopoly returns permitting managerial discretion.[15] Managerial discretion leads to the substitution of various forms of individual gratification at the expense of the firm's goal of profit maximization.[16]

But bureaucratic behavior is not proof of the absence of competition. Furthermore, the evidence of managerial discretion or organization slack is fragmentary at best. For example, the evidence cited by Williamson in his book devoted to the subject, is that firms laid off staff during a decline in sales [47, pp. 170-71]. But this is also consistent with maximization.[17] Bureaucracy and the divergence of organization and individual goals is found in every type of institution [4] [17] [26]. They are a characteristic of organizational behavior rather than of the economic milieu. They are associated with institutional age and encrustation rather than with size alone. They can occur under strict atomistic industry structure. With a large number of decision variables of complex dimensions and with uncertainty, an organization does not have to achieve an optimum or have maximized for survival [48]. An optimum-seeking organization need only "on-the-average" be on par with its rivals or competitors to survive in its environment.

In efficient business firms and other well-managed organizations continuous efforts are made to counter the tendency toward bureaucratization resulting from specialization and departmentation. Reviews in continuous communication, information feedback systems are one means of countering this tendency. One of the functions of corporate staff is to aid in developing an effective communication system in the firm between the headquarters and operating divisions to achieve optimum-seeking behavior toward the firm's goals.[18] For both atomistic and large firms, performance sufficient for survival is required. Within the average performance over a large number of complex decisions under uncertainty, organization slack may also develop. Organization slack may arise from lack of atomistic conditions, but this lack is not the necessary and only source. Hence the existence of organization slack is not evidence of lack of competitive behavior. *Optimum seeking goals are consistent with satisficing or survival*

---

levels to wealth maximization has been made by Clement G. Krouse, "Multiple Objectives and Adaptive Decision-Making in the Theory of the Firm" (MS).

15. "For purposes of studying behavior in the monopoly sector where conditions of discretion frequently prevail, the discretion models may often be the most appropriate: they provide a fruitful and orderly way with which to structure a broad range of monopoly practices" [47, pp. 170-71].

16. The theory postulates maximization with respect to nondiscretionary expenditures; individual goals are substituted for organization goals with respect to discretionary expenditures—managerial staff and "other perquisites" [47].

17. Williamson's regression analysis [47, pp. 132-3] of executive compensation with general and administrative expenses, concentration, entry barrier level, and percentage of managers to the total board membership is not conclusive. The direction of causality of the omitted profit variable is not "obvious."

18. This has been recognized in more recent writing in the behavioral tradition as an important function of the headquarters staff in contributing to the superior efficiencies of the multidivisional form of firm organization [46].

performance. The gains from specialization in large organizations are offset to some degree by the increased tendencies toward bureaucratization. But there is no a priori basis for arguing the superiority of large vs. small firms from organization-scale considerations. Nor is there a basis for arguing superiority of atomistic conditions for achieving competitive pressures.[19]

V. TESTS OF ALTERNATIVE INFERENCES

Previous studies, utilizing a deterministic model, have drawn a variety of inferences about the performance of large firms. The use of target-return pricing based on standard costs is held to result in inflexible prices that lag in response to changes in demand. The thrust of the argument is that standard-cost target-return pricing is used to discipline oligopolistic behavior. It is further assumed that each firm's standard costs are known to all other firms and that to maintain oligopolistic collusion large firms do not engage in price competition.[20]

The Implications of Standard Cost Systems. These inferences stem from a misconception of the role of standard cost systems in accounting control. Standard volume and cost standards are utilized along with related price estimates as the basis for improving managerial performance by seeking to separate influences on the measured results of operations. Standard costing procedures are another illustration of the use of target projections as reference points and the use of rule-of-thumb formulae for reaching tentative decisions. But these tentative formulations are followed by periodic reviews to determine required changes in strategies. The use of standard cost systems enables top management to distinguish variations from targeted performance due to departures from standard volume (volume variance), from standard cost (cost variance), and from targeted prices (price variance). Variance analysis implies adaptive processes in the firm. The frequency of reviews has been increased by managerial expertise and by the technology of handling information. With computer-assisted management control systems, frequent reviews of "actual" versus "standard" may be utilized to achieve "real time control."

The economic significance of variance analysis in managerial accounting control systems is that it represents one of the methods of achieving adaptive learning behavior. It is a misinterpretation of the nature of standard cost procedures to contrast "competitive" and "oligopolistic" pricing behavior on the basis of models distinguishing between actual unit labor cost and standard unit labor cost on the ground that "oligopolists lag in their adjustment to changes in the cost of labor." (Cf. Eckstein and Fromm [14].) Standard cost systems should not be regarded as evidence of oligopolistic control, since they are used by all firms independent of size in an effort to improve managerial performance. Indeed, the concept is applicable to all types of economizing organizations. Instead of representing a procedure for institutionalizing "oligopolistic lethargy," standard cost sys-

---

19. The discretionary behavior theory also implicitly assumes separation of owner and managerial control. In a multiple regression analysis Lewellen and Huntsman [23] have found a significant net relation between executive compensation and profits, but no significant net relation between executive compensation and sales, suggesting that the traditional view of divergence of owner and managerial interests is not supported by the evidence.

20. Ironically, it is extremely difficult to obtain information on cost accounting procedures and standard cost systems from individual firms because such information is regarded as highly proprietary and as being of great potential value to competitors.

Decision Making in the Private Sector

tems are a part of financial control systems seeking to achieve adaptive behavior in a dynamic world.

The Issue of Price Flexibility. A convincing explanation has not been given for the view that the prices of monopolists or of oligopolists in collusion should be less flexible than prices in atomistic industries, given the view that each is a "profit maximizer." Each should respond promptly to demand or cost changes that move them from their "maximizing" position. The rationalization sometimes offered is that firms in concentrated industries find it easier to maintain their tenuous and imperfect collusion if price changes are not required too often. But this rationale ignores their reaction to other dynamic variables that would be more destructive to the tenuous collusion than adjusting to price changes. Differences among industries in cost structures, the frequency of cost and demand changes, and variations in income elasticity of demand for different products would also be disruptive and would make price inflexibility an unsound policy.

Stigler and Kindahl [42] provide evidence that "effective" price changes in individual products are much wider and more frequent than conventionally assumed. They also found (in a regression analysis of the standard deviation of individual price changes about the mean change as the dependent variable) that the number of price reporters was a highly significant explanatory factor. Other individual pieces of evidence provide further support for the proposition that prices are actually much more flexible than has frequently been assumed. One such bit of evidence is drawn from the automobile industry, which is widely taken as the archetype of disciplined oligopoly in which prices are highly rigid. The conventional view is based on the beginning-of-the-year dealer-recommended prices and initial manufacturing charges to the dealers. But Congressional Hearings have revealed that individual automobile manufacturers begin changing their prices to dealers in a wide variety of ways, at various times and degrees depending upon the reception of a particular model of the manufacturer's car [34]. Price changes to dealers take many forms: special bonuses for cars sold in excess of the dealer's quota, special product promotions, price variations for specified optional equipment, etc. Pricing programs are modified and adapted throughout the model year in response to changing conditions of demand and the competitive efforts of other producers.

Another illustration is the divergence between list price and actual prices in the aluminum industry [52]. The price list is a reference point for determining discounts. For example, while the list price of 29 cents a pound for aluminum ingots does not fluctuate greatly, actual prices vary widely. In early 1972 ingot prices were 22 cents a pound, a reduction of more than 30 percent from list. Prices of some aluminum products have fluctuated so frequently that they are not even included in company price lists. Furthermore, customers are sensitive to the trade-off between service and price, one of the advantages of smaller firms being their ability to vary "prices" by varying the quantity of special services provided.

Another example can be drawn from the steel industry. In connection with a change in list prices [50], Bethlehem Steel announced a change in its policy for charging for extras "giving individual customers specific gauges, width, quantities, or other special treatment. These extras have come to number in the hundreds, making it easier to shade prices." Yet steel has been generally regarded as a "homogeneous product." With product variations in the hundreds, official price data must greatly understate actual price changes. These examples and the broader evidence assembled by Stigler and Kindahl contradict the general view that there is little price competition among oligopolists. Stronger assertions, such as Galbraith's, that oligopolists do not engage in "destructive" price competition are also inconsistent with the evidence.[21]

Another variation of the administered prices thesis is that collusive behavior and market control by oligopolists is evidenced by administered profits. Profit data on 20 companies were set forth by Lanzillotti [22] to support this position. The evidence reproduced in Table 1 is not persuasive. First, only seven of the 20 companies could be characterized as having a target-return on investment. Second, of the seven, two were slightly below, while five firms were above the target by an average of 3.1 percentage points. Third, the return on investment is defined by business firms as the ratio of income before interest charges to total operating assets (gross or net). In the evidence presented, the profit rate measured was the return on net worth. The relevant comparison to the target specified is set forth in Column 4. These average returns were in every case below the target-return on investment by substantial percentages. Fourth, average returns on net worth over any two time periods differ greatly as inspection of Columns 2 and 3 readily demonstrates. This evidence does not support the conclusion that leading firms are able to "plan or administer their profits."

Industry Structure and Pressures for Efficiency. Another argument is that an atomistic industry structure is a necessary condition for continuous pressures for increased efficiency. Although this view is consistent with a deterministic model, in a dynamic world other forces may produce similar results. Repeated emphasis in the interview discussions was placed on the importance of achieving cost reduction and cost leadership. In a dynamic environment with numerous forms of rivalrous behavior, and with long lags involved in responding to actions by rivals such as changes in product quality or product differentiation, cost reduction reduces vulnerability to unfavorable events. Cost leadership reduces vulnerability to rival's strategies. A related emphasis was on price reductions over time. The rationalization provided was "enlarging the market," which is consistent with a static model. But additionally, secular price reduction is a strategy for dealing with uncertainty. A massive type of risk faced by business firms is competition from new and substitute products which threaten not only a declining total market, but also intensification of rival's efforts for increasing their share of a declining market. Since product substitution involves performance-price comparisons between existing and new products, secular price reduction is a strategy for insuring against this form of uncertainty.

---

21. "And, to repeat, rivalry continues in advertising, product improvement, gadgetry and the like where it is not destructive. The automobile industry with three large and strong firms and one weaker one is cited more often than any other as the classical manifestation of oligopoly" [16, p. 911]. It is ironical that in the very statement in which Galbraith argues that there is absence of "destructive" rivalry, he refers to the few survivors of an industry in which hundreds of firms had existed in earlier years and which since 1950 has witnessed the disappearance of Nash and Hudson (into American Motors) and the "destruction" of the Studebaker and Packard motor car companies. Galbraith's assertions are internally inconsistent.

Decision Making in the Private Sector

Table 1—Target Rates of Return on Investment, Average Returns on Net Worth, and Average Returns on Total Assets of 20 Large Industrial Corporations, 1947-1967

	Target ROI per Lanzillotti (1)	Average Return on Net Worth (2) 1947-55	(3) 1956-67	Earnings, before Interest, on Total Assets (4) 1956-67
Alcoa	10%	13.8%	8.5%	5.8%
American Can		11.6	9.4	
A & P		13.0	11.6	
du Pont		25.9	16.7	
Esso (Standard Oil N.J.)		16.0	12.1	
General Electric	20	21.4	16.6	9.7
General Foods		12.2	17.2	
General Motors	20	26.0	19.9	14.5
Goodyear		13.3	12.5	
Gulf		12.6	12.5	
International Harvester	10	8.9	7.4	6.3
Johns-Manville	15	14.9	10.2	8.5
Kennecott		16.0	11.5	
Kroger	10	12.1	12.2	6.4
National Steel		12.1	10.0	
Sears Roebuck		5.4	14.5	
Standard Oil (Indiana)		10.4	7.6	
Swift		6.9	4.4	
Union Carbide		19.2	15.3	
U.S. Steel	8	10.3	8.2	6.0
Average for the 20		14.1	11.9	

Sources: Columns 1 and 2 [22]. Columns 3 and 4 calculated from company data in Moody's *Investment Manuals, Industrials.*

In short, uncertainty induces strategies reflecting the same types of pressures for efficiency and performance improvement ascribed to atomistic industry structures in a deterministic model. Some evidence in support of this hypothesis is provided by analysis of price movements in concentrated versus atomistic industries as shown in Table 2. Three time periods during 1953-70 are covered. During the period ending in 1958, the consumer price index (CPI) rose 1.6 percent per annum. Both household durables, a concentrated industry, and apparel, an unconcentrated industry, registered price declines. During 1958-66, the CPI rose at a 1.5 percent rate and the prices of apparel increased at a 1.1 percent rate, while prices of new cars and household durables declined. In the third period, 1966-70, the rate of price increase in the concentrated industries was lower than any of the other categories in Table 2. Multiple regression studies of these relations between price changes and industry concentration over time, show a positive relation between concentration and the rate of price increase for the period 1953-58, but a negative relation in the other three post-war periods, 1948-53, 1958-63, and 1963-68 [25]. The evidence does not establish the proposition that large firms uniquely seek to achieve secular cost reduction and price reduction in response to uncertainty. The theory embraces atomistic firms as well. In addition, the evidence is consistent with the proposition suggested by survey responses that firms in concentrated markets in a dynamic uncertainty model are subject to pressures for optimizing performance of the kind generally attributed to competitive forces.

Table 2—Compound Annual Rates of Price Change in GNP, CPI, and Illustrative Concentrated and Unconcentrated Industries, U.S., 1953-1970
(based on the BLS Consumer Price Index and Components)

Time Periods	All Items CPI	Concentrated Industries		Unconcentrated Industries			Gross National Product	
		New Cars	Household Durables	Apparel Commodities	Total Services	Medical Care Services	Real	Current Dollars
1953-58	1.6	1.2	-.7	.3	3.6	4.1	1.6	4.2
1958-66	1.5	-.3	-.4	1.1	3.1	4.2	4.9	6.6
1966-70	4.8	2.0	2.9	5.2	7.4	8.6	1.9	6.8

Source: [51, pp. 250-51, Tables C-46, C-47]

VI. CONCLUSIONS

In this reformulation of the analysis of the pricing behavior of large firms within the framework of probabilistic economics, some new generalizations emerge. Behavioral characteristics regarded as irrational in the context of deterministic models are seen as dynamic strategies for dealing with uncertainty.

In a dynamic model, the forms and dimensions of competitive behavior are multiplied. The probabilities of effective collusion are reduced, and the probable gains from independent actions are increased. The price inflexibility doctrine, which lacks the support of consistent economic logic in a deterministic model, is even less supportable in an uncertainty model. Evidence is growing that large firms in concentrated industries have been responsive to changes in demand as well as to changes in cost conditions. The profit data used in the attempt to bolster the administered price doctrine is consistent with alternative hypotheses. Revision of the administered profits thesis is required. The motivations for efficiency conventionally attributed to atomistic industry structures alone are shown to be exerted also in large firms in concentrated markets through continued pressures to develop sequential strategies in response to uncertainty.

The behavioral theory of the firm was formulated on the basis of evidence on organizational processes similar to that obtained in my interviews. This theory has emphasized elements such as bureaucratic tendencies, divergence of organization and individual goals, organization slack, and managerial discretion, protected in some degree from the rigors of competition. But these organizational imperfections are common to all types of institutions, not unique to business firms. Specialization and departmentation in large firms increases efficiency, but at the cost of increased tendencies toward bureaucratization. Whether a given firm is too large or not large enough by these criteria depends on the facts of each particular case.

REFERENCES

1. A. A. Alchian, "Uncertainty, Evolution, and Economic Theory," *Jour. Pol. Econ.*, June 1950, 58, 211-21.
2. H. I. Ansoff, *Corporate Strategy*. New York 1965.

Decision Making in the Private Sector

3. P. W. S. Andrews, *On Competition in Economic Theory*. London 1964.
4. M. Alexis and C. Z. Wilson, *Organizational Decision Making*. Englewood Cliffs 1967.
5. W. J. Baumol, *Business Behavior, Value and Growth* New York 1967.
6. _____ and R. E. Quandt, "Rules of Thumb and Optimally Imperfect Decisions," *Am. Econ. Rev.*, March 1964, *54*, 23-46.
7. W. T. Baxter and A. R. Oxenfeldt, "Costing and Pricing: The Cost Accountant *versus* the Economist," in *Studies in Cost Analysis*, ed., D. Solomons, Homewood 1968.
8. D. Brown, "Pricing Policy in Relation to Financial Control," *Management and Administration*, Feb., March, April 1924, *7*, 3-15.
9. R. M. Cyert and M. I. Kamien, "Behavioral Rules and the Theory of the Firm," in *Prices: Issues in Theory, Practice, and Public Policy*, eds., A. Phillips and O. E. Williamson, Philadelphia, 1967, pp. 1-10.
10. R. M. Cyert and J. G. March, *A Behavioral Theory of the Firm*. Englewood Cliffs 1963.
11. H. Demsetz, "The Welfare and Empirical Implications of Monopolistic Competition," *Econ. Jour.*, Sept. 1964, *74*, 623-41.
12. J. S. Earley, "Recent Developments in Cost Accounting and the 'Marginal Analysis,'" *Jour. Pol. Econ.*, June 1955, *63*, 227-42.
13. O. Eckstein, "A Theory of the Wage-Price Process in Modern Industry," *Rev. Econ. Stud.*, Oct. 1964, *31*, 267-86.
14. _____ and G. Fromm, "The Price Equation," *Am. Econ. Rev.*, Dec. 1968, *58*, 1159-83.
15. E. F. Fama, "Risk, Return and Equilibrium: Some Clarifying Comments," *Jour. Finance*, March 1968, *23*, 29-40.
16. J. K. Galbraith, *The New Industrial State*. Boston 1967.
17. O. Grusky and G. A. Miller, *The Sociology of Organizations*. New York 1970.
18. R. L. Hall and C. J. Hitch, "Price Theory and Business Behavior," *Oxford Econ. Papers*, May 1939, *2*, 12-45.
19. J. Hirshleifer, *Investment, Interest, and Capital*. Englewood Cliffs 1970.
20. A. D. H. Kaplan, J. B. Dirlam and R. F. Lanzillotti, *Pricing in Big Business*. Washington, D.C. 1958.
21. O. Langholm, *Full Cost and Optimal Price: A Study in the Dynamics of Multiple Production*. Oslo 1969.
22. R. F. Lanzillotti, "Pricing Objectives in Large Companies," *Am. Econ. Rev.*, Dec. 1958, *48*, 921-40.
23. W. G. Lewellen and B. Huntsman, "Managerial Pay and Corporate Performance," *Am. Econ. Rev.*, Sept. 1970, *60*, 710-20.
24. J. Lintner, "The Valuation of Risk Assets and the Selection of Risky Investments in Stock Portfolios and Capital Budgets," *Rev. Econ. Stat.*, Feb. 1965, *67*, 13-37.
25. S. H. Lustgarten, *Industrial Market Structure and Administered Price Inflation*. Unpublished doctoral dissertation, Univ. of Calif., 1971.
26. J. G. March, *Handbook of Organizations*. Chicago 1965.
27. J. Marschak, "Decision Making: Economic Aspects," *International Encyclopedia of the Social Sciences*, New York 1968, *4*, 42-55.
28. J. J. McCall, "Probabilistic Microeconomics," *Bell Jour. of Econ. and Mgmt.*, Autumn 1971, *2*, 403-33.
29. F. Modigliani and M. H. Miller, "The Cost of Capital, Corporation Finance and the Theory of Investment," *Am. Econ. Rev.*, June 1958, *48*, 261-97.
30. J. Monsen, Jr. and A. Downs, "A Theory of Large Managerial Firms," *Jour. Pol. Econ.*, June 1965, *73*, 228-29.
31. J. Mossin, "Equilibrium in a Capital Asset Market," *Econometrica*, Oct. 1966, *34*, 768-83.
32. _____, "Security Pricing and Investment Criteria in Competitive Markets," *Am. Econ. Rev.*, Dec. 1969, *59*, 749-55.
33. S. C. Myers, "Procedures for Capital Budgeting under Uncertainty," *Indus. Mgmt. Rev.*, Spring 1968, *9*, 1-19.
34. G. Nelson, Chairman, Subcommittee on Monopoly, Senate Select Committee on Small Business, Planning, Regulation, and Competition: *Automobile Industry–1968*, Hearings before Subcommittees of the Select Committee on Small Business, United States Senate, July 10 & 23, 1968, U.S. Government Printing Office, 1968.
35. A. Robinson, "The Pricing of Manufactured Products," *Econ. Jour.*, Dec. 1950, *60*, 771-80.

36. M. E. Rubinstein, "A Synthesis of Corporate Financial Theory," *Jour. Finance*, forthcoming.
37. W. F. Sharpe, "Capital Asset Prices: A Theory of Market Equilibrium under Conditions of Risk," *Jour. Finance*, Sept. 1964, *19*, 425-42.
38. A. Silberston, "Price Behavior of Firms," *Econ. Jour.*, Sept. 1970, *80*, 511-82.
39. A. P. Sloan, Jr., *My Years with General Motors*. New Jersey 1964.
40. G. A. Steiner, *Managerial Long-Range Planning*. New York 1963.
41. _____, *Top Management Planning*. New York 1969.
42. G. J. Stigler and J. K. Kindahl, *The Behavior of Industrial Prices*. New York 1970.
43. J. E. Stiglitz, "A Re-Examination of the Modigliani-Miller Theorem," *Am. Econ. Rev.*, Dec. 1969, *59*, 784-93.
44. D. Vickers, *The Theory of the Firm: Production, Capital and Finance*. New York 1968.
45. T. F. Walton, *Corporate Capital Accumulation*. Unpublished doctoral dissertation, Univ. of Calif., 1971.
46. O. E. Williamson, *Corporate Control and Business Behavior: An Inquiry into the Effects of Organization Form on Enterprise Behavior*. Englewood Cliffs 1970.
47. _____, *The Economics of Discretionary Behavior: Managerial Objectives in a Theory of the Firm*. Englewood Cliffs 1964.
48. S. Winter, Jr., "Economic 'Natural Selection' and the Theory of the Firm," *Yale Econ. Essays*, Spring 1964, *4*, 225-72.
49. T. Wilson and P. W. S. Andrews, *Oxford Studies on the Price Mechanism*. Oxford 1951.
50. *Business Week*, "Bethlehem Steel's New Price Gambit," May 9, 1970, p. 21.
51. *Economic Report of the President*, 1971.
52. *Wall Street Journal*, "Aluminum Book Prices Have Been Boosted, But Competition Keeps Actual Quotes Down," Feb. 1, 1972, p. 28.

READING

16 A MODEL OF PHYSICIAN PRICING

Joseph P. Newhouse*
THE RAND CORPORATION

Knowledge about the economics of medical care is still so scanty that it is not clear whether the market for physician services can be better characterized as monopolistic or competitive. This paper attempts to shed some light upon that question. Although physicians are commonly cited in the literature as an example of discriminating monopoly, supporting evidence is generally lacking.[1] Gaston Rimlinger and Henry Steele have presented some evidence that fees vary with patient income, although the main focus of their article is on the spatial distribution of physicians.[2] Their evidence, which we do not believe is conclusive, will be considered below. Reuben Kessel, in a 1958 article, assumes that physicians are discriminating monopolists and directs his attention toward analyzing mechanisms to prevent price cutting.[3] The major mechanism he cites is sanctions applied by organized medicine against physicians who may be price cutters. There is reason to think, however, that such sanctions may no longer be important, so that if they underlay monopolistic pricing, it may no longer exist.[4] Further, the spread of insurance for physician's services may have reduced the physician's ability to discriminate. Thus, the empirical evidence for the proposition that physicians are discriminating monopolists is less than completely convincing.

The view that physicians are not profit-maximizing monopolists has also appeared in the literature. Arrow, in something of an aside, pointed out that the observed low price elasticities for physician's services are incompatible with profit-maximizing monopolistic pricing.[5] Gabarino, in a 1959 article on the market for physicians' services, writes as though the market were competitive and price determined by the intersection of demand and supply curves [8]. Andersen and Anderson wrote in 1967, "The expenditure and use patterns are, accordingly, the results of a more or less spontane-

---

* Any views expressed in this paper are those of the author. They should not be interpreted as reflecting the views of The RAND Corporation or the official opinion or policy of any of its governmental or private research sponsors.

[1] For references to textbooks which cite physicians as a case of discriminating monopoly, see [11, 21].

[2] [15, 10–11]. Rimlinger and Steele point out that discriminatory pricing leads high income areas to have more physicians than they otherwise would have.

[3] [10]. In an argument somewhat related to Kessel's, Elton Rayack [14] has argued that the American Medical Association has in the past tried to control the number of physicians. We do not consider his arguments here for two reasons: (1) it is not clear they hold today; (2) even assuming total supply were limited, price might still be set competitively (it would include, in that case, economic rent). We are interested in how price is determined.

[4] The American Medical Association has the power to certify the hospital for internship and residency programs. Kessel points to this power as an instrument to promote cartel-like behavior. He argues that the marginal revenue product of interns and residents exceeds their marginal cost, so that hospitals are eager to obtain certification. The AMA has a rule, however, that no hospital can be certified for intern and resident training unless all of its staff are members of the local medical society. Hence, expulsion from the local medical society is a strong sanction against price cutting, for "lack of membership [in the local medical society] implies inability to become a member of a hospital staff." [10, 31] However, the spread of third party payment mechanisms which reimburse the hospital on the basis of its cost has meant the hospital has a smaller incentive to keep costs down. Kessel also points out that membership in the local medical society is required for admission to specialty board examinations, and that this gives organized medicine a control over those most likely to be potential price cutters, the young physicians establishing practices.

[5] [2, 957]. Price elasticity for a profit-maximizing monopolist must be equal to or greater than one (in absolute value). Although Arrow presents no evidence that the price elasticities facing a particular physician are low, we believe the demand curve faced by the individual physician differs little from the "industry" demand curve. See below.

ous play of supply and demand forces..." [1, 148–149]. Klarman notes that "authoritative opinion, supported by some facts, holds that a sliding scale of fees is not so widely applied today as formerly."[6]

Since the question appears to be unsettled, it seems worthwhile to examine the evidence to see if the market can be characterized as monopolistic or competitive. Knowledge of market characteristics is fundamental to sound public policy in the area. It is also important for the proper specification of an econometric model of the medical care sector. We first consider what might be said about the question a priori and then present some empirical evidence.

The market for physicians' services has special features which set it apart from more traditional markets [13, chs. 2–4; 11, chs. 2, 4]. Prominent among these features is consumer ignorance about price and about the product. We believe that consumer ignorance introduces a significant monopolistic element into the market. Since medical ethics frown upon advertising, and physician services are used relatively infrequently, the consumer is usually ignorant about prices charged by various physicians. Further, he is somewhat hampered in learning from the experience of others; since the physician provides a wide variety of services, the probability that a patient can readily find comparable prices is reduced. This is one aspect of consumer ignorance. Another is that the consumer often lacks the ability to judge which physician gives him higher quality service. For lack of other information he may partially judge quality by price.[7] For both these reasons, physicians who lower prices stand to gain few patients. That is, the cross-elasticity of demand between any two physicians is likely to be low, since consumers are unlikely to know about price differences, and if they do, may treat them as reflecting differences in the quality of care. That raises the question of what the mechanism is which distributes patients among physicians. Our view is that the mechanism has a large random component. Patient loads are equalized to some extent, however, by the queueing time necessary to use any particular physician. If a certain physician would randomly receive a large patient load, some patients may change to a relatively less utilized physician. Further, the physician's location, his manner, and other amenities surely influence patient choice of physician. Price, however, is unlikely to play a large role.

Hence, the mechanism for insuring that price equals average cost in the long run in a competitive market is not present in this market. A physician who charges his patients a monopolistic price is not likely to be effectively undersold. Because of low cross-elasticity of demand, each physician can act like a monopolist toward those patients who choose to use him.[8] In effect, the "firm" demand cuve (or the demand curve faced by the individual physician) is very nearly equal to the "industry" demand curve. Our hypothesis, therefore, is that the market for physicians' services is monopolistic, although we do not attempt to distinguish simple and discriminating monopoly.

A partial test of this hypothesis is the following: if physicians are discriminating monopolists, price per visit should increase with income. Data gathered by the National Health Survey show that the average expenditure per visit does increase with income. The figures are shown in Table I.[9] Similar figures are available for dentists. If Kessel's explanation for monopolistic pricing (namely American Medical Association sanctions) is correct, dentists should be less able to discriminate, since the sanctions are not readily available to them. The figures for dentists are also shown in Table I.[10] It

---

[6] [11, 22]. Klarman cites Joseph Gabarino, *Health Plans and Collective Bargaining* (1960) and Somers and Somers, *Doctors, Patients, and Health Insurance* (1961) as evidence.

[7] Andre Gabor and C. W. J. Granger have recently presented evidence that consumers do not purchase goods below a certain price level because their quality is suspect. This leads to an upward sloping demand curve at low levels of price. In the case of physicians, the curve might be upward sloping over the relevant range. See [9].

[8] It is well known that low cross-elasticity of demand is a necessary condition for monopoly to exist. See, for example [17, 198].

[9] The expenditure data are from [20] and the visit data from [22]. The expenditure data were gathered from July 1962 to December 1962 and the visit data from July 1963 to June 1964. This discrepancy would only cause error if either series changed and the change were not proportional across income groups.

[10] The expenditure data are from [20], and the visit data from [21]. The dental visit data were

Decision Making in the Private Sector

TABLE I

EXPENDITURE PER VISIT FOR PHYSICIAN AND DENTIST SERVICES BY INCOME CLASS

Income Class	Physician Expenditures	Physician Visits	Average Expenditure per Visit	Dental Expenditures	Dentist Visits	Average Expenditure per Visit
Less than $2000	$36	4.3	$8.37	$9	.8	$11.25
$2000–$3999	38	4.3	8.84	11	.9	12.22
$4000–$6999	41	4.5	9.11	16	1.4	11.43
$7000–$9999	46	4.7	9.79	24	1.9	12.63
Over $10,000	60	5.1	11.76	37	2.8	12.50

is clear that the association between expenditure per visit and income is much less marked for dentists than physicians. Rimlinger and Steele cite similar evidence from earlier surveys of expenditures on physicians in support of their assertion that physicians are discriminating monopolists.[11]

Although this test supports our hypothesis, it is not a powerful one. It is probable that the quality of care changes as one's income increases. For example, the higher income patient may utilize higher priced specialists' services.[12] Also the physician may spend more time and order more ancillary services (e.g., laboratory tests and X-rays) when treating a higher income patient. Further, for technological reasons quality may vary more for physician services than dentist services. Hence, differences in price among income levels may only reflect quality differences. Thus, another hypothesis is equally consistent with these data. To characterize this market as monopolistic or competitive it is necessary to rely upon indirect inferences which economic theory provides, as well as attempting to control for quality of services provided.

Our tests are based upon inferences from two alternative models of the market for pyhsician services. The first model is that of a monopoly, and is the model which the foregoing discussion of the market leads us to formulate. In the second model price is set by the intersection of supply and demand curves, as in a competitive market.

Suppose the demand curve of the representative consumer is:

(1) $\quad q_d = a - bp + cy + e,$

where q_d is quantity demanded, p is price, y is income, a, b, and c are constants, and e is a randomly distributed error term. We assume the monopolist ignores e in determining his price. If the cost function is also linear, the price a profit-maximizing sample monopolist will charge is then:

(2) $\quad p = (a + cy + bd)/2b,$

where d is marginal cost.[13] This model, a model of simple monopoly, will be known as Model I. To make it operational, we measure y in per capita terms. If we assumed discriminating monopoly, the empirical measures of price would be ambiguous and non-linearities would be introduced.[14] To avoid complexity, therefore, we continue to work with an analytical model based on simple monopoly.

There is no variable in Model I for the number of practitioners. This is a consequence of the assumption that each physi-

---

also gathered from July 1963 to June 1964 so that the same discrepancy exists as was cited in the previous footnote.

[11] [15]. They are not concerned about the market for dental services.

[12] [1, 16]. Note that the specialist-general practitioner distinction is one piece of information the consumer has in judging quality, but this does not help him in judging the merits of individual specialists or general practitioners. Hence, cross-elasticity of demand between specialists or between general practitioners is still likely to be low.

[13] We assume for convenience that marginal cost is constant and hence can be included in the intercept. If marginal cost is not constant, it becomes part of the error term in the estimated equation.

[14] The theory for a discriminating monopolist can be developed as follows: Suppose the demand curve faced by the discriminating monopolist is $q_d = a - bp + cy$. He then produces to where his marginal cost d, intersects the demand curve. Suppose it intersects the demand curve at q_0. Taking the inverse of the demand curve, $p = (1/b)(a - q + cy)$, the monopolist receives the area under the demand curve, or $q \int_0^{q_0} (1/b)(a - q + cy) \, dq = (1/b)(aq_0 - (q_0^2/2) + cyq_0)$. Since q_0 is a function of y, income enters non-linearly. For example, suppose $d = 0$. Then $q_0 = a + cy$ and the amount received by the physician is $(1/b)(a^2 + acy - [(a^2 + 2acy + c^2y^2)/2] + acy + c^2y^2) = (1/2b)(a^2 + 2acy + c^2y^2) = [(a + cy)^2/2b]$.

110

cian is a monopolist. The model would also apply if physicians were a cartel, since the short-run profit-maximizing price for a cartel is independent of the number of firms.[15]

In a competitive model there must be a supply curve. Suppose the supply of physician services per representative consumer in area i is a linear function of price and the number of physicians in area i. Price is included because it may affect the number of hours which the existing stock of physicians is willing to work (either positively or negatively) and it may affect the number of minutes a physician is willing to devote to any individual visit. In symbols, this supply curve is:

$$(3) \qquad q_s = f + gp + hn + u,$$

where q_s is quantity supplied per person, n is the number of physicians per person, f, g, and h are constants, and u is a randomly distributed error term. We do not make any assumptions about the sign of g, but do assume that the number of physicians in area i in year j is independent of q_d in that year.[16] This assumption, which is important to the argument, is based on the observation that physicians, once having established a practice, will face high moving costs. Thus, if n in area i is to increase, the increase must come mostly from recent medical school graduates. But these are only 3-4 percent of total physicians.[17] Hence physicians in area i in year j are taken to be a predetermined variable. If we assume the market clears, so that:

$$(4) \qquad q_s = q_d,$$

equations 1, 3, and 4 can be solved for the reduced form equation for price. The reduced form equation is:

$$(5) \quad p = (a - f + cy - hn + e - u)/(b + g).$$

If the supply curve has a positive slope, $b + g$ will be positive, so that the partial derivative of price with respect to income in equation 5 is positive and with respect to the number of physicians is negative. In any event, if c and h are both positive in the structural equations 1 and 3, one derivative is necessarily positive and the other negative in the reduced form equation. This model of competitive pricing we call Model II.

Data on general practitioner office visit prices and the number of general practitioners are available for 1966, and data on per capita income are available for 1965 for 18 cities.[18] Price and income were deflated by the Consumer Price Index for each area. When equation 2 (Model I) was estimated from these data, the results were:

$$p = 0.3 + 2.2y \qquad R^2 = 0.41.[19]$$
$$(0.7)**$$

Thus, the prediction of Model I is corroborated by these data. But the *partial* correlation of n with p is *+0.55*, which is strong evidence against Model II.[20] If Model II were correct, the sign of the partial correlation coefficient should be negative. That is, since $c/(b + g)$ is positive, $h/(b + g)$ should be negative.

Similar results appear when Models I and II are applied to the market for dental services. Data on prices charged for tooth fillings are available for 18 cities in 1961, and income data can be found in the 1960 census. No data on the number of dentists by city were found, but the 1961 dentist/population ratios are available for the counties in which the 18 cities are located. Using that ratio as n, and again deflating price and income by the Consumer Price Index, the resulting estimate of equation 2 (Model I) for dentists is:

$$p = 3.2 + 4.1 \text{ Income per Capita} \quad R^2 = 0.54.$$
$$(1.0)**$$

The partial correlation coefficient of n with p is small but positive, +0.13, which is again evidence against Model II.[21] Thus,

---

[15] The short-run maximizing price for a cartel is not, however, independent of the distribution of firms with respect to costs. If this model were to be a test of Kessel's assumptions, we would need to make the additional assumption that this distribution did not vary across areas.

[16] Years are used because our data are annual data.

[17] Computed from [18].

[18] Data sources and dates of measurement are given in the appendix.

[19] ** will be used to indicate significance at the 0.5 percent level (one-tail test) and * at the 2.5 percent level (one-tail test).

[20] If entered, n would be significant at the 1 percent level using a two-tail test. For an explanation of the positive sign, see below, n. 30.

[21] If entered, n would be insignificant at a 50 percent confidence level using a two-tail test.

the market for dental services can also be characterized as monopolistic. If dentists do not differ from physicians in this respect, it is probably something other than American Medical Association sanctions which leads to monopoly in the market for physicians' services. Since consumers are likely to be almost as ignorant about dental services as physician services, the consumer ignorance argument can explain the results.

Though we believe these results to be rather striking, there is additional evidence against Model II. Suppose Model II were correct, but there were a dynamic disequilibrium, in which income and thus demand increased relatively rapidly in some areas. Since supply does not immediately adjust, price would rise to clear the market. First differences are correlated definitionally with levels, and it may be that correlation between the first differences of income and price is responsible for correlation between the levels reported above. This explanation cannot satisfactorily explain the positive partial correlation of n and p, but if it is correct, there ought to be a close association between the first differences of price and income, perhaps even closer than between the levels. If Model I is correct, there may be a weak association, if any, between these variables. Although a change in income raises demand, physicians, if they act as monopolists, may treat the change as transitory or they may simply be slow to react to demand changes. Therefore, we have regressed the change in price (in real terms) from 1961 to 1966 on the change in income from 1960 to 1965. (These dates are chosen because data for those years are readily available.[22]) This yields:

change in $p = -4.7$
$\qquad + 0.4$ change in $y \qquad R^2 = 0.02.$
$\qquad (0.7)$

[22] What evidence there is on the speed on convergence to equilibrium physician supply indicates that little of the adjustment is accomplished within five years. [3] finds no relationship between changes in per capita income and changes in the physician/population ratio for consecutive ten-year periods beginning in 1930 and ending in 1960. This implies the lag is infinite. [5] finds that specialist/population and general practitioner/population do adjust to changes in the percent of families with incomes less than $3,000, but that only around 15 percent of the adjustment is accomplished within five years. These figures are quite crude econometrically, and are cited only because they are consistent with plausible a priori notions.

As can readily be seen the association is much weaker than the association between the levels, and so is further evidence in favor of Model I.

Although no data on the distribution of physicians for 1961 apear to be available, Model I can be tested further by using 1961 price and income data. As measures of price we have used the customary charge for a general practitioner office visit as well as four well-defined procedures: an obstetrical case; an appendectomy; a tonsillectomy, and a tooth filling. Although obstetrical cases, appendectomies, and tonsillectomies may be done by either a specialist or a nonspecialist, the sample of prices attempts to adjust for this [10, 4]. Thus, we attempt to control for the higher prices a specialist may charge. Second, we have included two variables which are designed to be proxies for certain dimensions of quality of care. These variables come from research on cross-sectional variation in mortality and morbidity rates [13]. Several demographic, economic, and medical characteristics of an area were used to explain the variation in these rates. Making the assumption that the residual variation in these rates can be attributed to the quality of care rendered in a given area, we have used the residuals from equations explaining variation in mortality due to cardiovascular disease and infant mortality as independent variables.

It is unclear what the relevant geographical market is for physicians' services. It could be the city or the standard metropolitan statistical area (SMSA) or even broader area. We have used data on the independent variables from both cities and SMSA's to see which have more explanatory power.

Data on price are available for 20 of the largest cities for 1955 and 1961 and for 39 cities for 1966.[23] We have excluded the 1955 data because of probable measurement error and because it is difficult to obtain data on the independent variables for that year.[24]

[23] But for 1966 only data from SMSAs are available for the independent variables.
[24] For 1966, the data are in the form of expenditure by city workers on physicians' services. Expenditure is defined as 13.1 × General Practitioner Office Visit Price + 0.6 × General Practitioner Home Visit Price. We have multiplied the resulting figure by 0.06778 to obtain an approximation to the office visit price. The figure 0.06778 =

Two of the 1961 observations and seven of the 1966 observations have been excluded because of a lack of data on the independent variables. Data sources and dates of measurement are listed in the Appendix.

The results are partially listed in Tables II and III. They are consistent with Model I as a characterization of both physician and dentist pricing, since the income variable is consistently quite significant.

The quality variables are never significant at the 5 percent level, but in all eight cases of physician pricing their partial correlation coefficients have the correct (negative) sign, given that income is in the equation. This has only a 1/256 chance of happening, if the probability of a negative sign is 0.5, and so would indicate that part of the price difference among areas may be due to quality variation.[25] The insignificance of the quality variables in Table II can be readily explained by measurement error; quality variation is surely only one element in the residuals. Inclusion of the quality variables, however, changes the coefficient of income little as can be seen by an inspection of Table II. The results using city data are uniformly much better than those using SMSA data. Hence, only the results using city data are presented.

Unfortunately, the results in Tables II and III do not assist in answering the question whether monopolistic pricing is simple or discriminatory. The question is important both for its welfare implications and if income elasticities are to be estimated using expenditure data, but the answer will have to await data on charges made to individual patients.[26]

$$\left(13.1 + \left(\frac{\begin{pmatrix} 0.6 \text{ Unweighted Average of GP} \\ \text{Home Visit Price in 20 Cities 1961} \end{pmatrix}}{\begin{matrix}\text{Unweighted Average of GP} \\ \text{Office Visit Price in 20 Cities 1961}\end{matrix}}\right)\right)$$

[25] Note also that one of the "quality" variables in the tooth filling equation has the "wrong" sign; it was not expected that these variables should be a measure of the quality of dental services.

[26] The welfare implications of discriminating monopoly for physician services are not clear. On the assumption of continuous utility functions, it is well known that discriminating monopoly creates a situation where mutually beneficial trades are possible and hence is not efficient. The problem with the argument in this case is the assumption of continuous utility functions. Suppose the service in question is a physical examination or a surgical operation. The value of one examination or operation in a given time period may be considerable, but the value of a second negligible or

TABLE II
18 CITIES—REAL PRICE AND INCOME, 1961

General practitioner price for an office visit = 0.9 + 1.8 income per capita $R^2 = 0.56$
                                                         (0.4)**

General practitioner price for an office visit = 0.9 + 1.8 income per capita − 0.3 cardiovascular
                                         (0.5)**   (0.4)

residuals − 0.01 infant residuals $R^2 = 0.58$.
      (0.1)

Obstetrical case price = 51.7 + 59.2 income per capita $R^2 = 0.24$.
                        (26.4)*

Obstetrical case price = 31.1 + 69.2 income per capita − 39.5 cardiovascular residuals + 4.8 in-
                        (29.2)*   (26.8)   (7.8)

fant residuals $R^2 = 0.34$. (See Note 1).

Appendectomy price = 9.4 + 75.5 income per capita $R^2 = 0.50$.
                  (18.8)**

Appendectomy price = 27.8 + 66.3 income per capita − 0.09 cardiovascular residuals − 6.1 infant
                  (21.3)**   (19.5)   (5.7)

residuals $R^2 = 0.55$.

Tonsillectomy price = 20.6 + 26.7 income per capita $R^2 = 0.32$.
                 (9.7)**

Tonsillectomy price = 21.4 + 26.3 income per capita − 8.4 cardiovascular residuals − 0.7 infant
                 (11.1)*   (10.2)   (3.0)

residuals $R^2 = 0.37$.

Tooth filling price = −3.2 + 4.1 income per capita $R^2 = 0.54$
                (1.0)**

Tooth filling price = −4.3 + 4.7 income per capita − 1.4 cardiovascular residuals + 0.3 infant
                (1.0)**   (1.0)   (0.3)

residuals $R^2 = 0.60$.

Note 1: The partial correlation of the infant residuals variable if the cardiovascular residuals variable is excluded is negative.

Decision Making in the Private Sector

It is interesting to compute the elasticities of the various prices with respect to income. For a monopolist facing the demand curve shown in equation 1 with constant marginal cost, such an elasticity is 0.5 (income elasticity of demand/price elasticity of demand).[27] The elasticities of price with respect to income computed at the means of the variables are shown in Table IV. Other estimates using household data of the income elasticity/price elasticity ratio for physician visits have placed this ratio around 3 or higher, so that the results in Table IV seem low by a factor of about 2 [7, 75–76]. Considering the small size of our sample, the aggregate nature of our data, and the simplifying assumptions in our model, this error in a point estimate is understandable. However, the results do indicate that the responsiveness of price to income is markedly higher for dental services. Little, if anything, is known about the price elasticity of demand for dental services, but others have estimated the income elasticity of demand for dental services to be considerably higher than for physician services.[28] Thus, unless price elasticity of demand for dental services is also considerably higher, the results in Table IV are qualitatively consistent with what is known about the relative income elasticities of physician and dental services.

Another question which may be asked of these data is whether physicians are profit-maximizers. An answer to this question as well as further evidence in favor of the hypothesis of monopoly is provided by including variables which other studies have indicated influence demand.[29] Such variables

TABLE III

32 CITIES—MONEY PRICE AND INCOME, 1966[a]

General practitioner price for an office visit = 3.7 + 1.0 income per capita $R^2 = 0.14$.
(0.4)*

[a] Deflators are not available for all cities.

TABLE IV

18 CITIES—ELASTICITY OF PRICE WITH RESPECT TO INCOME, 1961

Price	"Income Elasticity"
Office visit to a general practitioner 1961	0.8
Office visit to a general practitioner 1966	0.9
Obstetrical Case	0.7
Appendectomy	0.9
Tonsillectomy	0.7
Tooth Filling	1.6

are: the percent of the population over 65 years of age, the percent of the population with hospital or surgical insurance; the percent of the population with a high school education; and the percent of population change from 1950 to 1960 (since supply does not immediately adjust, this changes demand per physician). These variables, when included, are never significant. Furthermore, they often have the "wrong" sign. This could be because the sample is small and the variables intercorrelated. More likely, it is because physicians do not fully maximize profits, but do charge higher prices when income raises demand. Physicians may fear the political consequences of maximizing profits in the short run, so that the observed prices are long-run profit maximizing prices. Alternatively, they may be satisficers rather than maximizers.[30] That physicians are not short-run profit maximizers is consistent with Arrow's observation about price elasticity. Note that the insignificance of these variables, if it is due to a real lack of association rather than a lack of independent variation in the sam-

---

even negative. In other words, the consumer may not be able to make his marginal rate of substitution between the medical care service and the numeraire good exactly equal to their price ratio. In this case there may be no welfare loss from discriminating monopoly.

[27] Income elasticity of demand from equation 1 equals cy/q, while price elasticity of demand equals bp/q. Using equation 2 the elasticity of price with respect to income equals cy/2bp.

[28] On the observed higher income elasticity of demand for dental services, see [11, 26], [7], and [1, 29, 46, 47]. Estimated income elasticities are obscured by possible price discrimination if expenditure data are used. Andersen and Anderson, however, find higher income elasticities for dental services using data in physical units.

[29] For a survey of demand studies see [6] and [11, ch. 2].

[30] Satisficing behavior may explain the high positive partial correlation of the number of practitioners with price. Suppose physicians have a certain income target. As the number of physicians in an area increases, visits per physician will tend to fall. To achieve any given target income, each physician will then have to charge higher fees.

ple, provides an inference that the monopoly hypothesis is correct. If the market were competitive, price would be higher in areas with higher demand, provided supply curves have a positive slope.[31] If physicians are monopolists, price is necessarily higher in areas with higher demand only if physicians are short-run profit maximizers.

One explanation for the rapid increase in physician fees after the passage of the Medicare and Medicaid legislation is that the legislation probably shifted the demand curve physicians faced outwards and made it less elastic.[32, 33] This factor may account for much of the rise.[34] However, if physicians are monopolists, but are not short-run profit maximizers, there is an additional explanation for the price increase. Physicians may be less reluctant to charge the government a fee closer to their short-run profit maximizing fee than they were to charge aged patients who paid their own bill.

CONCLUSION

Although our tests are relatively weak because of the small number of observations, they all accord with a priori expectations in indicating that the market for physicians' services is monopolistic rather than competitive. This result also appears to hold in the market for dentists' services. Consumer ignorance about price and quality which leads to low cross elasticities of demand is therefore a more likely explanation than collusion by the American Medical Association. If this explanation is correct, the system is inherently monopolistic, since competitive forces of the marketplace cannot readily drive price to average cost. Nevertheless, there is some evidence that physicians do not maximize short-run profits, since price does not vary with age, education, or insurance variables. The relevant geographical market for physicians' and dentists' services appears to be the city rather than the SMSA. Part of the price difference among cities may be due to variation in the quality of care, although it is difficult to say how much of the difference in price can be attributed to quality variation.

APPENDIX

Data Sources and Dates of Measurement

Physician Prices, 1961: United States Bureau of the Census, *Statistical Abstract*, 1963; Washington: GPO, 1963, p. 363.

Price and Income Deflators; *ibid.*, pp. 357, 358.

Physician Prices, 1966: "City Worker's Family Budget," United States Department of Labor Bulletin 1570–1; Washington, D. C., 1967, pp. 9–12.

Number of Physicians 1966: Christ Theodore and Gerald Sutter, "Distribution of Physicians, Hospitals, and Hospital Beds in the U. S." Chicago: American Medical Association, 1966.

Number of Dentists 1961; American Dental Association, "Distribution of Dentists in the United States by State, Region, District, and County." Chicago: American Dental Association, 1962.

Income in 1959 of the population in 1960, population in 1960, % of population with income under $3,000 in 1960, population change 1950–1960, % of population over 65 years of age in 1960, % of population over 25 with a high school education in 1960: All from United States Bureau of the Census, *County and City Data Book*, 1967; Washington, D. C., 1967 (1960 Census data).

Income in 1965: United States Internal Revenue Service, *Statistics of Income 1965*; Washington, D. C., 1966.

Percent of population with hospital insurance coverage: United States Public Health Service, "Health Insurance Coverage," July 1962–June 1963. (Publication No. 1000, Series 10, No. 11); Washington, D. C., 1964.

---

[31] If supply curves do not have a positive slope, the positive associations between income and price are most difficult to explain using competitive assumptions.

[32] Physicians' fees rose at 2.8 percent per year from December 1960 to December 1965, but 7.0 percent per year from December 1965 to December 1967 [4, 2]. It should be noted, however, that the entire CPI also more than doubled its rate of price increase; in the earlier period it increased at 1.3 percent per year and in the later period at 2.8 percent. The Medicare legislation took effect on July 1, 1966, although it was signed into law on July 30, 1965. It is quite possible that physicians, who realized that reimbursement was to be made on the basis of customary charges, made anticipatory price increases before July 1966.

[33] For this explanation see [16, 259–260] and [12].

[34] Visits by the over 65 age group are 12.9 percent of total physician visits, and visits by under 65 with incomes under $3000 are another 9.3 percent of total visits [23].

Decision Making in the Private Sector

Mortality Residuals: from equations computed in Joseph P. Newhouse, "Toward a Rational Allocation of Medical Care Resources," unpublished Ph.D. dissertation, Harvard University, 1968.

REFERENCES

1. Andersen, Ronald and Odin Anderson, *A Decade of Health Services*, Chicago: University of Chicago Press, 1967.
2. Arrow, Kenneth J., "Uncertainty and the Welfare Economics of Medical Care," *American Economic Review*, December 1963, 941–973.
3. Benham, L., A. Maurizi, and M. Reder, "Migration, Location, and Remuneration of Medical Personnel: Physicians and Dentists," *Review of Economics and Statistics*, August 1968, 332–347.
4. Berry, William F., and James C. Daugherty, "A Closer Look at Rising Medical Costs," *Monthly Labor Review*, November 1968, 1–9.
5. Feldstein, Martin S., "An Aggregate Planning Model of the Health Care Sector," *Medical Care*, November–December 1967, 369–381.
6. Feldstein, Paul J., "Research on the Demand for Health Services," *Millbank Memorial Fund Quarterly*, October 1966, 128–165.
7. ——— and Ruth M. Severson, "The Demand for Medical Care," in American Medical Association *Report of the Commission on the Cost of Medical Care*. Chicago: American Medical Association, 1964.
8. Gabarino, Joseph, "Price Behavior and Productivity in the Medical Market," *Industrial and Labor Relations Review*, October 1959, 3–15.
9. Gabor, Andre and C. W. J. Granger, "Price as an Indicator of Quality: Report of an Enquiry," *Economica*, February 1966, 43–70.
10. Kessel, Reuben, "Price Discrimination in Medicine," *Journal of Law and Economics*, October 1958, 20–53.
11. Klarman, Herbert, *The Economics of Health*. New York: Columbia University Press, 1965.
12. "Medicare and Medical Inflation," *Hospital Practice*, November 1968, 23–32.
13. Newhouse, Joseph P., "Toward a Rational Allocation of Medical Care Resources," unpublished Ph.D. dissertation, Harvard University, 1968.
14. Rayack, Elton, *Professional Power and American Medicine*. New York: World Publishing Company, 1967.
15. Rimlinger, Gaston V., and Henry B. Steele, "An Economic Interpretation of the Spatial Distribution of Physicians in the U.S.," *Southern Economic Journal*, July 1963, 1–12.
16. Somers, Herman M. and Anne R., *Medicare and the Hospitals*. Washington: The Brookings Institution, 1967.
17. Stigler, George J., *The Theory of Price*, 3rd edition. New York: The Macmillan Company, 1966.
18. United States Bureau of the Census, *Statistical Abstract 1967*. Washington, D.C., 1967.
19. United States Bureau of Labor Statistics, "The Consumer Price Index, Technical Notes," Bulletin 1554. Washington, D.C., 1967, 4.
20. United States National Center for Health Statistics, "Personal Expenses," Publication No. 1000, Series 10, No. 27; Washington, D.C., 1966.
21. ——— "Volume of Dental Visits," Publication No. 1000, Series 10, No. 23. Washington, D.C., 1965.
22. ——— "Volume of Physician Visits," Publication No. 1000, Series 10, No. 18; Washington, D.C., 1965.
23. ——— "Volume of Physician Visits," Publication No. 1000, Series 10, No. 49; Washington, D.C., 1968.

READING

17 WHY DOES GASOLINE COST MORE IN CHARLEVOIX THAN IT DOES IN DETROIT?

Bruce T. Allen
ASSISTANT PROFESSOR OF ECONOMICS, MICHIGAN STATE UNIVERSITY

Petroleum refining is an oligopolistic industry. By this, we mean that there are relatively few refiners serving any market. Each is fully aware of the existence, the strategies, and the retaliatory power of the others. Any attempt to deal with the question of pricing and price differentials must begin here.

Frequently, this kind of market structure produces results that are little different from those from an unregulated, single-firm monopoly. If each seller in a market is aware that his moves can be immediately matched, each seller will try to play it safe. This means that no seller will try to increase his market share by shading his price, since all his rivals would counter his move, leaving all with lower prices, revenues, and profits. There is an unfortunate converse to this situation: If each seller becomes resigned to or contented with his market share, each can raise his price—and trust others to do likewise—until all companies have prices as high as an unregulated monopoly would charge. Economists call this phenomenon "mutual dependence recognized" or "tacit collusion."[*] It is quite legal, although the result is the same as that of a well-managed price-fixing cartel.

This is a fairly accurate picture of the marketing and pricing of petroleum products in that part of Michigan located above the Muskegon-Bay City area. The market is relatively small, sellers are few. A price cut by one cannot go undetected for long—and the market is not large enough to warrant any firm's making the attempt.

LARGE MARKETS

Where the market is larger, competitive strategies become somewhat more flexible. The reason is largely in the cost structure of petroleum refining. A refinery's costs, except for crude oil, are largely fixed and are the same whatever the level of throughput. The extra cost of another barrel of gasoline to a refinery that has excess capacity is essentially just the cost of the crude. If a customer offers to take refined products from such a seller at a price which covers little more than the variable costs involved, the refiner has a substantial temptation to sell. Why not? The extra revenues are greater than the extra costs. In fact, the spread between price and variable costs constitutes an enormous temptation to shade price just a little bit and try to capture a little larger market share. It is this "incremental barrel," whose extra costs are so much lower than its extra revenues, that gives rise to the only price competition that exists in the industry.

Prices will be shaded in only two instances. They may be cut to particular customers because the refiner thinks the extra gasoline can be kept out of normal marketing channels so that it does not upset the general market—for example, discounts to truck fleets. Or the refiner may think (sometimes erroneously) that a special price cut may get or retain a particular customer without the refiner's rivals finding out about the special deal. The customer may be a branded dealer or jobber, or possibly an independent marketer who buys incremental barrels (or tankwagons) here and there from the majors and sells them at cut-rate outlets for about 2¢ a gallon less than the going rate for major branded gasoline. The key to both these situations is the *secrecy* with which the price cut is made and the expectation that rivals will not find out and retaliate. This condition is most likely to be met in large urban areas; Detroit is a prime example.

Word of a secret price cut in, say, Benzie County is likely to spread fast: there are too few sellers and too

---

[*] As the president of the American Economic Association puts it: "Where firms are few and large they can, without overt collusion, establish and maintain a price that is generally satisfactory to all participants. Nor is this an especially difficult calculation, this exercise of power. This is what we economists with our genius for the neat phrase have come to call oligopolistic rationality. And this market power is legally immune or very nearly so." Statement of J. K. Galbraith in *Planning, Regulation, and Competition: Hearing before the Select Committee on Small Business of the U.S. Senate* (Washington, D.C.; U.S. Government Printing Office, 1967), p. 8.

Decision Making in the Private Sector

few customers. In other words, there is little if any temptation for a refiner to cut prices upstate. Why should he? He has a good thing going if he keeps his prices up, and a minor disaster on his hands if he does not. Not so in the large cities. With hundreds of stations among which a secret price cut could be hidden, with thousands of motorists looking for gasoline bargains, with independent marketers and commercial customers by the hundreds, some gasoline is bound to be sold at less than a full monopoly price.* Nor is the temptation to cut prices selectively confined to the refining level of the industry; if anything, this temptation is a factor which the majors have striven mightily to overcome. An occasional "maverick"—a dealer who is willing to let the service go and just pump lots of gallons for a lower margin— can upset a market to the point where his competitors' suppliers must either lower prices to his competitors or lose the business to someone who will.

The beauty of this situation, then, is the continued—and continually frustrated—hope of the major refiner that this or that price concession can be kept secret. Incremental barrels inevitably find their way into the regular marketing channels of the major cities. The resulting competiton lowers prices generally. What makes price competition in retail motor fuel so spectacular is its infrequency (except in the large cities) and the fact that it can be traced to the actions and reactions of individual, identifiable sellers. All it takes to start the process is one refiner or a few dealers who are disgusted with the amount of business they are doing and who experiment with a few selected price reductions. Once it is under way, the competition gives all sellers a hard choice: cut prices, to costs if necessary, or lose the business. It is the motorist who benefits from the situation.

THE PRICE DIFFERENTIAL

Data in the accompanying table lend support to this analysis. Although they are subject to an unknown amount of sampling error, the average gasoline prices *are* higher upstate. (The averages are based on a five-station sample taken by the Michigan Consumers Council in each city.[1]) There are fewer gas stations, as one would expect, suggesting that word of any secret discounting by a refiner would get around more rapidly and lessen any incentive to shade prices.

---

*The total demand for gasoline is inelastic: a price drop will produce a less-than-proportionate increase in quantity and a fall in total sales revenue. However, enough customers are willing to look for a gas station with the cheapest gas, so the demand facing an individual branded seller is highly elastic.

Moreover, the lower numbers of vehicle registrations and lower amounts of sales indicate that the payoff in increased sales from even successful price cutting would be much lower upstate than in the metropolitan areas of southern Michigan. Essentially, there is a lot of competition in the larger cities and virtually no real competition upstate. The result is a lower price in the cities than upstate.

What, then, should be done about the price differential? Granted, it works a relative hardship on northern Michiganians, is there any remedy for it that does not cost more than the benefits the remedy confers? In general, the answer is probably "no."

Often proposed is the direct elimination, by statute or administrative regulation, of any price differential (price discrimination, in legal and economic jargon) not justified by differences in (largely transportation) cost. This remedy was proposed in 1971 as House Bill 4660 and is enacted on the federal level as the Robinson-Patman Act of 1936. This remedy does nothing about the differences in market structure that cause the price differences, however.

As explained above, price discrimination—in the form of selective (the refiner hopes), secret, price concessions—is an essential ingredient in the price competition that does take place. The major refiner selling gasoline in Detroit has to keep tabs on scores of different retail and tankwagon prices just to know what his competitors are doing. Forbid price discrimination, and he need track only a few prices to accomplish the same result. If each competitor knows accurately what his rivals are doing, it is a simple matter for all to advance prices to monopoly levels in the cities—after all, they have been doing it upstate for years.

If the law tells a refiner that he cannot discriminate, he may choose to lower the high (upstate) price or raise the lower (downstate) price. Or he may split the difference; exactly what he does depends on the circumstances of the specific case. The circumstances of *this* case are such that the lower price is likely to rise and the higher price to remain where it is. If in order to lessen discrimination *between* cities, we must eliminate it *within* cities, we will open the way to tacit collusion and higher prices downstate, with no corresponding benefit to northern Michiganians. Statutory elimination of the discrimination would likely have eliminated most of the remaining competition as well.

Actually, the differential is a problem of varying, and probably diminishing, importance. The 10¢ per gallon differential observed in July 1971 by the Michigan Consumers Council was down to less than 3¢ by September.[2] One would expect the differential to be most serious in the summer when tourists bring

Table 1
Michigan Gasoline Marketing Data, Selected Areas

Area	Average Price per Gallon 7/16/71	Average Price per Gallon 9/3/71	Number of Stations 1967	Vehicle Registrations 1971 Total	Vehicle Registrations 1971 Per Gas Station	Gasoline Station Sales 1967 ($000) Total	Gasoline Station Sales 1967 ($000) Per Station
Standard Metropolitan Statistical Area[1]							
Lansing	30.9	37.1	351	237,064	675	46,077	131
Detroit	26.4	37.9	3,082	2,397,170	778	472,335	153
Grand Rapids	27.7	35.3	528	356,345	675	67,722	128
Flint	27.5	38.3	403	313,319	777	60,278	150
Kalamazoo	32.1	38.1	190	122,773	646	23,815	125
Average	28.9	37.3					
City/County[1]							
Mt. Pleasant/Isabella	38.9	38.9	30	23,586	786	3,159	105
Traverse City/Grand Traverse	39.9	39.9	52	33,304	640	5,710	110
Cadillac/Wexford	38.9	38.9	35	14,998	429	3,507	100
Alpena/Alpena	37.2	38.9	39	21,780	558	3,557	91
Cheboygan/Cheboygan	41.3	41.5	46	11,708	255	3,831	83
Marquette/Marquette	39.6	39.6	69	36,430	538	6,415	93
Sault Ste. Marie/Chippewa	40.7	40.9	47	18,891	402	3,180	68
Menominee/Menominee	38.6	38.2	28	16,146	577	1,804	64
Escanaba/Delta	39.1	39.1	47	23,862	508	3,600	77
Ironwood/Gogebic	37.5	38.9	42	12,588	300	3,088	74
Average	39.2	39.5					

Source: (Prices) Michigan Consumers Council, *Report to the Governor on the Survey of Retail Gasoline Prices in Michigan and Possible Reasons for Price Differences;* (Gasoline stations and sales) U.S. Bureau of the Census, *Census of Business, 1967;* (Vehicle registrations) *Michigan Statistical Abstract,* Ninth ed.

[1]Price data usually collected within city limits. Other data are for SMSA or county, as indicated.

their higher incomes upstate and buy more gasoline, and when the heating-oil season is over, releasing more spare refining capacity for those incremental barrels in the cities.

The differential is likely to diminish further as time passes because domestic crude oil supplies are declining relative to demand levels. This cuts off the raw materials for independent refiners and the throughput for the majors' incremental barrels. The independent marketers are already feeling the pinch and are resorting to imported petroleum products whenever the economics and the administration permit.[3] Only one major refinery is under construction as this is written. Sooner or later there will not be any incremental barrels for Detroit, and its prices can be expected to rise to tacitly collusive levels.

CONCLUDING REMARKS

What this means is that the issue of unfairness to northern Michigan is a temporary one and that the prospects for motorists throughout the state are pretty grim. Shrinking supplies of crude oil and gasoline appear to be in prospect for the foreseeable future; is there anything we can do about *them?*

First, and most obvious, is the elimination of import quotas on crude oil and refined products. Senator Hart has been arguing for this for a long time. This would be of benefit to motorists throughout the state. How much cheaper elimination of quotas would make gasoline is not clear, but a barrel of imported crude costs roughly two-thirds to three-fourths the price of the domestic equivalent.

Second, and somewhat more controversial, is the increasing realization by motorists that "gas is gas," and that the customer may well benefit slightly by shopping around where he can. The fact that the majors are experimenting with "fighting" second brands and frequently have supplied sub-regular grades offers some hope here: the consumer isn't as dumb as paternalistic economists or many advertising agencies seem to think.

Gasoline is unlikely to become really inexpensive again, however. Ultimately there is little we can do about this. In fact, I suspect we have expected more of the political process than it can deliver when it comes to regulating the petroleum industry. Politics has given us import quotas, cartelized production, depletion allowances, antidiscrimination proposals, cartelized retailing (in Wisconsin), and special favors here and there. But it has not and cannot cope with the hard fact of deficient supplies. In fact, except for a rather technical problem in property rights and conservation,* it is doubtful that any regulation of the

---

*Production from any oil pool must be regulated centrally. Otherwise, a single leasehold operator will attempt to extract the oil before the others working the same pool and too much oil will be taken up too soon. Even here, production control has had the effect of keeping prices up and conservation is often a secondary outcome.

Decision Making in the Private Sector

oil industry has aided any consumer since the Standard Oil Trust was "busted" in 1911. That's not compelling evidence for more regulation.

CITATIONS

1. Michigan Consumers Council, *Report to the Governor on the Survey of Retail Gasoline Prices in Michigan and Possible Reasons for the Price Differences* (Lansing, Michigan: processed, 20 January 1972), Appendix I.
2. Ibid.
3. *Business Week,* 18 November 1972, p. 21.

CASE

18 A RATE INCREASE FOR THE ALABAMA POWER COMPANY

The Alabama Public Service Commission (APSC) is located in the State office building in Montgomery, Alabama. On the morning of August 10, 1974, Ken Hammond, President of APSC entered the auditorium on the second floor and was greeted by the Associate Commissioner, the Hearings Examiner, and the Chief of the Utilities Division. At about the same time, Joseph Farley, President of the Alabama Power Company (APCO) entered with his entourage through another door. After proper introductions, the meeting was called to order by Ken Hammond, who announced the opening of the investigation proceedings in the matter of Alabama Power Company's request for electrical power rate hikes. A synopsis of that meeting follows:

Mr. Farley was called to testify first.

Q. Please state your name and by whom you are employed.

A. My name is Joseph M. Farley. My Employer is the Alabama Power Company, sometimes referred to as APCO. I am President and Chief Executive Officer.

Q. Mr. Farley, this present filing for changes in APCO's retail rate schedules for electric service is taking place 18 months after this Commission granted partial rate relief from the company's previous request for rate schedule changes. What caused APCO to file this request for additional revenues this year?

A. Insufficient earnings to carry on its public utility responsibilities. Having planned for sales of first mortgage bonds and preferred stock in the first half of 1974 to provide the necessary capital to continue building more electrical capacity to serve increased loads, we realized that after such sales we would be bordering on the edge of those limitations which would prevent further sales of secured capital, and then, with the 1974 earnings declining beyond our expectations, it became apparent that after the sales of those securities, APCO for the first time in its history would have restrictions imposed upon it which would deny future sales until its earnings position improved sufficiently to rise above restrictive limitations.

Unrestrained inflation since the last retail rate increase and the massive need for more and more capital eroded the benefits received from that increase.

Q. Mr. Farley, for those on the Commission, and for those in our audience who are unaware of its operation, please describe generally the business of APCO.

A. APCO operates in 56 of Alabama's 67 counties. At the end of 1973, it serviced 863,000 customers in 639 cities and communities. At the end of 1973 APCO employed 7,693 employees. It owned and operated 13 hydroelectric generating plants, five thermal-electric plants, and two combustion turbine plants. The system includes more than 59,435 circuit miles of transmission and distribution lines.

Q. Is APCO interconnected with any other electric system?

A. Yes, APCO is one of the operating subsidiaries of the Southern Company. Other operating companies in the system are Georgia Power Company, Gulf Power Company, and Mississippi River Company.

Q. What has been the recent growth of the APCO system?

A. Nationally, the usage of electricity has doubled in the last ten years; on our system electrical consumption has doubled in the last nine years. In 1953, our customers consumed 5.4 billion kilowatt-hours of electrical energy, and last year, 1973, consumed 24.8 billion kilowatt-hours. Average consumption per residential customer increased 297% over the same twenty year period.

Q. Mr. Farley, upon what basis have your forecasts been made?

A. We arrived at the estimates through load forecasting procedures developed over many years of business. In part, the conclusion represents an extension of "historical" trend lines reflecting long-term rate of growth. However, we have constantly under study load growth patterns, prospective new loads, the use saturation of electrical equipment and

---

*This case was prepared by Thomas M. Tole, Assistant Professor of Finance, Auburn University. It is a basis for classroom discussion and is not intended to illustrate either effective or ineffective handling of an administrative situation.

Decision Making in the Private Sector

appliances, new service applications, past performances, and the like.

In addition, there has been an unprecedented increase in industrial development in Alabama. The Mobile area, because of its Port, industrial sites on deep water, proposed superport, and so on, saw the announcement of new companies requiring an additional demand for 60,000 kilowatts. We are receiving enquiries from companies seeking locations with electrical demands in the range of 200,000 to 300,000 kilowatts. I see this activity continuing.

Q. How is APCO intending to meet these new electrical demands?

A. As shown in Exhibit 1, we have several projects under construction, or in the planning stage. In addition to this exhibit, another nuclear generating plant comprised of four 1,200,000-kilowatt units has been proposed and is scheduled for completion, one each year, in 1982, 1983, 1984 and 1985. All of these units together total over nine million kilowatts of new capacity.

Q. Mr. Farley, what is the impact of the proposed construction on the financial plans of the Company?

A. The company will be required to construct plant additions costing $1.3 billion in the period 1974 through 1976. However, extending this projection through 1978, shows that the Company will be required to expend $2.4 billion for plant and systems additions. It is not possible to raise all these funds internally and it is essential that APCO maintain an acceptable financial standing in the marketplace to ensure its ability to secure these needed funds in competition with other sellers of securities.

Q. What percent of APCO's cash requirements is internally generated?

A. Through retained earnings, depreciation, deferral of income taxes, and similar sources, in the order of 50% in the recent past. During 1974, the Company can expect to generate about 18%! The balance will have to be raised through he sale of new securities and capital contributions from the Southern Company, which in turn can only come from the sale of securities by the Southern Company. We see no significant change in this ratio over the next several years, without substantial rate relief.

Q. To whom would APCO sell these large amounts of new securities?

A. The policies and practices of the SEC have required that sales of bonds and preferred stock be at competitive bids to the investment community. Common equity is derived through investment in the common stock of APCO by Southern Company. Of course, if the income of the operating subsidiaries of the Southern Company show inadequate earnings to

Exhibit 1 (Farley)   Electrical Capacity Under Construction

Project*	Electrical Capacity	Total Projected Expenditures	Percent Complete	Completion Date
N Farley #1	880 MW	$463,483,000	84%	5/1/76
N Farley #2	880 MW	376,105,000	36%	2/15/77
H Mitchell	80 MW	27,139,000	—	1980
H Harris	135 MW	62,000,000	15%	1979
H Martin	60 MW	14,087,000	1%	1981
F Miller #1	660 MW	223,729,000	7%	1978
F Miller #2	660 MW	161,228,000	—	1979
F Miller #3	660 MW	188,070,000	—	1980

*N = Nuclear, H = Hydro, and F = Fossil

pay attractive dividends, Southern Company would be unable to market its securities on an attractive basis.

I should point out, that SEC surveillance, as well as investment community acceptability, make it imperative for APCO to maintain a proper balance in its capital structure.

At this point, Mr. Ken Hammond thanked Mr. Farley for his testimony and excused him. To obtain a more detailed understanding of the operations of APCO, the Public Service Commission called Mr. Walter Johnsey to testify.

Q. Please state your name and employer.

A. My name is Walter F. Johnsey. I am vice-president in charge of Administration and Finance of the Alabama Power Company.

Q. What is the primary intent of your testimony?

A. I shall supply evidence to support in full the increased revenues to be derived from the rate schedule changes filed with this Commission. Included in this evidence are exhibits relating to the accounting and finance functions of the company.

Exhibit 2 contains condensed balance sheets and income statements. In this exhibit, line 6 shows that the proprietary capital, the capital supplied by both the preferred & common stockholders, has more than doubled in the period shown, while capital obtained from long-term debt (line 7) has also doubled. On lines 9 and 13, you see other forms of capital, which is provided from deferral of investment tax credits and of income taxes resulting from the use of accelerated depreciation.

Line 19, the allowance for funds used during construction, is often ignored by analysts because it represents a future cash flow, not realized in the current period. It represents a capitalized value of funds which are tied up in construction-in-progress. Some think of it as an opportunity cost. Disregarding

Pricing

Exhibit 2 (Johnsey) — Alabama Power Company

Condensed Balance Sheets as of the Year-End for the Years 1969 through 1973 and as of May 31, 1974, as Well as Condensed Income Accounts for Such Years and the Twelve Months Ended May 31, 1974 (Thousands of Dollars)

Line No.	Condensed Balance Sheets	1969	1970	1971	1972	1973	May 31, 1974
	Assets						
1	Net Utility Plant	$899,715	$998,448	$1,170,572	$1,387,504	$1,726,007	$1,871,620
2	Other Property and Investments	19,123	18,883	18,602	18,657	18,835	18,788
3	Current and Accrued Assets	42,562	60,651	76,422	106,097	114,515	137,333
4	Deferred Debits	2,381	3,914	4,371	6,389	8,709	10,204
5	Total Assets	$963,781	$1,081,896	$1,269,967	$1,518,647	$1,868,066	$2,037,945
	Liabilities						
6	Proprietary Capital	$376,709	$418,729	$469,379	$577,209	$711,508	$770,089
7	Long-Term Debt	473,826	533,739	618,614	738,418	905,045	922,766
8	Current and Accrued Liabilities	44,790	57,524	92,862	94,922	123,707	209,133
	Deferred Credits —						
9	Unamortized Investment Credit	12,597	12,205	15,759	23,063	24,699	24,558
10	Other	1,172	1,079	2,997	2,053	2,114	2,408
11	Operating Reserves	304	174	198	217	321	177
12	Contributions in Aid of Construction	272	305	395	652	—	—
13	Earned Surplus Restricted for Future Income Taxes	54,111	58,141	69,763	82,113	100,672	108,814
14	Total Liabilities	$963,781	$1,081,896	$1,269,967	$1,518,647	$1,868,066	$2,037,945
15	Total Utility Plant — End of Period	$1,198,436	$1,321,457	$1,516,539	$1,760,171	$2,130,174	$2,293,161
	Condensed Income Accounts						
16	Utility Operating Revenues	$235,170	$249,714	$278,725	$326,325	$397,532	$416,609
17	Utility Operating Expenses	177,762	189,814	213,594	250,720	301,214	327,122
18	Net Utility Operating Income	57,408	59,900	65,131	75,605	96,318	89,487
	Other Income and Deductions —						
19	Allowance for Funds Used During Construction	4,247	4,472	10,667	14,954	23,872	32,023
20	Other	2,379	2,702	2,116	1,822	10,137	12,083
21	Interest Charges	(21,432)	(25,481)	(33,157)	(42,709)	(55,472)	(61,477)
22	Net Income	42,602	41,593	44,757	49,672	74,855	72,116
23	Dividends on Preferred Stock	3,884	3,979	4,808	9,027	9,766	11,861
24	Net Income After Dividends on Preferred Stock	$38,718	$37,614	$39,949	$40,645	$65,089	$60,255

line 19 results in even smaller net income available for common stockholders.

In other words, during this time electric construction work in progress has increased from $70,733,000 to $649,715,000 or an increase of nine times. It is draining the Company of its cash resources. While it is true that the investment in this work in progress is creating "below-the-line" bookkeeping income, it is not providing cash income. The company needs cash—and large amounts of it—to meet the commitments of the construction program and to pay the interest and other costs of added investment.

In addition to this exhibit, I wish to point out the change of capitalization from May 31, 1969 to May 31, 1974 as follows:

	May, 1969	May, 1974	Percent Change
Debt	$451,785,000	$978,450,000	117%
Preferred Stock	82,546,000	235,861,000	186
Common Stock	282,220,000	534,228,000	89
Total Capitalization	$816,551,000	$1,748,539,000	114%

It should be noted that while debt increased 117%, the cost of carrying that debt increased 187%. Similarly, the dividend cost of preferred stock increased 205% during the same period.

However, the account suffering most is the account for common stock equity. One must not be misled by the fact that the gross dollars of earnings increased so much. They represent earnings on a vastly increased investment by the common stockholder. The investor is earning a smaller return. At the same time, that investment is attended with a substantially higher risk; namely, the cost to the Company of carrying the interest and dividends on debt and preferred stock which increased over 200%. Capital cannot be attracted in such circumstances.

For the year 1974, it is estimated that the company will be able to claim only $604,000 as an investment tax credit, although the potential investment tax credit to be generated that year from eligible property to be placed in service is estimated at $11.5 million. This heavy loss in potential funds stems from the minor

Decision Making in the Private Sector

Federal income tax liability to be experienced in 1974 as a consequence of depressed taxable income. This completes my observations on Exhibit 2.

Q. Mr. Johnsey, both you and Mr. Farley have testified about the enormous sums being expended on, and to be expended for, additional plant facilities to match the growing demand for electricity. Do you have an exhibit which accounts for such expenditures?

A. Yes, my next exhibit (See Exhibit 3) illustrates the expenditures required for additional plant capacity. It shows actual expenditures for 1973 plant additions and estimated expenditures through 1985 which will be required to meet supply demands now projected to occur.

Q. Why did you carry these projects all the way to 1985?

A. First of all, this Commission has issued certificates of convenience and necessity to APCO which authorized the construction of additional electric power generating stations for which expenditure will be extended through 1985. Another reason is to show how essential long-range planning is for mushrooming growth. And, furthermore, this Commission is entitled to come face to face with the enormity of its regulatory responsibilities as time passes on.

Q. Please go on with your explanation of the exhibit!

A. The entries are largely self-explanatory. Of course, any change in the rate of inflation, either up or down, would change these numbers; and I must add, the unrelenting rise in the rate of inflation brought about an overrun of expenditures in 1973.

Q. How does the Company propose to finance these vast expenditures?

A. We must find the money from both ratepayers and investors. And we all know that investors will not provide capital unless a satisfactory return can be realized from the funds invested. For us to obtain investor capital, ratepayers must provide more and more revenues to leave sufficient earnings which will continue to attract investors.

Q. What about issuing additional first mortgage bonds and preferred stock?

A. In an expanding business which has little control over demand, there is an urgent need for profits to provide protection to investors. The holders of bonds and preferred stock have built-in safeguards in the indenture and corporate charter. Each of these instruments will not allow issuance of additional securities when the rate of earnings has fallen below specified limits. My next exhibit (See Exhibit 4) explains earnings requirements for first mortgage bonds and preferred stock. The exhibit clearly shows that under existing rates and earnings resulting therefrom, APCO cannot sell additional first mortgage bonds or preferred stock. An inferior fixed charge coverage is a signal that the return on common equity is too low, which in turn tends to make it virtually impossible to raise new equity without diluting the equity interest of present stockholders. Any attempt at further financing under current conditions may be so disruptive as to cause bond rating companies to reevaluate the A-rating of our bonds. If this occurs, not only will bond prices fall, but bonds will become appreciably less marketable even at a lower price.

At existing levels of earnings the Company is prevented from selling any additional amount of senior securities.

Q. Our last question, Mr. Johnsey. What would be the effect on revenues if the proposed rate increase were approved?

A. Based upon actual customer usage over the past twelve months (May, 1973 to May, 1974), overall revenues would have increased by $64,484,114 had the new rates been in effect.

Mr. Johnsey was thanked for his testimony. In order to obtain more information regarding the ramifications of a possible rate increase, the Public Service Commission requested hearing the next witness on the docket, Mr. Eugene Meyer.

Q. Please state your name and occupation.

A. My name is Eugene W. Meyer. I am a Vice President of Kidder, Peabody, and Company, an

Exhibit 3 (Johnsey)   Alabama Power Company

Construction Expenditures for the Year 1973 and Projected Expenditures for the Years 1974 through 1985 (Thousands of Dollars)

Year	Annual Totals	Year	Annual Totals	Year	Annual Totals
1973	383,114	1978	511,016	1983	1,208,618
1974	466,900	1979	691,256	1984	1,213,961
1975	452,785	1980	989,504	1985	1,384,866
1976	424,710	1981	1,027,473		
1977	504,743	1982	1,089,594		

Pricing

investment banking company located in New York City. I am the Director of the Utility Corporate Finance Department of our firm. I am responsible for price negotiations in all utility offerings where Kidder, Peabody is chosen to manage, or co-manage the transaction.

Q. What will be the basic thrust of your testimony?

A. I will get right to the heart of investor requirements. Specifically, I shall testify regarding the earnings necessary to provide a sufficient return to investors to enable Alabama Power Company and the parent firm, the Southern Company, to attract capital on a reasonable basis.

Q. How do you view the current outlook for

Exhibit 4 (Johnsey)   Page 1
                             Alabama Power Company

Fixed Charge Coverage Requirement for Issuance of Additional First Mortgage Bonds Under Terms of the Company's Mortgage Indenture

Requirement
Before there can be an issuance of additional first mortgage bonds, an "interest earnings requirement" must be met; that is, all income after operating expenses and taxes but before federal and state income taxes, shall be no less than two (2) times the aggregate annual interest charges on all outstanding indebtedness at the date of new issue of bonds plus the annual interest on the proposed new issue, provided, however, that the amount of net non-operating revenues included in income must be the smallest of the following three items:

1. Net non-operating revenues
2. 10% of net earnings
3. 15% of the interest earnings requirement

Coverage Experience

Year Ended December 31	Times Earned
1969	4.26
1970	3.33
1971	2.73
1972	2.23
1973	2.50

Twelve Months Ended	
January 1974	2.51
February	2.48
March	2.39
April	2.36
May	1.93[1]
September	1.76[2]

[1] After giving effect to $100,000,000 principal amount of First Mortgage Bonds, 9-3/4% Series, sold in June 1974.
[2] Based upon actual earnings from October 1973 through May 1974 plus budget earnings June 1974 through September 1974 and giving effect to the proposed sale in November 1974 of $80,000,000 principal amount of first mortgage bonds at an assumed interest cost of 9-3/4%.

Exhibit 4 (Johnsey)   Page 2
                             Alabama Power Company

Fixed Charge and Preferred Stock Dividend Coverage Requirement for Issuance of Additional Preferred Stock Under Terms of the Company's Corporate Charter

Requirement
Before there can be any issuance of additional shares of preferred stock, the gross income available for the payment of interest must be at least equal to one and one-half (1-1/2) times the aggregate of the annual interest requirements (adjusted by provision for amortization of debt discount and expense or of premium on debt as the case may be) on all outstanding indebtedness of the corporation and the annual dividend requirements (adjusted for provision for amortization of preferred stock premium and expense) on all outstanding shares of preferred stock plus the shares proposed to be issued.

Coverage Experience

Year Ended December 31	Times Earned
1969	2.41
1970	2.04
1971	1.87
1972	1.61
1973	1.71

Twelve Months Ended	
January 1974	1.75
February	1.75
March	1.69
April	1.63
May	1.48[1]
September	1.44[2]

[1] After giving effect to $100,000,000 principal amount of First Mortgage Bonds, 9-3/4% Series, sold in June 1974.
[2] Based upon actual earnings from October 1973 through May 1974 plus budget earnings June 1974 through September 1974 and giving effect to the proposed sale in November 1974 of $80,000,000 principal amount of first mortgage bonds at an assumed interest cost of 9-3/4%.

utility securities from the investment banking standpoint?

A. Electric utilities face a severely declining ability to attract the capital it needs for construction necessary to provide electrical output. The percentage of total capital requirements provided by funds internally generated has dropped from 56% in 1968 to 44% in 1973. This has put increasing pressure on the capital markets and caused utilities to pay more for the use of capital.

Despite that fact, providers of that capital did not receive returns which protected the principal amount of their investment. For instance, consider the data presented in Exhibit 6. This Exhibit indicates that the dividends per share for the Moody's 24 Electric Power Common Stock Index have remained fairly stable, but that investors are requiring a much higher return on

Decision Making in the Private Sector

their investment. This is due, in some part, to the dividend omission of Consolidated Edison, and to generally reduced bond ratings.

In addition, until investors are convinced that the earnings problem is rectified, I expect utility debt to carry higher interest rates than industrial company debt. Utility stock price/earning ratios will remain at low levels. And utility stock current yields will have to be higher than yields available on utility bonds.

It should not go unnoticed that for all practical purposes, institutional holdings of utility common stock and institutional interest in them disappeared by 1970. Virtually all of the new common stock issued by utilities since that time has been purchased by individuals out of their savings. This individual market can be maintained only so long as the industry pays dividends regularly without fail.

Q. There has been discussion that Southern Company may have to sell common stock below book value to be able to supply capital funds to Alabama Power Company. What occurs when a company is forced to sell below book value?

A. The earnings per share and the assets per share of the existing stockholders are diluted. In effect, existing shareholders are told that the value of the assets which they own has been reduced and allocated in part to new shareholders and in return they will receive absolutely nothing. Furthermore, this happens at a time when the company is required to make additional investments at a rate of return level below that being earned on the already existing assets of the company. Therefore, the rate of return on equity drops and dilution of earnings per share also results. This has substantially reduced investor

Exhibit 5 (Johnsey)   Page 1
Alabama Power Company

Balance Sheet as of May 31, 1974

Line No.	Assets and Other Debits		
	Utility Plant		
1	Electric plant in service	$1,619,582,337	
2	Accumulated provision for depreciation	(420,510,410)	
3	Electric plant held for future use	1,613,060	
4	Construction work in progress—Electric	649,715,354	
5	Electric plant acquisition adjustments	121,317	$1,850,521,658
6	Steam heat plant in service	7,407,655	
7	Accumulated provision for depreciation	(1,030,641)	
8	Construction work in progress—Steam heat	92,453	6,469,467
9	Nuclear fuel in process of fabrication		14,628,693
10	Net utility plant		1,871,619,818
	Other Property and Investments		
11	Nonutility property (net)	2,098,518	
12	Investment in subsidiary companies	16,682,231	
13	Other investments	1	
14	Special funds	7,677	18,788,427
	Current and Accrued Assets		
15	Cash	3,907,844	
16	Special deposits	39,649,096	
17	Working funds	391,394	
18	Notes and accounts receivable	28,834,813	
19	Receivables from associated companies	6,150,800	
20	Materials and supplies	51,074,040	
21	Prepayments	6,941,626	
22	Rents receivable	382,944	137,332,557
	Deferred Debits		
23	Unamortized debt expense	2,590,895	
24	Preliminary survey and investigation charges	804,753	
25	Clearing accounts	1,648,525	
26	Research and development expenditures	1,244,108	
27	Unamortized leasehold improvements	616,467	
28	Miscellaneous deferred debits	3,299,300	10,204,048
			$2,037,944,850

Pricing

willingness to make further investment in utility stocks.

In the case of Southern Company, it requires $180.0 million from the sale of common shares in 1974. The book value of the company is $18.35 while its market price is currently $11.875. Therefore, it will have to issue approximately 5,348,000 more shares of common to obtain the necessary financing than if it could sell its common stock at book.

Q. In your opinion, Mr. Meyers, what is

Exhibit 5 (Johnsey) Page 2
Alabama Power Company

Balance Sheet as of May 31, 1974

Line No.	Liabilities and Other Credits		
	Proprietary Capital		
1	Common stock issued	$224,358,200	
2	Preferred stock issued	235,400,000	
3	Premium on capital stock	460,920	
4	Other paid-in capital	180,000,000	
5	Capital stock expense	(99,237)	
6	Unappropriated retained earnings	129,918,587	
7	Unappropriated undistributed subsidiary earnings	50,231	$770,088,701
	Long-Term Debt		
8	Bonds (less $89,000 reacquired)	905,045,000	
9	Other long-term debt	18,611,000	
10	Unamortized premium on long-term debt	1,206,597	
11	Unamortized discount on long-term debt — Debit	(2,096,187)	922,766,410
	Interim Indebtedness		
12	Accrued nuclear fuel payments	9,654,140	
13	Notes payable	46,030,000	55,684,140
	Current and Accrued Liabilities		
	(Excluding Interim Indebtedness)		
14	Accounts payment	39,494,387	
15	Payables to associated companies	13,958,492	
16	Customer deposits	8,291,703	
17	Taxes accrued	15,359,703	
18	Interest accrued	17,140,744	
19	Dividends declared	15,819,264	
20	Matured long-term debt	303,518	
21	Matured interest	36,614,788	
22	Tax collections payable	1,589,770	
23	Miscellaneous current and accrued liabilities	4,876,627	153,448,996
	Deferred Credits		
	Customer advances for construction —		
24	Electric department	850,739	
25	Steam heat department	11,303	
	Unamortized investment credit —		
26	Electric department	24,274,176	
27	Steam heat department	283,396	
28	Other deferred credits	1,546,233	26,865,847
	Operating Reserves		
29	Injuries and damages reserve		177,045
	Earned Surplus Restricted for Future Income Taxes		
30	Accelerated amortization (electric)	9,420,924	
	Liberalized depreciation —		
31	Electric department	75,462,443	
32	Steam heat department	256,037	
	Other —		
33	Electric department	23,659,677	
34	Steam heat department	14,630	108,813,711
35	Total Liabilities and Other Credits		$2,037,944,850

Decision Making in the Private Sector

required by investors in common stock of the Southern Company?

A. The return to the investor is derived from the dividend he receives and any market appreciation he realizes. In the current marketplace, the investor has the option of buying First Mortgage Bonds of the subsidiary companies of the Southern Company. These carry a lower risk than the common stock of the Southern Company and yield about 10.50%. To buy the common of Southern Company, the investor would require a price appreciation and dividend yield combined which would be higher than the yield available on the subsidiary bond. Historically, investors have required a return on investment in common 3-5% higher than the yield available on the company's bond. The yield on first Mortgage bonds

Exhibit 5 (Johnsey) Page 3
Alabama Power Company

Statement of Income for the Twelve Months Ended May 31, 1974

Line No.		Electric Utility	Steam Heat Utility	Total
	Utility Operating Income			
1	Operating Revenues	$415,896,918	$711,961	$416,608,879
	Operating Expenses:			
2	Operation expense	188,889,584	846,071	189,735,655
3	Maintenance expense	28,142,920	222,011	28,364,931
4	Depreciation expense	42,314,960	200,050	42,515,010
5	Amortization of utility plant acquisition adjustments	10,110	—	10,110
6	Amortization of investment tax credit — Credit	(869,898)	(6,149)	(876,047)
7	Taxes other than income taxes	31,740,904	110,880	31,851,784
8	Income taxes — Federal	16,673,676	(559,464)	16,114,474
9	State	(418,880)	(20,464)	(439,344)
10	Provision for deferred income taxes	21,448,894	50,375	21,499,269
11	Provision for deferred income taxes — Credit	(2,419,295)	(822)	(2,420,117)
12	Provision for investment tax credits	661,803	104,239	766,042
13	Total utility operating expenses	426,174,778	946,989	327,121,767
14	Net utility operating income	$ 89,722,140	$(235,028)	89,487,112
	Other Income and Deductions			
	Other Income:			
	Allowance for funds used during construction —			
15	Electric department			31,853,629
16	Steam heat department			69,415
17	Interest and dividend income			1,166,482
18	Other income			1,680,050
19	Total other income			34,869,576
	Other Income Deductions:			
20	Donations			269,771
21	Other income deductions			37,571
22	Total other income deductions			307,342
	Taxes Applicable to Other Income and Deductions:			
23	Taxes other than income taxes			77,878
24	Income taxes — Federal			(9,107,915)
25	State			(513,748)
26	Total taxes on other income and deductions			(9,543,785)
27	Net other income and deductions			44,106,019
28	*Income Before Interest Charges*			133,593,131
	Interest Charges			
29	Interest on long-term debt			56,466,327
30	Amortization of Debt Discount, Premium and Expense			185,972
31	Other Interest Expense			4,824,675
32	Total interest charges			61,476,974
33	*Net Income*			72,116,157
34	Dividends on Preferred Stock			11,861,045
35	*Net Income After Dividends on Preferred Stock*			$ 60,255,112

Exhibit 6 (Meyer)   Assorted Data: Utility Securities

Year	Moody's 24 Electric Power Common Stock Index — Average Dividends per Share	Book Value per Share	Year-End Price per Share	Moody's Public Utility Bond Yield Range	Moody's Public Utility Bond Yield Average
1968	$4.50	$57.94	$104.04	6.27%-6.85%	6.56%
1969	4.61	60.54	84.62	7.02%-8.39%	7.71%
1970	4.70	64.09	88.59	8.34%-9.06%	8.70%
1971	4.77	66.37	85.56	7.92%-8.39%	8.16%
1972	4.87	70.41r	83.61	7.48%-7.88%	7.68%
1973	5.01	71.67	60.87	7.51%-8.17%	7.84%
Latest Available 1974	4.82+	——	46.42	9.08%-9.27%	8.68%
% Increase (Decrease) 1968-1973	11.3%	23.7%	(41.5%)		19.5%
Compound Annual Growth (Decline) Rate 1968-1973	2.2%	4.3%	(10.1%)		3.6%

r = revised
+ Actual dividend index, adjusted for Consolidated Edison Company's reduced annual dividend rate of $.80 per share.
Source: Moody's Investors Services.

has been averaging 10.5%. The yield on preferred has been greater than 11.0%. In this case, such a total return on common stock would be 13.5% to 15.5% comprised of 7.6% current yield ($1.40 ÷ $18.35) and 5.9% to 7.9% earnings per share growth rate. If the retention rate of Southern Company is 35%, rate of return on book value of 16.9% to 22.6% must be achieved to maintain a growth rate of 5.9% to 7.9%.*

As we all know, utilities, including Southern Company, have been unable to actually earn the returns necessary to provide for sufficient earnings per share growth.

    Q. Mr. Meyer, if Southern Company must achieve a 16.9% to 22.6% return on book value, you are saying that APCO has not requested a large enough rate increase?

    A. I am only endeavoring to point out the investor requirements in today's financial marketplace if new equity capital is to be raised.

So long as the American people have freedom to put their savings where they wish, a return on that investment must be provided which will induce them to invest in the utility industries which are so vital to our economic well being.

After Mr. Meyer's testimony, Mr. Ken Hammond moved toward adjournment of the hearing. He thanked all those who testified, and concluded by saying that the Alabama Public Service Commission would like the opportunity to review the testimony and exhibits presented. He felt sure that the Alabama Public Service Commission and the Alabama Power Company would have another round before any decisions concerning rate increases were made.

Questions for Discussion

1. Identify specific financial problems faced by an electric utility that are not generally applicable to a private profit seeking firm.
2. Discuss the treatment of projecting demand for electric power in the future.
3. What are the prevailing capital market conditions which generally influence public utility financing? Why have electrical utilities faced special problems in recent years in raising necessary capital needs? What would you suggest as a remedy for this apparent capital shortage?
4. What technique is used in calculating the cost of capital in this rate case? Are there any special problems of deriving cost of capital for a public utility?
5. Develop a sources and needs statement of future funds for the Alabama Power Company.

*from g = 5.9% to 7.9%, b = 35%.
Since r = g/b,   r = $\frac{5.9\% \text{ to } 7.9\%}{35\%}$ = 16.9% to 22.6%

EXERCISES
19

19-1. Assume that a firm sells its product in a perfectly competitive market. The firm's fixed costs (including a "normal" return on the funds the entrepreneur has invested in the firm) are equal to $100 and its variable cost schedule is as follows:

Output (Units)	Variable Cost per Unit
50	$5.00
100	4.50
150	4.00
200	3.50
250	3.00
300	2.75
350	3.00
400	3.50

a. Find the marginal cost and average total cost schedules for the firm.
b. If the prevailing market price is $4.50, how many units will be produced and sold?
c. What are total profits and profit per unit at the output level determined in b.?
d. Is the industry in long-run equilibrium at this price? Explain.

19-2. Exotic Metals, Inc., a leading manufacturer of zirilium, which is used in many electronic products, estimates the following demand schedule for its product:

Price ($/Pound)	Quantity (Pounds/Period)
$25	0
18	1,000
16	2,000
14	3,000
12	4,000
10	5,000
8	6,000
6	7,000
4	8,000
2	9,000

Fixed costs of manufacturing zirilium are $14,000 per period. The firm's variable cost schedule is as follows:

Output (Pounds/Period)	Variable Cost per Pound
0	$ 0
1,000	10.00
2,000	8.50
3,000	7.33
4,000	6.25
5,000	5.40
6,000	5.00
7,000	5.14
8,000	5.88
9,000	7.00

a. Find the total revenue and marginal revenue schedules for the firm.
b. Determine the average total cost and marginal cost schedules for the firm.
c. What are Exotic Metal's profit maximizing price and output level for the production and sale of zirilium?
d. What is Exotic's profit (or loss) at the solution determined in c.?
e. Supose that the federal government announces that it will sell zirilium, from its extensive wartime stockpile, to anyone who wants it at $6.00 per pound. How does this affect the solution determined in c.? What is Exotic Metal's profit (or loss) under these conditions?

19-3. Wyandotte Chemical Company sells various chemicals to the automobile industry. Wyandotte currently sells 30,000 gallons of polyol per year at an average price of $15 per gallon. Fixed costs of manufacturing polyol are $90,000 per year and total variable costs equal $180,000. The operations research department has estimated that a 15 percent increase in output would not affect fixed costs, but would reduce average variable costs by $ .60 per gallon. The marketing department has estimated the arc elasticity of demand for polyol to be —2.0.

a. How much would Wyandotte have to reduce the price of polyol in order to achieve a 15 percent increase in the quantity sold?
b. Evaluate the impact of such a price cut on (1) total revenue, (2) total costs, and (3) total profits.

19-4. Tennis Products, Inc. produces three models of high quality tennis racquets. The following table contains recent information concerning the sales, costs, and profitability of the three models:

Model	Average Quantity Sold (Units/ Month)	Current Price	Total Revenue	Variable Cost per Unit	Contribution Margin per Unit	Contribution Margin*
A	15,000	$30.00	450,000	$15.00	$15.00	$225,000
B	5,000	35.00	175,000	18.00	17.00	85,000
C	10,000	45.00	450,000	20.00	25.00	250,000
Total			$1,075,000			$565,000

*Contribution to fixed costs and profits.

The company is considering lowering the price of Model A to $27.00 in an effort to increase the number of units sold. Based upon the results of price changes that have been instituted in the past, Tennis Products' chief economist has estimated the arc price elasticity of demand to be —2.5. Furthermore, he has estimated the arc cross elasticity of demand between Model A and Model B to be

Decision Making in the Private Sector

approximately .5 and between Model A and Model C to be approximately .2. Variable costs per unit are not expected to change over the anticipated changes in volume.

a. Evaluate the impact of the price cut on the (1) total revenue, and (2) contribution margin of Model A. Based upon this analysis, should the firm lower the price of Model A?

b. Evaluate the impact of the price cut on the (1) total revenue and (2) contribution margin for the entire line of tennis racquets. Based upon this analysis, should the firm lower the price of Model A?

19-5. The Lumins Lamp Company, a producer of old-style oil lamps, has estimated the following demand function for their product:

$$Q = 120,000 - 10,000P$$

where Q is the quantity demanded per year and P is the price per lamp. The firm's fixed costs are \$12,000 and variable costs are \$1.50 per lamp.

a. Write an equation for the total revenue (TR) function in terms of Q.
b. Specify the marginal revenue function.
c. Write an equation for the total cost (TC) function in terms of Q.
d. Specify the marginal cost function.
e. Write an equation for total profits (π) in terms of Q. At what level of output (Q) are total profits maximized? What price will be charged? What are total profits at this output level?
f. Check your answers in e. by equating the marginal revenue and marginal cost functions, determined in b. and d., and solving for Q.
g. What model of market pricing behavior has been assumed in this problem?

19-6. Consolidated Sugar Company has two divisions, a farming-preprocessing (p) division and a processing-marketing (m) division. The farming-preprocessing division grows sugar and crushes it into juice which it may sell to the processing-marketing division or sell externally in the perfectly competitive open market. The processing-marketing division buys cane juice, either from the farming-preprocessing division or externally in the open market, and then evaporates and purifies it and sells it as processed sugar.

The processing-marketing division's demand function for processed sugar is:

$$P_m = 24 - Q_m$$

where P_m is the price, in dollars per unit, and Q_m is the quantity sold, in units, and its cost function (excluding cane juice) is:

$$C_m = 8 + 2Q_m$$

The farming-preprocesing division's total cost function for cane juice is:

$$C_p = 10 + 2Q_p + Q_p^2$$

where Q_p is the quantity produced, in units. Assume that one unit of cane juice is converted into one unit of processed sugar. Furthermore, assume that the open market price for cane juice is \$14.

Pricing

   a. What is the profit-maximizing price and output level for the farming-preprocessing division?

   b. What is the profit-maximizing price and output level for the processing-marketing division?

   c. How much of its output (i.e., cane juice) should the farming-preprocessing division sell (1) internally to the processing-marketing division and (2) externally on the open market?

   d. How much of its input (i.e., cane juice) should the processing-marketing division buy (1) internally from the farming-preprocessing division and (2) externally on the open market?

   e. What is the minimum price that the farming-preprocessing division would be willing to sell cane juice to the processing-marketing division? Explain.

   f. What is the maximum price that the processing-marketing division would be willing to buy can juice from the farming-preprocessing division? Explain.

   g. In order to maximize the overall profits of Consolidated Sugar, what price should the company use for intracompany transfers of cane juice from the farming-preprocessing division to the processing-marketing division?

19-7. Phillips Industries manufactures a certain product that can be sold directly to retail outlets or to the Superior Company for further processing and eventual sale by them as a completely different product. The demand function for each of these markets is:

$$\text{Retail Outlets: } P_1 = 60 - 2Q_1$$
$$\text{Superior Company: } P_2 = 40 - Q_2$$

where P_1 and P_2 are the prices charged and Q_1 and Q_2 are the quantities sold in the respective markets. Phillips' total cost function for the manufacture of this product is:

$$TC = 10 + 8(Q_1 + Q_2)$$

   a. Determine Phillips' total profit function.

   b. What are the profit-maximizing price and output levels for the product in the two markets?

   c. At these levels of output, calculate the marginal revenue in each market.

   d. What are Phillips' total profits if the firm is effectively able to charge different prices in the two markets?

   e. Calculate the profit-maximizing level of price and output if Phillips is required to charge the same price per unit in each market. What are Phillips' profits under this condition?

Chapter 6 Capital Budgeting

READING
20 INVESTMENT DECISIONS USING THE CAPITAL ASSET PRICING MODEL

J. Fred Weston*

The Capital Asset Pricing Model permits the criteria for asset expansion decisions to be set out unambiguously and compactly. It generalizes the traditional weighted average cost of capital approach. This presentation emphasizes implementation and communication of the ideas. First, the theoretical framework is briefly summarized [3,9]. Second, an example illustrates concepts and computation procedures. Third, some practical implications are discussed.

Summary of Underlying Theory

The underlying model was set forth succinctly in an article in *Financial Management* by Logue and Merville [4] in Equation 1, repeated here with slight changes in notation.

$$E(R_j) = R_f + [E(R_m) - R_f]\beta_j \quad (1)$$

where $E(R_j)$ is the expected return on a security or real investment (these concepts are treated interchangeably as claims on a future income stream). R_f is a risk-free interest rate, $E(R_m)$ is the expected return on a broad-based market index (a portfolio of securities or real assets), and β_j is a measure of volatility of the individual security relative to market returns. β_j is measured by the ratio of the covariance of the returns of the individual security with market returns divided by the variance of market returns.

*Dr. Weston is Professor of Business Economics and Finance, University of California, Los Angeles. He is author and coauthor of a number of books and articles in finance.

Equation 1 states that the expected return on an individual security or real investment is represented by a risk-free rate of interest plus a risk premium. Earlier literature did not provide a theory for the determination of the risk premium. Capital market theory shows the risk premium to be equal to the market risk premium weighted by the index of the systematic risk of the individual security or real investment.

The nature of β was developed in detail by Logue and Merville [4]. For an individual security it reflects industry characteristics and management policies that determine how returns fluctuate in relation to variations in overall market returns. If the general economic environment is stable, if industry characteristics remain unchanged, and if management policies have continuity, the measure of β will be relatively stable when calculated for different time periods. However, if these conditions of stability do not exist, the value of β would vary.

The great advantage of Equation 1 is that all its factors other than β are market-wide constants. If β's are stable, the measurement of expected returns is straightforward. For example, the returns on the market for long periods have been shown by the studies of Fisher [2] to be at the 9%-10% level. The level of R_f has been characteristically at the 4%-5% level. Thus the expected return on an individual investment, using the lower of each of the two numbers and a β of 2, would be:

$$E(R_j) = 4\% + (9\% - 4\%)2 = 14\% \quad (1a)$$

The higher of each of the two figures gives an $E(R_j)$ of 15%:

$$E(R_j) = 5\% + (10\% - 5\%)2 = 15\%. \qquad (1b)$$

Under the conditions just described, the basic relation expressed in Equation 1 may become a criterion for capital budgeting decisions [8]. That is, the relation in Equation 1 can be extended to apply to the expected return $E(R_j^o)$ on an individual project and its volatility measure, β_j^o, as set forth in Equation 2:

$$E(R_j^o) > R_f + [E(R_m) - R_f]\,\beta_j^o. \qquad (2)$$

In inequality 2 the market constants remain. Variables for the individual firm now become variables for the individual project by addition of an appropriate superscript. Inequality 2 expresses the condition that must hold if the project is to be acceptable. The expected return on the new project must exceed the pure rate of interest plus the market risk premium weighted by β_j^o, the measure of the individual project's systematic risk.

The general relationship is illustrated in Exhibit 1. The criterion in graphical terms is to accept all projects that plot above the market line and reject all those that plot below the market line. Managers seek to find new projects such as A and B with returns in excess of the levels required by the risk-return market equilibrium relation illustrated in Exhibit 1. When such projects are added to the firm's operations, the expected returns on the firm's common stock (at its previous existing price) will be higher than required by the market line. These "excess returns" induce a rise in price until the return on the stock $E(R_j)$ is at an equilibrium level represented by the capital market line in Exhibit 1.

A comparison with the weighted average cost of capital ($WACC_j$) approach is also facilitated by this exhibit, where the weighted average cost of capital is shown as a horizontal line extending to the right from point $WACC_j$. If the WACC criterion is interpreted as "accept a project if $E(R_j^o)$ exceeds $WACC_j$," conflicting results may be obtained. The market price of risk (MPR) criterion would reject Project C while the WACC criterion would accept it. The opposite would exist for Project B. However, admittedly, it may be inappropriate to draw the WACC line as shown in Exhibit 1, since the weighted average cost of capital applies to a "given risk class" while the systematic risk of the firm clearly varies along the horizontal axis. The general concepts may now be illustrated more concretely.

Exhibit 1. Illustration of the Use of Investment Hurdle Rates

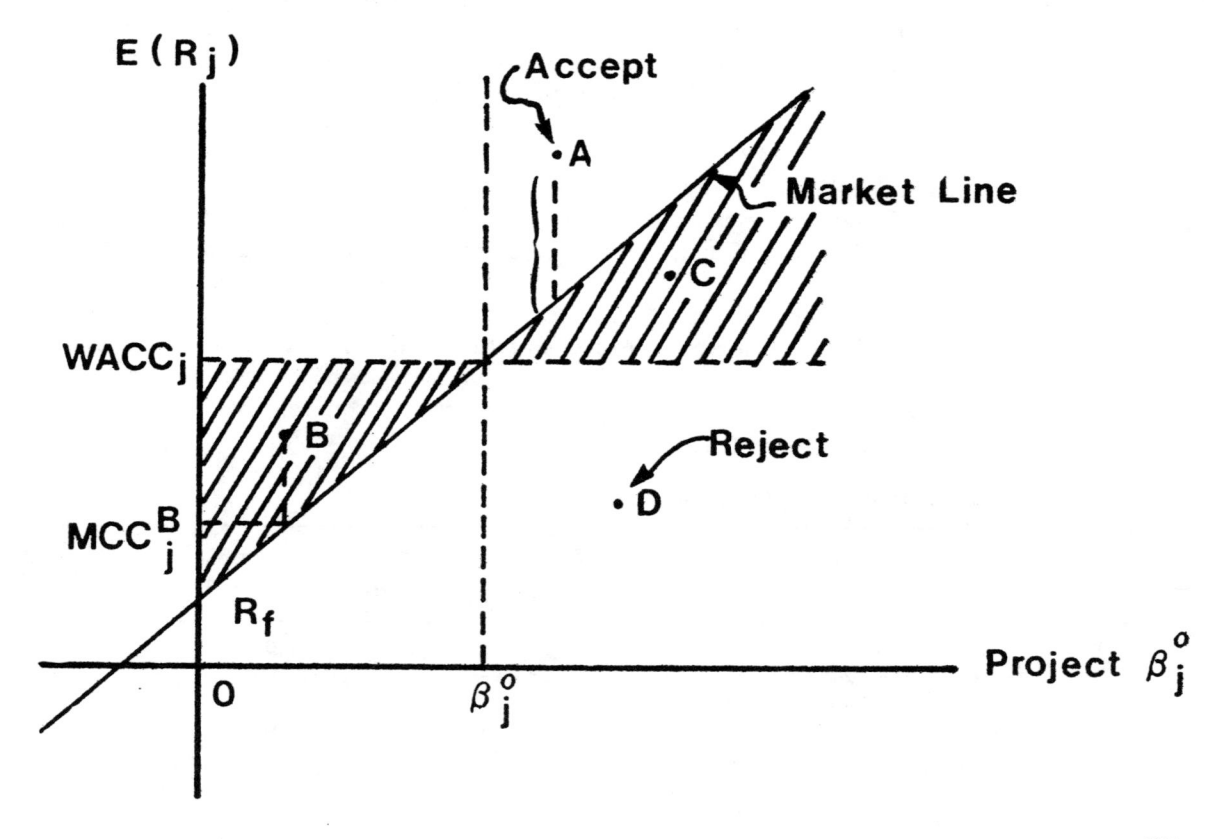

Decision Making in the Private Sector

Exhibit 2. Summary of Information—Mostin Case

(1) State of world (s)	(2) Subjective probability (π_s)	(3) Market return R_{ms}	(4) Proj. #1	(5) Proj. #2	(6) Proj. #3	(7) Proj. #4
			\multicolumn{4}{c}{Project rates of return}			
s = 1	.1	−.30	−.46	−1.00	−.40	−.40
s = 2	.2	−.10	−.26	− .50	−.20	−.20
s = 3	.3	.10	.46	.00	.00	.60
s = 4	.4	.30	.00	1.00	.70	.00

The Mostin Company Case

In the case that follows four states-of-the-world are considered with respect to future prospects for real growth in Gross National Product. State 1 represents a relatively serious recession, State 2 is a mild recession, State 3 is a mild recovery and State 4 is a strong recovery. The probabilities of these alternative future states-of-the-world are set forth in column 2 of Exhibit 2. Estimates of market returns and project rates of return are set forth in the remaining columns.

The Mostin Company is considering four projects in a capital expansion program. The Vice-President of Finance has estimated that the firm's weighted average cost of capital (WACC) is 12%. The Economics Staff projected the future course of the market portfolio over the estimated life span of the projects under each of the four states-of-the-world (first three columns in Exhibit 2); it recommended the use of a risk-free rate of return of 4%. The Finance Department provided the estimates of project returns conditional on the state-of-the-world (columns 4 through 7 in Exhibit 2). Each project involves an outlay of approximately $50,000.

Assuming that the projects are independent and that the firm can raise sufficient funds to finance all four projects, which projects would be accepted using the WACC and MPR criteria?

Solution Procedure

In Exhibit 3 the data provided by market relationships are utilized to calculate the expected return on the market along with its variance and standard deviation. The probabilities of the future states-of-the-world are multiplied by the associated market returns and their products are summed to obtain the expected market return $E(R_m)$ of 10%.

The expected market return $E(R_m)$ is used in calculating the variance and standard deviation of the market returns. This is shown in columns 4 through 6. The expected return is deducted from the return under each state, and deviations from $E(R_m)$ in column 4 are squared in column 5. In column 6 the squared deviations are multiplied by the probabilities of each expected future state (which appear in column 1). These products are summed to give the variance of the market return. The square root of the variance is its standard deviation.

A similar procedure is followed in Exhibit 4 for calculating the expected return and the covariance for each of the four individual projects. The expected return is obtained by multiplying the probability of each state times the associated forecasted return. The deviations of the return under each state from the expected return are next calculated in column 5. The deviations of the market returns from their mean are repeated for convenience. In column 8, the

Exhibit 3. Calculation of Market Parameters

(1) π	(2) R_m	(3) πR_m	(4) $R_m - E(R_m)$	(5) $[R_m - E(R_m)]^2$	(6) $\pi[R_m - E(R_m)]^2$
.1	−.30	−.03	−.40	.16	.016
.2	−.10	−.02	−.20	.04	.008
.3	.10	.03	0	0	0
.4	.30	.12	.20	.04	.016
		$E(R_m) = 10$		Var $R_m = .040$	$\sigma_m = .20$

136

Capital Budgeting

Exhibit 4. Calculation of Expected Returns and Covariances for the Four Hypothetical Projects

(1) Project number	(2) π	(3) R_j	(4) πR_j	(5) $[R_j - E(R_j)]$	(6) $[R_m - E(R_m)]$	(7) $[R_j - E(R_j)][R_m - E(R_m)]$	(8) $\pi[R_j - E(R_j)][R_m - E(R_m)]$
P1	.1	−.46	−.046	−.50	−.40	.200	.0200
	.2	−.26	−.052	−.30	−.20	−.060	.0120
	.3	.46	.138	.42	.00	.000	.0000
	.4	.00	.000	−.04	.20	−.008	−.0032
		$E(R_1) = .040$					$Cov(R_1, R_m) = .0288$
P2	.1	−1.00	−.10	−1.20	−.40	.480	.0480
	.2	−.50	−.10	−.70	−.20	.140	.0280
	.3	0	.00	−.20	.00	.000	.0000
	.4	1.00	.40	0.80	.20	.160	.0480
		$E(R_2) = .20$					$Cov(R_2, R_m) = .1400$
P3	.1	−.40	−.04	−.60	−.40	.240	.0240
	.2	−.20	−.04	−.40	−.20	.080	.0160
	.3	.00	.00	−.20	−.00	.000	.0000
	.4	+.70	.28	.50	.20	.100	.0400
		$E(R_3) = .20$					$Cov(R_3, R_m) = .0800$
P4	.1	−.40	−.04	−.50	−.40	.200	.0200
	.2	−.20	−.04	−.30	−.20	.060	.0120
	.3	.60	.18	.50	.00	.000	.0000
	.4	.00	.00	−.10	.20	−.020	−.0080
		$E(R_4) = .10$					$Cov(R_4, R_m) = .0240$

deviations of project returns are multiplied by the deviations of the market returns and by the probability factors to determine the covariance for each of the four projects.

In Exhibit 5, the beta for each project is calculated as the ratio of its covariance to the variance of the market return, and they are employed in Exhibit 6 to estimate the required return on each project in terms of the market line relationship. The risk-free rate of return is assumed to be 4% and market risk premium of 6%.

Required returns as shown in column 2 of Exhibit 6 are deducted from the estimated returns for each individual project to derive the "excess returns." These relations are depicted graphically in Exhibit 7.

The MPR criterion accepts the projects with positive excess returns, which appear above the MPR line. It rejects those with negative excess returns (plotted below the MPR line). The WACC criterion as portrayed in Exhibit 7 accepts projects with returns above 12% and rejects those with returns less than 12%. The two criteria give conflicting results for Project 2 and for Project 4.

It may be argued with justice that projects with different risk are in different risk classes and, therefore, the WACC line cannot be employed in this frame. This emphasizes the direct adjustments of the MPR criterion for risk differences and its development of the appropriate return-risk relations for making a determination of whether to accept or reject an individual project.

Applications

The same calculation procedures are now applied to the data of General Motors and Chrysler in Exhibits 8 and 9. In Exhibit 8, the return on the market is first calculated. Initially, the yearly percentage change in a broadly based stock market

Exhibit 5. Calculation of the Betas

$$\beta_1^0 = .0288/.04 = 0.72$$

$$\beta_2^0 = .1400/.04 = 3.50$$

$$\beta_3^0 = .0800/.04 = 2.00$$

$$\beta_4^0 = .0240/.04 = 0.60$$

Decision Making in the Private Sector

Exhibit 6. Calculation of Excess Returns

(1) Project number	Measurement of required return	(2)	(3) Estimated return	(4) Excess return
P1	$E(R_1) = .04 + .06(0.72) =$	.083	.040	−.043
P2	$E(R_2) = .04 + .06(3.50) =$	.250	.200	−.050
P3	$E(R_3) = .04 + .06(2.00) =$	.160	.200	.040
P4	$E(R_4) = .04 + .06(0.60) =$	.076	.100	.024

Exhibit 7. Application of the Asset Expansion Criterion

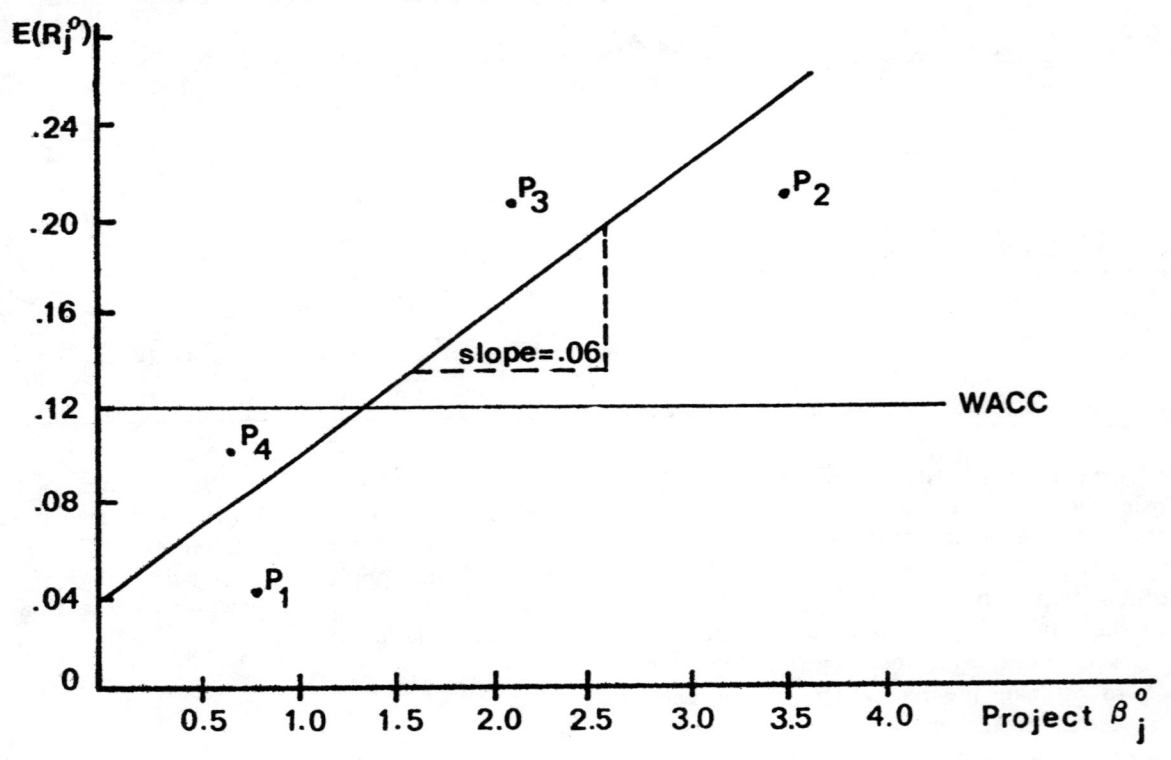

index is calculated. To each year's percentage change is added the dividend yield on the same index to obtain annual return on the market (column 2). Then, in a fashion similar to that used in Exhibit 3, the variance and standard deviation of market returns are calculated.

The risk-free return is calculated as an average of the risk-free returns over the previous ten-year period on 9- to 12-month U.S. government security issues. Theoretically, the use of shorter maturities would minimize the influence of price level rises. However, since these measures will be utilized to calculate expected returns on individual securities, there is good reason for calculating a risk-free return that includes the inflation influence. Exhibit 8 presents computations of a market return of 8.2%, a variance of approximately 1% and an estimated risk-free rate of 4.3%.

In the next step the analysis of the individual securities—General Motors Corporation and Chrysler Corporation—is undertaken (Exhibit 9). The requisite data on stock prices and dividend yields are readily available in widely used publications and financial services. From such sources the prices (P_t) are listed in column 1. In column 2 the annual percent change in price or capital gain percentage over the previous year is calculated $[(P_t/P_{t-1})-1]$. In column 3 the dividend yield is recorded. Column

Exhibit 8. Estimates of Market Parameters

(1) Year	(2) R_{mt}^*	(3) $[R_{mt}-E(R_m)]$	(4) $[R_{mt}-E(R_m)]^2$	(5) R_{ft}^{**}
1960	.07	(.01)	.0001	.05
1961	.18	.10	.0100	.03
1962	(.02)	(.10)	.0100	.03
1963	.20	.12	.0144	.03
1964	.16	.08	.0064	.04
1965	.11	.03	.0009	.04
1966	(.06)	(.14)	.0196	.04
1967	.16	.08	.0064	.05
1968	.11	.03	.0009	.05
1969	(.09)	(.17)	.0289	.07
	.82/10		.0976/9	.43/10

$E(R_m) = .082$ or approximately 8% $VAR(R_m) = .0108$ est $R_f = .043$

*Annual rates of return on market portfolio of 500 Standard & Poor's Stock Index (including dividend yields but before individual income taxes and individual transactions costs) compiled from the *Federal Reserve Bulletin*, various issues.

**Annual yields on 9-to-12 month U.S. government issues compiled from the *Federal Reserve Bulletin*, various issues.

4 is the sum of columns 2 and 3, representing the annual returns which are utilized to calculate an expected return of approximately 10% for General Motors and 21% for Chrysler Corporation.

On the basis of the numbers and calculations implicit in columns 5 through 7 the covariance is estimated for each company.

Beta values of 1.09 for General Motors Corporation and 2.94 for the Chrysler Corporation are obtained by dividing the covariance for each of the two companies by the market variance. In Exhibit 10 the expected returns for General Motors and Chrysler are calculated by utilizing market line relations. To the risk-free return is added the market risk differential times the individual company beta, indicating a return of 8.6% for General Motors and a return of 15.8% for Chrysler.

The orders of magnitude and the relations are highly plausible. Because these companies produce consumer durables with relatively high income elasticities of demand, their beta values are expected to be greater than one. The emphasis on forecasting initiated in the early 1920's along with other management qualities has apparently enabled GM to keep its beta close to one. Chrysler is a more risky security than GM. An overall required return on equity for GM in the range 9% to 11% and for Chrysler in the range of 15% to 20% seem reasonable first approximations. As is generally true, theory provides a basis for narrowing the boundaries for decisions. Analysis of additional economic and financial variables then provides a basis for determination of the appropriate cost of capital (or its range) to be employed in some variant of a sensitivity analysis of outcomes.

Further Implementation Aspects

The central practical implementation problem is the calculation of the betas for individual projects or for individual divisions in a company. This may represent a problem because market price data are not available either for individual projects or for individual divisions. One approach has already been provided in the illustrative Mostin Company Case. Estimates are required of alternative future states-of-the-world, and probabilities are attached to them which correspond to returns in the alternative future states. The prospective returns on the individual projects or divisions can be calculated in the same manner as illustrated in the Mostin Company Case.

An alternative procedure can also be used as a check on the previous calculations [8]. It involves multiplying three factors: (1) the price less variable cost margin, (2) the standard deviation of the turnover of operating investment to produce the product, normalized by the standard deviation of the market

Decision Making in the Private Sector

Exhibit 9. Calculation of Betas for GM and Chrysler

General Motors Corporation

	(1) P_t	(2) $\left[\frac{P_t}{P_{t-1}}\right]-1$	(3) $\frac{D_t}{P_t}$	(4) R_{jt}	(5) $[R_{jt}-E(R_j)]$	(6) *$[R_m-E(R_m)]$	(7) $[R_m-E(R_m)]$ $[R_{jt}-E(R_j)]$
1959	52						
1960	48	(.08)	.04	(.04)	(.14)	(.01)	.0014
1961	49	.02	.05	.07	(.03)	.10	(.0030)
1962	52	.06	.06	.12	.02	(.10)	(.0020)
1963	74	.42	.05	.47	.37	.12	.0444
1964	90	.22	.05	.27	.17	.08	.0136
1965	102	.13	.05	.18	.08	.03	.0024
1966	87	(.15)	.05	(.10)	(.20)	(.14)	.0280
1967	78	(.10)	.05	(.05)	(.15)	.08	(.0120)
1968	81	.04	.05	.09	(.01)	.03	(.0003)
1969	74	(.09)	.06	(.03)	(.13)	(.17)	.0221
				.98/10			.0946/8

$E(R_j) = .098$ or approximately 10%

$Cov(R_j, R_m) = .0118 \quad \beta_j = \frac{.0118}{.0108} = 1.093$

Chrysler Corporation

	(1)	(2)	(3)	(4)	(5)	(6)	(7)
1959	15						
1960	13	(.13)	.03	(.10)	(.31)	(.01)	.0031
1961	12	(.08)	.02	(.06)	(.27)	.10	(.0270)
1962	14	.17	.02	.19	(.02)	(.10)	.0020
1963	33	1.36	.01	1.37	1.16	.12	.1392
1964	51	.55	.02	.57	.36	.08	.0288
1965	54	.06	.02	.08	(.13)	.03	(.0039)
1966	45	(.17)	.04	(.13)	(.34)	(.14)	.0476
1967	44	(.02)	.05	.03	(.18)	.08	(.0144)
1968	60	.36	.03	.39	.18	.03	.0054
1969	44	(.27)	.05	(.22)	(.43)	(.17)	.0731
				2.12/10			.2539/8

$E(R_k) = .21$

$Cov(R_k, R_m) = .0317 \quad \beta_k = \frac{.0317}{.0108} = 2.94$

*$[R_m-E(R_m)]$ computed from column 4 in Exhibit 8.

returns, and (3) the correlation relation between the fluctuations in the economy as a whole and the output of the individual product or division of a company. The first two relations, which are calculated as a part of planning and control analysis, are fundamental determinants of the return on investment. They represent basic elements used in implementing the du Pont system of financial planning and control [10]. The third factor properly brings in the impact of the economic environment on fluctuations in the volume of sales for individual products or divisions.

The problem is somewhat more complex in planning a new product activity since historical data are not available. In this instance estimates will have to be made of the three factors described. From the pro-forma statements and budgets for the new project, sales estimates and total investment estimates can be utilized to formulate an estimate of sales turnover. Similarly, from the pro-forma income statements, a price less variable cost margin can be estimated. Covariance between the output of the pro-

Exhibit 10. Required Return for GM and Chrysler

$E(R_j) = R_f + [E(R_m) - R_f] \beta_j$

$E(R_j) = .043 + (.082 - .043) 1.09 = .086$ GM

$E(R_k) = .043 + (.082 - .043) 2.94 = .158$ Chrysler

duct and variations in the economy is related to the concept of income elasticity. From data on income elasticity, the correlation coefficient or beta may be estimated. The effort required is similar to that involved in sales and cost forecasting.

The assumptions of stability in the underlying relations will not always be met. As the characteristics of the economy change, different influences with different impacts on industries and firms vary from one time period to another. One period may be characterized by extreme monetary stringency, another by changes in tax rates, another by international factors. The firm must anticipate these broad economic changes and make the requisite adjustments.

Breen and Lerner have calculated betas for three companies over a large number of different monthly intervals [1] They observed that the wide range in the values of the betas raised doubts about the usefulness of the concept in practical applications. Their calculations of betas for General Motors, a company used in this article for illustration, for annual time intervals over periods of 6 or more years, were very close to the calculations reported here slightly over 1. Differences resulted when their calculations involved only one or two time periods or involved relatively short time intervals. As Professor Myers pointed out in commenting on their article, their calculations, based on a small number of observations, will result in standard errors so large that one would not reasonably utilize such estimates in practical application [6,7].

Concluding Comments

It should not be inferred that the procedures proposed for developing investment hurdle rates will be calculated or utilized mechanically. The methodology recommended provides another useful procedure for estimating the relevant cost of equity capital and, since leverage considerations have not been introduced, the overall cost of capital as well. Capital structure variations under leverage pose additional issues treated by Rubinstein [8].

Traditional methods of calculating the cost of equity capital have been based on either a variant of the Gordon model or regression studies. The use of the Gordon model prescribes calculating the cost of equity capital by Equation 3.

$$k = \frac{D}{P} + G \qquad (3)$$

Equation 3 states that the cost of equity capital is the dividend yield plus the expected growth rate of the firm. In practical application the expected growth rate is estimated by the use of historical data. Covariance is not likely to change as much as past growth rates versus future growth rates. Another alternative, of course, is to estimate a future growth rate. This would involve the same kind of forecasting required for forward-looking estimates of beta.

Another method of estimating the cost of capital, the more sophisticated regression studies, involve massive data collection. Problems of defining risk class must be met. The computation procedures make the use of a computer essential and the task of preparing the data for computer use is time consuming. Even after such massive efforts the results are not free from considerable disagreement and also require the use of managerial judgments for application.

Thus the MPR procedures involve smaller estimating difficulties and provide information on risk as well as return. Hence the MPR method provides a useful managerial aid. It is economical to develop. It is based on relevant theory. The resulting estimates cannot help but improve managerial judgments.

One great practical advantage of the market price of risk (MPR) criterion is that all but one of its statistical factors are market constants, applicable to all firms and to all projects. Also, since the required return is related to the project's beta, acceptance or rejection is a function of the investment's own systematic risk. By implication, application of the firm's overall cost of capital or some weighted average risk premium of the firm to individual divisions or projects with different risk characteristics is conceptually invalid.

The MPR criterion also underscores Myers' demonstration that diversification can be ignored in capital budgeting decisions [5]. Under the assumptions of his model, "homemade diversification" by investors is superior to diversification by business firms. However, if there is interdependence between the returns of individual projects, these "synergies" would have to be taken into account in the comparison of diversification by firms versus diversification by investors.

A great strength of the use of the capital asset pricing model is that it extends the application of neoclassical economic theory to a broad range of financial decisions. At a minimum, it provides a general framework for clarifying the assumptions of alternative criteria that have been employed. A great practical advantage of the new financial theory is utilization of the abundance of heretofore relatively neglected but readily available financial information such as that provided in the Standard & Poor's

Summary Sheets or the summary sheets provided in Moody's *Handbook of Common Stocks* (quarterly).

REFERENCES

1. W.J. Breen and E.M. Lerner, "On the Use of β in Regulatory Proceedings," *Bell Journal of Economics and Management Science* (Autumn 1972), p. 612.

2. L. Fisher, "Some New Stock-Market Indexes," *Journal of Business* (January 1966), p. 191.

3. M.C. Jensen, "Capital Markets: Theory and Evidence," *Bell Journal of Economics and Management Science* (Autumn 1972), p. 357.

4. D.E. Logue and L.J. Merville, "Financial Policy and Market Expectations," *Financial Management* (Summer 1972), p. 37.

5. S.C. Myers, "Procedures for Capital Budgeting Under Uncertainty," *Industrial Management Review* (Spring 1968).

6. S.C. Myers, "The Application of Finance Theory to Public Utility Rate Cases," *Bell Journal of Economics and Management Science* (Spring 1972), p. 58.

7. S.C. Myers, "On the Use of β in Regulatory Proceedings: A Comment," *Bell Journal of Economics and Management Science* (Autumn 1972), p. 622

8. M.E. Rubinstein, "A Synthesis of Corporate Financial Theory," *Journal of Finance* (March 1973), p. 167.

9. W.F. Sharpe, *Portfolio Theory and Capital Markets*, New York, McGraw-Hill Book Company, 1970.

10. J.F. Weston, "ROI Planning and Control: A Dynamic Management System," *Business Horizons* (August 1972), p. 35.

CASE

21 GENERAL MEDICAL CENTER—
CAPITAL BUDGETING PROBLEMS
OF AN URBAN HOSPITAL

General Medical Center is a medium-large, metropolitan hospital facility, serving an area of approximately one million people. The facility contains about 550 beds and a total staff of over 1,580 people as of the end of 1972. Included in the facility is a school of nursing and in-house training for non-nursing graduates and technical personnel. There is a house staff of medical doctors of about sixty-five, including five department chiefs (See Table 1 for report of services for 1971-72).

A partial listing of the types of units contained in the medical facility includes family practice, internal medicine, orthopedic surgery, surgery, urology, clinic, research lab, radiology, physical therapy, and pharmacy. The total revenues earned by this community not-for-profit hospital in 1972 were about $20 million.

The hospital financial staff prepares a 3-year capital budget for the entire Medical Center. All departments conduct an administrative review, list proposed projects, and establish priorities to be submitted to the executive committee of the Board of Directors for final approval. The total capital budget requested for the fiscal year 1973 was approximately $1,200,000. Of this total, about $350,000 was initially approved. Later, ten additional major projects were added to the list of requests for 1973 (See Table 2). The executive board of the Board of Directors of General Medical Center decided that only three of the supplemental proposals warranted further analysis at this time. Medical personnel representing the respective divisions proposing the major projects submitted supporting information for each proposal and gave a verbal presentation.

Dr. Evans, Chief of Surgery, spoke on behalf of a new cadiac surgery unit to be added to the surgery division. Due to the size and complexity of the project, a more thorough cost/benefit analysis was provided than is normally the case at the hospital.

The single most important factor giving social justification for the project is the emergency status of many cardiac patients. Often the patient is in need of immediate surgery, yet with the hospital's present facilities (heart catheterization laboratory) all that can be done is diagnostic work and minor treatment. Patients must be sent to the only clinic performing major open heart surgery; there was presently a 6-month waiting list for all but the most urgent cases.

During an average year, General Medical Center handled about 260 heart cases in its Heart Cathorization Laboratory, with about 75 percent of the total patients being referred to other hospitals. The remaining 25 percent were treated at General Medical. On average, about 195 cases needing further health care are generated by area cardiologists. For analysis of the proposed cardiovascular surgery unit, it was assumed that 120 of the 195 cases would be referred to General Medical Center by area cardiologists.

Presently, there are only two doctors performing open heart surgery in the area. It is necessary for them to travel to the only medical clinic with a cardiovascular surgery unit. General Medical Center sent a team of four administrators and doctors to Milwaukee, Wisconsin to observe open heart surgery and determine the equipment and support needs of such a facility.

One of the leading area heart surgeons, Dr. Milford, spent 6 months of intensive training at the Heart Clinic in Milwaukee, Wisconsin, actually performing open heart surgery. General Medical Center was recently able to attract Dr. Milford to join the full-time staff in residence. His duties would include overseeing the setting up of the cardiovascular surgery unit, if it were approved. In addition to Dr. Milford, another doctor on the hospital's staff was qualified to perform open heart surgery, and two operating room nurses were also sent to the Milwaukee, Wisconsin Heart Clinic for additional training.

Dr. Milford absorbed the cost of his training, but General Medical did pay him per diem. However, the entire cost of the training of the operating room nurses was absorbed by the hospital. The total training costs amounted to approximately $7,000.

One major cost savings of a new cardiovascular surgery unit would be the ability to utilize the existing facilities and operating room. Thus, there was no need to seek approval for new construction or plans. Also, since the project was under $100,000, it was

Decision Making in the Private Sector

Table 1 General Medical Center Report of Medical Services

	1972		1971
Beds in Service	as of 11/9/72	548	as of 11/1/71 546
Patients in Hospital			
First day		332	337
Admissions for			
Year		16,683	14,734
Medicine	4,052		3,181
Surgery	8,661		7,867
Family Practice	983		838
Maternity	2,217		2,304
Psychiatry	632		415
Pediatric	138		129
Total Treated		17,015	15,071
Discharges		16,664	14,739
In Hospital Last Day		351	332
Average Census		463	446
Medicine	125.6		122.6
Surgery	230.2		226.2
Family Practice	29.7		26.5
Maternity	30.0		32.5
Psychiatry	45.1		35.8
Pediatric	2.6		2.7
% of Occupancy		84.6	86.9
Average Length of			
Stay—Days		10.3	11.0
Medicine	12.3		15.0
Surgery	9.7		10.2
Family Practice	13.5		13.2
Maternity	4.8		5.0
Psychiatry	24.6		27.7
Pediatric	7.2		7.7

	1972	1971
Days of		
Patient Care	171,877	162,490
Medicine	46,606	44,635
Surgery	85,406	82,349
Family Practice	11,010	9,665
Maternity	11,160	11,845
Psychiatry	16,734	13,025
Pediatric	961	971
Newborn Days	9,163	9,741
Births	2,067	2,104
Operations	8,280	7,607
Deliveries	2,051	2,087
Deaths	533	530
Autopsies	278	231

Ambulatory Departmental Patient Visits

	1972	1971
Emergency Room	26,287	22,705
Clinic	15,523	13,134
Radiology	24,702	21,388
Laboratories	30,548	26,932
Physical Therapy	2,283	1,937
Pulmonary Function	557	241
Respiratory Therapy	34	89
Neurology	465	433
Operating Room	994	828
ElectroShock Therapy	57	95
Total	101,450	87,782

Comparison of statistics are for the year December 27, 1971 through December 31, 1972 and December 28, 1970 through December 26, 1971.

decided that it would not need outside financing, but it could be financed out of general operating funds of the hospital.

In further support of the investment proposal for the cardiovascular surgery unit, Dr. Evans submitted a "Proposed Capital Equipment and Operating Budget" (See Table 3) and a "Charge Proposal and Revenue Projection" for the first year (See Table 4).

The Capital Equipment and Operating Budget for the first year (Table 3) lists the total new equipment costs for the operating room ($37,994) and a two-bed recovery area ($32,800) for a total capital budget for the first year of $70,794. In addition, the operating budget for one year for the heart unit is estimated to cost $90,800.

Table 4 shows the Charge Proposal and Revenue Projection for the cardiovascular surgery unit for one year. Total operating costs for both the operating room and recovery area for the proposed cardiovascular surgery unit is $112,560 ($548 times 120 procedures annual plus $130 times 360 days of care).

Under the existing Medicare law, the Medical Center would be able to charge Medicare for 27 percent of the cost of the new equipment for the cardiac unit ($70,794) the first year, which would result in additional savings.

There were two potential problems for the Medical Center, stemming from the planned investment. First was the question of Medicare reimbursement for some percentage of patient health care resulting from the planned cardiovascular surgery unit. A second problem stemmed from the existing price controls on medical procedures.

The General Medical Center was presently on

Table 2 General Medical Center List of Ten Proposed Major Investment Projects 1973 Priorities

1. Purchase of Real Estate	$ 92,000
2. Ultrasonography	32,500
3. Relocate Hemodialysis	25,000
4. Expansion of Laboratories	10,000
5. Cardiac Surgery	71,000
6. Parking Deck #1 — $1,000,000. 1/4th	250,000
7. Radiation Therapy & Oncology — $425,000. 1/4th	106,000
8. Convert Delivery Rooms to GYN O.R.	35,000
9. Pocket Page	40,000
10. Remodel Nursing Office	20,000
	$681,500

Table 3 Cardiovascular Surgery Proposed Capital Equipment and Operating Budget
June 6, 1973

Capital Equipment—Operating Room

Monitoring Equipment	$26,900
Anesthesia Machine	6,500
Esophageal Stethoscope	94
Blood Gas Machine	2,500
Flame Photometer	500
Modification — Remco Pump	1,500
Total Operating Room	$37,994

Capital Equipment—Two-Bed Recovery Area

Monitoring Equipment	$25,000
Two MA-1 Respirators	6,000
Refrigerator	600
Defibrillator	1,200
Total Recovery Area	$32,800

Total Capital Budget — $70,794

Operating Budget—One Year

Salaries — O.R. (1)	$26,000
Salaries — Recovery (2)	36,000
Employee Benefits (3)	7,440
Depreciation (4)	14,160
Supplies	6,000
Misc. Expense	1,200

Total Operating Budget — $90,800

(1) 1 Perfusionist (operates heart machine) and 1 Technician
(2) 4 Nurses
(3) 12 Percent of Payroll
(4) 5-Year Equipment Life

Note: At the outset, three nurses and one technician presently employed in the Operating Room will be utilized for Cardiovascular Surgery. This salary and benefit cost is $40,800 per year with 60% or $24,480 used to determine direct expenses of performing cardiovascular surgery.

Table 4 Cardiovascular Surgery Charge Proposal and Revenue Projection
June 6, 1973

Operating Room (5)
Costs based upon 120 procedures annually:

Personnel Costs	$	435
Depreciation		63
Supplies and Miscellaneous		60
Total Direct Cost	$	548

Proposed Charge — $1,200 per procedure
Per Year Revenue — $144,000 for 120 procedures

Recovery Area (5)
Costs based upon 360 days of care annually (4):

Personnel Costs	$	112
Depreciation		18
Total Direct Cost	$	130

Proposed Charge — $200.00 per day
Per Year Revenue — $72,000 for 360 days of care

Total Revenue — $216,000

Notes: (1) INCU and CCU charge $122.
(2) St. Luke's, Milwaukee charges $194 for Surgical INCU and $800 for the Operating Room on a volume of 17 procedures per week.
(3) Massachusetts General charges $218 for Surgical INCU and $1,500 for the Operating Room—volume unknown.
(4) Each procedure requires approximately three days in recovery/intensive area.
(5) These costs are in addition to those shown in Table 3.

annual filing for Medicare reimbursements from the federal government. Their present average daily operating cost was $110, but the Medicare reimbursement was calculated at $103 per day. With the addition of the new equipment and machinery of the cardiac unit, the Center's daily operating costs will increase. The Center had filed for reimbursement in April, 1973. Also, they were planning to go to periodic interim payment (P.I.P) which would allow bi-weekly payments to be readjusted by auditing for Medicare services performed. Under the present annual filing procedure, the Medical Center had over $800,000 in Medicare receivables. This was being financed currently up to $207,000, at $17,000 per month.

The price freeze (Phase IV) caused some problem regarding shifting to the P.I.P. as planned by the Medical Center. Moreover, they could not increase the reimbursed rate for Medicare payments until after the price freeze was lifted.

The Center also faced a problem with existing price controls in establishing a planned pricing policy for medical treatment and care in the new cardiovascular surgery unit. It was felt by the Center's financial experts that the service of the open heart surgery unit would be fairly price inelastic; that is, people needing the surgery would not quibble over a "few extra dollars" for the operation, and in most cases the care was covered by a third party anyway.

General Medical Center's financial experts decided that the charges for the cardiac unit could be intially set at $1,200 per procedure in operating room and $200 per day in recovery area (See Table 4). According to the chief financial officer of the Medical Center, this charge was "way below" that charged by the nearest open heart surgery unit 30 miles away. Moreover, it was in line with the charges for similar facilities at St. Luke's Hospital, Milwaukee, and Massachusetts General (See footnotes, Table 4).

The two other projects (of the added 10 proposed shown in Table 2) being considered besides the cardiac surgery unit were a parking deck ($250,000) and the radiation therapy and oncology unit ($106,000). The overall proposal for the parking deck envisioned an eventual $1,000,000 investment, but one-fourth of the total would be in the fiscal 1973 capital budget. There were two possible means of financing this

Decision Making in the Private Sector

proposed project. Since the total project cost involved $1,000,000 or more, it qualified as a project eligible for outside, long-term funding.

The first type of possible financing for the parking deck would be for a group of doctors on the Center's staff to form a subchapter-S corporation and build the parking deck. This would allow the doctors to lease the facility back to the Center, while taking a rapid write-off for tax purposes of the new corporation. Moreover, the facility would earn revenues by charging parking fees. Once the doctors had fully recovered the cost of the facility, they could donate the parking deck back to the Medical Center at the "fair market value," dissolve the corporation, and deduct the gift from their personal income taxes.

The other possibility for financing the parking deck would be to issue a tax-exempt bond through the municipality. It was felt, however, by the Center's financial experts that the issue would be too small to gain any benefits. There would be 4 percent closing costs plus the interest cost of the debt for issues of $2-$5 million.

The final investment project considered by the Executive Committee of the Board of Directors was a radiation therapy and oncology unit at a cost of $425,000. One-fourth of the total would be spent in fiscal 1973 ($106,000).

Neither the parking deck nor the radiation therapy unit were supported by detailed cost/benefit analysis, as was attempted for the cardiac surgery unit. The

Appendix A   Statement of Operations

	Year Ended	
	December 31 1972 (53 weeks)	December 26 1971 (52 weeks) Restated Note C
Patient service revenue	$19,975,774	$16,673,332
Less:		
Allowances and contract adjustments	603,924	229,396
Provision for doubtful accounts	507,000	438,371
	1,110,924	667,767
	18,864,850	16,005,565
Other operating revenue	374,711	323,671
Total Operating Revenue	19,239,561	16,329,236
Operating expenses:		
Hospital:		
Patient services	9,973,348	8,693,228
Building operations	2,046,992	1,899,511
Food service	1,235,686	1,183,676
General and administrative	3,008,359	2,538,008
Provision for depreciation	867,517	823,255
Interest (principally on long-term debt)	433,861	445,614
	17,565,763	15,583,292
Education programs, less tuition (1972—$99,484; 1971—$68,935)	1,064,814	876,829
Total Operating Expenses	18,630,577	16,460,121
Income (Loss) from Operations before Nonoperating Revenues and Extraordinary Credit	608,984	(130,885)
Nonoperating revenues:		
Unrestricted gifts and bequests	47,554	17,708
Income and gains (losses) from Board-designated funds	(166)	11,526
	47,388	29,234
Income (Loss) before Extraordinary Credit	656,372	(101,651)
Extraordinary credit—increase in prior year Medicare reimbursement arising from legislative enactment—Note C	—0—	55,854
Net Income (Loss)	$ 656,372	$(45,797)

See notes to financial statements

Capital Budgeting

reasons given by the chief financial officer was the desire on the part of the chief of surgery to get quick approval for the cardiac unit. Also, the parking deck involved little controversy; there seemed to be a consensus of the need for such a facility. All that remained in doubt was the manner in which it would be financed.

Finally, the radiation therapy unit was a favorite project of the Women's Board of the Medical Center. They pledged to donate $125,000 toward the total cost of $425,000 for the entire unit. The Women's Board was in charge of running the gift shop, boutique, flower shop and snack bar in the Center. The Women's Board pledge would be paid over the four year period.

The Medical Center relied heavily on outside donations and internally generated funds to finance most of their projects. Since they were a private, nonprofit corporation, they felt that access to outside funds would be quite limited to them. Also, the prevailing attitude of the Board of Directors tended to mitigate against outside sources of funds. Moreover, it was the feeling of the financial officers that with a low rate of return for the Center their calculated cost of capital was about 2 or 3 percent, making it "cheaper" to finance themselves.

The Center did have open lines of credit with an outstanding balance of $600,000 in short-term loans at 6.25 percent. They generally get a lower interest charge from local banks. (See Appendix A for financial statements of General Medical Center.)

At their monthly meeting the executive committee decided to approve the parking deck and radiation therapy proposals. There was some question, however, relative to the cardiac surgery unit, and the board postponed a decision until their next meeting.

Appendix A (Page 2) Balance Sheet
Unrestricted Funds

	December 31 1972	December 26 1971 Restated Note C
Assets		
Current Assets		
Cash	$ 7,697	$ 82,859
Receivables:		
Patients and third-party payors	5,431,551	4,104,181
Medicare settlements—Note C	755,000	855,000
Allowances (deduction)	(735,000)	(510,000)
	5,451,551	4,449,181
Due from restricted funds	55,498	2,064
Inventories	290,842	307,039
Prepaid expenses	58,974	42,123
Total Current Assets	5,864,562	4,883,266
Board-Designated Assets		
Cash	39,703	38,461
Marketable securities	11,025	—0—
	50,728	38,461
Property, Plant, and Equipment—Note D		
Land and improvements	1,134,636	1,074,360
Buildings	17,619,990	17,599,777
Equipment	6,993,086	7,242,768
	25,747,712	25,916,905
Allowances for depreciation (deduction)	(5,281,025)	(4,930,277)
	20,466,687	20,986,628
	$26,381,977	$25,908,355

Appendix A (Page 3)

	December 31 1972	December 26 1971 Restated Note C
Liabilities and Equity		
Current Liabilities		
Notes payable to banks	$ 350,000	$ 535,000
Trade accounts payable	773,162	732,586
Employee compensation	750,501	789,985
Accrued expenses	700,918	380,154
Building project payables	61,476	275,478
Due to restricted funds	73,136	243,378
Current portion of mortgage note payable	322,876	302,601
Total Current Liabilities	3,032,069	3,259,182
Mortgage Note Payable, less portion classified as current liability—Note D	6,113,904	6,436,754
Deferred Credits		
Deferred pension costs	393,300	393,300
Deferred Medicare revenues	340,923	242,885
	734,223	636,185
Equity in Unrestricted Funds		
Working capital	2,832,493	1,624,084
Deferred credits (deduction)	(734,223)	(636,185)
Unallocated Equity	2,098,270	987,899
Board-designated assets	50,728	38,461
Property, plant, and equipment, less mortgage note payable	14,352,783	14,549,874
Total Equity	16,501,781	15,576,234
	$26,381,977	$25,908,355

See notes to financial statements

Appendix A (Page 4)

Balance Sheet Restricted Funds

	December 31 1972	December 26 1971
Special Purpose Funds		
Assets		
Cash	$ 49,185	$ 29,539
Marketable securities	2,978	3,116
Notes and accounts receivable	68,774	62,999
Due from unrestricted funds	73,136	140,323
Total	$194,073	$235,977
Liabilities and Equity		
Accounts payable	$ 3,088	$ 560
Due to unrestricted funds	498	2,064
Fund equity	190,487	233,353
Total	$194,073	$235,977
Building Fund		
Assets		
Cash	$ 5,224	$ 23,325
Marketable securities	1,654	1,654
Grant receivable	65,000	—0—
Pledges receivable, less allowance	10,524	12,893
Due from unrestricted funds	—0—	103,055
Total	$ 82,402	$140,927
Equity		
Due to unrestricted funds	$ 55,000	$ —0—
Fund equity	27,402	140,927
Total	$ 82,402	$140,927

See notes to financial statements

Appendix A (Page 5)   Statement of Changes in Equity Balances

Years ended December 31, 1972 and December 26, 1971

	Unrestricted Purposes	Restricted to Special Purposes	Restricted to Building Purposes
Balances at December 28, 1970:			
As previously reported	$14,643,192	$ 218,409	$ 694,887
Adjustments—Note C	89,876	—0—	—0—
As restated	14,733,068	218,409	694,887
Net loss for 1971—restated	(45,797)	—0—	—0—
Restricted gifts and bequests	—0—	95,491	—0—
Income from restricted investments	—0—	641	3,056
Grants	—0—	—0—	270,947
Additions to property, plant, and equipment from restricted sources	888,963	(61,000)	(827,963)
Fund expenditures	—0—	(20,188)	—0—
Balances at December 26, 1971	15,576,234	233,353	140,927
Net income for 1972	656,372	—0—	—0—
Restricted gifts and bequests	—0—	70,788	—0—
Income from restricted investments	—0—	1,590	270
Grant	—0—	—0—	65,000
Additions to property, plant, and equipment from restricted sources	269,175	(90,380)	(178,795)
Fund expenditures	—0—	(24,864)	—0—
Balances at December 31, 1972	$16,501,781	$ 190,487	$ 27,402

( ) Indicates negative figure
See notes to financial statements

Decision Making in the Private Sector

Appendix A (Page 6) — Statement of Changes in Financial Position

	Year Ended	
	December 31, 1972 (53 weeks)	December 26, 1971 (52 weeks) Restated Note C
Source of Funds		
From operations:		
Net income (loss) before extraordinary credit	$ 656,372	$(101,651)
Add items included in operations not requiring funds:		
Provision for depreciation	867,517	823,255
Increase in deferred Medicare revenues	98,038	113,349
Total from operations before extraordinary credit	1,621,927	834,953
Extraordinary credit	—0—	55,854
Total from Operations	1,621,927	890,807
Transfers from restricted funds	269,175	888,963
Other	—0—	14,935
Totals	$1,891,102	$1,794,705
Application of Funds		
Additions to property, plant and equipment	$ 347,576	$1,194,029
Payments and transfer to current maturity on mortgage note payable	322,850	302,566
Other	12,267	—0—
Increase in working capital	1,208,409	298,110
Totals	$1,891,102	$1,794,705
Increases (Decreases) in the Components of Working Capital		
Cash	$(75,162)	$ 30,047
Receivables	1,002,370	34,158
Due from special purpose funds	53,434	2,064
Inventories	(16,197)	66,224
Prepaid expenses	16,851	7,379
Notes payable to banks	185,000	(355,000)
Trade account and building project payables	173,426	405,806
Employee compensation and accrued expenses	(281,280)	(301,097)
Due to restricted funds	170,242	450,450
Current portion of mortgage note payable	(20,275)	(41,921)
Increase in Working Capital	$1,208,409	$ 298,110

See notes to financial statements

Appendix A (Page 7) — Notes to Financial Statements

December 31, 1972 and December 26, 1971

Note A — The Corporation

General Medical Center was incorporated on December 6, 1928, as an organization exempt from federal income taxes, for the purpose of providing health care services to the community. No capital has been paid or contributed to the Corporation.

The Medical Center's reporting period is the fifty-two, fifty-three week fiscal year. The one week differential between 1972 and 1971 does not significantly affect the comparability of the accompanying financial statements. The Medical Center has adopted the calendar year for future reporting purposes.

Note B — Accounting Policies and Practices

The Medical Center's financial statements are prepared in accordance with the Hospital Audit Guide promulgated by the American Institute of Certified Public Accountants. A summary of the more significant policies and practices, which have been consistently followed in the preparation of the financial statements, are set forth below.

Capital Budgeting

Unrestricted Funds—These funds have originated from unrestricted gifts or income accumulated in previous years and their use is totally within the discretion of the governing board. Gifts and bequests that are not restricted by the donor and the investment income thereon are reported in the statement of operations as nonoperating revenues.

Restricted Funds—Gifts and bequests which are restricted as to use by the donor are reported as restricted assets. Restricted assets and related income are credited directly to the respective fund balance.

Board-designated Funds—Unrestricted cash has been designated by the governing board generally for the payment of the mortgage note. An accumulation of funds for these debt payments is made in an amount equivalent to the depreciation reported as operating expenses in the statement of operations.

Inventories—Inventories are stated at cost (first-in, first-out method) not in excess of market.

Property, Plant, and Equipment—Property, plant, and equipment is recorded at cost. Routine maintenance, repairs, renewals, and replacement costs are charged against income. Expenditures which significantly increase values, change capacities, or extend useful lives are capitalized. Depreciation is computed by the straight-line method at rates calculated to amortize the cost of the assets over their estimated useful lives. The estimated useful lives of buildings is 50 years and 4 to 16-2/3 years for equipment.

Patient Service Revenues—Patient service revenues are reported on the accrual basis in the period in which services are provided, at established rates regardless of whether collection in full is expected. Services rendered to patients under contractual arrangements, principally the Medicare program, are reimbursed at the cost per patient day, as defined, which is generally less than the established billing rate. Accordingly, arrangements for services at less than established rates, as well as the recognition of charity allowances and uncollectible accounts, are provided for in the financial statements and are reflected as reductions of patient service revenues.

Deferred Medicare Revenues—The Medical Center uses an accelerated depreciation method for Medicare reimbursement purposes as opposed to the straight-line method for financial statement purposes. The reimbursement arising from the additional depreciation for Medicare reporting purposes is deferred, and will be subsequently recognized as revenue in the statement of operations over the years the related depreciation is recognized as expense in the same statement.

Pension Plan—The Medical Center's policy is to fund current pension costs accrued.

Appendix A (Page 8)   Notes to Financial Statements — Continued

Note C — Estimated Medicare Settlements

Revenues and receivables arising from services to Medicare patients are subject to audit and final settlement between the Medical Center and the Medicare intermediary. The Medicare reports for 1971 and 1972 are subject to audit.

Early in 1973 the Medicare reports for 1968, 1969, and 1970 were finally settled with the Medicare intermediary. The settlements for 1969 and 1970 were cumulatively $219,412 ($89,876 after giving effect to deferred Medicare revenues) greater than the amounts estimated by the Medical Center. Accordingly, the accompanying financial statements have been restated to reflect these prior year adjustments. In addition, the settlement amount for 1971 was also redetermined and the results of operations for 1971 have also been restated.

During 1971, legislation was enacted, retroactive to July 1, 1969 and increasing the amounts reimbursable under the Medicare program, which gave recognition to the greater amount of nursing care required by elderly patients. The amount of nursing differential relative to years prior to 1971 has been reflected as an extraordinary credit in 1971.

Note D — Mortgage Note

The Medical Center has executed a note in the amount of $7,000,000, secured by a first mortgage on substantially all of the Medical Center's plant and property. The note requires monthly payments of $60,980, including interest at 6½ percent per annum.

Note E — Pension Plan

The Medical Center has a contributory pension plan covering substantially all employees. Total pension expense was approximately $303,000 and $221,000 for 1972 and 1971, respectively. The expense for 1972 included the amortization of past service costs over 30 years. No provision for past service costs was made in 1971 as deferred pension costs approximated unfunded past service costs.

The total value of the fund assets and balance sheet accruals exceeds the actuarially computed value of vested benefits at January 1, 1973.

Questions for Discussion

1. List and discuss the unique aspects of a capital budgeting decision for a large medical facility.
2. Use the payback and net present value methods to arrive at an evaluation of the investment decision in the cardiovascular unit.
3. How should the expected flow of earnings from medical care investments be assessed when there are substantial social as well as economic benefits?
4. Should the executive committee of the medical center approve the investment in a cardiovascular surgery unit?

EXERCISES
22

22-1. The engineering department of a company is proposing to buy a new computer-controlled drafting machine for $1,000,000. It is expected to save 20,000 drafting work-hours per year, with each work-hour costing the company $10 in wages and fringe benefits. The firm uses straight-line depreciation and the drafting machine is expected to have a useful life of 10 years with a zero salvage value at the end of that period. The firm's cost of capital is 9 percent and its marginal income tax rate is 50 percent. Compute the following quantities:
   a. payback period
   b. internal rate of return
   c. net present value

   Based on the net present value criterion, should the company buy the drafting machine?

22-2. Equipment replacement. Alliance Manufacturing Company is considering the purchase of a new, automated drill press to replace an older one. The machine now in operation has a book value of zero and a salvage value of zero. However, it is in good working condition with an expected life of 10 additional years. The new drill press is more efficient than the existing one and, if installed, will provide an estimated cost savings (i.e. labor, materials, maintenance) of $6,000 per year. The new machine costs $25,000 delivered and installed. It has an estimated useful life of 10 years, and a salvage value of $1,000 at the end of this period. The firm's cost of capital is 14 percent and its marginal income tax rate is 40 percent. The firm uses the straight-line depreciation method.
   a. What is the net cash flow in year zero (i.e. initial outlay)?
   b. What are the net cash flows after taxes in each of the next 10 years?
   c. What is the net present value of the investment?
   d. Should Alliance replace its existing drill press?

22-3. Equipment replacement. Let us reconsider the Alliance Manufacturing Company equipment replacement problem discussed above (See Problem 22-2). Suppose that the old drill press, rather than having a current book and salvage value of zero, has a book value of $10,000 and a salvage value of $5,000. Assume that it was purchased 5 years ago for $15,000 and is being depreciated on a straight-line basis over a 15-year life with an estimated salvage value of zero at the end of this period. How does this alter the results obtained above (in Problem 22-2)? First, in year zero, Alliance will receive the proceeds from the sale of the old drill press. Also, the firm will incur a book loss on the disposal of the old drill press. The book loss, which is not a cash flow, is equal to the difference between its book value and its salvage value. While this book loss is not a cash flow, it will reduce Alliance's taxable income and, hence, reduce income taxes in year zero. What will be the tax saving? Second, in years 1 to 10, Alliance will forego the depreciation of its old drill press if it purchases the new automated one. This will reduce yearly depreciation expenses, increase net income before taxes, and, hence, increase income taxes (a cash flow). How much additional income taxes will be paid each year as a result?

Answer questions a.-d. of Problem 22-2 taking into account these additional cash flows.

22-4. **Equipment replacement.** The Wilcox Company purchased a metal lathe 5 years ago at a cost of $7,500. The machine had a life expectancy of 15 years at the time of purchase and a zero estimated salvage value at the end of the 15-year period. It is being depreciated on a straight-line basis and has a book value of $5,000. Its current market (i.e. salvage) value is $1,000. The plant manager reports that the firm can buy a new lathe for $10,000 including installation, and it will reduce labor and raw materials usage sufficiently to cut annual operating costs from $7,000 to $5,000 per year for 10 years. Depreciation will be on a straight-line basis with an estimated salvage value of zero. Corporate income taxes are at a 50 percent rate and the firm's cost of capital is 10 percent.
   a. What is the net cash flow in year zero?
   b. What are the net cash flows after taxes in each of the next 10 years?
   c. What is the net present value of the investment?
   d. Should Wilcox purchase the new lathe?

22-5. The Audio Warehouse Company, a wholesale distributor of stereo equipment, has decided to purchase a small computer system to automate the accounting department. Two computer companies are bidding for the order—each requiring an initial investment of $7,500 with an expected life of 5 years and a zero salvage value at the end of this period. One of the computers utilizes more advanced technology and is expected to be more efficient than the other computer. However, the more advanced computer has not been fully tested in an operational setting and, consequently, the estimated annual savings are more uncertain. The probability distributions of the estimated cost savings for each computer are given below. The firm uses the risk-adjusted discount rate approach in evaluating investment projects and has assigned a risk premium of 5 percent to the computer whose estimated savings are more uncertain. Audio Warehouse's cost of capital is 9 percent and its marginal income tax rate is 40 percent. The firm uses the straight-line depreciation method.

Computer A		Computer B	
Annual Savings	Probability	Annual Savings	Probability
$2,000	.1	$ 0	.2
2,500	.4	3,000	.3
3,000	.4	4,000	.3
3,500	.1	5,000	.2

Decision Making in the Private Sector

a. What are the expected annual savings for each computer?*
b. What are the expected annual net cash flows after taxes for each computer?
c. Calculate the standard deviation of the annual savings for each computer.** Based on the standard deviation as measure of risk, which computer has more uncertain annual savings?
d. What is the net present value of each investment when evaluated at its appropriate risk-adjusted discount rate?
e. Which computer (A or B) would you recommend that Audio Warehouse purchase?

22-6. Michigan Engineering Company has the following capital structure (December 31, 1975):

Long-term Debt	
Bank loan†	$ 4,000,000
Debentures (8's 30 year, due 2000)††	14,000,000
Total Long-term Debt	$18,000,000
Stockholders' Equity	
Common stock (5 million shares, $1 par value)‡	5,000,000
Capital in excess of par value	7,500,000
Retained earnings	1,500,000
Total Stockholders' Equity	$14,000,000
Total Long-term Debt and Stockholder's Equity	$32,000,000

Dividends have been growing at an average compound yearly rate of 5 percent over the past several years and this rate of increase is expected to continue for the foreseeable future. Based on this assumption, next year's dividend is forecasted to be $.30 per share. The marginal corporate income tax rate is 35 percent. Using market weights, compute Michigan Engineering Company's weighted-average cost of capital.

---

*Recall that the formula for the expected value is

$$E(X) = \Sigma X \cdot P(X)$$

where X is the annual savings and P(X) is the probability of the annual savings.

**Recall that the formula for the standard deviation is

$$\sigma(X) = \sqrt{\sum_{\text{All outcomes (X)}} [X - E(X)]^2 P(X)}$$

where X is the annual savings, E(X) is the expected annual savings, and P(X) is the probability of the annual savings.

† The bank loan represents the amount outstanding under a revolving credit agreement with a bank, bearing an interest rate of 10.0% (2% above the prime rate).

††The current yield to maturity on the debentures is 9.0% and the current price is $90 (per $100 of principal).

‡The stock currently sells for $5 per share.

Part Three Issues in Regulation, Market Structure, Conduct, and Performance

Chapter 7 Regulating the Private Corporation

READING
23 THE THEORY OF ECONOMIC REGULATION
George J. Stigler
THE UNIVERSITY OF CHICAGO

The potential uses of public resources and powers to improve the economic status of economic groups (such as industries and occupations) are analyzed to provide a scheme of the demand for regulation. The characteristics of the political process which allow relatively small groups to obtain such regulation is then sketched to provide elements of a theory of supply of regulation. A variety of empirical evidence and illustration is also presented.

■ The state—the machinery and power of the state—is a potential resource or threat to every industry in the society. With its power to prohibit or compel, to take or give money, the state can and does selectively help or hurt a vast number of industries. That political juggernaut, the petroleum industry, is an immense consumer of political benefits, and simultaneously the underwriters of marine insurance have their more modest repast. The central tasks of the theory of economic regulation are to explain who will receive the benefits or burdens of regulation, what form regulation will take, and the effects of regulation upon the allocation of resources.

Regulation may be actively sought by an industry, or it may be thrust upon it. A central thesis of this paper is that, as a rule, regulation is acquired by the industry and is designed and operated primarily for its benefit. There are regulations whose net effects upon the regulated industry are undeniably onerous; a simple example is the differentially heavy taxation of the industry's product (whiskey, playing cards). These onerous regulations, however, are exceptional and can be explained by the same theory that explains beneficial (we may call it "acquired") regulation.

Two main alternative views of the regulation of industry are

The author obtained the B.B.A. degree from the University of Washington, the M.B.A. degree from Northwestern, and the Ph.D. degree from the University of Chicago. He is presently Charles R. Walgreen Distinguished Service Professor of American Institutions at the University of Chicago, and has published numerous articles and texts in the field of economics. Dr. Stigler is Vice Chairman of the Securities Investor Protective Commission.

widely held. The first is that regulation is instituted primarily for the protection and benefit of the public at large or some large subclass of the public. In this view, the regulations which injure the public—as when the oil import quotas increase the cost of petroleum products to America by $5 billion or more a year—are costs of some social goal (here, national defense) or, occasionally, perversions of the regulatory philosophy. The second view is essentially that the political process defies rational explanation: "politics" is an imponderable, a constantly and unpredictably shifting mixture of forces of the most diverse nature, comprehending acts of great moral virtue (the emancipation of slaves) and of the most vulgar venality (the congressman feathering his own nest).

Let us consider a problem posed by the oil import quota system: why does not the powerful industry which obtained this expensive program instead choose direct cash subsidies from the public treasury? The "protection of the public" theory of regulation must say that the choice of import quotas is dictated by the concern of the federal government for an adequate domestic supply of petroleum in the event of war—a remark calculated to elicit uproarious laughter at the Petroleum Club. Such laughter aside, if national defense were the goal of the quotas, a tariff would be a more economical instrument of policy: it would retain the profits of exclusion for the treasury. The non-rationalist view would explain the policy by the inability of consumers to measure the cost to them of the import quotas, and hence their willingness to pay $5 billion in higher prices rather than the $2.5 billion in cash that would be equally attractive to the industry. Our profit-maximizing theory says that the explanation lies in a different direction: the present members of the refining industries would have to share a cash subsidy with all new entrants into the refining industry.[1] Only when the elasticity of supply of an industry is small will the industry prefer cash to controls over entry or output.

This question, why does an industry solicit the coercive powers of the state rather than its cash, is offered only to illustrate the approach of the present paper. We assume that political systems are rationally devised and rationally employed, which is to say that they are appropriate instruments for the fulfillment of desires of members of the society. This is not to say that the state will serve any person's concept of the public interest: indeed the problem of regulation is the problem of discovering when and why an industry (or other group of like-minded people) is able to use the state for its purposes, or is singled out by the state to be used for alien purposes.

1. What benefits can a state provide to an industry?

■ The state has one basic resource which in pure principle is not shared with even the mightiest of its citizens: the power to coerce. The state can seize money by the only method which is permitted by the laws of a civilized society, by taxation. The state can ordain

[1] The domestic producers of petroleum, who also benefit from the import quota, would find a tariff or cash payment to domestic producers equally attractive. If their interests alone were consulted, import quotas would be auctioned off instead of being given away.

the physical movements of resources and the economic decisions of households and firms without their consent. These powers provide the possibilities for the utilization of the state by an industry to increase its profitability. The main policies which an industry (or occupation) may seek of the state are four.

The most obvious contribution that a group may seek of the government is a direct subsidy of money. The domestic airlines received "air mail" subsidies (even if they did not carry mail) of $1.5 billion through 1968. The merchant marine has received construction and operation subsidies reaching almost $3 billion since World War II. The education industry has long shown a masterful skill in obtaining public funds: for example, universities and colleges have received federal funds exceeding $3 billion annually in recent years, as well as subsidized loans for dormitories and other construction. The veterans of wars have often received direct cash bonuses.

We have already sketched the main explanation for the fact that an industry with power to obtain governmental favors usually does not use this power to get money: unless the list of beneficiaries can be limited by an acceptable device, whatever amount of subsidies the industry can obtain will be dissipated among a growing number of rivals. The airlines quickly moved away from competitive bidding for air mail contracts to avoid this problem.[2] On the other hand, the premier universities have not devised a method of excluding other claimants for research funds, and in the long run they will receive much-reduced shares of federal research monies.

The second major public resource commonly sought by an industry is control over entry by new rivals. There is considerable, not to say excessive, discussion in economic literature of the rise of peculiar price policies (limit prices), vertical integration, and similar devices to retard the rate of entry of new firms into oligopolistic industries. Such devices are vastly less efficacious (economical) than the certificate of convenience and necessity (which includes, of course, the import and production quotas of the oil and tobacco industries).

The diligence with which the power of control over entry will be exercised by a regulatory body is already well known. The Civil Aeronautics Board has not allowed a single new trunk line to be launched since it was created in 1938. The power to insure new banks has been used by the Federal Deposit Insurance Corporation to reduce the rate of entry into commercial banking by 60 percent.[3] The interstate motor carrier history is in some respects even more striking, because no even ostensibly respectable case for restriction on entry can be developed on grounds of scale economies (which are in turn adduced to limit entry for safety or economy of operation). The number of federally licensed common carriers is shown in Figure 1: the immense growth of the freight hauled by trucking common carriers has been associated with a steady secular decline of numbers of such carriers. The number of applications for new certificates has been in excess of 5000 annually in recent years: a rigorous proof that hope springs eternal in an aspiring trucker's breast.

We propose the general hypothesis: every industry or occupation that has enough political power to utilize the state will seek to control entry. In addition, the regulatory policy will often be so fashioned

[2] See [7], pp. 60 ff.
[3] See [10].

Issues in Regulation, Market Structure, Conduct, and Performance

as to retard the rate of growth of new firms. For example, no new savings and loan company may pay a dividend rate higher than that prevailing in the community in its endeavors to attract deposits.[4] The power to limit selling expenses of mutual funds, which is soon to be conferred upon the Securities and Exchange Commission, will serve to limit the growth of small mutual funds and hence reduce the sales costs of large funds.

One variant of the control of entry is the protective tariff (and the corresponding barriers which have been raised to interstate movements of goods and people). The benefits of protection to an industry, one might think, will usually be dissipated by the entry of new domestic producers, and the question naturally arises: Why does the industry not also seek domestic entry controls? In a few industries (petroleum) the domestic controls have been obtained, but not in most. The tariff will be effective if there is a specialized domestic resource necessary to the industry; oil-producing lands is an example. Even if an industry has only durable specialized resources, it will gain if its contraction is slowed by a tariff.

A third general set of powers of the state which will be sought by the industry are those which affect substitutes and complements. Crudely put, the butter producers wish to suppress margarine and encourage the production of bread. The airline industry actively supports the federal subsidies to airports; the building trade unions have opposed labor-saving materials through building codes. We shall examine shortly a specific case of inter-industry competition in transportation.

The fourth class of public policies sought by an industry is directed to price-fixing. Even the industry that has achieved entry control will often want price controls administered by a body with coercive powers. If the number of firms in the regulated industry is even moderately large, price discrimination will be difficult to maintain in the absence of public support. The prohibition of interest on demand deposits, which is probably effective in preventing interest payments to most non-business depositors, is a case in point. Where there are no diseconomies of large scale for the individual firm (e.g., a motor trucking firm can add trucks under a given license as common carrier), price control is essential to achieve more than competitive rates of return.

☐ **Limitations upon political benefits.** These various political boons are not obtained by the industry in a pure profit-maximizing form. The political process erects certain limitations upon the exercise of cartel policies by an industry. These limitations are of three sorts.

First, the distribution of control of the industry among the firms in the industry is changed. In an unregulated industry each firm's influence upon price and output is proportional to its share of industry output (at least in a simple arithmetic sense of direct capacity to change output). The political decisions take account also of the political strength of the various firms, so small firms have a larger influence than they would possess in an unregulated industry. Thus, when quotas are given to firms, the small firms will almost always receive larger quotas than cost-minimizing practices would allow.

[4] The Federal Home Loan Bank Board is the regulatory body. It also controls the amount of advertising and other areas of competition.

FIGURE 1

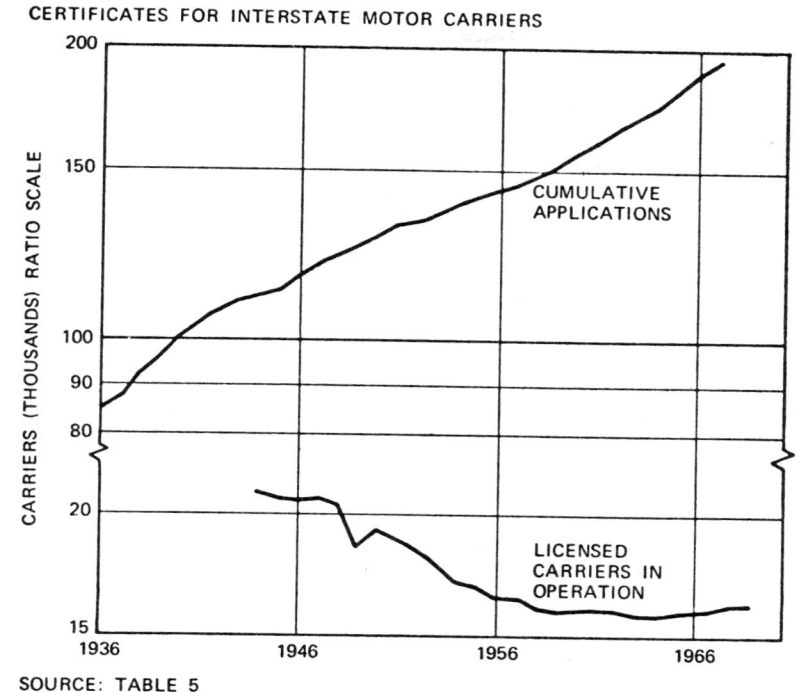

CERTIFICATES FOR INTERSTATE MOTOR CARRIERS

[Figure: Graph showing cumulative applications rising from about 85 thousand in 1936 to nearly 200 thousand by 1966, while licensed carriers in operation decline from about 25 thousand to around 16 thousand over the same period. Y-axis: Carriers (thousands) ratio scale, 15 to 200. X-axis: 1936 to 1966.]

SOURCE: TABLE 5

The original quotas under the oil import quota system will illustrate this practice (Table 1). The smallest refiners were given a quota of 11.4 percent of their daily consumption of oil, and the percentage dropped as refinery size rose.[5] The pattern of regressive benefits is characteristic of public controls in industries with numerous firms.

Second, the procedural safeguards required of public processes are costly. The delays which are dictated by both law and bureaucratic thoughts of self-survival can be large: Robert Gerwig found the price of gas sold in interstate commerce to be 5 to 6 percent higher than in intrastate commerce because of the administrative costs (including delay) of Federal Power Commission reviews [5].

Finally, the political process automatically admits powerful outsiders to the industry's councils. It is well known that the allocation of television channels among communities does not maximize industry revenue but reflects pressures to serve many smaller communities. The abandonment of an unprofitable rail line is an even more notorious area of outsider participation.

These limitations are predictable, and they must all enter into the calculus of the profitability of regulation of an industry.

☐ **An illustrative analysis.** The recourse to the regulatory process is of course more specific and more complex than the foregoing sketch suggests. The defensive power of various other industries which are affected by the proposed regulation must also be taken into account. An analysis of one aspect of the regulation of motor trucking will illustrate these complications. At this stage we are concerned only with the correspondence between regulations and economic interests;

[5] The largest refineries were restricted to 75.7 percent of their historical quota under the earlier voluntary import quota plan.

Issues in Regulation, Market Structure, Conduct, and Performance

TABLE 1
IMPORT QUOTAS OF REFINERIES AS PERCENT
OF DAILY INPUT OF PETROLEUM
(DISTRICTS I – IV, JULY 1, 1959 – DEC. 31, 1959)

SIZE OF REFINERY (THOUSANDS OF BARRELS)	PERCENT QUOTA
0–10	11.4
10–20	10.4
20–30	9.5
30–60	8.5
60–100	7.6
100–150	6.6
150–200	5.7
200–300	4.7
300 AND OVER	3.8

SOURCE: HEARING, SELECT COMMITTEE ON SMALL BUSINESS, U. S. CONGRESS, 88th CONG., 2nd SESS., AUG. 10 AND 11, 1964, [12] P. 121.

later we shall consider the political process by which regulation is achieved.

The motor trucking industry operated almost exclusively within cities before 1925, in good part because neither powerful trucks nor good roads were available for long-distance freight movements. As these deficiencies were gradually remedied, the share of trucks in intercity freight movements began to rise, and by 1930 it was estimated to be 4 percent of ton-miles of intercity freight. The railroad industry took early cognizance of this emerging competitor, and one of the methods by which trucking was combatted was state regulation.

By the early 1930's all states regulated the dimensions and weight of trucks. The weight limitations were a much more pervasive control over trucking than the licensing of common carriers because even the trucks exempt from entry regulation are subject to the limitations on dimensions and capacity. The weight regulations in the early 1930's are reproduced in the appendix (Table 6). Sometimes the participation of railroads in the regulatory process was incontrovertible: Texas and Louisiana placed a 7000-pound payload limit on trucks serving (and hence competing with) two or more railroad stations, and a 14,000-pound limit on trucks serving only one station (hence, not competing with it).

We seek to determine the pattern of weight limits on trucks that would emerge in response to the economic interests of the concerned parties. The main considerations appear to be the following:

(1) Heavy trucks would be allowed in states with a substantial number of trucks on farms: the powerful agricultural interests would insist upon this. The 1930 Census reports nearly one million trucks on farms. One variable in our study will be, for each state, trucks per 1000 of agricultural population.[6]

[6] The ratio of trucks to total population would measure the product of (1) the importance of trucks to farmers, and (2) the importance of farmers in the state. For reasons given later, we prefer to emphasize (1).

(2) Railroads found the truck an effective and rapidly triumphing competitor in the shorter hauls and hauls of less than carload traffic, but much less effective in the carload and longer-haul traffic. Our second variable for each state is, therefore, length of average railroad haul.[7] The longer the average rail haul is, the less the railroads will be opposed to trucks.

(3) The public at large would be concerned by the potential damage done to the highway system by heavy trucks. The better the state highway system, the heavier the trucks that would be permitted. The percentage of each state's highways that had a high type surface is the third variable. Of course good highways are more likely to exist where the potential contribution of trucks to a state's economy is greater, so the causation may be looked at from either direction.

We have two measures of weight limits on trucks, one for 4-wheel trucks (X_1) and one for 6-wheel trucks (X_2). We may then calculate two equations,

$$X_1 \text{ (or } X_2) = a + bX_3 + cX_4 + dX_5,$$

where

X_3 = trucks per 1000 agricultural labor force, 1930,
X_4 = average length of railroad haul of freight traffic, 1930,
X_5 = percentage of state roads with high-quality surface, 1930.

(All variables are fully defined and their state values given in Table 7 on page 20.)

The three explanatory variables are statistically significant, and each works in the expected direction. The regulations on weight were less onerous; the larger the truck population in farming, the less competitive the trucks were to railroads (i.e., the longer the rail hauls), and the better the highway system (see Table 2).

☐ The foregoing analysis is concerned with what may be termed the industrial demand for governmental powers. Not every industry will have a significant demand for public assistance (other than money!), meaning the prospect of a substantial increase in the present value of the enterprises even if the governmental services could be obtained gratis (and of course they have costs to which we soon turn). In some economic activities entry of new rivals is extremely difficult to control—consider the enforcement problem in restricting the supply of domestic servants. In some industries the substitute products cannot be efficiently controlled—consider the competition offered to bus lines by private car-pooling. Price fixing is not feasible where every unit of the product has a different quality and price, as in the market for used automobiles. In general, however, most industries will have a positive demand price (schedule) for the services of government.

2. The costs of obtaining legislation

■ When an industry receives a grant of power from the state, the benefit to the industry will fall short of the damage to the rest of the

---

[7] This is known for each railroad, and we assume that (1) the average holds within each state, and (2) two or more railroads in a state may be combined on the basis of mileage. Obviously both assumptions are at best fair approximations.

TABLE 2

REGRESSION ANALYSIS OF STATE WEIGHT LIMITS ON TRUCKS
(T VALUES UNDER REGRESSION COEFFICIENTS)

DEPENDENT VARIABLE	N	CONSTANT	X_3	X_4	X_5	R^2
X_1	48	12.28 (4.87)	0.0336 (3.99)	0.0287 (2.77)	0.2641 (3.04)	0.502
X_2	46	10.34 (1.57)	0.0437 (2.01)	0.0788 (2.97)	0.2528 (1.15)	0.243

X_1 = WEIGHT LIMIT ON 4-WHEEL TRUCKS (THOUSANDS OF POUNDS), 1932-33

X_2 = WEIGHT LIMIT ON 6-WHEEL TRUCKS (THOUSANDS OF POUNDS), 1932-33

X_3 = TRUCKS ON FARMS PER 1,000 AGRICULTURAL LABOR FORCE, 1930

X_4 = AVERAGE LENGTH OF RAILROAD HAUL OF FREIGHT (MILES), 1930

X_5 = PERCENT OF STATE HIGHWAYS WITH HIGH-TYPE SURFACE, DEC. 31, 1930

SOURCES: X_1 AND X_2: THE MOTOR TRUCK RED BOOK AND DIRECTORY [11], 1934 EDITION, P. 85-102, AND U.S. DEPT. OF AGRIC., BUR. OF PUBLIC ROADS, DEC. 1932 [13].

X_3: CENSUS OF AGRICULTURE, 1930, VOL. IV, [14].

X_4: A.A.R.R., BUR. OF RAILWAY ECONOMICS, RAILWAY MILEAGE BY STATES, DEC. 31, 1930 [1] AND U.S.I.C.C., STATISTICS OF RAILWAYS IN THE U.S., 1930 [18].

X_5: STATISTICAL ABSTRACT OF THE U.S., 1932 [16].

community. Even if there were no deadweight losses from acquired regulation, however, one might expect a democratic society to reject such industry requests unless the industry controlled a majority of the votes.[8] A direct and informed vote on oil import quotas would reject the scheme. (If it did not, our theory of rational political processes would be contradicted.) To explain why many industries are able to employ the political machinery to their own ends, we must examine the nature of the political process in a democracy.

A consumer chooses between rail and air travel, for example, by voting with his pocketbook: he patronizes on a given day that mode of transportation he prefers. A similar form of economic voting occurs with decisions on where to work or where to invest one's capital. The market accumulates these economic votes, predicts their future course, and invests accordingly.

Because the political decision is coercive, the decision process is fundamentally different from that of the market. If the public is asked to make a decision between two transportation media comparable to the individual's decision on how to travel—say, whether airlines or railroads should receive a federal subsidy—the decision must be abided by everyone, travellers and non-travellers, travellers this year and travellers next year. This compelled universality of political decisions makes for two differences between democratic political decision processes and market processes.

---

[8] If the deadweight loss (of consumer and producer surplus) is taken into account, even if the oil industry were in the majority it would not obtain the legislation if there were available some method of compensation (such as sale of votes) by which the larger damage of the minority could be expressed effectively against the lesser gains of the majority.

(1) The decisions must be made simultaneously by a large number of persons (or their representatives): the political process demands simultaneity of decision. If A were to vote on the referendum today, B tomorrow, C the day after, and so on, the accumulation of a majority decision would be both expensive and suspect. (A might wish to cast a different vote now than last month.)

The condition of simultaneity imposes a major burden upon the political decision process. It makes voting on specific issues prohibitively expensive: it is a significant cost even to engage in the transaction of buying a plane ticket when I wish to travel; it would be stupendously expensive to me to engage in the physically similar transaction of voting (i.e., patronizing a polling place) whenever a number of my fellow citizens desired to register their views on railroads versus airplanes. To cope with this condition of simultaneity, the voters must employ representatives with wide discretion and must eschew direct expressions of marginal changes in preferences. This characteristic also implies that the political decision does not predict voter desires and make preparations to fulfill them in advance of their realization.

(2) The democratic decision process must involve "all" the community, not simply those who are directly concerned with a decision. In a private market, the non-traveller never votes on rail versus plane travel, while the huge shipper casts many votes each day. The political decision process cannot exclude the uninterested voter: the abuses of any exclusion except self-exclusion are obvious. Hence, the political process does not allow participation in proportion to interest and knowledge. In a measure, this difficulty is moderated by other political activities besides voting which do allow a more effective vote to interested parties: persuasion, employment of skilled legislative representatives, etc. Nevertheless, the political system does not offer good incentives like those in private markets to the acquisition of knowledge. If I consume ten times as much of public service A (streets) as of B (schools), I do not have incentives to acquire corresponding amounts of knowledge about the public provision of these services.[9]

These characteristics of the political process can be modified by having numerous levels of government (so I have somewhat more incentive to learn about local schools than about the whole state school system) and by selective use of direct decision (bond referenda). The chief method of coping with the characteristics, however, is to employ more or less full-time representatives organized in (disciplined by) firms which are called political parties or machines.

The representative and his party are rewarded for their discovery and fulfillment of the political desires of their constituency by success in election and the perquisites of office. If the representative could confidently await reelection whenever he voted against an economic policy that injured the society, he would assuredly do so. Unfortunately virtue does not always command so high a price. If the representative denies ten large industries their special subsidies of money or governmental power, they will dedicate themselves to the election of a more complaisant successor: the stakes are that important. This does not mean that every large industry can get what it wants or all

[9] See [2].

that it wants: it does mean that the representative and his party must find a coalition of voter interests more durable than the anti-industry side of every industry policy proposal. A representative cannot win or keep office with the support of the sum of those who are opposed to: oil import quotas, farm subsidies, airport subsidies, hospital subsidies, unnecessary navy shipyards, an inequitable public housing program, and rural electrification subsidies.

The political decison process has as its dominant characteristic infrequent, universal (in principle) participation, as we have noted: political decisions must be infrequent and they must be global. The voter's expenditure to learn the merits of individual policy proposals and to express his preferences (by individual and group representation as well as by voting) are determined by expected costs and returns, just as they are in the private marketplace. The costs of comprehensive information are higher in the political arena because information must be sought on many issues of little or no direct concern to the individual, and accordingly he will know little about most matters before the legislature. The expressions of preferences in voting will be less precise than the expressions of preferences in the marketplace because many uninformed people will be voting and affecting the decision.[10]

The channels of political decision-making can thus be described as gross or filtered or noisy. If everyone has a negligible preference for policy A over B, the preference will not be discovered or acted upon. If voter group X wants a policy that injures non-X by a small amount, it will not pay non-X to discover this and act against the policy. The system is calculated to implement all strongly felt preferences of majorities and many strongly felt preferences of minorities but to disregard the lesser preferences of majorities and minorities. The filtering or grossness will be reduced by any reduction in the cost to the citizen of acquiring information and expressing desires and by any increase in the probability that his vote will influence policy.

The industry which seeks political power must go to the appropriate seller, the political party. The political party has costs of operation, costs of maintaining an organization and competing in elections. These costs of the political process are viewed excessively narrowly in the literature on the financing of elections: elections are to the political process what merchandizing is to the process of producing a commodity, only an essential final step. The party maintains its organization and electoral appeal by the performance of costly services to the voter at all times, not just before elections. Part of the costs of services and organization are borne by putting a part of the party's workers on the public payroll. An opposition party, however, is usually essential insurance for the voters to discipline the party in power, and the opposition party's costs are not fully met by public funds.

The industry which seeks regulation must be prepared to pay with the two things a party needs: votes and resources. The re-

[10] There is an organizational problem in any decision in which more than one vote is cast. If because of economies of scale it requires a thousand customers to buy a product before it can be produced, this thousand votes has to be assembled by some entrepreneur. Unlike the political scene, however, there is no need to obtain the consent of the remainder of the community, because they will bear no part of the cost.

sources may be provided by campaign contributions, contributed services (the businessman heads a fund-raising committee), and more indirect methods such as the employment of party workers. The votes in support of the measure are rallied, and the votes in opposition are dispersed, by expensive programs to educate (or uneducate) members of the industry and of other concerned industries.

These costs of legislation probably increase with the size of the industry seeking the legislation. Larger industries seek programs which cost the society more and arouse more opposition from substantially affected groups. The tasks of persuasion, both within and without the industry, also increase with its size. The fixed size of the political "market," however, probably makes the cost of obtaining legislation increase less rapidly than industry size. The smallest industries are therefore effectively precluded from the political process unless they have some special advantage such as geographical concentration in a sparsely settled political subdivision.

If a political party has in effect a monopoly control over the governmental machine, one might expect that it could collect most of the benefits of regulation for itself. Political parties, however, are perhaps an ideal illustration of Demsetz' theory of natural monopoly [4]. If one party becomes extortionate (or badly mistaken in its reading of effective desires), it is possible to elect another party which will provide the governmental services at a price more closely proportioned to costs of the party. If entry into politics is effectively controlled, we should expect one-party dominance to lead that party to solicit requests for protective legislation but to exact a higher price for the legislation.

The internal structure of the political party, and the manner in which the perquisites of office are distributed among its members, offer fascinating areas for study in this context. The elective officials are at the pinnacle of the political system—there is no substitute for the ability to hold the public offices. I conjecture that much of the compensation to the legislative leaders takes the form of extra-political payments. Why are so many politicians lawyers?—because everyone employs lawyers, so the congressman's firm is a suitable avenue of compensation, whereas a physician would have to be given bribes rather than patronage. Most enterprises patronize insurance companies and banks, so we may expect that legislators commonly have financial affiliations with such enterprises.

The financing of industry-wide activities such as the pursuit of legislation raises the usual problem of the free rider.[11] We do not possess a satisfactory theory of group behavior—indeed this theory is the theory of oligopoly with one addition: in the very large number industry (e.g., agriculture) the political party itself will undertake the entrepreneurial role in providing favorable legislation. We can go no further than the infirmities of oligopoly theory allow, which is to say, we can make only plausible conjectures such as that the more concentrated the industry, the more resources it can invest in the campaign for legislation.

☐ **Occupational licensing.** The licensing of occupations is a possible

---

[11] The theory that the lobbying organization avoids the "free-rider" problem by selling useful services was proposed by Thomas G. Moore [8] and elaborated by Mancur Olson [9]. The theory has not been tested empirically.

Issues in Regulation, Market Structure, Conduct, and Performance

use of the political process to improve the economic circumstances of a group. The license is an effective barrier to entry because occupational practice without the license is a criminal offense. Since much occupational licensing is performed at the state level, the area provides an opportunity to search for the characteristics of an occupation which give it political power.

Although there are serious data limitations, we may investigate several characteristics of an occupation which should influence its ability to secure political power:

(1) *The size of the occupation.* Quite simply, the larger the occupation, the more votes it has. (Under some circumstances, therefore, one would wish to exclude non-citizens from the measure of size.)

(2) *The per capita income of the occupation.* The income of the occupation is the product of its number and average income, so this variable and the preceding will reflect the total income of the occupation. The income of the occupation is presumably an index of the probable rewards of successful political action: in the absence of specific knowledge of supply and demand functions, we expect licensing to increase each occupation's equilibrium income by roughly the same proportion. In a more sophisticated version, one would predict that the less the elasticity of demand for the occupation's services, the more profitable licensing would be. One could also view the income of the occupation as a source of funds for political action, but if we view political action as an investment this is relevant only with capital-market imperfections.[12]

The average income of occupational members is an appropriate variable in comparisons among occupations, but it is inappropriate to comparisons of one occupation in various states because real income will be approximately equal (in the absence of regulation) in each state.

(3) *The concentration of the occupation in large cities.* When the occupation organizes a campaign to obtain favorable legislation, it incurs expenses in the solicitation of support, and these are higher for a diffused occupation than a concentrated one. The solicitation of support is complicated by the free-rider problem in that individual members cannot be excluded from the benefits of legislation even if they have not shared the costs of receiving it. If most of the occupation is concentrated in a few large centers, these problems (we suspect) are much reduced in intensity: regulation may even begin at the local governmental level. We shall use an orthodox geographical concentration measure: the share of the occupation of the state in cities over 100,000 (or 50,000 in 1900 and earlier).

(4) *The presence of a cohesive opposition to licensing.* If an occupation deals with the public at large, the costs which licensing imposes upon any one customer or industry will be small and it will not be economic for that customer or industry to combat the drive for licensure. If the injured group finds it feasible and profitable to act jointly, however, it will oppose the effort to get licensure, and (by

[12] Let n = the number of members of the profession and y = average income. We expect political capacity to be in proportion to (ny) so far as benefits go, but to reflect also the direct value of votes, so the capacity becomes proportional to $(n^a y)$ with $a > 1$.

increasing its cost) weaken, delay, or prevent the legislation. The same attributes—numbers of voters, wealth, and ease of organization—which favor an occupation in the political arena, of course, favor also any adversary group. Thus, a small occupation employed by only one industry which has few employers will have difficulty in getting licensure; whereas a large occupation serving everyone will encounter no organized opposition.

An introductory statistical analysis of the licensing of select occupations by states is summarized in Table 3. In each occupation the dependent variable for each state is the year of first regulation of entry into the occupation. The two independent variables are

(1) the ratio of the occupation to the total labor force of the state in the census year nearest to the median year of regulation,
(2) the fraction of the occupation found in cities over 100,000 (over 50,000 in 1890 and 1900) in that same year.

We expect these variables to be negatively associated with year of licensure, and each of the nine statistically significant regression coefficients is of the expected sign.

The results are not robust, however: the multiple correlation

TABLE 3

INITIAL YEAR OF REGULATION AS A FUNCTION OF
RELATIVE SIZE OF OCCUPATION AND DEGREE OF URBANIZATION

OCCUPATION	NUMBER OF STATES LICENSING	MEDIAN CENSUS YEAR OF LICENSING	SIZE OF OCCUPATION (RELATIVE TO LABOR FORCE)	URBANIZATION (SHARE OF OCCUPATION IN CITIES OVER 100,000*)	R^2
BEAUTICIANS	48	1930	−4.03 (2.50)	5.90 (1.24)	0.125
ARCHITECTS	47	1930	−24.06 (2.15)	−6.29 (0.84)	0.184
BARBERS	46	1930	−1.31 (0.51)	−26.10 (2.37)	0.146
LAWYERS	29	1890	−0.26 (0.08)	−65.78 (1.70)	0.102
PHYSICIANS	43	1890	0.64 (0.65)	−23.80 (2.69)	0.165
EMBALMERS	37	1910	3.32 (0.36)	−4.24 (0.44)	0.007
REGISTERED NURSES	48	1910	−2.08 (2.28)	−3.36 (1.06)	0.176
DENTISTS	48	1900	2.51 (0.44)	−22.94 (2.19)	0.103
VETERINARIANS	40	1910	−10.69 (1.94)	−37.16 (4.20)	0.329
CHIROPRACTORS	48	1930	−17.70 (1.54)	11.69 (1.25)	0.079
PHARMACISTS	48	1900	−4.19 (1.50)	−6.84 (0.80)	0.082

SOURCES: THE COUNCIL OF STATE GOVERNMENTS, "OCCUPATIONAL LICENSING LEGISLATION IN THE STATES", 1952 [3], AND U.S. CENSUS OF POPULATION [15], VARIOUS YEARS.

* 50,000 IN 1890 AND 1900.

coefficients are small, and over half of the regression coefficients are not significant (and in these cases often of inappropriate sign). Urbanization is more strongly associated than size of occupation with licensure.[13] The crudity of the data may be a large source of these disappointments: we measure, for example, the characteristics of the barbers in each state in 1930, but 14 states were licensing barbers by 1910. If the states which licensed barbering before 1910 had relatively more barbers, or more highly urbanized barbers, the predictions would be improved. The absence of data for years between censuses and before 1890 led us to make only the cruder analysis.[14]

In general, the larger occupations were licensed in earlier years.[15] Veterinarians are the only occupation in this sample who have a well-defined set of customers, namely livestock farmers, and licensing was later in those states with large numbers of livestock relative to rural population. The within-occupation analyses offer some support for the economic theory of the supply of legislation.

A comparison of different occupations allows us to examine several other variables. The first is income, already discussed above. The second is the size of the market. Just as it is impossible to organize an effective labor union in only one part of an integrated market, so it is impossible to regulate only one part of the market. Consider an occupation—junior business executives will do—which has a national market with high mobility of labor and significant mobility of employers. If the executives of one state were to organize, their scope for effective influence would be very small. If salaries were raised above the competitive level, employers would often recruit elsewhere so the demand elasticity would be very high.[16] The third variable is stability of occupational membership: the longer the members are in the occupation, the greater their financial gain from control of entry. Our regrettably crude measure of this variable is based upon the number of members aged 35–44 in 1950 and aged 45–54 in 1960: the closer these numbers are, the more stable the membership of the occupation. The data for the various occupations are given in Table 4.

The comparison of licensed and unlicensed occupations is consistently in keeping with our expectations:

---

[13] We may pool the occupations and assign dummy variables for each occupation; the regression coefficients then are:
    size of occupation relative to labor force: -0.450 ($t = 0.59$)
    urbanization   : -12.133 ($t = 4.00$).
Thus urbanization is highly significant, while size of occupation is not significant.

[14] A more precise analysis might take the form of a regression analysis such as:
    Year of licensure = constant
                        $+b_1$ (year of critical size of occupation)
                        $+b_2$ (year of critical urbanization of occupation),
where the critical size and urbanization were defined as the mean size and mean urbanization in the year of licensure.

[15] Lawyers, physicians, and pharmacists were all relatively large occupations by 1900, and nurses also by 1910. The only large occupation to be licensed later was barbers; the only small occupation to be licensed early was embalmers.

[16] The regulation of business in a partial market will also generally produce very high supply elasticities within a market: if the price of the product (or service) is raised, the pressure of excluded supply is very difficult to resist. Some occupations are forced to reciprocity in licensing, and the geographical dispersion of earnings in licensed occupations, one would predict, is not appreciably different than in unlicensed occupations with equal employer mobility. Many puzzles are posed by the interesting analysis of Arlene S. Holen in [6], pp. 492-98.

(1) the licensed occupations have higher incomes (also before licensing, one may assume),
(2) the membership of the licensed occupations is more stable (but the difference is negligible in our crude measure),
(3) the licensed occupations are less often employed by business enterprises (who have incentives to oppose licensing),
(4) all occupations in national markets (college teachers, engineers, scientists, accountants) are unlicensed or only partially licensed.

The size and urbanization of the three groups, however, are unrelated to licensing. The inter-occupational comparison therefore provides a modicum of additional support for our theory of regulation.

3. Conclusion

■ The idealistic view of public regulation is deeply imbedded in professional economic thought. So many economists, for example, have denounced the ICC for its pro-railroad policies that this has become a cliché of the literature. This criticism seems to me exactly

TABLE 4

CHARACTERISTICS OF LICENSED AND UNLICENSED PROFESSIONAL OCCUPATIONS, 1960

OCCUPATION	MEDIAN AGE (YEARS)	MEDIAN EDUCATION (YEARS)	MEDIAN EARNINGS (50-52 WKS.)	INSTABILITY OF MEMBERSHIP*	PERCENT NOT SELF-EMPLOYED	PERCENT IN CITIES OVER 50,000	PERCENT OF LABOR FORCE
LICENSED:							
ARCHITECTS	41.7	16.8	$ 9,090	0.012	57.8%	44.1%	0.045%
CHIROPRACTORS	46.5	16.4	6,360	0.053	5.8	30.8	0.020
DENTISTS	45.9	17.3	12,200	0.016	9.4	34.5	0.128
EMBALMERS	43.5	13.4	5,990	0.130	52.8	30.2	0.055
LAWYERS	45.3	17.4	10,800	0.041	35.8	43.1	0.308
PROF. NURSES	39.1	13.2	3,850	0.291	91.0	40.6	0.868
OPTOMETRISTS	41.6	17.0	8,480	0.249	17.5	34.5	0.024
PHARMACISTS	44.9	16.2	7,230	0.119	62.3	40.0	0.136
PHYSICIANS	42.8	17.5	14,200	0.015	35.0	44.7	0.339
VETERINARIANS	39.2	17.4	9,210	0.169	29.5	14.4	0.023
AVERAGE	43.0	16.3	8,741	0.109	39.7	35.7	0.195
PARTIALLY LICENSED:							
ACCOUNTANTS	40.4	14.9	6,450	0.052	88.1	43.5	0.698
ENGINEERS	38.3	16.2	8,490	0.023	96.8	31.6	1.279
ELEM. SCHOOL TEACHERS	43.1	16.5	4,710	(a)	99.1	18.8	1.482
AVERAGE	40.6	15.9	6,550	0.117(b)	94.7	34.6	1.153
UNLICENSED:							
ARTISTS	38.0	14.2	5,920	0.103	77.3	45.7	0.154
CLERGYMEN	43.3	17.0	4,120	0.039	89.0	27.2	0.295
COLLEGE TEACHERS	40.3	17.4	7,500	0.085	99.2	36.0	0.261
DRAFTSMEN	31.2	12.9	5,990	0.098	98.6	40.8	0.322
REPORTERS & EDITORS	39.4	15.5	6,120	0.138	93.9	43.3	0.151
MUSICIANS	40.2	14.8	3,240	0.081	65.5	37.7	0.289
NATURAL SCIENTISTS	35.9	16.8	7,490	0.264	96.3	32.7	0.221
AVERAGE	38.3	15.5	5,768	0.115	88.5	37.6	0.242

(*) 1-R, WHERE R = RATIO: 1960 AGE 45-54 TO 1950 AGE 35-44.

(a) NOT AVAILABLE SEPARATELY; TEACHERS N.E.C. (INCL. SECONDARY SCHOOL AND OTHER) = 0.276

(b) INCLUDES FIGURE FOR TEACHERS N.E.C. IN NOTE (a)

SOURCE: U.S. CENSUS OF POPULATION, [15], 1960.

Issues in Regulation, Market Structure, Conduct, and Performance

as appropriate as a criticism of the Great Atlantic and Pacific Tea Company for selling groceries, or as a criticism of a politician for currying popular support. The fundamental vice of such criticism is that it misdirects attention: it suggests that the way to get an ICC which is not subservient to the carriers is to preach to the commissioners or to the people who appoint the commissioners. The only way to get a different commission would be to change the political support for the Commission, and reward commissioners on a basis unrelated to their services to the carriers.

Until the basic logic of political life is developed, reformers will be ill-equipped to use the state for their reforms, and victims of the pervasive use of the state's support of special groups will be helpless to protect themselves. Economists should quickly establish the license to practice on the rational theory of political behavior.

Appendix

TABLE 5
COMMON, CONTRACT AND PASSENGER MOTOR CARRIERS, 1935–1969[1]

YEAR ENDING	CUMULATIVE APPLICATIONS			OPERATING CARRIERS	
	GRAND-FATHER	NEW	TOTAL	APPROVED APPLICATIONS[3]	NUMBER IN OPERATION[2]
OCT. 1936	82,827	1,696	84,523	–	–
1937	83,107	3,921	87,028	1,114	–
1938	85,646	6,694	92,340	20,398	–
1939	86,298	9,636	95,934	23,494	–
1940	87,367	12,965	100,332	25,575	–
1941	88,064	16,325	104,389	26,296	–
1942	88,702	18,977	107,679	26,683	–
1943	89,157	20,007	109,164	27,531	–
1944	89,511	21,324	110,835	27,177	21,044
1945	89,518	22,829	112,347		20,788
1946	89,529	26,392	115,921		20,632
1947	89,552	29,604	119,156		20,665
1948	89,563	32,678	122,241		20,373
1949	89,567	35,635	125,202		18,459
1950	89,573	38,666	128,239		19,200
1951	89,574	41,889	131,463		18,843
1952	(89,574)[4]	44,297	133,870		18,408
1953	"	46,619	136,192		17,869
1954	"	49,146	138,719		17,080
1955	"	51,720	141,293		16,836
JUNE 1956	"	53,640	143,213		16,486
1957	"	56,804	146,377		16,316
1958	"	60,278	149,851		16,065
1959	"	64,171	153,744		15,923
1960	"	69,205	158,778		15,936
1961	"	72,877	162,450		15,967
1962	"	76,986	166,559		15,884
1963	"	81,443	171,016		15,739
1964	"	86,711	176,284		15,732
1965	"	93,064	182,637		15,755
1966	"	101,745	191,318		15,933
1967	"	106,647	196,220		16,003
1968	"	(6)	(6)		16,230[5]
1969	"	(6)	(6)		16,318[5]

SOURCE: U.S. INTERSTATE COMMERCE COMMISSION ANNUAL REPORTS [17].

1 EXCLUDING BROKERS AND WITHIN-STATE CARRIERS.
2 PROPERTY CARRIERS WERE THE FOLLOWING PERCENTAGES OF ALL OPERATING CARRIERS: 1944–93.4%; 1950–92.4%; 1960–93.0%; 1966–93.4%.
3 ESTIMATED.
4 NOT AVAILABLE; ASSUMED TO BE APPROXIMATELY CONSTANT.
5 1968 AND 1969 FIGURES ARE FOR NUMBER OF CARRIERS REQUIRED TO FILE ANNUAL REPORTS.
6 NOT AVAILABLE COMPARABLE TO PREVIOUS YEARS; APPLICATIONS FOR PERMANENT AUTHORITY DISPOSED OF (I.E., FROM NEW AND PENDING FILES) 1967-69 ARE AS FOLLOWS: 1967–7,049; 1968–5,724; 1969–5,186.

Regulating the Private Corporation

TABLE 6

WEIGHT LIMITS ON TRUCKS, 1932-33*, BY STATES (BASIC DATA FOR TABLE 2).

STATE	MAXIMUM WEIGHT (IN LBS.) 4-WHEEL[1]	MAXIMUM WEIGHT (IN LBS.) 6-WHEEL[2]	STATE	MAXIMUM WEIGHT (IN LBS.) 4-WHEEL[1]	MAXIMUM WEIGHT (IN LBS.) 6-WHEEL[2]
ALABAMA	20,000	32,000	NEBRASKA	24,000	40,000
ARIZONA	22,000	34,000	NEVADA	25,000	38,000
ARKANSAS	22,200	37,000	NEW HAMPSHIRE	20,000	20,000
CALIFORNIA	22,000	34,000	NEW JERSEY	30,000	30,000
COLORADO	30,000	40,000	NEW MEXICO	27,000	45,000
CONNECTICUT	32,000	40,000	NEW YORK	33,600	44,000
DELAWARE	26,000	38,000	NO. CAROLINA	20,000	20,000
FLORIDA	20,000	20,000	NO. DAKOTA	24,000	48,000
GEORGIA	22,000	39,600	OHIO	24,000	24,000
IDAHO	24,000	40,000	OKLAHOMA	20,000	20,000
ILLINOIS	24,000	40,000	OREGON	25,500	42,500
INDIANA	24,000	40,000	PENNSYLVANIA	26,000	36,000
IOWA	24,000	40,000	RHODE ISLAND	28,000	40,000
KANSAS	24,000	34,000	SO. CAROLINA	20,000	25,000
KENTUCKY	18,000	18,000	SO. DAKOTA	20,000	20,000
LOUISIANA	13,400	N. A.	TENNESSEE	20,000	20,000
MAINE	18,000	27,000	TEXAS	13,500	N. A.
MARYLAND	25,000	40,000	UTAH	26,000	34,000
MASSACHUSETTS	30,000	30,000	VERMONT	20,000	20,000
MICHIGAN	27,000	45,000	VIRGINIA	24,000	35,000
MINNESOTA	27,000	42,000	WASHINGTON	24,000	34,000
MISSISSIPPI	18,000	22,000	WEST VA.	24,000	40,000
MISSOURI	24,000	24,000	WISCONSIN	24,000	36,000
MONTANA	24,000	34,000	WYOMING	27,000	30,000

* RED BOOK [11] FIGURES ARE REPORTED (P. 89) AS "BASED ON THE STATE'S INTERPRETATIONS OF THEIR LAWS [1933] AND ON PHYSICAL LIMITATIONS OF VEHICLE DESIGN AND TIRE CAPACITY." PUBLIC ROADS [13] FIGURES ARE REPORTED (P. 167) AS "AN ABSTRACT OF STATE LAWS, INCLUDING LEGISLATION PASSED IN 1932."

1. 4-WHEEL: THE SMALLEST OF THE FOLLOWING 3 FIGURES WAS USED:

   (A) MAXIMUM GROSS WEIGHT (AS GIVEN IN RED BOOK, P. 90-91).

   (B) MAXIMUM AXLE WEIGHT (AS GIVEN IN RED BOOK, P. 90-91), MULTIPLIED BY 1.5 (SEE RED BOOK, P. 89).

   (C) MAXIMUM GROSS WEIGHT (AS GIVEN IN RED BOOK, P. 93).

   EXCEPTIONS: TEXAS AND LOUISIANA—SEE RED BOOK, P. 91.

2. 6-WHEEL: MAXIMUM GROSS WEIGHT AS GIVEN IN PUBLIC ROADS, P. 167. THESE FIGURES AGREE IN MOST CASES WITH THOSE SHOWN IN RED BOOK, P. 93, AND WITH PUBLIC ROADS MAXIMUM AXLE WEIGHTS MULTIPLIED BY 2.5 (SEE RED BOOK, P. 93). TEXAS AND LOUISIANA ARE EXCLUDED AS DATA ARE NOT AVAILABLE TO CONVERT FROM PAYLOAD TO GROSS WEIGHT LIMITS.

TABLE 7

INDEPENDENT VARIABLES
(BASIC DATA FOR TABLE 2 — CONT'D)

STATE	TRUCKS ON FARMS PER 1,000 AGRICULTURAL LABOR FORCE	AVERAGE LENGTH OF RAILROAD HAUL OF FREIGHT (MILES)	PERCENT OF STATE HIGHWAYS WITH HIGH-TYPE SURFACE
ALABAMA	26.05	189.4	1.57
ARIZONA	79.74	282.2	2.60
ARKANSAS	28.62	233.1	1.72
CALIFORNIA	123.40	264.6	13.10
COLORADO	159.50	244.7	0.58
CONNECTICUT	173.80	132.6	7.98
DELAWARE	173.20	202.7	21.40
FLORIDA	91.41	184.1	8.22
GEORGIA	32.07	165.7	1.60
IDAHO	95.89	243.6	0.73
ILLINOIS	114.70	207.9	9.85
INDIANA	120.20	202.8	6.90
IOWA	98.73	233.3	3.39
KANSAS	146.70	281.5	0.94
KENTUCKY	20.05	227.5	1.81
LOUISIANA	31.27	201.0	1.94
MAINE	209.30	120.4	1.87
MARYLAND	134.20	184.1	12.90
MASSACHUSETTS	172.20	144.7	17.70
MICHIGAN	148.40	168.0	6.68
MINNESOTA	120.40	225.6	1.44
MISSISSIPPI	29.62	164.9	1.14
MISSOURI	54.28	229.7	2.91
MONTANA	183.80	266.5	0.09
NEBRASKA	132.10	266.9	0.41
NEVADA	139.40	273.2	0.39
NEW HAMPSHIRE	205.40	129.0	3.42
NEW JERSEY	230.20	137.6	23.30
NEW MEXICO	90.46	279.0	0.18
NEW YORK	220.50	163.3	21.50
NO. CAROLINA	37.12	171.5	8.61
NO. DAKOTA	126.40	255.1	0.01
OHIO	125.80	194.2	11.20
OKLAHOMA	78.18	223.3	1.42
OREGON	118.90	246.2	3.35
PENNSYLVANIA	187.60	166.5	9.78
RHODE ISLAND	193.30	131.0	20.40
SO. CAROLINA	20.21	169.8	2.82
SO. DAKOTA	113.40	216.6	0.04
TENNESSEE	23.98	191.9	3.97
UTAH	101.70	235.7	1.69
VERMONT	132.20	109.7	2.26
VIRGINIA	71.88	229.8	2.86
WASHINGTON	180.90	254.4	4.21
WEST VIRGINIA	62.88	218.7	8.13
WISCONSIN	178.60	195.7	4.57
WYOMING	133.40	286.7	0.08

(1) AVERAGE LENGTH OF RR HAUL OF (REVENUE) FREIGHT = AVERAGE DISTANCE IN MILES EACH TON IS CARRIED = RATIO OF NUMBER OF TON-MILES TO NUMBER OF TONS CARRIED. FOR EACH STATE, AVERAGE LENGTH OF HAUL WAS OBTAINED BY WEIGHTING AVERAGE LENGTH OF HAUL OF EACH COMPANY BY THE NUMBER OF MILES OF LINE OPERATED BY THAT COMPANY IN THE STATE (ALL FOR CLASS I RR'S).

(2) PERCENTAGE OF STATE ROADS WITH HIGH-QUALITY SURFACE: WHERE HIGH-QUALITY (HIGH-TYPE) SURFACE CONSISTS OF BITUMINOUS MACADAM, BITUMINOUS CONCRETE, SHEET ASPHALT, PORTLAND CEMENT CONCRETE, AND BLOCK PAVEMENTS. ALL STATE RURAL ROADS, BOTH LOCAL AND STATE HIGHWAYS SYSTEMS, ARE INCLUDED.

References

1. ASSOCIATION OF AMERICAN RAILROADS, BUREAU OF RAILWAY ECONOMICS. *Railway Mileage by States.* Washington, D. C.: December 31, 1930.
2. BECKER, G. S. "Competition and Democracy." *Journal of Law and Economics,* October 1958.
3. THE COUNCIL OF STATE GOVERNMENTS. "Occupational Licensing Legislation in the States." 1952.
4. DEMSETZ, H., "Why Regulate Utilities?" *Journal of Law and Economics,* April 1968.
5. GERWIG, R. W. "Natural Gas Production: A Study of Costs of Regulation." *Journal of Law and Economics,* October 1962, pp. 69-92.
6. HOLEN, A. S. "Effects of Professional Licensing Arrangements on Interstate Labor Mobility and Resource Allocation." *Journal of Political Economy,* Vol. 73 (1915), pp. 492-98.
7. KEYES, L. S. *Federal Control of Entry into Air Transportation.* Cambridge, Mass.: Harvard University Press, 1951.
8. MOORE, T. G. "The Purpose of Licensing." *Journal of Law and Economics,* October 1961.
9. OLSON, M. *The Logic of Collective Action.* Cambridge, Mass.: Harvard University Press, 1965.
10. PELTZMAN, S. "Entry in Commercial Banking." *Journal of Law and Economics,* October 1965.
11. *The Motor Truck Red Book and Directory,* 1934 Edition, pp. 85-102.
12. U. S. CONGRESS, SELECT COMMITTEE ON SMALL BUSINESS. *Hearings,* 88th Congress, 2nd Session, August 10 and 11, 1964.
13. U. S. DEPARTMENT OF AGRICULTURE, BUREAU OF PUBLIC ROADS. *Public Roads.* Washington, D. C.: U. S. Government Printing Office, December 1932.
14. U. S. DEPARTMENT OF COMMERCE, BUREAU OF THE CENSUS. *United States Census of Agriculture, 1930,* Vol. 4. Washington, D. C.: U. S. Government Printing Office, 1930.
15. ———. *United States Census of Population.* Washington, D. C.: U. S. Government Printing Office, appropriate years.
16. ———, BUREAU OF FOREIGN AND DOMESTIC COMMERCE. *Statistical Abstract of the U. S., 1932.* Washington, D. C.: U. S. Government Printing Office, 1932.
17. U. S. INTERSTATE COMMERCE COMMISSION. *Annual Report.* Washington, D. C.: U. S. Government Printing Office, appropriate years.
18. ———. *Statistics of Railways in the United States, 1930.* Washington, D. C.: U. S. Government Printing Office, 1930.

READING

24 BANK ENTRY AND BANK PERFORMANCE

Donald R. Fraser and Peter S. Rose*

THE IMPACT OF CHANGES in banking structure on bank performance has been the focus of considerable scholarly effort during the past decade. Most of the studies have taken a cross section of different banking markets, applied a multiple regression technique to isolate the effect of changes in structure on bank performance, and then used the coefficient of the structure variable to infer what would happen if the number of banks in a given market were, in fact, altered. In general, the results indicate that changes in banking structure affect both the price and quantity of banking services, but that the impact is quite small. However, many contradictory results have been obtained in these studies.[1]

Only a few studies have approached the impact of structure on bank performance *directly* by investigating the question: What has happened to bank performance in communities where the structure of the market actually has been altered? One of these[2] attempted to determine whether the opening of new branches in New York state by commercial banks, mutual savings banks, and savings and loan associations had significantly adverse effects on the growth and profitability of competing institutions. The study found that, despite some evidence of slowing in the growth rate of deposits, the profitability of existing institutions was not adversely affected by the opening of new branches by their competitors. A second study[3] examined the change in the performance of unit banks acquired by branch systems. In most cases, there appeared to be a strong tendency to make the policies of the acquired bank conform to those of the branch system. This generally resulted in higher rates paid on savings accounts and lower rates and more liberal terms on loans. On the other hand, there was a tendency toward higher service charges on checking accounts. Finally, a third important study examined the impact of the acquisition of a bank by a holding company.[4] The conclusion was that a substantially greater proportion of potential bank credit was made available to local individuals and businesses because the subsidiary banks held fewer U.S. Government securities and balances due from banks.[5]

The purpose of the present study is to examine the applicability of these findings to the case of *de novo* entry by independent unit banks into relatively small, well-defined banking markets. The study focuses upon the impact of the entry of new banks into isolated market areas served by only one, two, or three independent unit banks. In this type of market environ-

---

* The University of Texas at El Paso and Texas A&M University respectively. The authors gratefully acknowledge the helpful comments of George G. Kaufman and Robert H. Marshall on an early draft. However, the interpretation and conclusions are those of the authors and do not necessarily reflect the views of their respective institutions or of the reviewers.

1. See, for example, the studies by Edwards (2), Flechsig (3), Kaufman (9), and the present authors (4).
2. See Kohn and Carlo (12).
3. See Horvitz and Shull (7).
4. See Lawrence (13).
5. For some additional work on actual changes in banking structure see Motter and Carson (16) and Kaufman and Detz (10).

ment, the addition of just one bank represents a very substantial change in the structure of the market. Theory would suggest that where the number of banks in the market is small, the impact of *de novo* entry is likely to be most pronounced and most easily observed.[6]

In addition, problems in defining the relevant market area—the critical consideration in determining actual structure-performance relationships—appear to be significantly reduced in the case of small, relatively isolated communities. In banking, the relevant product market often differs widely for different products and services. It seems reasonable to suggest, however, that in small nonmetropolitan area communities with small banks, the various product markets are roughly coterminous. Unit banks of the size typically found in rural communities deal almost exclusively within the local market.[7]

I. The Analytical Framework

The subsequent analysis focuses upon two basic questions. The first is whether banks operating in comunities about to experience the entry of a new bank have performance characteristics different from a set of banks similar in size and location but not experiencing new competition. Substantial differences in bank performance during the period before entry may explain some of the reasons why new banks are formed. The second question, and perhaps the crucial one, is whether the appearance of new competition affects the performance of the existing institutions.

The pace of new bank formations has accelerated sharply in the past decade following a period of large-scale consolidation during the earlier postwar years. One of the periods of most rapid growth in new banks occurred during the years 1962-64, when over 800 banks were chartered—nearly as many as in the entire decade of the 1950s. Of these, 124 banks (15 percent) were established in that portion of the nation served by the Eleventh Federal Reserve District.[8] While almost three-quarters of the new Eleventh District banks were opened in the region's major metropolitan centers, 24 new banks were established in 23 one-, two-, and three-bank nonmetropolitan area communities. These 23 towns, ranging in population size from about 1,000 to 33,000, were selected for a detailed analysis of the effects of *de novo* bank entry. Important characteristics of the previously operating banks in these communities—the "entry" sample of banks—are presented in Table 1.

All of the entry towns were relatively isolated communities in predominantly rural counties with the nearest metropolitan area (SMSA) almost 70 miles away and the nearest town with a bank almost 15 miles distant. About 80 percent were located in the unit-banking states of Oklahoma and Texas.[9]

While market structure and performance are closely related in economic theory, structure is not the sole determinant of bank performance. There are many factors other than the entry of a new bank in the market area which may influence the performance of the previously operating banks. A few of

---

6. As Kaufman notes, "it may reasonably be expected that the impact of a change in structure on performance becomes greater the closer structure approaches total concentration." (9, p. 438).

7. Although several studies in recent years have been devoted to the problem of defining bank market areas, the subject continues to be surrounded with considerable controversy. For a discussion of the significant issues see, for example, Alhadeff (1), Shull (18), and Gelder and Budzeika (5).

8. The Eleventh Federal Reserve District includes all of Texas, 26 parishes in northern Louisiana, 18 counties in southern New Mexico, eight counties in southern Oklahoma, and five counties in southern Arizona.

9. Full-service branches are prohibited in Oklahoma and Texas. Arizona permits statewide branching without significant limitations. Louisiana allows practically unlimited branching in the parish where a bank's head office is located but only one branch in other parishes. There is a home-office protection rule, however. New Mexico permits branching countywide and also branching in an adjoining county or within a radius of 100 miles of the head office subject to home-office protection.

Issues in Regulation, Market Structure, Conduct, and Performance

these include changes in the community's economic base, demand for banking services by local households and business firms, bank operations, monetary policy, and the nature of nonbank competition.

To separate the impact of *de novo* bank entry from effects attributable to these and other factors, the performance of the entry banks was compared with a "control group" of similar-size banks operating in a similar economic and structural environment. In addition to providing a yardstick against which to measure the "before-and-after" performance of banks faced with new competition, this "nonentry" sample of banks provided evidence on whether banks with certain operating characteristics were more likely to generate the appearance of new competition.

A number of key economic and structural characteristics of the entry towns were used as benchmarks from which to construct the nonentry sample of banks. Among these were the number and size of the banks in the community, the level of income, the agricultural-industrial mix of the area, and the rate of growth of population. Also, because important differences in bank performance have been attributed to national—as opposed to state—chartered and member versus nonmember banks, the entry and nonentry samples of banks were cross-matched to insure a roughly equal balance of nationally chartered, Federal Reserve member institutions.[10]

Using these criteria, a total of 56 independent unit banks in 49 one-, two-, and three-bank towns were selected as benchmarks.[11] (Information on these banks is also shown in Table 1.) All of the banks in the nonentry sample were in different counties from the entry banks.

A total of 26 measures of bank performance were computed for each entry and nonentry bank from the year-end reports of condition and from income and dividend reports the banks filed with the appropriate regulatory agency. Included were measures of profitability, revenue, expenses, and the composition

---

10. See, for example, Gray (6) and Mayne (14).

11. None of the banks included in either sample changed ownership over the sample period and none were affiliates of bank holding companies. All were situated at least 5 miles from the nearest community with a bank.

TABLE 1
Characteristics of Commercial Banks Operating in Entry and Non-Entry Communities
(Unit Banks in One-, Two, and Three-Bank Towns)

	Entry	Non-Entry
Number of Banks	34	56
Average Deposit Size, 1960 (Millions of Dollars)	11.7	10.5
Deposit Size Distribution (Percentage of Banks)		
0-$6	18	11
6-12	59	54
Over 12	23	35
Community Composition Before Entry (Percentage of Communities)		
1-Bank Towns	54	22
2-Bank Towns	42	63
3-Bank Towns	4	14
Percentage of Banks Classified as:		
Member Banks	73	66
National Banks	62	53

of assets, liabilities, and loans. These measures of performance were computed for 1960-61 (pre-entry years) and 1965-66 (post-entry years). Performance measures for both samples are shown in Table 2.

The basic hypothesis submitted to empirical testing was that the mean performance levels ($\overline{X}$) of the entry (E) and the nonentry (NE) banks, before and after entry, were identical (i.e., from the same underlying population). In symbols, $\overline{X}^B_E = \overline{X}^B_{NE}$ and $\overline{X}^A_E = \overline{X}^A_{NE}$. This hypothesis was tested by determining the probability of "t" from the ratio

$$t = \frac{\overline{X}_E - \overline{X}_{NE}}{\hat{\sigma}_{(E+NE)}}$$

where $\hat{\sigma}_{(E+NE)}$ is the estimated standard error of the difference between the two sample means. This approach assumes that the two samples are from the same population with regard to variance, σ^2. In order to test this assumption, an F-ratio test for homogeneity of variances was made for each performance measure. The computed "F" values were generally not significant at the 5 percent risk level with the exception of those performance measures involving service charges on demand deposits, which should, therefore, be interpreted with caution. The results of the "t" tests using a two-tailed test of significance are shown in Table 3.

II. The Impact of Bank Entry on Bank Performance

The Situation Before Entry

A comparison of the performance ratios for the entry and nonentry samples in 1960 and 1961 provides some important insights into the reasons why a new bank was organized and a charter granted in the entry towns. In particular, it is interesting to note that the profitability of the banks in the entry sample was definitely not higher than the profitability of the banks in the nonentry sample. This is somewhat surprising since the majority of entry banks were monopolists prior to the appearance of new competition.[12] Why did the new banks enter markets where the profitability of existing institutions was not higher than the average for similar communities? An analysis of the other performance measures provides a plausible explanation.

The ratio of loans to total assets—one measure of bank output—at the entry banks was almost 5 percentage points lower in 1960 and more than 6 percentage points lower in 1961, on average, than at the nonentry banks. Moreover, the ratio of U.S. Government securities to total assets was almost 6 percentage points higher for the entry banks.[13]

These differences in asset composition are, of course, also reflected in the income statement. For the entry sample in both 1960 and 1961, the ratio of revenue on loans to total operating revenue was significantly lower while that for interest and dividends on U.S. Government securities to total operating revenue was significantly higher.

The lower revenue resulting from an allocation of assets heavily in favor of U.S. Government securities and away from loans was offset, however, by the fact that the liability structure of the banks in the entry sample was more heavily weighted toward demand deposits which have lower explicit costs. Thus, time deposits represented only 17.3 percent of total deposits, on average,

---

12. Economic theory suggests that if an area is served by a monopolist, that firm can earn the maximum potential profits which can be generated in the market. Of course, in banking there is no regulation concerning the maximum rate of return as is the case with public utilities.

13. These findings are consistent with theory which suggests that in the absence of effective local competition the volume of loans outstanding will tend to be smaller than in a more competitive market setting. For further discussion of this point, see Horvitz and Shull (7, pp. 143-44).

at the entry banks in 1960—almost 6 percentage points less than at banks in the nonentry sample.[14] This difference in liability structure was reflected in a significantly lower ratio of interest paid on time and savings deposits to total operating revenue.

The lower expenses appeared to about balance off the lower revenue, with the result that the profitability of the entry and nonentry banks was not statistically different except when related to total capital. The ratio of net current earnings to total capital was significantly lower for the banks in the entry sample, at the 5-percent level, because these banks financed a larger share of their assets through capital account.

In summary, the entry of new banks into these Southwestern communities did not appear to result from excessive profits earned by the previously operating institutions. Rather, it appeared to stem from the anticipation of a probable stream of future profits arising from an expansion of credit to the local area. The conservative management of the established banks as reflected in their low loan-asset ratios, high ratios of U.S. Government securities to total assets, and low proportions of time to total deposits ostensibly encouraged the entry of new banking institutions drawn by the lure of long-run profits at favorable levels of risk.[15]

The Impact of Bank Entry

The entry of new banks into these relatively isolated markets exerted a profound impact upon the performance of the existing banks. In particular, the composition of assets and liabilities changed dramatically relative to the control group. Moreover, the rate of growth of deposits was altered markedly, although not in the direction suggested by earlier studies.

Following the entry of a new bank, the ratios of loans and of U.S. Government securities to total assets changed dramatically as the portfolios of the established banks were shifted away from riskless assets toward loans. In the post-entry period, banks in the entry communities had ratios of loans and of U.S. Government securities to total assets not significantly different from the norm. While it cannot be proven that the additional loans were purchased by local firms and households, the entry of new banks appeared to have produced a significant change in the allocation of bank credit towards local customers.[16]

The composition of total loans also appears to have been substantially changed. While agricultural loans remained roughly constant relative to total assets, increased emphasis was placed on both business and consumer loans. Real estate loans also moved higher relative to the norm, but the change was not significant.[17]

14. The presence or absence of competing nonbank financial institutions, such as mutual savings banks and savings and loan associations, has been shown to be important in determining the ratio of time to total deposits. (See, for example, Kaufman (9, pp. 436-7) and Kaufman and Latta (11, pp. 539-42).) The two samples, however, were almost identical in this respect with three-quarters of the nonentry towns and a slightly higher percentage—four-fifths—of the entry towns having at least one office of a savings and loan association.

15. Of course, it may be argued that the conservative stance of the previously operating banks in the entry communities reflected a relatively low level of local demand for banking services. However, a low level of local demand would not serve as a strong incentive for starting a new bank. Moreover, if the existing bank is able to fully satisfy local needs while still maintaining a substantial level of liquidity, it is doubtful that a new charter would be issued.

16. Similar conclusions were reached by Motter (15) for the case of *de novo* entry. These findings also parallel those of Jessup and Lawrence in their studies of small-town banks which changed ownership. See, in particular, Jessup (8) and Lawrence (13).

17. These changes are consistent with Motter's observation that "the forte of a new bank is its ability to provide flexible and personalized service to its individual and small business customers. Thus, it is rational for a new bank to specialize in consumer and small business loans, especially if a

Regulating the Private Corporation

Substantial changes in the sources of funds were also evident in the entry communities. The ratio of time to total deposits, which was significantly lower in the entry communities during the 1960-61 period, was not statistically different during the post-entry period. Moreover, the ratio of total capital to risk assets in the entry communities declined in significance relative to the norm and became insignificant in 1966. These changes reflect a more aggressive mode of behavior by banks faced with a new market situation.

The substantial shifts in the sources and uses of bank funds in the entry communities between 1960 and 1966 were also reflected in changes in revenues, expenses, and profits. The ratio of revenue on loans to total operating revenue was not statistically different after entry, whereas it was significantly lower at the entry banks before the appearance of new competition. In addition, the entry banks reduced their reliance on service charge income. The ratio of service charges on deposit accounts to total operating revenue fell sharply, and by the end of the period was not statistically different from banks in the nonentry communities.

On the expense side of the income statement, the most important change was in interest paid on time and savings deposits. Reflecting the rapid growth of these deposits, the ratio of interest on time and savings deposits to total operating revenue—2.5 to 3.5 percentage points below the norm in the pre-entry period—was not statistically different after entry. The ratio of total current operating expenses to assets was not significantly different before or after.

The profitability and also the average return earned on assets of the banks in the entry communities remained about the same as in the nonentry communities. The ratio of net current earnings to total capital, which was significantly less in the entry communities before the appearance of a new bank, was not statistically different after.[18] The development reflected the change in the capital account rather than the change in earnings and is another indication of the more aggressive behavior of the entry banks.

With reference to the capital account, the capital adequacy of the established banks does not appear to have been adversely affected by new competition. The ratio of capital to risk assets (total assets minus cash and U.S. Government securities) declined relative to the norm in the post-entry period, but was still somewhat greater than norm. Moreover, total capital at the entry banks increased, on average, at a slightly faster rate than at the nonentry banks.

It is interesting to note that these important changes in bank performance occurred without significant changes in many of the conventionally used measures of performance. For example, the two most frequently used measures of performance—the effective rate charged on loans and the average rate paid on time deposits—were not significantly different in either the pre-entry or post-entry periods, although the effective rate charged in the entry towns fell relative to the norm.[19] Similarly, the average service charge collected

---

credit void previously existed . . . Once a new bank begins to emphasize this type of credit, other banks must, in some degree, follow suit in order to retain the other banking business of their customers." (15, pp. 342-43).

18. This result is directly contrary to the argument that charterings of new banks tend to reduce the profits of local banking institutions. The findings are, however, fully consistent with those of Kohn and Carlo (12) and Motter and Carson (16).

19. Similar conclusions concerning the most commonly used measures of performance were reached by both Jessup (8, p. 22) and Lawrence (13, p. 20).

Changes in the composition of the loan portfolio may have had a more significant impact upon the average yield on loans than changes in market structure. In this particular case the increases in consumer and mortgage loans relative to other assets at the entry banks would tend to increase the

TABLE 2
MEAN OPERATING RATIOS FOR ENTRY AND NONENTRY BANKS 1960, 1961, 1965, 1966
(Unit Banks in One-, Two-, and Three-Bank Towns)

Pre-entry Period

Operating Ratios	Entry Banks 1960	Entry Banks 1961	Nonentry Banks 1960	Nonentry Banks 1961	Operating Ratios	Entry Banks 1960	Entry Banks 1961	Nonentry Banks 1960	Nonentry Banks 1961
Net Current Earnings/Total Capital	16.44%	14.27%	19.99%	16.69%	All Other Expenses/Total Operating Revenue	25.62%	24.71%	23.88%	24.14%
Net Current Earnings/Total Assets	1.36	1.19	1.49	1.24	Total Operating Revenue/Total Assets	4.12	3.81	4.22	4.02
Net Current Earnings/Total Operating Revenue	34.16	31.57	35.32	30.72	Revenue on Loans/Total Loans	6.79	6.66	6.84	6.54
Government Securities/Total Assets	26.42	26.47	20.81	20.76	Total Capital/Total Assets	8.39	8.23	7.67	7.61
Other Securities/Total Assets	11.01	11.59	12.96	12.82	Total Capital/Total Risk Assets	18.95	18.45	14.66	14.12
Loans (Net)/Total Assets	35.10	34.62	39.75	41.15	Time Deposits/Total Deposits	17.34	18.00	23.08	23.44
Cash Assets/Total Assets	25.39	25.15	24.71	23.47	Interest on Time Deposits/Time Deposits	2.16	2.24	2.20	2.68
Interest and Dividends on U.S. Governments/Total Operating Revenue	23.36	21.14	18.48	16.59	Consumer Loans/Total Assets	10.01	9.95	9.61	9.13
Revenue on Loans/Total Operating Revenue	55.51	58.65	62.77	64.98	Farm Loans/Total Assets	7.88	7.79	8.88	11.15
Service Charges on Deposit Accounts/Total Operating Revenue	7.84	8.22	5.96	6.01	Real Estate Mortgages/Total Assets	5.83	5.50	5.88	5.74
Salaries and Wages/Total Operating Revenue	29.94	33.19	29.37	31.03	Business Loans/Total Assets	10.23	10.37	14.84	14.68
					All Other Expenses/Total Assets	1.06	0.95	1.01	0.97
Interest on Time and Savings Deposits/Total Operating Revenue	8.90	10.53	11.42	14.13	Total Current Operating Expenses/Total Assets	1.36	2.63	1.49	2.78
					Service Charges on Demand Deposits/Demand Deposits	0.46	0.44	0.37	0.36

TABLE 2 (*Continued*)

Post-entry Period

Operating Ratios	Entry Banks 1965	Entry Banks 1966	Nonentry Banks 1965	Nonentry Banks 1966	Operating Ratios	Entry Banks 1965	Entry Banks 1966	Nonentry Banks 1965	Nonentry Banks 1966
Net Current Earnings/Total Capital	14.34%	15.83%	15.14%	15.10%	All Other Expenses/Total Operating Revenue	22.27%	24.11%	23.31%	25.27%
Net Current Earnings/Total Assets	1.12	1.24	1.16	1.19	Total Operating Revenue/Total Assets	22.56	21.84	22.05	21.51
Net Current Earnings/Total Operating Revenue	25.94	26.67	25.22	24.56	Revenue on Loans/Total Loans	6.54	6.98	6.82	7.19
Government Securities/Total Assets	19.04	17.35	16.54	15.79	Total Capital/Total Assets	8.06	7.99	7.61	7.83
Other Securities/Total Assets	12.96	14.72	14.71	18.10	Total Capital/Total Risk Assets	14.76	13.14	12.19	12.17
Loans (Net)/Total Assets	44.35	44.84	46.66	45.51	Time Deposits/Total Deposits	31.34	36.15	35.00	38.01
Cash Assets/Total Assets	21.08	19.78	17.69	17.49	Interest on Time Deposits/Time Deposits	3.38	3.37	3.31	3.48
Interest and Dividends on U.S. Governments/Total Operating Revenue	18.08	15.72	14.62	15.63	Consumer Loans/Total Assets	13.73	13.71	10.69	11.01
Revenue on Loans/Total Operating Revenue	64.39	65.98	67.87	66.52	Farm Loans/Total Assets	7.27	6.88	11.43	9.68
Service Charges on Deposit Accounts/Total Operating Revenue	5.80	5.72	5.40	5.56	Real Estate Mortgages/Total Assets	8.26	8.93	7.08	7.77
Salaries and Wages/Total Operating Revenue	29.24	27.38	29.42	28.61	Business Loans/Total Assets	14.03	13.91	16.67	15.89
					All Other Expenses/Total Assets	1.02	1.04	1.01	1.06
Interest on Time and Savings Deposits/Total Operating Revenue	22.27	24.11	23.31	25.27	Total Current Operating Expenses/Total Assets	3.31	3.47	3.42	3.68
					Service Charges on Demand Deposits/Demand Deposits	0.43	0.48	0.44	0.50

TABLE 3
"t" VALUES FOR ENTRY AND NONENTRY BANKS 1960, 1961, 1965, 1966
(Unit Banks in One-, Two-, and Three-Bank Towns)

Operating Ratio	Pre-Entry Years 1960	Pre-Entry Years 1961	Post-Entry Years 1965	Post-Entry Years 1966	Operating Ratio	Pre-Entry Years 1960	Pre-Entry Years 1961	Post-Entry Years 1965	Post-Entry Years 1966
Net Current Earnings/Total Capital	−2.61##	−2.21##	− .84	.71	All Other Expenses/Total Operating Revenue	1.35	.44	.47	.24
Net Current Earnings/Total Assets	−1.32	− .59	− .44	.56	Total Operating Revenue/Total Assets	− .72	−1.30	− .84	−1.17
Net Current Earnings/Total Operating Revenue	− .49	.37	.39	1.08	Revenue on Loans/Total Loans	− .18	.40	−1.28	−1.03
Government Securities/Total Assets	2.69###	2.67##	1.17	.74	Total Capital/Total Assets	1.88#	1.52	1.01	.39
Other Securities/Total Assets	−1.21	− .76	−1.08	−1.89##	Total Capital/Total Risk Assets	3.16###	3.34###	2.12##	1.08
Loans (Net)/Total Assets	−2.14##	−2.86###	− .93	− .33	Time Deposits/Total Deposits	−2.23##	−2.17##	−1.52	− .80
Cash Assets/Total Assets	.41	1.21	2.70###	2.12##	Interest on Time Deposits/Time Deposits	− .26	−2.53##	.50	− .63
Interest and Dividends on U.S. Governments/Total Operating Revenue	2.33##	2.29##	1.71#	.05	Consumer Loans/Total Assets	.29	.61	2.17##	1.90#
Revenue on Loans/Total Operating Revenue	−3.04###	−2.68##	−1.55	− .25	Farm Loans/Total Assets	− .47	−1.27	−1.67	1.32
Service Charges on Deposit Accounts/Total Operating Revenue	2.16##	2.52##	.53	.22	Real Estate Mortgages/Total Assets	− .06	− .27	1.07	1.09
Salaries and Wages/Total Operating Revenue	.51	1.92#	− .14	− .97	Business Loans/Total Assets	−3.02###	−2.61##	−1.35	−1.16
Interest on Time and Savings Deposits/Total Operating Revenue	−1.68#	−2.33#	− .58	− .60	All Other Expenses/Total Assets	.80	− .40	.04	− .19
					Total Current Operating Expenses/Total Assets	−1.32	−1.04	− .67	−1.40
					Service Charges on Demand Deposits/Demand Deposits	1.38	1.28	.06	.26

Note: #Significant at 0.10 level. ##Significant at 0.05 level. ###Significant at 0.01 level.

per dollar of demand deposits was not significantly different before or after.[20]

A potentially important impact of bank entry performance may occur through the rate of growth of the established banks, thus affecting the viability of these institutions over time. In particular, in the absence of an increase in the rate at which an area generates deposits, the entry of a new bank would force previously existing institutions to share the growth potential of their communities with the new bank. If there is considerable dissatisfaction with the established banks, the new bank may be able to claim a disproportionate share of the total increase in local deposits plus some deposits from the existing banks. On the other hand, the rate of growth of a bank's deposits are a proxy for the quality of bank services rendered. Thus, if the entry of a new competitior spurs the existing banks into offering more and better services, their rate of deposit growth may accelerate relative to banks not faced with new competition.

The banks in the entry communities, contrary to the results found by Kohn and Carlo,[21] did not experience less rapid growth in total deposits than the banks in the nonentry towns. In fact, the opposite was the case. Total deposits for banks in the entry sample expanded at a 7-percent annual rate during the 1960-66 period, while total deposits for banks in the nonentry sample grew at only 5.6-per cent average annual rate. The difference can be attributed largely to the growth of time deposits which expanded at a 20.7-per cent annual rate at the entry banks but only a 15.6-per cent annual rate at the nonentry banks.[22] Considering the fact that *de novo* entry exerted little or no impact on rates paid, the entry of a new competitior seems to have had a much greater impact on the willingness of the existing banks to accept interest-bearing deposits at going rates rather than on the rates actually offered.

III. CONCLUSION

Preceding research on *actual* changes in banking structure has focused largely on changes in the performance of banks acquired by branch systems or holding companies. These studies have generally found that the impact of branch or holding company acquisitions or of other changes in ownership has generally proven beneficial to the communities involved. Loan-asset ratios rose, while consumer and business loans became more important relative to the norm. This study extends the findings of earlier research by demonstrating that similar changes can occur in the performance of established banks as a result of *de novo* entry.

The appearance of a new independent bank in the situations analyzed brought about significant changes in the nature of banking services offered to the local communities by the established banks. Loan-asset ratios increased, greater emphasis was placed on business and consumer loans, while the prices for key banking services, as measured by revenue on loans to total loans and service charges on deposit accounts to demand deposits, did not

---

average yield on the whole loan portfolio, offsetting the rate-depressing effects of new competition.

The poor results obtained for the time deposit rate appear to be consistent with Shull's findings for Illinois unit banks that "over time, the influence of local structure has been diluted by regional or even national competition for time and savings funds." (19, p. 2).

20. This measure is of questionable significance, however. See Kaufman (9, p. 432, n. 13).

21. Kohn and Carlo (12, p. 113). These results are, however, not contrary to Motter's findings (15, p. 333).

22. The newly chartered banks were not included in the calculation of these growth rates. However, several earlier studies have examined the performance of new banks in terms of profitability and deposit growth. See, for example, Motter (15) and Shea (17). The results of these studies generally suggest that new banks fare very well relative to normative rates of return and deposit growth.

appear to rise relative to the norm. Also, established banks in the new entry communities were spurred into entering the competition for time deposits.

These benefits to the public occurred without an adverse impact upon bank profitability or growth. The force of new competition appeared to result in competing banks that better served their communities and, at the same time, provided at least a normal rate of return on capital to their stockholders. These findings are particularly significant in view of the high social priority placed upon the provision of bank credit to local areas, especially in relatively isolated communities where both bank and nonbank alternatives tend to be limited and costly. At the very least, the results reported here imply that *de novo* bank entry, at least in unit banking areas, does not create unusually repressive conditions for existing financial institutions, even relatively small ones.

The results also suggest the importance of adopting a multi-dimensional point of view in analyzing structure-performance relationships. Analysis of the composition of bank credit, earnings, and expenses, as well as the traditional measures of price and profitability, may yield significant information about the impact of structural changes. Given the oligopolistic or quasi-monopolistic nature of most banking markets, so-called "price" effects appear to severely understate the true impact of structural changes.

The study has several important limitations which suggest avenues for future research. It does not, for example, examine the impact of *de novo* entry on the service dimensions of performance in banking—the "quality" and "convenience" of banking services provided to the local community. Moreover, the methodology adopted may not have permitted enough time to elapse in order to capture fully the impact of new entry upon bank operating policies. Bankers in rural communities might be expected to react cautiously to the appearance of new competition. In addition, a longer period of time may be necessary to judge which benefits accruing to the banking public will be permanent and which only temporary. With the passage of time it seems likely that both the new and the established banks will recognize the interdependence of their operations and this recognition will gradually erode many of the initial benefits stemming from *de novo* entry. Without question, it is important that the findings of the study be replicated using data from different time periods and from other regions with different banking laws.

REFERENCES

1. David A. Alhadeff, *Monopoly and Competition in Banking* (Berkeley, California: University of California Press, 1954).
2. Franklin R. Edwards, "Concentration in Banking and its Effects on Business Loan Rates," *The Review of Economics and Statistics*, XLVI (August 1964), 294-300.
3. Theodore G. Flechsig, *Banking Market Structure and Performance in Metropolitan Areas* (Washington, D.C.: Board of Governors of the Federal Reserve System, 1965).
4. Donald R. Fraser and Peter S. Rose, "More on Banking Structure and Performance: The Evidence from Texas," *The Journal of Financial and Quantitative Analysis*, VI (January 1971), 601-11.
5. Ralph H. Gelder and George Budzeika, "Banking Market Determination—The Case of Central Nassau County," *Monthly Review*, Federal Reserve Bank of New York, November 1970, 258-66.
6. H. Peter Gray, "Bank Regulation, Bank Profitability, and Federal Reserve Membership," *The National Banking Review*, I (December 1963), 207-20.
7. Paul M. Horvitz and Bernard Shull, "The Impact of Branch Banking on Bank Performance," *The National Banking Review*, II (December 1964), 143-88.
8. Paul F. Jessup, *Changes in Bank Ownership: The Impact on Operating Performance* (Washington, D.C.: Board of Governors of the Federal Reserve System, 1969).
9. George G. Kaufman, "Bank Market Structure and Performance: The Evidence from Iowa," *The Southern Economic Journal*, XXXII (April 1966), 429-39.
10. George G. Kaufman and Roberta Detz, *Customers View a Bank Merger—A Resurvey of Elkhart, Indiana*, Federal Reserve Bank of Chicago, October 1969.

11. George G. Kaufman and Cynthia Latta, "Near Banks and Local Savings," *The National Banking Review*, III (June 1965), 539-42.
12. Ernest Kohn and Carmen J. Carlo, *The Competitive Impact of New Branches*, New York State Banking Department, December 1969.
13. Robert J. Lawrence, *The Performance of Bank Holding Companies* (Washington, D.C.: Board of Governors of the Federal Reserve System, 1967).
14. Lucille S. Mayne, *The Effect of Federal Reserve System Membership on the Profitability of Illinois Banks, 1961-63*, The Pennsylvania State University, 1967.
15. David C. Motter, "Bank Formation and the Public Interest," *The National Banking Review*, Vol. No. (March 1965), 299-350.
16. David C. Motter and Deane Carson, "Bank Entry and the Public Interest: A Case Study," *The National Banking Review*, I (June 1964), 465-512.
17. Maurice P. Shea, III, "New Commercial Banks in Massachusetts," *New England Business Review*, Federal Reserve Bank of Boston September 1967, 2-9.
18. Bernard Shull, "Commercial Banking as a 'Line of Commerce,'" *The National Banking Review*, I (December 1963), 187-206.
19. Bernard Shull, *Nonlocal Competition for Time Deposits in Isolated One- and Two-Bank Towns*, Staff Economic Studies, Board of Governors of the Federal Reserve System, 1967.

CASE 25 PRODUCT LIABILITY: WHAT ARE THE LIMITS?*

BACKGROUND: SHIFT IN EMPHASIS FOR PRODUCT LIABILITY

Use of consumer products may often result in accidents and injury to purchaser, user, or sometimes to a bystander. The question of who should be held liable has been a matter of concern both to the courts and to businesspeople attempting to cope with a changing legal environment.

There are two important aspects to the question of product liability: first, the legal question of assessment of liability for damage; and, second, the economic aspect of accidental damages since this involves a special case of externalities. Externalities are either costs or benefits that are not mutually or voluntarily accepted by the parties involved in some transaction or relationship. An accident, therefore, contains an element of externality in that the parties involved in the accident usually do not agree mutually or voluntarily to the relationship.

The existence of an externality is related to both the rules for, and the costs of assigning and exchanging certain property rights. Products may be thought of as packages of rights to do things that are embodied in their specific physical features. Roland McKean has pointed out regarding property rights and externalities that,

If all rights were clearly defined and assigned, *if* there were zero transaction costs, and *if* people agreed to abide by the results of voluntary exchange, there would be no externalities. Accidental damage is no exception. Wherever it results in an externality, this is related to the rules for and costs of assigning and exchanging rights.[1]

Roland McKean sees the issue of product liability in terms of specific assignment of property rights. Therefore, if a seller possesses the right to avoid liability under law, this is similar to a right, say, to resell one's land, which becomes a feature of an asset that gives it added value. Various kinds of assignment of rights (from complete avoidance of liability to total responsibility for liability) would tend to have different impacts on equity (from the point of view of the individual).

LEGAL DEVELOPMENTS CONCERNING PRODUCT LIABILITY

With the development of industrial societies, one of the most important conditions for the existence of product liability was privity; that is, a direct contractual relationship (privity) between, say, a retailer and consumer, but not between a manufacturer and a consumer. A decisive change occurred in a case in 1916, *MacPherson v. Buick Motor Company*,[2] in which a manufacturer was held liable, regardless of privity, for injuries resulting from the use of a product, whether or not it was inherently dangerous, as long as there was evidence of "negligence" in the manufacture or assembly of the product.

This rule became widespread, although the product usually had to pose significant damages to life and limb, and the courts often refused to make rewards for minor hazards. The courts, for the most part, were uneasy about proceeding to strict liability by a producer lest it result in more harm than good; however, it was generally felt that various small steps with relatively unambiguous cut-offs would yield more good than harm. For instance, there was the development of the doctrine of *res ipsa loquitur*, that is, let the matter speak for itself. Thus, if a sealed unit in a machine caused damage, the courts often concluded that this manufacturer could be held responsible since it obviously had assembled the unit in question.

In recent years, expressed warranty and especially implied warranty have been extended by the courts, further reflecting a shift toward the concept of "let the seller beware." There may now be an implied warranty of fitness of a product for any specific purpose as distinct from the product's ordinary or intended purpose. Moreover, a manufacturer's advertisement to consumers can generate a warranty to them. In *Baxter v. Ford Motor Company*,[3] the producer was held to be liable because a windshield

---

*Material contained in this case is based in part upon the thesis of Donald M. Jenkins, "The Product Liability of Manufacturers: An Understanding and Exploration," School of Law, Western Reserve University, June, 1971.

[1] Roland N. McKean, "Products Liability: Implications of Some Changing Property Rights," *The Quarterly Journal of Economics*, Nov. 1970, p. 611.

[2] 217 N.Y. 382, 111 N.E. 1050 (1916).
[3] 168 Wash. 456, 12 P. 2d 409.

advertised as shatterproof did in fact shatter when struck by a stone.

The emerging doctrine regarding product liability appears to be strict liability under tort, which can be roughly defined as liability simply because an alleged wrong was done, thus eliminating privity or the failure to fulfill a contractual relationship. A crucial case in this respect was that of *Henningsen v. Bloomfield Motors, Inc.* in 1960.[4] An individual suffered injuries when her car suddenly turned right and ran into a wall, allegedly due to a defective steering gear. Without any evidence of negligence, the court held Chrysler Corporation as well as the selling dealer liable, stating: "... an implied warranty that it (the car) is reasonably suitable for use as such accompanies it into the hands of the ultimate purchaser. Absence of agency ... is immaterial."[5] Within several years this doctrine of strict liability under tort was applied to a wide variety of products, including a glass door, shotgun, and dental chair. In addition, liability to bystanders, as well as to other extensions of manufacturer liability have been established.

However, even strict tort liability requires that there be some defect in the product, and issues regarding proof of injury and defect, abnormal use, intervening conduct, and knowledge of the defect may still relieve the producer of liability in many circumstances.[6] The full development of strict liability under tort goes further in raising the probability that a manufacturer can be held liable resulting from an accident or injury from its product. From a legal-economic point of view, there has been a reassignment of certain valuable property rights in a probabilistic sense.

LARSEN V. GENERAL MOTORS CORPORATION

A precedent-breaking decision was issued in 1968 that completely upset the previous position of the courts that the responsibility of the manufacturer is the duty to design the product to be reasonably fit for its intended purpose, its normal and proper use, and not for an unintended use.[7] This decision involved *Larsen v. General Motors Corporation*, where the plaintiff alleged that the design of the steering column assembly constituted an increased hazard to the occupant of the automobile when it was involved in an accident.[8] The alleged defective design did not cause the collision. The accident, involving the plaintiff, was a head-on collision with another vehicle.

The District Court granted summary judgment for the defendant. The Circuit Court asserted that the manufacturer's "duty" is to design a product that is reasonably fit for its intended use and free of hidden defects that could render it unsafe for such use. The Court thus turned its attention to the "intended use" of the automobile. The Court ruled that it is foreseeable that an auto will be involved in some type of injury-producing accident and that the manufacturer cannot say that such use is not intended.

Moreover, when the design of the product causes an unreasonable risk to the users of the product, manufacturer liability should follow. Such injuries, according to the Court, are readily foreseeable as an incident of the normal and intended use of an automobile. The duty of reasonable care must be viewed in light of the risks involved. The court concluded the following:

> While all risks cannot be eliminated nor can a crash-proof vehicle be designed under the present state of the art, there are many common sense factors in design, which are or should be well-known to the manufacturer that will minimize or lessen the injurious effects of a collision.[9]

This decision made it clear that this duty applies to all manufacturers with the customary limitations of unintended or unforeseeable use. The Court, while emphasizing that its holdings were relevant to the issue of negligence, indicated it could be carried further to cover a concept of strict liability.

The *Larsen v. General Motors* case represents a major change in the law concerning the design liability of manufacturers and has been accepted by some other courts.[10] There have been, however, some courts that have taken contrary positions regarding this issue.

The trend of the past several years concerning product liability indicates the direction in which the courts have been moving because emphasis has been placed on the tendency to expand the application of strict liability through interpretation. Sellers are defined to include not only the original producer, but also the producer of component and subcomponent parts. The exposure time for potential liability is measured from the time of the injury. Moreover,

---

[4]32 N.J. 358, 161 A 2d 69 (1960). See also Willious R. Prosser, "The Fall of the Citadel (Strict Liability to the Consumer)," *Minnesota Law Review* (1966), pp. 791-848.

[5]Id. 32 N.J. 384, 161 A. 2d. 84.

[6]Prosser, *Op. cit.*, pp. 824-848.

[7]*Shumard v. General Motors Corp.*, 270F. Supp. 311 (S.D. Ohio 1967).

[8]*Larsen v. General Motors Corp.*, 391F. 2nd 495 (8th Cir. 1968).

[9]*Ibid.* p. 503.

[10]See: *Dyson v. General Motors Corp.*, 298 F. Supp 1064 (E.D.P.A. 1969); *DeFelice v. Ford Motor Co.*, 28 Conn. sup. 164, 255 A. 2d 636 (1969); and *Storey v. Exhaust Specialists & Parts, Inc.*, 464 P. 2d 831 (Or. 1970).

resale of the product does not preempt the manufacturer from liability.

Strict liability reaches the manufacturer of all products, although some by their nature are more apt to be defective and unreasonably dangerous. A defect may be shown by inferential evidence where direct evidence cannot be produed. Instead of requiring proof of a specific defect, proof that the product was not fit for its intended purpose has been accepted as sufficient evidence of a defect. The design duty of a producer has been broadened and his or her failure to perform this duty may result in a defective product for the purposes of establishing strict liability. In addition, the elements of recoverable damages have been expanded to include commercial or monetary losses in some contexts, in addition to personal injuries and property damage.

ECONOMIC IMPLICATIONS OF STRICT PRODUCER LIABILITY

What would be the economic implications of moving completely to total producer liability, first, in the case of a defective product and, second, for a product without defect but improperly used? If the trend of court decisions continues to increase the probability of the producer being held strictly liable, in the case of a defective product, several factors would tend to result.

First, it would be reasonable to expect more court cases and court costs, since under complete producer liability the potential for gain from suits by alleged injured parties would greatly increase. It would be more difficult and costly for producers to encourage purchasers to exercise care in the use of their products, thus it would be entirely possible for the accident rate to rise.[11] Producers faced with rising injury suits and/or accident rates involving their products would be expected to turn increasingly to liability insurance.

Under the "protection" of liability insurance, some producers might find it efficient to neglect safety features altogether, since there will be lesser demands from consumers that would dilute the shift toward safer products, which has been the apparent desire of public policy and consumer groups.[12] With the customer facing a lower probability of being liable, relatively hazardous designs for products would tend to become more attractive to the producer, which would tend to result in increased demand for such products relative to comparatively safer products.

[11]McKean, *Op. cit.*, p. 622.
[12]Oliver E. Williamson, Douglas G. Olson, et. al. "Externalities, Insurance, and Disability Analysis," *Economica*, Vol. 34, August 1967, pp. 235-53.

Producers, facing a greater probability of being held liable and having to carry liability insurance or pay damages, would find relatively hazardous designs becoming more costly; thus, the supply curve for such products would tend to decline. On the basis of the shift in liability assignment itself, there is no presumption that the quality of hazardous products sold would be improved. However, the buyer would have to pay a higher price to the producer being forced to bear the higher costs of marketing relatively hazardous products.

It is not entirely clear what will be the actual outcome due to the continual movement of courts toward strict producer liability. Where will it stop? As with automobile accident insurance, there may be a development of producer liability without fault or defect. The manufacturer might be held liable for all injuries occurring with the use of this product, regardless of the circumstances. This would bring a whole new set of economic effects as a result. Moreover, there are some who believe it would be more equitable to spread costs even more widely, that is, instituted general taxpayer liability. For instance, in the case of an airline crash, instead of holding the airline, supplier, or manufacturer at fault, why not put the burden on taxpayers in general and have the government compensate people for all injuries regardless of fault? However, this would also have substantial repercussions upon the market and individual freedom of choice.

Questions for Discussion

1. If you were a manufacturer of a consumer product might you logically ask: what are the limits to your liability? Most state legislatures have not defined any limits. The courts are attempting to answer the question. What is your answer?
2. Discuss the implications of carrying these court decisions to their logical end in relation to incentives and innovation by American manufacturers.
3. Discuss the economic effects of various liability assignments upon producers, suppliers, customers, taxpayers, as would occur with, say, complete producer liability without defect or total taxpayer liability regardless of fault.
4. Analyze present trends of court cases and state legislatures regarding products liability and no-fault insurance. See, for instance, James C. Gardner v. Q.H.S., Inc. and J.M. Fields, Inc. U.S. Court of Appeals, 4th Circuit, No. 15, 393, August 1971.
5. In your opinion, what type assignment of rights and degree of product liability would be best, and in what sense?

Chapter 8 Merger Regulation

CASE 26 PROCTOR & GAMBLE-CLOROX MERGER: A LANDMARK DECISION

The Proctor & Gamble-Clorox merger case is a significant one because it was an early application of the Celler-Kefauver antimerger act to a conglomerate or product-extension merger.

Following the FTC hearings on Proctor's acquisition of Clorox in 1957, the hearing examiner rendered his decision in which he concluded that the acquisition was unlawful and ordered divestiture. After appeal to the entire Commission, the hearing examiner's decision was reversed, holding that the record as then constituted was inadequate. The examiner was remanded to hold additional hearings for the express purpose of taking added evidence on the postmerger situation in the liquid bleach industry.

After additional hearings, the examiner again held the acquisition unlawful and ordered divestiture, this time with the concurrence of the entire Commission. The Court of Appeals reversed the FTC decision and directed the complaint be dismissed. The Court of Appeals said that the Commission's findings of illegality had been based on "treacherous conjecture," mere possibility and suspicion.[1]

The findings of the FTC are briefly summarized as follows: (1) substitution of Proctor with its huge assets and advertising advantages for already dominant Clorox would dissuade new entrants and discourage active competition from firms already in industry due to fear of retaliation by Proctor; (2) possibility of retailers giving Proctor preferred shelf space for Clorox; (3) danger that Proctor might underprice Clorox in order to drive out competition, and subsidize this predatory pricing with revenue from other products; (4) the "practical tendency" of the merger would be to transform the structure of the liquid bleach industry into an arena of big business competition only, with the few small firms eventually falling by the wayside; and, (5) merger would diminish potential competition by eliminating Proctor as a potential entrant into the industry.

The Court of Appeals in dismissing the FTC ruling set forth the following arguments. First, it pointed out that, in addition to the six large producers sharing 80 percent of the liquid bleach market, there were 200 smaller producers. As for the possibility that Proctor would use its tremendous advertising budget and volume discounts to push Clorox, the court found "it difficult to base a finding of illegality on discounts in advertising."[2] The court rejected the FTC's finding that the merger eliminated the potential competition of Proctor because there was no reasonable probability that Proctor would have entered the household bleach market but for the merger.[3] The lower court concluded that there "was no evidence that Proctor at any time in the past engaged in predatory practice, or that it intended to do so in the future."[4]

The Court of Appeals heavily relied on post-acquisition evidence to the effect that the other producers subsequent to the merger were selling more bleach for more money than ever before, and that there had been no significant change in Clorox's market share in the 4 years subsequent to the merger.[5]

The Supreme Court in its infinite wisdom reversed the lower court's decision, stating that the FTC's findings were amply supported by the evidence; therefore, the Court of Appeals erred. The Supreme Court rested its decision on three alleged findings of anticompetitive effects: (1) substitution of the power of acquiring firm for already dominant Clorox raised entry barriers and made the market more rigid; (2)

---

[1] FTC vs. The Proctor & Gamble Company, 358 F. 2d 74.
[2] Ibid., 358 F. 2d, p. 81.
[3] Ibid., 358 F 2d, p. 82.
[4] Ibid., 358 F. 2d, p. 83.
[5] Ibid., 358 F. 2d, p. 80.

elimination of potential competition from acquiring firm; and, (3) entrance of Proctor would dissuade smaller firms in liquid bleach industry from aggressively competing.

There were four important guides to the adjudication of conglomerate mergers under the Celler-Kefauver act that were set forth by the Supreme Court. First, the decision can rest on analysis of market structure without resorting to evidence of postmerger, anticompetitive behavior. Second, the operation of the premerger market must be understood as a foundation for successful analysis. Third, if it is reasonably probable that there will be a change in the market structure which will allow the exercise of substantially greater market power, then a *prima facie* case has been made under section 7 as amended. Finally, where the case against the merger rests on the probability of increased market power the defendants may attempt to prove that there are countervailing economies reasonably probable which should be weighed against adverse effects.

Mr. Justice Harlan, although concurring with the final decision disagreed with the cavalier manner in which the majority of the Court blithely overthrew the lower court decision without providing sufficient guidelines. Justice Harlan saw this case as a landmark decision that had important effects upon future administrative and judicial application of the Celler-Kefauver act. He states that:

> ... more refined analysis is required before putting the stamp of approval on what the Commission has done in this case. It is regrettable to see this Court as it enters this comparatively new field of economic adjudication starting off with what has almost become a kind of *res ipsa loquitur* approach to antitrust cases.[6]

Justice Harlan argues in vain for the formulation of standards for application of section 7 to conglomerate mergers, and then makes a valiant attempt to singlehandedly do so.

Justice Harlan first examines each of the findings of alleged anticompetitive effects of the merger. Examining the contention of the Court that the liquid bleach market was "oligopolistic" and that Proctor would make the oligopoly "more rigid" because in the opinion of the Court, "... (t)here is every reason to assume that the smaller firms would become more cautious in competing due to their fear of retaliation by Proctor."[7] Justice Harlan points out that the Court fails to show what reasons lie behind this assumption or by what standard such an effect is deemed "reasonably probable."[8]

It could equally be assumed that smaller firms would become more aggressive in competing since Proctor, as a new entrant in the bleach field, was vulnerable to attack. In fact, the postacquisition evidence gathered by the FTC appears to support this second proposition over the first.

The Court next stressed the rise in alleged barriers to new entry in the liquid bleach resulting from the larger advertising capabilities of Proctor for those of Clorox. The Court, however, fails to show why it considers this change to have significance under the Celler-Kefauver act, nor does it indicate when or how the alleged entry barriers affect competition in a relevant market.[9]

Finally, Justice Harlan points out that the Court placed great emphasis on the loss of a potential entrant in the liquid bleach market—Proctor & Gamble. Two entirely separate anticompetitive effects might result from this loss, yet the Court fails to distinguish between them. The first is simply the loss of the most likely entrant that tends to increase the operative barriers by decreasing the likelihood of attempted entry from outside the industry. But this effect is simply a reinforcement of the Court's previous entry-barrier argument, which was not very convincing. Further doubt is cast upon the creditability of the argument that Proctor was a potential entrant aside from merger by Proctor's memorandum discussing the question of entry into the liquid bleach market which stated:

> We would not recommend that the Company consider trying to enter this market by introducing a new brand or by trying to expand a sectional brand. This is because we feel it would require a very heavy investment to achieve a major volume in the field, and with a low "available" (a reference to profit margin) ... .[10]

A second possible effect of elimination of Proctor as a potential entrant is that one measure of horizontal competition has been lost. The exclusion of what would promise to be an important independent competitor may be sufficient to support a finding of illegality under Clayton section 7 when the market has few competitors. But, Justice Harlan points out:

> The Commission ... expressly refused to find a reasonable probability that Proctor would have entered this market on its own, and the Sixth Circuit was in emphatic agreement. ... it seems clear to me that no consequence can be attached to the possibility of loss of Proctor as an actual competitor.[11]

---

[6]FTC vs. The Proctor & Gamble Co., 386 U.S. 568 (Apr. 1967).
[7]*Ibid.*, p. 575.
[8]*Ibid.*, p. 584.
[9]*Ibid.*, p. 585.
[10]FTC vs. Proctor & Gamble Co., 386 U.S. 568, p. 584
[11]*Ibid.*, p. 586.

Merger Regulation

Relating to the question of mergers in so-called oligopoly industries, Justice Harlan wonders whether the state of economic knowledge is sufficiently advanced to enable a sure-footed administrative or judicial determination to be made of the alleged anticompetitive effect in mergers of this type. There is no doubt that Congress desired that conglomerate mergers be brought under section 7 scrutiny, but many economists have argued that such scrutiny can not conclusively lead to a valid finding of illegality. The simple fact remains that if a firm purchases another producing an item that is neither competing, nor a raw material for its own product, there is no competition between them to be extinguished or the possibility of fewer alternatives for customers or suppliers.[12]

In fact, several arguments can be put forth supporting product extension or conglomerate mergers on efficiency grounds which argue against excessive controls being imposed on them. First, the ability to merge brings large firms into the market for capital assets and encourages economic development by holding out the incentive of quick and profitable liquidation to others. The owners of Clorox who had built the business, were able to liquify their capital on profitable terms without dismantling their enterprise. Second, merger allows an active management to move rapidly into new markets bringing with its entrance, competitive stimulation and innovation. Third, a merger of this type permits a large corporation to protect its shareholders from business fluctuation through diversification. And finally, it may facilitate the introduction of capital resources allowing significant economies, both production and financial, into a stagnating market.[13]

Justice Harlan concludes with a stern warning: "... the statute does not leave us free to strike down mergers on the basis of sheer speculation or a general fear of bigness."[14]

Questions for Discussion

1. Aside from the question of guilt in this case, who appears to present the most convincing argument—the lower court, the Supreme Court majority, or Justice Harlan? Why?
2. Why is this decision so important? Are sufficient guidelines provided for future prospective mergers by this decision? How could the guidelines be improved?
3. Discuss the pros and cons of a conglomerate or product extension merger. Is there anything unique or different regarding legality of this type of merger as opposed to a vertical or horizontal merger?
4. As a manager, what can be implied from the activity of the FTC and the decisions of the Supreme Court relative to merger activity?

[12]*Ibid.*, p. 587.

[13]*Ibid.*, p. 588.

[14]*Ibid.*, p. 590; also, see FTC vs. General Foods Corp. 3 Trade Reg. Rep. 17,465 at 22,749 (Commissioner Elman dissenting).

CASE 27 BANK MERGERS AND ANTITRUST: PROVIDENT NATIONAL BANK AND CENTRAL-PENN NATIONAL BANK MERGER

BACKGROUND

In many respects, antimerger law, as applied to banking and finance, is identical to that applied to nonfinancial institutions; however, there does exist specific bank merger legislation, e.g., Bank Holding Company Act (1956) amended in 1970 and the Bank Merger Acts (1960 and 1966). Two important antimerger cases involving banks were the Philadelphia Bank Case (1963) and the Manufacturers Hanover Case (1965). Both cases involved mergers between large banks, and in the case of Philadelphia National Bank (PNB) and Girard Trust, the second and third largest banks in the vicinity, respectively, the merger would have resulted in the largest bank in the area.

The Supreme Court struck down both mergers applying a strict interpretation of the Celler-Kefauver antimerger act, which prohibits any merger with anticompetitive effects resulting in increased concentration in the relevant product market and geographical area. The proposed merger of PNB with 21 percent of the market as defined by the Justice Department and Girard with 15 percent would have resulted in a single bank with 36 percent of the market.[1] Congress was intensely concerned that under the rigid test propounded in the PNB case a "floundering" or "stagnating" bank could not be saved by merging with a stronger and healthier bank. Thus, the 1966 Bank Merger Act carved out a new exception or defense for an otherwise anticompetitive merger in the form of a convenience and needs test. Lower courts have taken opposing views on the meaning of this new test.

THE PROVIDENT NATIONAL BANK CASE

The U.S. vs. Provident National Bank case (1968)[2] is significant for several reasons. First, it is a recent application of all relevant bank merger legislation. Second, it involves the same banking area as the original PNB case, i.e., the four-county area including Philadelphia. Finally, the case never went to the Supreme Court; thus, certain issues still remain in doubt.

The Department of Justice in 1966 filed to enjoin a merger of the Provident National Bank and Central-Penn National Bank of Philadelphia. The Comptroller of the Currency, who as the relevant regulator had approved the merger under the Bank Merger Act provisions, intervened as a party and filed to dismiss this case along with the defendants. Chief Judge Clary of the U.S. District Court rejected the Government's request for an injunction against the merger.

The Justice Department maintained that the Court should grant the motion to enjoin the merger; it took the position that the sole purpose of Congress was to halt all mergers after suit was filed until there had been a final determination on the merits.[3] Judge Clary stated:

> It appears throughout the legislative history that the Congress was concerned with the problems of divestiture as well as the tremendous expense to the applicant banks when mergers were unduly delayed, and that stay should be granted only when the Government... in good faith proceeded promptly to a trial on the merits... It is, therefore, the decision of this Court that it will not stay the merger...[4]

The Government continued its suit and the case returned to Judge Clary under a civil action without a jury, and a final decision was rendered in February, 1968. The merger involved the fifth and seventh largest banks in a four-county area by which the resultant bank would have controlled approximately 10 percent of the relevant market. In making the decision in the case, the Court was faced with a dilemma stated by Judge Clary as follows:

---

[1] Eugene M. Singer, *Antitrust Economics*, New York: Prentice-Hall, 1968, p. 128.
[2] U.S. vs. Provident National Bank and Central-Penn National Bank of Philadelphia, U.S. District Ct. ED. Pa., 280 F. Supp.
[3] This appears to have been the opinion of the lower court in the White Consolidated-White Motors merger case.
[4] U.S. vs. Provident National Bank and Central-Penn National Bank of Philadelphia, D.C., 262 F. Supp. 397.

The dilemma confronting the Court is that . . . a jury would have no difficulty in finding qualitatively that the proposed merger would be a good merger . . . However, because of the quantitative (mechanical rules) approach to the question of antitrust violations declared as a policy by the Supreme Court and its decisions supporting that policy, this Court is constrained, *albeit* reluctantly, to declare that this merger may not be consummated.[5]

Judge Clary clearly and systematically presents the findings in this case. In December, 1965 Provident and Central-Penn National banks filed with the Comptroller of the Currency an application to merge under the provisions of the Bank Merger Act (1960), which requires approval of all bank mergers by the relevant regulating agency—Comptroller of Currency, Federal Reserve Board, or Federal Deposit Insurance Corporation. Prior to the Comptroller's approval of this merger, the Bank Merger Act was amended in 1966 to create a new defense for anticompetitive mergers. It allowed that if the anticompetitive effects of the proposed merger are clearly outweighed in the public interest by the probable effect in meeting the convenience and needs of the community to be served, then the merger is legal. Moreover, the amended act deleted the words "line of commerce" which appeared in the 1960 Act, thus leaving open the question whether commercial banking is still to be considered as the area of effective competition.

The F.D.I.C. filed no report, but both the Federal Reserve and the Justice Department reported that the merger's effect on competition would be significantly adverse and therefore should not be approved. If approved, the resultant merged bank would become the fourth largest bank in the four-county area.

Judge Clary followed the approach developed for applying Clayton Section 7 (as amended) standards. Thus, he examined the impact and effect of the proposed merger on the (1) relevant geographic market, (2) relevant product market, (3) effects on market concentration and anticompetitive behavior, and finally adding (4) convenience and needs of the community.

THE RELEVANT GEOGRAPHIC MARKET

The four-county area of Bucks, Montgomery, Delaware, and Philadelphia was proposed by the Government as the relevant section of the country for this case, which was the same as in the earlier Philadelphia National Bank case (1963). The Government showed that by number, 95 percent of Provident's total deposit accounts were within the four-county area, and 98 percent of Central-Penn's deposit accounts also were located within the area.

The Comptroller of the Currency disagreed with the assertion that the four-county area was the relevant geographic market. He contended that the Standard Metropolitan Statistical Area (SMSA), which comprised three New Jersey counties and five Pennsylvania counties, was more relevant. He argued that this case is not bound by the PNB ruling since a different factual record was developed in this case. The Court agreed with the Government in finding the four-county area as appropriate for this case, but set forth a distinction between wholesale accounts, which in some cases should be considered in a national market, and retail accounts, which essentially are relegated to the local community. This point will be discussed in detail later.

THE RELEVANT PRODUCT MARKET

The Justice Department maintained that commercial banking is the appropriate product market in which to assess this merger's competitive effects as in the PNB-Girard Trust case. In 1963, the Supreme Court ruled in the PNB case that the unique cluster of products and services offered by commercial banks was sufficiently distinctive to constitute a relevant product market.

However, Judge Clary disagreed, and he pointed out that since the PNB decision, the Bank Merger Act was amended and the phrase "line of commerce" was deleted. Judge Zirpoli, in U.S. vs. Crocker-Anglo National Bank,[6] in 1967, ruled that a broader test was intended by Congress which was construed to comprise all institutions competing either for savings or investment dollar or for the extension of credit. Under cross examination, one of the expert witnesses for the Government admitted that in the area of mortgages, loans, and savings, there are other alternative, and sometimes better, sources than commercial banks, such as mutual savings banks and savings and loan associations.[7]

Judge Clary extended the line of commerce to include only particular financial institutions (mutuals and savings and loan associations) because they "alone offer *direct* and meaningful competition to commercial banks."[8] This interpretation is supported by the Supreme Court's ruling in U.S. vs. Continental Can Company,[9] which involved a merger between the nation's second largest can producer and the

---

[5] U.S. vs. Provident National Bank, et al., Op. cit., 280 F. Supp. 4.

[6] U.S. vs. Crocker-Anglo National Bank, D.C. D. Col. 277 F. Supp. 133.

[7] Donald R. Hodgman's testimony N.T. 48-49, op. cit., p. 8.

[8] U.S. vs. Provident National Bank, et al., 280 F. Supp. 9.

[9] U.S. vs. Continental Can Co., et al., 378 U.S. 441, 84 S. Ct. 1738, 12 L. Ed 2d 953 (1964).

third largest producer of glass containers. There the Court found that Section 7 is not limited to identical products and lumped together the glass and container industries into one product market. The Court emphasized cross-elasticity of demand and interchangeability of use as its reason for broadening the market.

Judge Clary pointed out that the same reason exists in this case, only the competition for certain financial services is more direct and meaningful. Thus, he stated:

> If such interchangeability can be used negatively in antitrust jurisprudence, surely the same concept can be used positively. The underlying question remains the same in each instance, i.e., to construct reasonable product markets in which to measure probable competitive effects realistically.[10]

THE ANTICOMPETITIVE EFFECTS OF THE MERGER

The Justice Department maintained the proposed merger between Provident and Central-Penn was anticompetitive based on the traditionally accepted structural approach to antitrust analysis. Given a certain industry structure one can reasonably predict a kind of conduct and perhaps ultimate economic performance of the industry. The prediction is more valid when the composition of the industry remains static and new firms are not entering at a rapid rate.[11]

However, there are significant differences between product markets in the usual economic sense and commercial banking. Unlike two steelmakers, two commercial banks from the same counties do not always compete for the same retail or wholesale customer. This is due mainly to the so-called convenience factor on the retail level and the differences in services offered by large and small commercial banks on the wholesale level. Therefore, Judge Clary stated:

> ... concentration ratios for *non-banking industries* are more realistic in that competition is usually more even and equal and all firms dealing in that one or several products are justifiably lumped together. This is not true of commercial banks.[12]

Judge Clary argued for inclusion of savings and loan associations and mutual savings banks as well as breaking commercial banking into two subproducts, wholesale and retail banking. Wholesale banking meant dealing with a number of large accounts, primarily with large corporations, governmental bodies, financial institutions, and wealthy individuals. Retail banking, on the other hand, catered "to the mass needs of the general public and small business."[13]

By dividing commercial banking in this manner, the Government's concentration ratios and market shares became invalid. The Government's data found that the merged bank would control about 14 percent of the total assets, loans and deposits in the four-county area, and 15 percent of the commercial banking offices. The five-bank concentration ratio would allegedly increase from 73.1 percent to 77.7 percent in terms of assets, 73.1 to 77.8 percent in terms of deposits, and 73.9 to 78.6 percent in terms of loans.

The defendant banks, in support of the contention of a national market for wholesale accounts, referred to a Federal Reserve system report that refers to the composition of the national credit market. The banks maintained that the bulk of corporate loans and related deposit balances are really in this wholesale market. In addition, some bank services are so specialized, i.e., international business and pension trust services, that they can be obtained only from large banks in the national market. Moreover, there was direct testimony from corporate officials in the Philadelphia area that they bank in New York, Boston, or elsewhere, to obtain large loans or sophisticated and expert advice and are solicited by banks across the country for their banking business.

Once a broader product market and geographic market definition is accepted, the Court faces the task of formulating realistic concentration ratios. Judge Clary adopted the "shading procedure" used by the Supreme Court in the PNB case. In the PNB case the Supreme Court scaled down the aggregate share of the market held by PNB and Girard as a merged bank from 36 to 30 percent, or by about 6 percent. By applying the same reduction formula between Provident and Central-Penn, Judge Clary reduced their market share from 14 percent to 11.7 percent, which was an attempt to account for the wholesale (national) aspect of their business.

A further adjustment was necessary to account for competition from savings and loan associations. The inclusion of savings and loan and mutual savings banks broadened the structure base even more. Judge Clary recognized that in recent years commercial banks have become increasingly interested in securing time deposits, and as a result their ratio between time and demand deposits approached equal parity. Time deposits at the time of the case comprised about 40 percent of the total deposits held by commercial banks in the four-county area.

---

[10] U.S. vs. Provident National Bank, et al., Op. cit., 280 F. Supp. 9.

[11] See: Willard F. Mueller, "The New Antitrust: A 'Structural' Approach," Vol. 12, *Vill. Law Review*, 764 (1967).

[12] U.S. vs. Provident National Bank, et al., 280 F. Supp. 11.

[13] U.S. vs. Manufacturers Hanover Trust Co., 240 F. Supp. 867, 896 (S.D.N.Y., 1965).

When competition from savings and loan associations and mutual savings banks is included for time deposits, it is found that in 1965 commercial banks held only 19.49 percent of the total savings dollar in the four-county area. Mutual savings banks held 45.73 percent, savings and loan associations 32.95 percent, and credit unions 1.88 percent. Provident and Central-Penn held 1.88 percent and 1.11 percent respectively. The resultant bank would control 2.74 percent of the total savings dollar in the four-county area. Therefore, Judge Clary further shaded the 11.7 percent of market controlled by the merged bank to account for competition for savings deposits from savings and loan associations. Since 2.74 percent represented the resultant bank's share of all time and savings deposits in the four-county area, Judge Clary used this to adjust downward the 11.7 percent to arrive at a final aggregate share of 9.74 percent.[14] Judge Clary stated:

> After arriving at a more realistic concentration ratio, we can now consider whether a merger, which produces a firm controlling some 9.8 percent of the relevant market, is anticompetitive.[15]

Judge Clary indicated that there is a distinct difference between competition and the number of competitors, especially in commercial banking.

The defendant banks contended that the merger between the fifth and seventh largest banks in the four-county area would produce a bank better able to compete with the four leading commercial banks on a qualitative basis, since it would have more resources to be innovators rather than mere followers. Similarly, Provident and Central-Penn maintained that their merger would also be pro-competition in the retail market since the improvement of services resulting therefrom should intensify the competition with other banks and financial institutions.

Moreover, the banks argued that despite the substantial reduction of independent commercial banks as contended by the Government in the four-county area, the competitive options for the retail customer increased, and the services offered increased both quantitatively and qualitatively. As an example, a study of the area indicated that 35 of the 40 communities had experienced an increase in the number of bank and other financial institution offices.

Finally, this merger would tend to increase the quality of competition among commercial banks for the wholesale customer. Most of the existing 37 commercial banks in the area were limited severely by their size, location, and staff; thus, they could not seriously compete for wholesale accounts. Wholesale transactions usually require large lending limits, reserve city status, and a large expert staff in diversified areas. Most small independent banks do not fit into this category. Central-Penn was not a major competitive factor in the wholesale market. However, the merger would produce another bank on par with the other leading wholesale banks in the city.

Congress and the Supreme Court, in carrying out the mandate of Section 7 (Clayton) stated that one purpose of the law is to arrest the alleged trend toward concentration or tendency toward monopoly before the consumer's alternatives disappear through mergers. Therefore, despite the fact that the aggregate share of total deposits that the resultant bank would hold was less than 10 percent, the merger still ran counter to the Supreme Court's precept that competition is most vital when there are many sellers, none of which has any significant market share.

Judge Clary concluded from the law that if a market can be characterized as oligopolistic, any merger which strengthens this oligopolistic structure must be struck down. Herein lies the dilemma which confronted the Court. Judge Clary stated:

> Philadelpia concededly has an oligopolistic banking structure . . . Barring significant new entries into commercial banking in the four-county area, and the prospect of divestiture of the large banking institutions seemingly remote, it seems the necessary result of such a policy will only strengthen the present leaders while the lesser banking institutions are correspondingly weakened.[16]

THE CONVENIENCE AND NEEDS OF THE COMMUNITY

The defendant banks stated that the merger would serve the convenience and needs test in the following ways: (1) The merged bank will be more comparable in resources, services and prestige to larger banks in other cities; (2) the merged bank would provide more competition for the larger banks in Philadelphia; and (3) they would provide better service to individuals and small businesses in their area.

Judge Clary examined the legislative intent and history for guidance in applying the new convenience and needs test and concluded that it must be interpreted restrictively, i.e., merely allowing bank mergers in those cases where the needs and convenience of the community are so compelling that competition will be enhanced rather than decreased

---

[14]U.S. vs. Provident National Bank, et al., 280 F. Supp. 15.
[15]Ibid., p. 16.

[16]Ibid., pp. 18-19.

by the merger. Concluding that the Bank Merger Act (1966) requires that convenience and needs of the community must clearly outweigh any anticompetitive effects before a merger can be approved, Judge Clary stated:

> This burden has not been met in the instant case. At best, it has resulted in a tie. Justice [Department] has shown anticompetitive effects and the banks have pointed to convenience and needs. However, in a tie situation, the banks necessarily lose.[17]

Judge Clary is led to the unfortunate conclusion that:

> Although we are persuaded that this merger would be good for Philadelphia and its banking community, this Court has seen no compelling evidence which would except this merger from our antitrust laws.[18]

[17]*Ibid.*, p. 24.
[18]U.S. vs. Provident National Bank, *et al.*, 280 F. Supp. 25.

Questions for Discussion

1. Assume that you are the Supreme Court and this case is appealed by the Provident and Central-Penn Banks. What would your decision be? Give careful supporting arguments.
2. Does this case point up a need for a change in the approach toward mergers in banking and finance?
3. In light of the present interpretation of antimerger law, is it possible for any bank merger to be successfully defended against an antitrust attack regardless of whether it is approved by the relevant regulator?
4. Is there a need for clarification of the precise roles of the regulators and antitrust agencies in approving or opposing mergers between banks? If so, what would you recommend?

CASE 28 ANTITRUST ASSAULT ON CONGLOMERATENESS: U.S. VS. LING-TEMCO-VOUGHT, JONES & LAUGHLIN STEEL, AND JONES & LAUGHLIN INDUSTRIES CASE

BACKGROUND

The United States of America, the Plaintiff, acting through its Department of Justice, filed a complaint against the defendants, Ling-Temco-Vought, Incorporated, Jones and Laughlin Steel Corporation, and Jones and Laughlin Industries, Incorporated, and sought an adjudication that the defendants were in violation of Section 7 of the Clayton Act; that the defendants Ling-Temco-Vought and Jones and Laughlin Industries be directed to divest themselves of all ownership interests in Jones and Laughlin Steel and that in connection therewith injunctive processes issue.[1]

The defendant Ling-Temco-Vought is a Delaware corporation having its principal place of business in Dallas, Texas; the defendant Jones and Laughlin Steel is a Pennsylvania corporation having its principal place of business in Pittsburgh, Pennsylvania; and the defendant Jones and Laughlin Industries is a Delaware corporation having its principal place of business in Dallas, Texas. The parties involved have stipulated that all were transacting business within the Western District of Pennsylvania at the time the suit was filed by the Plaintiff.

Jones and Laughlin Industries, acting as intermediary for its parent company Ling-Temco-Vought, acquired in excess of 81.4 percent of the outstanding common stock of Jones and Laughlin Steel for Ling-Temco-Vought through offerings to the holders of Jones and Laughlin Steel common stock.

The parties originally entered into and agreed upon a preliminary injunction that was then directed by the court to be filed. Then, discovery procedures were commenced and during the course of such procedures an agreement was reached for finally determining the entire action. The court was presented a stipulation and a suggested decree concerning the matter; these were then directed to be filed. To determine whether the settlement entered into between the parties in their proffered decree was in the best public interest, and since no evidence was presented in support of such decree, an open public hearing was scheduled for June 1, 1970.

Meanwhile, the court received many letters from interested persons, and these letters were ordered to be filed and became part of the record. Those who wished to speak at the hearing on June 1, 1970, were given the opportunity to do so. Persons who communicated their feelings, either by letter or in the courtroom, were categorized generally as: (1) those persons who are owners of Ling-Temco-Vought stock and have been severely affected financially because of the decline in the market price of Ling-Temco-Vought stock and who, for the most part, condemn the Justice Department as intermeddling in the free enterprise activities of Ling-Temco-Vought; (2) those persons who own stock or are investors in debt securities of Jones and Laughlin Steel and who condemn Ling-Temco-Vought for its self-serving efforts in acquiring control of a corporation such as Jones and Laughlin Steel and who fear that Ling-Temco-Vought will divert Jones and Laughlin Steel's assets for the advantage of various other holdings; and, (3) those employees of Jones and Laughlin Steel who, for the most part, are concerned with possible disruption of their employment security, and their employment rights, particularly unemployment and pension benefits, as a result of the acquisition of Ling-Temco-Vought.[2]

A main complaint of these individuals was concerned with the precipitous decline in the stock market values of Ling-Temco-Vought and Jones & Laughlin Steel stocks and bonds or debentures. These individuals blamed either the Government or Ling-Temco-Vought for the rapid decline in value of these securities during 1969 and 1970, in particular. However, it seems that the fact that the securities market in general had shown a severe decline during the same period was not taken into consideration by these individuals.

The effect of this acquisition upon individual

---

[1] "United States of America vs. Ling-Temco-Vought, Incorporated, Jones and Laughlin Steel Corporation, and Jones and Laughlin Industries, Incorporated," Civil Action number 69-438, p. 2.

[2] Ibid., pp. 3-4.

persons was shown through the letters received by the court and the presentations of those who attended the hearing. It was learned that there were heavy investors in Ling-Temco-Vought who had seen their fortunes reduced to practically nothing. Taking into consideration all of the unfortunate circumstances, however, determination by the court had to be made in accordance with the provisions of the Clayton Act and the court's decision also had to best effectuate the public welfare.

On April 19, 1970, Judge Rosenberg directed that the parties present support by way of affidavits, stipulation, or other evidence upon which the court might base the requested decree. A stipulation of facts had been filed on October 24, 1969, and a Stipulated Statement of Facts was filed pursuant to the court's order of April 10 on May 8, 1970. Thus, the following findings of fact were evident:

(1) On May 14, 1968, Ling-Temco-Vought offered to purchase for cash outstanding common stock of Jones & Laughlin Steel for $85 per share, while at the same time, at or near that time, the market price of the common stock of Jones & Laughlin Steel on the New York Stock Exchange ranged from a low of $51.875 to a high of $55.75.

(2) As a result of the offer, Ling-Temco-Vought acquired approximately 63 percent of the shares then outstanding, for approximately $425,000,000.

(3) On January 21, 1969, Ling-Temco-Vought caused Jones & Laughlin Industries to be incorporated under the laws of the state of Delaware, and on March 13, 1969, Ling-Temco-Vought transferred to Jones & Laughlin Industries all of the shares of the common stock of Jones & Laughlin Steel owned by it in exchange for certain shares of common stock and certificates of indebtedness obligations, and that on March 17, 1969, became the owner of all outstanding stock of Jones & Laughlin Industries.

(4) Ling-Temco-Vought, a highly diversified company, as of April 14, 1969, was engaged, through its operating subsidiaries, in a variety of businesses, including the manufacture and sale of fighter planes and aerospace equipment, copper wire, sporting goods, meat products, chemical and pharmaceutical products, electronic equipment, carpeting products, and steel and steel products. It also controlled one of the nation's major commercial airlines, Braniff Airways, Inc. (Braniff) and one of the country's three major car rental firms, National Car Rental System, Inc.

(5) Jones & Laughlin Steel is a fully integrated steel company which produces most basic steel products and accounts for approximately six percent of national steel shipments.

(6) Braniff purchases substantial quantities of jet fuel from oil producers and refiners who are actual or potential purchasers of steel products manufactured by Jones & Laughlin Steel, and that Braniff also purchases aircraft which incorporate components that are or can be manufactured by Ling-Temco-Vought's subsidiary, Ling-Temco-Vought Aerospace, Inc.

(7) The Okonite Company (Okonite) is a non-integrated producer of copper wire and also produces various types of insulated copper and aluminum cable and manufactures mining cable for which Jones & Laughlin Steel is an actual or potential customer in connection with the operation of its mining properties, and it also manufactures and sells a variety of carpeting products.

(8) The iron and steel industry is a highly concentrated oligopoly of which eight fully integrated steel companies have accounted for over 75 percent of the industry's total net shipments of steel products. The economies of scale in the production of steel are such that integrated steel plants must be large in size and therefore require very large capital investment, and thus the barrier to entry into the iron and steel industry as a fully integrated producer are high.

(9) Subsequent to the filing of the complaint, Ling-Temco-Vought disposed of its entire interest in its subsidiaries, Wilson Sporting Goods Company and National Car Rental System, Inc., the book value of whose combined assets exceeded 156 million dollars as of December 31, 1968.

(10) This action is one of several cases brought by the Department of Justice predicated in part on its claim that Section 7 of the Clayton Act prohibits the acquisition by large conglomerate corporations in the course of, and which tend to proliferate, a merger movement where concentration of control of manufacturing assets will be substantially increased and the trend to further concentration will be encouraged.

(11) As the alternative is presented for the divesture of Braniff and Okonite or of Jones & Laughlin interests, a divesture of more than 500 million dollars of assets is involved.[3]

The parties arrived at a settlement of their differences; thus, further elaboration by the court on the issues involved became unnecessary. The court needed only to state that the Government commenced this action pursuant to the Acts of Congress against the acquisition by Ling-Temco-Vought of Jones & Laughlin Steel stock "because of the conglomerate holdings which Ling-Temco-Vought had as of the time of the instant acquisition, and because of the impact which such an enlargement of conglomerate holdings might have upon the competitive economy involved, as well as the potential reciprocity which a conglomerate set up of this character might generate."[4]

[3]*Ibid.*, pp. 6-14.
[4]*Ibid.*, p. 14.

The proposed decree, according to the Government, reflects the view of the Justice Department that Congress, in enacting Section 7 was deeply concerned with the trend toward economic concentration in the American economy, particularly by external expansion of businesses through mergers, acquisitions, and consolidations. Thus, the decree would help to attain the Congressional purpose of halting the trend toward increased economic concentration in the United States' economy and would be a significant deterrent against other very large acquisitions by conglomerate firms which have characterized the accelerating merger trend in the United States in recent years.

In addition, the Government declares that "the relief which the decree will insure conforms to the belief of the Department of Justice that the Congressional intent was to prevent undue concentration of economic power through conglomerate acquisitions as well as those that are vertical or horizontal in character."[5]

The submitted decree states that Ling-Temco-Vought cannot use Jones and Laughlin Steel assets for its own purpose until the divesture is completed. Between the time judgment is entered and the divesture is actually accomplished, Ling-Temco-Vought is prohibited to liquidate any of Jones and Laughlin Steel, Braniff or Okonite assets to resolve any financial problems that Ling-Temco-Vought might encounter. These provisions are to prohibit piecemeal disposition, liquidation, or cannibalization of presently operating companies, with government approval required for certain exceptions. Another provision of the decrees required Ling-Temco-Vought and Jones and Laughlin Steel to obtain the consent of the government or of the court before acquiring any interest in excess of 1 percent in any corporation which has assets in the amount of 100 million dollars. The defendant is, therefore, prevented from acquiring any of the very large corporations in America, thus increasing economic concentration.

The submitted decree prohibits the defendant from engaging in the reciprocity or seller's practice of utilizing the volume or potential volume of its purchases to induce other companies to purchase its products. The Government, originally filing the complaint, asserted that the probability of anticompetitive effects was increased along with the enhanced opportunity for reciprocity practices resulting from the acquisition. Such reciprocity practices are prohibited for a period of 10 years by the proposed decree. Protective measures against anticompetitive reciprocity practices, policies, or arrangements are provided for by the decree, and it also attempts to insure the effectiveness of these measures by requiring the principal domestic subsidiaries of each defendant to file a submission to jurisdiction with the court and also consent to be bound by these provisions which prohibit reciprocity practices.

Adoption of the submitted decree was urged by the parties in order to bring the litigation to a speedy termination. The decree provides:

> . . . a vehicle by which the Department of Justice is vested with a certain amount of supervisory controls over the functions of Ling-Temco-Vought for the next ten years; and for the next three years Ling-Temco-Vought is granted an option of either retaining Jones and Laughlin Steel and divesting itself of Okonite and Braniff, or in the alternative of divesting itself of Jones and Laughlin Steel and retaining Okonite and Braniff.[6]

The background material presented here was extracted from the complaint filed by the Justice Department and the Opinion rendered by Judge Rosenberg of the Western District Court of Pennsylvania.

Questions for Discussion

1. Would the merger between Ling-Temco-Vought, Incorporated and Jones and Laughlin tend to substantially lessen competition and increase concentration that would not otherwise be as prevalent?
2. Would it be likely to cause a tendency toward a monopoly?
3. Would this merger enhance the reciprocal buying power of Ling-Temco-Vought, Incorporated and Jones and Laughlin Steel Corporation?

[5] *Ibid.*, p. 15.

[6] *Ibid.*, p. 18.

Part Four Decision Making in the Public Sector

Chapter 9 Cost-Benefit Analysis

READING

29 A BENEFIT-COST ANALYSIS OF THE UPWARD BOUND PROGRAM

Walter I. Garms

ABSTRACT

The private and social benefits and costs of the Upward Bound program are analyzed for white males, white females, nonwhite males, and nonwhite females, using older siblings of the same sex as a control group. Private net benefits are shown to be positive for all four sex-race classifications at discount rates of 5 and 10 percent. Social net benefits are positive at a discount rate of 5 percent, but negative at 10 percent. In addition, rather high rates of college attendance by siblings indicate that the Upward Bound program may function more as a device to identify those rather apt to go to college anyway rather than as a program to help those who would otherwise be very unlikely to go to college.

The Upward Bound program is a project, formerly in the Office of Economic Opportunity and now operated by the U.S. Office of Education, the goal of which is to find able high school students who would be unlikely to go on to college because of poverty or because of low perceptions of probable success associated with race or socioeconomic status. Typically, the program has attempted to identify these students in their sophomore year in high school. They are given an intensive program at a local college during the ensuing summers until college enrollment, and during the school year there are occasional Saturday sessions at the college. The work is designed to introduce these students to skills and attitudes that are helpful in college and to remedy those subject matter areas in which the student is weak. Special efforts are made to place the student in a college suited to his abilities. During the entire period of his participation in Upward Bound, the student is paid a small weekly stipend. Active participation in the Upward Bound program ceases with enrollment in a college.

This article represents a reworking of the data of a benefit-cost analysis done by the author for OEO.[1] The purpose of such an analysis is to attempt

The author is Associate Professor of Higher Education, Teachers College, Columbia University.

1 Contained in *Upward Bound, 1965–1969: A History and Synthesis of Data on the Program in the Office of Economic Opportunity* (New York: Greenleigh Associates, Inc., 1969). I am indebted to Harold Noah, Daniel Rogers, Robinson Hollister, Glen Cain, and the referees for this *Journal* for their critical comments on earlier drafts of this article.

Decision Making in the Public Sector

to determine whether, in an economic sense, the benefits of the Upward Bound program exceed its costs. However, it should be emphasized that the goals of Upward Bound are social as well as economic, and economic efficiency should not be the sole criterion by which the program is judged.

THE SAMPLE

An attempt to analyze rigorously an experimental program involves comparison with a control group, either defined or implied. One of the difficulties in analysis of the results of social programs is the definition of a satisfactory control group. Fortunately, for the purpose of this study a control group exists which is far better than usually is available, for data are available on the educational attainment of older siblings of the Upward Bound students. With cautions that will be discussed later, these older siblings can be thought of as being like the Upward Bound students in all ways except that they were not exposed to the Upward Bound program.

The sample for the study consists of 7,236 students who entered Upward Bound between June 1966 and August 1968, and the control group consists of their older siblings of the same sex as the students.[2]

In constructing the control group, each Upward Bound student was made to have the equivalent of only one older sibling of the same sex. For example, if a white female Upward Bound student had an older sister who dropped out of high school and another who had completed high school, one-half person was added to the sibling category "white female, dropped out of high school" and one-half was added to the sibling category "white female, graduated from high school." In this way account was taken of all older siblings of the same sex, but siblings from large families do not exert extra influence on the sample.

There are several biases that might be introduced by using older siblings as a control group. In excluding students who do not have an older sibling of the same sex, we exclude students from small families and those who are the eldest. Some studies seem to indicate that such students would tend to be brighter than average. Second, data on older siblings were obtained from Upward Bound students by means of a self-administered questionnaire. Because education is defined by our society as "good," the Upward Bound students may have been tempted to report their siblings' educational attainment as higher than it actually was. The effect in both cases is to bias benefits downward. On the other hand, there is the probability that the Upward Bound students are brighter, on the average, than their siblings, simply because they are a selected group. Students from similar families who were not as bright as their siblings would be less likely to be chosen for the Upward Bound program. A fourth bias arises because siblings attended

---

2 Basic data are from an extensive computerized data file maintained by OEO on all Upward Bound students, with updating even after the student has left the program. The sample for the study consists of all students whose files contained all of the necessary information, and who had older siblings of the same sex. Sample percentages by sex and race, compared with the Upward Bound population during the same time period, are as follows:

	Sample	*Population*
Whites	32.0%	31.2%
Nonwhites	68.0	68.8
Male	47.5	49.4
Female	52.5	50.6

Nonwhites include those with Spanish surnames. Data on the population calculated from *Upward Bound, 1965–1969*, pp. 76–77.

college (or did not attend) from one to several years before the Upward Bound students. College admissions policies with regard to students with nonstandard backgrounds have been changing rapidly in the last several years, and it is possible that a larger percentage of the siblings would have attended college had they graduated from high school at the same time as the Upward Bound students. The effect of these biases is to inflate the presumed benefits of the Upward Bound program. It is impossible to say what is the net effect of these biases involved with using older siblings as a control group, but the implicit assumption is that their effects tend to balance out.

The actual attainment of the Upward Bound students and their siblings as of the time that data were collected are shown in Table 1. However, for the purposes of this study it was necessary to estimate the *final* educational attainment for these groups, and these estimates are given in Table 2. Study

TABLE 1
ACTUAL PRESENT EDUCATIONAL ATTAINMENT

Category	Upward Bound Students	Siblings of Same Sex
White males		
Dropped out of high school	8.0%	28.1%
Still attending high school	15.4	6.7
Completed high school, not in college	26.5	36.7
1–3 years higher education, not attending	1.5	6.3
1–2 years junior college, still attending	11.5	—
Some business or technical training	—	6.0
1–3 years college, still attending	37.1	11.0
Completed college	0.0	5.2
White females		
Dropped out of high school	7.6	23.4
Still attending high school	12.3	6.3
Completed high school, not in college	29.2	44.3
1–3 years higher education, not attending	1.0	5.3
1–2 years junior college, still attending	14.4	—
Some business or technical training	—	8.1
1–3 years college, still attending	35.5	9.5
Completed college	0.0	3.1
Nonwhite males		
Dropped out of high school	6.9	25.4
Still attending high school	9.8	7.5
Completed high school, not in college	18.8	40.1
1–3 years higher education, not attending	0.7	7.2
1–2 years junior college, still attending	12.7	—
Some business or technical training	—	5.2
1–3 years college, still attending	51.1	11.5
Completed college	0.0	3.1
Nonwhite females		
Dropped out of high school	4.3	20.7
Still attending high school	7.4	7.1
Completed high school, not in college	22.8	38.4
1–3 years higher education, not attending	1.1	7.2
1–2 years junior college, still attending	15.1	—
Some business or technical training	—	8.2
1–3 years college, still attending	49.3	13.6
Completed college	0.0	4.8

Source: OEO data files. A dash in the data column indicates that the category is not included in the data file.

Decision Making in the Public Sector

TABLE 2
ESTIMATED FINAL EDUCATIONAL ATTAINMENT

Category	Upward Bound Students	Siblings of Same Sex
White males		
1–3 years high school	8.8%	30.3%
4 years high school	28.8	30.3
1–3 years college	34.3	26.1
4 or more years college	28.1	13.3
White females		
1–3 years high school	8.3	24.9
4 years high school	30.9	32.9
1–3 years college	33.8	29.3
4 or more years college	27.0	12.9
Nonwhite males		
1–3 years high school	7.3	27.9
4 years high school	20.4	33.2
1–3 years college	39.1	27.2
4 or more years college	33.2	11.7
Nonwhite females		
1–3 years high school	4.7	22.5
4 years high school	23.9	29.1
1–3 years college	39.4	32.2
4 or more years college	32.0	16.2

Source: Derived from Table 1 using assumptions about percentages of students currently at a given level of education who will go on to specified levels of education. Assumptions are derived from data in *Evaluations of the War on Poverty,* RMC Report UR-151 (Bethesda, Md.: Resource Management Corporation, 1969), which indicate that of the Upward Bound students still in high school, 5 percent would drop out, 15 percent would graduate but not attend college, 40 percent would drop out of college, and 40 percent would graduate from college. The corresponding percentages for male siblings are 33, 42, 19, and 6; and for female siblings, 25, 43, 22, and 10. For both Upward Bound students and siblings who enrolled in four-year colleges, the report estimated that 50 percent would graduate. Additional assumptions consistent with these estimates were made for students at other stages of their education.

of Tables 1 and 2 indicates that Upward Bound students do indeed go on to college in greater numbers than their siblings, and drop out of high school less frequently. But it is also worth noting that Upward Bound students do not come from families to which higher education is completely foreign. Based on the estimates made here, about 43 percent of siblings will enter college. Directly comparable figures for the nation as a whole are not available, but one indicator is the fact that nationally 47 percent of the students who were juniors in high school in 1966 were enrolled in college in 1968.[3] This does not include those who wait one or more years after high school graduation before enrolling in college. Another comparison shows that 46.6 percent of the population aged 18 to 21 years in 1967 were in college. This figure is also somewhat low to use for comparison, for included in the population 18 to 21 years of age are some who have not yet enrolled in college but will, and some who have already attended college but are no longer doing so.

However, with these comparisons in mind, one is forced seriously to question whether the selection process for Upward Bound students operated, as intended, to select students who would otherwise be very unlikely

---

[3] National data in this section from U.S. Office of Education, *Digest of Educational Statistics, 1969* (Washington: U.S. Government Printing Office, 1969).

to attend college. Instead, it appears that a group slightly below average in likelihood of college attendance has been selected, and that a result of the Upward Bound program has been that they have attended college in considerably greater proportion than the population as a whole. This gives some support to the criticism that Upward Bound's major function has been that of identifying promising students and that the costly training portion of the program is of little importance. On the other hand, only about 32 percent of the siblings who enter college are projected to complete a four-year degree, compared with a rate of 50 percent for the nation as a whole. The rate for Upward Bound students is about 45 percent. To the extent that the Upward Bound program has improved the completion rate, it can be said to have been of value aside from its selection function.

BENEFITS AND COSTS FROM THE INDIVIDUAL'S VIEWPOINT

It is important to examine the benefits and costs of the Upward Bound program from the individual's viewpoint, for if there are no net benefits for him he will not be interested in it, no matter how desirable the program may be from a social viewpoint. The categories of benefits considered in the analysis are increased lifetime income after taxes, the stipend received while in the Upward Bound program, and scholarships and grants received while in college. Benefits not calculated include the value of the option to obtain further education which is passed up if one drops out of high school, and intangible benefits to which no dollar amounts can be assigned. The costs to the individual included in the analysis are the tuition cost of attending college, extra living costs associated with attending college, foregone earnings while attending high school and college, and foregone unemployment and welfare payments as a result of being more fully employed during his working lifetime. Intangible costs are not considered.

Lifetime Incomes

The standard method of estimating lifetime incomes is to use data on present incomes for various ages and educational attainments and assume that these cross-sectional data represent the longitudinal data. Such a method does not hold constant some factors that are potentially of importance in determining income. Hanoch has held constant a number of factors, chiefly geographical region, urban or rural residence, mobility, marital status, and size of family, in making his estimates.[4] Weiss held constant marital status, rural-urban residence, and veteran status.[5] Data were unavailable for estimation of the effects of most variables of this sort in this study. A geographical region variable could have been used, but it was considered inappropriate because the increased mobility of people, particularly the college educated, and changes in regional economies during the working life of the Upward Bound students makes such a variable questionable.

Another way of looking at the same thing is to say that income differentials associated with education are caused by two things: education and a complex composed of all other causes. The other causes include all of those listed above and others, but most importantly innate ability, which

4 Giora Hanoch, "An Economic Analysis of Earnings and Schooling," *Journal of Human Resources* 2 (Summer 1967), pp. 310–29.
5 Randall D. Weiss, "The Effect of Education on the Earnings of Blacks and Whites," *Review of Economics and Statistics* 52 (May 1970), pp. 150–59.

is not considered by either Hanoch or Weiss. The question then is what percentage of the difference in incomes associated with education is caused by education. Denison has used a figure of 60 percent.[6] Weiss implies that for nonwhites the figure should be considerably lower than this.[7] Although Weiss's method is ingenious, the low R^2 values he gets leave the issue open to doubt. Hines cites studies indicating a range from 60 to 88 percent.[8] The author tends to lean toward the side of those who feel that a fairly high proportion of income differences associated with education are caused by education, and in this study a figure of 75 percent has been used.

But another element that must be accounted for is the long-term secular increase in real incomes. For purposes of this study it must be expressed in terms of the per annum growth of output per man-hour holding manpower quality (in terms of education) constant. Miller shows that from 1949 to 1959 real incomes of individuals in constant dollars expanded at a rate of about 3.5 percent per year,[9] but this is for a single decade and does not hold manpower quality constant. Becker notes that real economic growth per member of the working force has been about 2 percent per year.[10] Denison calculated the annual growth rate per person employed during the period 1929–57 at 1.60 percent and estimated that it would be 1.62 percent for the period 1960–80.[11] Cain selects a figure of 2 percent as representing fairly recent experience, while noting that the growth rate over longer periods would be considerably lower.[12] Hines et al. also choose 2.0 percent for the aggregate of all schooling groups, but note that it would be lower for those with a college education.[13] For this study the Denison estimate of 1.62 percent has been used because it represents an estimate based on a long period of years and because it is a generally conservative estimate. A model incorporating this estimate produces the figures shown in Table 3. Present values are calculated to age 16, the approximate age at which a decision is made to enter the Upward Bound program.

Having obtained present values of lifetime incomes, the determination of the lifetime income differential associated with the Upward Bound program is straightforward. For each of the sex-race groups, the proportion of Upward Bound students in each educational category is multiplied by the present value of lifetime income for that category, and the sum of these four products is the expected present value of average lifetime income of an Upward Bound student in that sex-race category. The same is done for siblings in that sex-race category, and the difference between income for Upward Bound students and that for siblings is assumed to be associated with the Upward Bound program. Taking 75 percent of this amount gives the income differential assumed to be *caused* by the Upward Bound program and the additional education obtained as a result of it. This differ-

6 Edward F. Denison, *The Sources of Economic Growth in the United States and the Alternatives Before Us,* Supplementary Paper No. 13 (Washington: Committee on Economic Development, 1962).
7 Weiss, "The Effect of Education...."
8 Fred Hines, Luther Tweeten, and Martin Redfern, "Social and Private Rates of Return to Investment in Schooling by Race-Sex Groups and Regions," *Journal of Human Resources* 5 (Summer 1970), pp. 318–40.
9 Herman P. Miller, "Lifetime Income and Economic Growth," *American Economic Review* 55 (September 1965), pp. 834–44.
10 Gary S. Becker, *Human Capital* (New York: Columbia University Press, 1964).
11 Denison, *The Sources of Economic Growth....*
12 Glen G. Cain, *Benefit/Cost Estimates for Job Corps* (Madison: Institute for Research on Poverty, University of Wisconsin, 1967), pp. 40–42.
13 Hines et al., "Social and Private Rates of Return...."

TABLE 3
VALUE OF LIFETIME INCOME ASSOCIATED WITH EDUCATION

Category	Total Income	Present Value at 5 Percent	Present Value at 10 Percent
White males			
1–3 years high school	$427,633	$132,262	$60,488
4 years high school	478,280	147,951	66,940
1–3 years college	534,013	153,187	63,151
4 or more years college	699,771	184,831	68,902
White females			
1–3 years high school	94,693	28,872	13,377
4 years high school	125,428	35,072	14,780
1–3 years college	147,986	40,580	16,729
4 or more years college	276,640	70,769	27,043
Nonwhite males			
1–3 years high school	268,268	86,543	40,636
4 years high school	309,765	99,817	46,323
1–3 years college	355,265	106,002	44,850
4 or more years college	423,395	116,268	44,622
Nonwhite females			
1–3 years high school	111,041	35,027	16,539
4 years high school	139,863	40,277	17,213
1–3 years college	176,101	49,494	20,515
4 or more years college	361,002	94,639	36,357

Notes: The assumption is made that real incomes in 1967 dollars at any given age will increase at 1.62 percent per year as a result of expansion of the economy.

Amounts shown are present values at age 16 of incomes from age 16 to 65, before taxes. Basic data are from U.S. Bureau of the Census, *Current Population Reports,* Series P-60, No. 60, "Income in 1967 of Persons in the United States" (Washington: U.S. Government Printing Office, 1969). Incomes during periods individuals are students are from Robert G. Spiegelman, *A Benefit/Cost Model to Evaluate Educational Programs* (Menlo Park, Calif.: Stanford Research Institute, 1968).

Median incomes were used, to help correct for the upward bias caused by using income rather than earnings data. Data, given by the Bureau of the Census at 10-year age intervals, were positioned at the midpoint of the interval and values for other years were determined by linear interpolation. A mortality correction is included.

Figures shown are for incomes *associated* with education. They include the effect of noneducational causal factors correlated with education.

ential was then reduced by 25 percent to give a net differential after taxes.[14]

There are still several sources of error in these esimates that are particularly associated with the Upward Bound program. One is that Upward Bound students may, on the average, attend colleges of lower quality than do the entire population, on which income figures are based. To the extent that this is so, income differentials are overstated. Second, the differentials for nonwhites are based on present incomes which reflect the operation of discrimination of various kinds. If, as seems likely, this discrimination is reduced in the future, nonwhite differentials may approach those for whites. Third, the assumption is made here that the incomes of Upward Bound students will be equal to present average incomes of people with the same education. This will be true only so long as Upward Bound remains a marginal program, and this constitutes a basic difficulty in generalizing from small programs to large ones.

---

[14] Joseph Pechman, in "The Rich, the Poor, and the Taxes They Pay," *The Public Interest* 17 (Fall 1969), pp. 21–43, shows that in the midrange of incomes, total federal, state, and local taxes take about 25 percent of the individual's income.

Decision Making in the Public Sector

Upward Bound Stipend

Upward Bound students received an average of $45.36 a month in stipends during the summer months and $5.60 a month during the school year.[15] Based on average length of time in the program, white males received a total stipend of $219, white females received $218, nonwhite males $223, and nonwhite females $233. The appropriately discounted values of these figures were shown in the tables as benefits.

Scholarships and Grants

Almost all of the Upward Bound students received scholarships and grants (loans were not considered a benefit), with the first-year amount ranging from $739 for white males to $793 for nonwhite females.[16] The assumption was made that these receipts would remain at this level during the time the student was in college, and present values at age 16 were calculated. No data were available on scholarships and grants received by older siblings, but the assumption was made that they received amounts equal to the amounts received by the Upward Bound students. Differentials were calculated by the same method used to calculate lifetime income differentials. The resulting net benefit is entirely the result of the different rates of college attendance for Upward Bound students and their siblings.

Tuition

The individual is not concerned with how much it costs to educate him, but with how much he must pay for it. The assumption was made that Upward Bound students attended colleges of all kinds in the same proportion as did the population as a whole. A weighted average of tuition for 1968-69 for all U.S. institutions is $602.[17] A present value of tuition for two and four years of college was calculated by discounting back to age 16, and then the same procedure was used as for lifetime income differentials in computing present value of differential tuition paid by Upward Bound students.

Extra Living Cost While in College

Based on a number of assumptions, an average figure of $425 per year in additional living costs while in college was calculated.[18] This was discounted and assigned in the same manner as was tuition.

Foregone Earnings While in School

Because the income series used in getting lifetime income differentials starts at age 16, the effect of foregone earnings while in school is automatically included as a reduction in lifetime earnings of those who attend school, and it need not be accounted for separately.

---

15 Data furnished by OEO officials.
16 Data from Upward Bound data bank.
17 *Digest of Educational Statistics, 1969*.
18 It was assumed that half of the students would live away from home while in college. Average cost of room and board in 1968-69 was $870 for all U.S. colleges, and transportation, books, and supplies were estimated at $190. But the family of the student can spend about $400 less for food while he is away. The net extra living cost of a student living away from home is $660 per year. For students living at home, the extra cost was estimated at $190, so that the average for all students was $425.

The individual who is more successful in finding and holding jobs as a result of his education will consequently receive less in unemployment and welfare payments during his working life. These foregone payments should be considered as an offset against the increased income resulting from education. Because the income series used includes these payments, their inclusion as an offset is automatic and it is not necessary to estimate them separately.

The results of the benefit-cost analysis from the individual's viewpoint are shown in Table 4.

BENEFITS AND COSTS FROM SOCIETY'S VIEWPOINT

While it is important that the program, to be successful, should be attractive to the individual, its value must ultimately be judged by its net benefit to society as a whole. The social benefits of the Upward Bound program considered here are limited to lifetime income differentials of those who enroll in the Upward Bound program, taken before taxes, as a measure of the increased production of those who take part in the program. External and intangible benefits are not considered, although they may be substantial. Unemployment and welfare payments are transfer payments from the social viewpoint. Since they are included in the income series as a reduction in net income differentials, their amount must be estimated and added back to the differentials.

We are concerned with the economic value of the Upward Bound program and the education that it stimulates, but not with the portion of income associated with education but really caused by innate ability, family connections, inherited wealth, etc. Therefore we show, as for the case of the individual, 75 percent of the lifetime income differential.

The social costs included in the analysis are the direct cost of the Upward Bound program to the government, less the amount paid in stipends (which are considered to be transfer payments); cost of the Upward Bound program to the participating colleges; cost of educating the Upward Bound students, both in high school and in college (starting with the junior year of high school, when the analysis starts); extra living costs of students while in school; and foregone income.

The additional calculations necessary for this section involve estimates of present value of unemployment and welfare payments foregone by Upward Bound students during their lifetimes, the costs of the Upward Bound program to the government and the colleges, and the cost of education. Estimates of welfare and unemployment are hard to make, particularly at a time when major changes in welfare programs may be imminent. The estimates made are rough, and probably low, thus biasing benefits downward. At the 5 percent discount rates, the present value of these payment differentials is estimated to range from $59 for white females to $231 for nonwhite males. The amount is relatively small compared with the other amounts involved in this analysis.

Cost of the Upward Bound program to the government was calculated from cost data furnished by OEO, on the basis of a cost per student-month; this was multiplied by the average number of months spent in the program by students of each sex-race group. The government cost, less stipends, per student came to $1,888 for white males, $1,874 for white females, $2,004 for nonwhite males, and $2,001 for nonwhite females. These figures were discounted to the start of the program at age 16.

Decision Making in the Public Sector

TABLE 4
BENEFITS AND COSTS FROM THE INDIVIDUAL'S VIEWPOINT[a]

	White Male	White Female	Nonwhite Male	Nonwhite Female
Discount rate 5 percent				
Benefits				
Lifetime income differentials (after taxes)[b]	$5,209	$3,549	$3,943	$5,843
Upward Bound stipend[c]	210	209	224	224
Scholarships and grants[d]	454	394	683	498
Total benefits	$5,873	$4,152	$4,850	$6,565
Cost differentials[e]				
Tuition[f]	370	319	537	378
Extra living costs[g]	260	225	379	267
Total costs	$ 630	$ 544	$ 916	$ 645
Net benefits	$5,243	$3,608	$3,934	$5,920
Discount rate 10 percent				
Benefits				
Lifetime income differentials (after taxes)[b]	$ 770	$1,152	$ 354	$1,902
Upward Bound stipend[c]	202	201	214	214
Scholarships and grants[d]	373	324	561	410
Total benefits	$1,345	$1,677	$1,129	$2,526
Cost differentials[e]				
Tuition[f]	308	264	446	314
Extra living costs[g]	215	185	312	220
Total costs	$ 523	$ 449	$ 758	$ 534
Net benefits	$ 822	$1,228	$ 371	$1,992

[a] All figures shown as present value at age 16, the approximate age at which a decision is made to include a student in Upward Bound.

[b] Differentials are calculated by multiplying the proportion of Upward Bound students in each educational category by the present value of lifetime income for that category, and summing over all four categories. The same is done for siblings, and the difference between those figures is the raw differential. The raw differential is reduced by 25 percent to allow for taxes paid, and the result is again reduced by 25 percent on the assumption that only 75 percent of income differentials are *caused* by education.

[c] Stipends averaged $45.36 per month during the summer and $5.60 per month during the school year. For the whole program, stipends ranged from $218 for white females to $233 for nonwhite females. Figures shown are present values of these amounts.

[d] Scholarships and grants ranged from $739 to $793 per year for Upward Bound students and were assumed to be identical for siblings. Differentials shown arise because of differential rates of college attendance between Upward Bound students and siblings.

[e] Because present values are computed at age 16, the income series automatically shows foregone income as a reduction in benefits, and it is not included separately as a cost. This is also true of the reduced receipts of unemployment and welfare payments by educated individuals.

[f] Based on average 1968–69 tuition of $602 for all U.S. institutions.

[g] Assumes an average of $425 per year in extra living cost while in college.

College costs for operating the Upward Bound program were also calculated on the basis of data furnished by OEO and amount to $271 for white males, $269 for white females, $287 for nonwhite males, and $288 for nonwhite females. However, the extent to which these "costs" (required of the colleges by the government) overstate actual economic costs is an open question, particularly if the college has excess capacity.

The cost of education was calculated on the assumption that the Upward Bound students attended schools and colleges all over the United States in the same proportions that all other students do. An average current cost of education in 1967 for high schools was calculated at $623 per pupil and for colleges at $1,470 per pupil.[19] These costs were discounted appropriately to a present value at age 16.

Extra living cost is a cost from the social point of view, and the figures in Table 5 are identical to those shown in Table 4. Table 5 summarizes the benefits and costs from society's viewpoint.

[19] U.S. Office of Education, *Digest of Educational Statistics, 1968* (Washington, U.S. Government Printing Office, 1968).

TABLE 5
BENEFITS AND COSTS FROM SOCIETY'S VIEWPOINT[a]

	White Male	White Female	Nonwhite Male	Nonwhite Female
Discount rate 5 percent				
Benefits				
Lifetime income differentials (before taxes)[b]	$7,020	$4,777	$5,491	$7,942
Cost Differentials[c]				
Upward Bound cost to the government[d]	$1,811	$1,798	$1,922	$1,919
Upward Bound cost to colleges[e]	260	257	275	275
Cost of education[f]	1,057	872	1,424	1,028
Extra living costs[g]	260	225	379	267
Total costs	$3,388	$3,152	$4,000	$3,489
Net benefits	$3,632	$1,625	$1,491	$4,453
Discount rate 10 percent				
Benefits				
Lifetime income differentials (before taxes)[b]	$1,066	$1,560	$598	$2,609
Cost Differentials[c]				
Upward Bound cost to the government[d]	$1,737	$1,724	$1,845	$1,842
Upward Bound cost to colleges[e]	249	247	264	264
Cost of education[f]	852	724	1,183	856
Extra living costs[g]	215	185	312	220
Total costs	$3,053	$2,880	$3,604	$3,182
Net benefits	—$1,987	—$1,320	—$3,006	—$573

[a] All figures are present values at age 16.
[b] Differentials are calculated as in Table 4, including the assumption that only 75 percent of differentials are caused by education, but excluding the reduction for taxes paid. The effect of decreased receipts of unemployment and welfare benefits by educated individuals has been removed because in the social context these are transfer payments.
[c] As in Table 4, foregone income is included in lifetime income differentials as a reduction in benefits.
[d] Excludes cost of stipends paid students, which are transfer payments. Cost calculated from data furnished by OEO.
[e] Calculated from data furnished by OEO.
[f] Based on total economic cost of education, estimated at $623 per pupil in high school and $1,470 per pupil in college.
[g] Extra living cost is estimated at $425 per year while in college.

An important caveat must be expressed here. From the social viewpoint (but not from the individual viewpoint) it is of vital importance to know whether or not the colleges to which the Upward Bound students go have excess capacity. If they do not, sending the Upward Bound students to college merely results in displacing other students. To the extent that this is true, there may be no social benefits at all from the Upward Bound program! Unfortunately, no data exist by which to answer this question. The high-prestige public and private universities clearly do not have excess capacity, but excess capacity probably exists in a great many public and private institutions that are below the top in prestige. The reader should be cautioned, then, that the benefits shown are based on the assumption that excess capacity exists in all cases, and the benefits are therefore overstated, perhaps substantially.

On the other hand, if excess capacity exists, the use of average college costs probably overstates them, although no data are available from which to make a reasonable estimate of the marginal costs of educating the Upward Bound students.

CONCLUSIONS

From the viewpoint of the individual, the Upward Bound program has net economic benefits for all sex-race groups even at the 10 percent discount rate (subject, of course, to the caveats expressed earlier). However, there would be no net benefits for nonwhite males at the 10 percent discount rate if it were not for the Upward Bound stipend and the scholarships and grants received. From the social viewpoint, substantial net benefits at the 5 percent discount rate become substantial net costs at the 10 percent discount rate. From the economic viewpoint, Upward Bound is at best a marginal program, and the justification for its continued existence must be sought in presumed benefits which are not accounted for here. In addition, the social benefits shown here are completely dependent upon the existence of excess capacity at the colleges attended by the Upward Bound students. If such excess capacity does not exist, there are no such benefits—only costs.

Finally, the data point out the possibility that the Upward Bound program is primarily a device for identification of students who would be rather likely to go to college anyway. If this were its only function, all social benefits would also be eliminated, and private benefits would be limited to the value of the Upward Bound stipend.

READING

30 COST-BENEFIT ANALYSIS FOR EVALUATING TRANSPORTATION PROPOSALS: LOS ANGELES CASE STUDY†

Thomas Peterson

Although most economists and public officials understand the theory of cost-benefit analysis, there seems to be great difficulty when it comes to applying this technique to "real world" problems. This paper critically examines a cost-benefit study undertaken for a proposed rapid transit system in the Los Angeles metropolitan area in order to illustrate the problems and to suggest alternative methods for treating them. For the proposed Los Angeles rapid transit system, the benefit cost ratio is favorable (exceeds unity) only because: (1) many benefits are incorrectly calculated due to such factors as inflation, anticipated unemployment reductions and expenditure decreases, along with double counting and the inclusion of nonquantifiable benefits; (2) many costs are understated or omitted entirely; and (3) the passenger estimates are overly optimistic. This last point is particularly important since passenger estimates are crucial to a cost-benefit study of any rapid transit system.[1]

In 1968 the voters of the Southern California Rapid Transit District (hereinafter referred to as SCRTD) rejected a $2.5 billion fixed rail transit system. The rejected proposal was an 89-mile, 66-station, 5-corridor rapid transit system.[2] Map 1 shows the proposed system; the rail network would operationally form an "X" pattern including four of the corridors, with the Airport-Southwest Route being operationally independent. The recommended system also included the inauguration of 250 miles of express feeder bus route and 300 miles of local feeder bus service. The estimated cost—$2,514,861,000—was almost equal to the maximum debt limit the SCRTD could incur.

The SCRTD paid Stanford Research Institute (hereinafter referred to as SRI) $68,000 to undertake a cost-benefit analysis of its proposed rapid transit system [SRI 1968]. Specifically, SRI was commissioned to: (1) evaluate the traveler benefits accruing to both rapid transit users and automobile travelers, (2) identify and appraise the community benefits accruing to the public, (3) compare traveler and community benefits with system costs, and (4) appraise the overall feasibility of the system.

TRAVELER BENEFITS

Travel time savings, based on 1980 trip patterns, are estimated by comparing trip travel times both with and without rapid transit. The difference in travel time after allowances for congestion from construction is valued at $39.5 million per year [SRI 1968, p. 15]. Travel time saving for airport patrons is valued at $3.05 million per year. Since no airport study was undertaken, these savings are based on the 1.4 million airport patrons required for the airport route to break even. The decrease in vehicle operating costs for motorists who switch to rapid transit and for those who continue to use the less congested street and freeway facilities is valued at $46.5 million annually.

The system would also reduce required parking spaces. SRI reported: "Rapid transit will result in an estimated reduction of 117,770 parking spaces needed, at an annual saving of $22.7 million in the cost of providing these spaces" [1968, p. 18]. The cost of providing parking spaces at the transit stations is included in the systems cost. SRI asserted that automobiles no longer needed for commuting are a benefit assigned to the rapid transit system. This benefit is due to the availability of rapid transit, which would allow some former automobile users to sell their cars or use them for other purposes. SRI valued the decrease of 10,000 automobiles at $3.4 million per year. Use of rapid transit is likewise expected to decrease the number of vehicle miles driven per

---
†I would like to acknowledge the helpful comments on an earlier draft by Jeffrey Barbour, anonymous reviewers. and the editors of *Land Economics*.

[1] This paper is a revised section of the author's doctoral dissertation. Peterson [1970].

[2] See SCRTD [1968].

Decision Making in the Public Sector

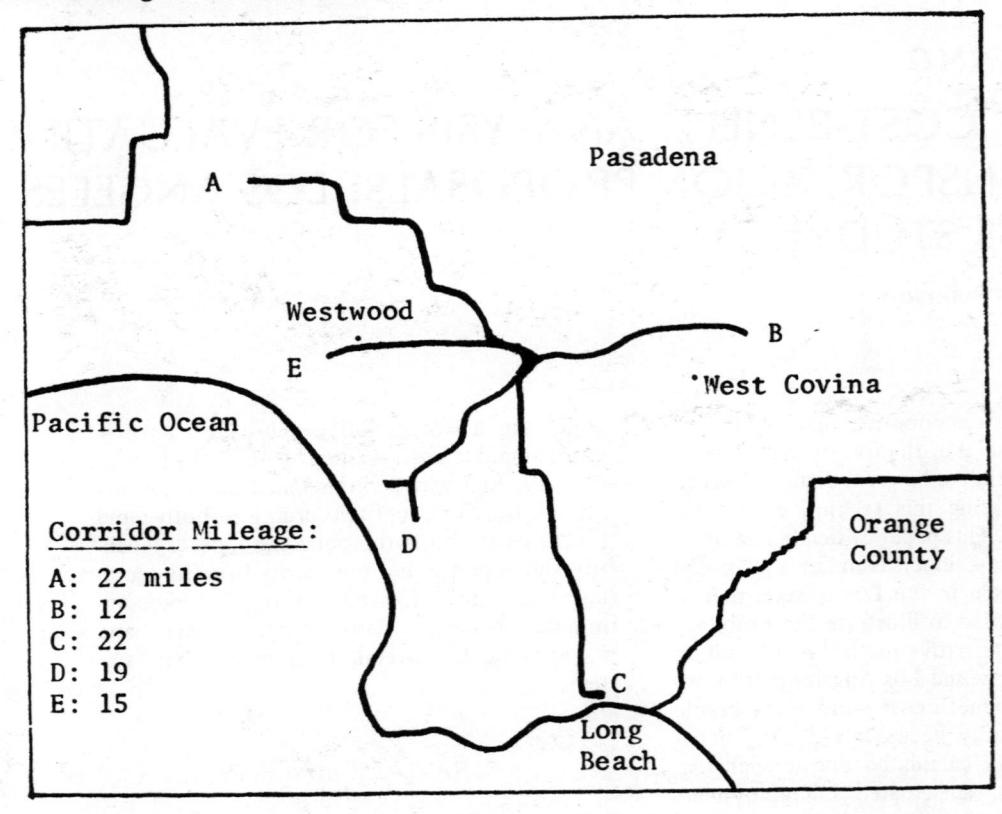

MAP 1

FIVE–CORRIDOR RAPID TRANSIT SYSTEM PROPOSED FOR LOS ANGELES

Corridor Mileage:
A: 22 miles
B: 12
C: 22
D: 19
E: 15

year, which would decrease the number of automobile accidents. The decrease in accidents is valued at $4.7 million per year. Also included under traveler benefits by SRI was a $14.9 million yearly "revenue surplus" used to improve bus service and to avoid fare increases. This alleged "benefit" is merely an income transfer payment because it is not generated from the investment in rapid transit.

The total value of all traveler benefits estimated by SRI is $134.8 million per year [1968, p. 25]. These benefits are greatly dependent on the number of passengers carried. If passenger estimates are not achieved, then these traveler benefits must likewise be reduced.

COMMUNITY BENEFITS

The second classification of benefits from the system are those that accrue to the population as a whole as a by-product or consequence of traveler benefits. Community benefits result from: (1) structural and functional unemployment reductions, (2) construction unemployment reductions, (3) improved business productivity, (4) improved government productivity, and (5) improvements in life style.

SRI estimated that by 1980 rapid transit improvements to labor mobility could reduce the monthly jobless total by 4,200 through improved access to areas of labor shortage. This benefit is questionable since rapid transit alone is not expected to have a major impact on the hard-core unemployment problem in the poverty areas of Los Angeles County. Improved transportation does not by itself increase job opportunities.[3] There are other equal or greater controlling factors. In other words, lack of public transportation may not be the major cause of unemployment in poverty areas of Los Angeles. SRI valued a permanent reduction in unemployment due to improvements in labor mobility at $30 million per year. SRI asserted that the construction of the rapid transit system would have a major impact on unemployment in the construction industry. The con-

[3] *Los Angeles Times*, July 1, 1968. The federally funded transportation-employment project director for Los Angeles "... found evidence that car ownership is a prime condition of employment regardless of job." See *Los Angeles Times*, February 24, 1969, and Wohl [1970], p. 23.

218

struction program was estimated to provide an average of 5,300 jobs for construction workers over a seven-year period, with one-half of the workers coming from the unemployed ranks. The increase in construction employment valued at $24 million per year is open to question since it is difficult to predict the level of unemployment that would exist without the project.[4]

If the employment of one-half of the workers who construct the system is counted as a benefit, one can ask why the decrease in parking space expense, valued at $22.7 million per year, is also counted as a benefit. Even if the gain from increased construction activity due to the rapid transit were counted, other individuals would be laid off—for example, gas station attendants and others associated with automotive transport, including insurance claim adjusters and freeway fence repairmen. In other words, why does SRI count only the positive effect on employment and not the negative effect? To solve this difficulty, the effect on employment due to construction and operation of the system should not be counted in a cost-benefit analysis. SRI also mentioned that millions of dollars of local expenditures for materials, machinery and services will be a further short-term aid to employment demand and a major boon to local industry. This erroneous statement of a secondary benefit is a superb example of what McKean meant when he wrote about multiple counting: "Right before our eyes ... the project's costs ... have suddenly turned into gains" [1958, p. 157].

A third source of benefits to the community from the system is an increase in business productivity. This benefit, estimated at $15 million per year, results from improved labor supply, so-called environmental factors, and business profit on increased labor employment. SRI admitted that most of these benefits are not susceptible to measurement, but wrote that "one indication of their value is the fact that the Los Angeles Chamber of Commerce publicly registered strong support for an extensive rapid transit system" [1968, p. 39]. However, if the gain to merchants located in the central district is at the expense of outlying business districts, then the system only provides an income transfer payment from merchants outside the central area to those located in the central area.

Another $15 million yearly benefit results from improved government productivity. Part of this productivity improvement was derived by SRI based on a "hypothetical city structure." SRI also estimated that the efficiencies through a mass improvement in labor supply would result in a cost reduction of 0.1 percent, which would produce $3 million in savings annually. SRI concluded that the "... dollar value of $15 million per year in increased government productivity ... is believed defendable because it is so conservative" [1968, p. 183].

SRI asserted that there "... are a number of non-monetary improvements that rapid transit will bring to many District residents to broaden their range of choice of mobility as well as residential possibilities that will enrich their 'style of urban life'" [1968, p. 43]. This benefit was estimated by SRI at $25 million annually. After the SCRTD *Final Report* was issued, an SRI representative, when questioned about the value of this benefit, answered that "... others were entitled to their opinion of the value of this particular benefit."[5] Indeed, opinions may differ but there is no way to quantify these benefits to the satisfaction of all voters.

The quantifiable community benefits estimated at $109 million-plus per year by SRI are reduced to only $60 million when the construction employment and "life-style" benefits, valued at $24 million and $25 million per year, respectively, are eliminated. These benefits are correctly excluded because the construction employment benefit, as pointed out, is erroneous and the "life-style" benefit is highly subjective and left for each individual to quantify himself.

COMPARISON OF COSTS AND BENEFITS OF SCRTD'S PROPOSAL

The SCRTD estimated the "equivalent annual cost" of the investment at $140.2 million [SRI 1968, p. 99]. In an attempt to reconcile the difference in the value of costs and benefits which accrue in different years, SRI took the estimated 1980 benefits of $194 million and assumed they would extend until 2016. The benefits were first expressed as constant in real terms to the end of the study period, but "... because the purchasing power of the dollar is expected to change the benefits are adjusted for *anticipated* inflation" [1968, p. 54]. (Emphasis added.) This annual adjustment was estimated at $58.5 million per year.

SRI reasoned that: "The amount required to pay the interest and principal may decline in value by today's standards because of the decreased purchasing power of the dollars used to make these payments. We have therefore increased the benefits at a constant annual rate to

---

[4] See Haveman and Krutilla [1968], for further discussion on this topic.

[5] *Los Angeles Times*, October 6, 1968.

measure the value of the benefits and the amount of money paid for bond service in any year in equivalent dollars" [1968, p. 54]. This procedure is incorrect since bondholders would anticipate the inflation, as did SRI, and therefore demand higher bond payments. If the inflation were unanticipated, then the SCRTD or taxpayers would gain as SRI indicates since the amount of interest and principal would decline in real terms as the purchasing power of the dollar declines. However, from a social point of view the inflation does not produce a net gain since the gain incurred by the SCRTD is exactly offset by the losses incurred by the bondholders or creditors. To avoid the inflation problem the entire comparison of costs and revenues should be calculated in constant dollars of the present period and the discount rate adjusted to what would be the ruling rate if, in fact, people were confident that dollars would have constant purchasing power.

A cost overlooked by SRI is the increase in police costs required to provide safety for users. An indication of this cost can be gained by considering the subway system of New York, where $11 million were spent in fiscal 1964–65 policing its trains and stations.[6] Another cost of the system which must always be considered when a public service replaces a private one is the foregone taxes that a private undertaking would pay, not only on the land right-of-way, but also on the equipment and on all the income earned from operations.

An important factor to consider in the rapid transit proposal is that it was to be financed entirely by bonds. This means that some allowance for risk should be calculated in the SCRTD's proposal, because a similar private undertaking could not be financed entirely by bonds. The riskiness of the project would require that there be some equity financing, the return on which is heavily taxed. As Hirshleifer et al. so clearly put it: "If this interaction is ignored ... any shoe store or macaroni factory could be shown to be more 'profitable' if government owned since the enterprise could be entirely debt financed escaping the corporate income tax" [1960, p. 142].

In summary, even when SRI's optimistic traffic estimates are used, the annual equivalent cost of the system, as computed by Carlin and Wohl, is still greater than the annual equivalent benefit [1968, p. 115]. Table 1, which compares the costs and benefits of the 89-mile system, shows that the estimated net annual benefit of $117.1 million calculated by SRI becomes a negative $10.8 million when recalculated.

[6] Assembly Interim Committee [1965], p. 155.

TABLE 1
COMPARISON OF NET EQUIVALENT ANNUAL BENEFITS OF PROPOSED RAPID TRANSIT SYSTEM
(Millions of 1968 Dollars)

	SCRTD Final Report	Carlin and Wohl
1. Traveler Benefits	$ 85.3	$119.9
2. Community Benefits	109.0	60.0
3. Adjustment for Inflation	58.5	–
4. Equivalent Annual Benefits	252.8	179.9
5. Annual Operating Costs	–	49.2
6. Equivalent Annual Capital Costs	140.2	146.0
7. Less Equivalent Annual Value of $700 million Salvage Value of ROW and Structures Received in 2017	–4.5	–4.5
8. Equivalent Annual Costs	135.7	190.7
9. Net Equivalent Annual Benefits	117.1	–10.8

Source: Carlin and Wohl [1968], p. 15.

PASSENGER ESTIMATES

Since the benefits estimated depend heavily on the level of system patronage, these passenger estimates must be examined very closely. The number of passengers using the 89-mile rapid transit system was estimated by forecasting the 1980 travel demands in a band surrounding the rail system called the "service area."[7] The 1980 travel demands, based on data provided by the Los Angeles Regional Transportation Study and private surveys, were estimated through the use of a transportation model.[8] Table 2, which summarizes the results

[7] The service area is defined as an area "extending 10 minutes in travel time outward from the stations except for the terminal stations which will draw from a more limited area" [Coverdale and Colpitts 1968, p. III–1].

[8] For a discussion of the factors that were assumed to affect future travel demands and the development

Cost-Benefit Analysis

TABLE 2
PROJECTED SOURCE OF 1980 RAPID TRANSIT REVENUE PASSENGERS
(1980 Average Weekday).

	Potential Service Area Trips	Trips Diverted to Rapid Transit	% of Service Area Trips Diverted to Rapid Transit
Trips Via Bus			
Peak	96,200	70,000	72.8%
Off-Peak	100,000	61,000	61.0
All Day	196,200	131,000	66.8%
Trips Via Auto			
Peak	1,604,800	307,000	19.1%
Off-Peak	3,911,100	39,000	1.0
All Day	5,515,900	346,000	6.3%
Trips Via Bus and Auto Combined			
Peak	1,701,000	377,000	22.2%
Off-Peak	4,011,000	100,000	1.5
All Day	5,712,000	477,000	8.4%

Source: Reproduced verbatim from the SCRTD, *Final Report*, p. CC-4.

of this model, shows that in the service area there are 5.7 million potential rapid-transit users, and that 1.7 million of these potential trips would take place during the peak hours.

From the estimate of potential riders, Coverdale and Colpitts estimated the number that would be diverted to the rapid transit system during both the peak and off-peak hours.

Expected Passenger Usage

The SCRTD's passenger estimates are used to show that even with their optimistic estimates the rapid transit system will not have much effect on traffic congestion in the Los Angeles area.

Table 2 shows that during the peak hours the rapid transit system is expected to carry 307,000 former automobile passengers on an average weekday, which is less than 20 percent of the potential automobile trips that take place in the service area during the peak hours. In other words, the system's greatest effect will be in the service area during peak hours. The benefits from this passenger switch have been discussed earlier. When the county is considered rather than the smaller service area, these passengers reduce the number of automobiles from the county's streets by about 5 percent during the peak hours.[9] Table 2 also shows that during the peak hours the bus and transit system will carry 377,000 passengers, roughly 80 percent of its passengers, with almost three-fourths of them being diverted from the bus system.

During the off-peak hours, when approximately two-thirds of the average daily trips take place, the rapid transit system will divert only one percent of the automobile passengers from the service area. The total system, both rapid transit and bus, is expected to carry slightly over eight percent of the total number of daily trips in the county.

The rapid transit system is expected to remove 74,327,000 automobiles per year from the streets and freeways during the peak hours, at a cost of at least $1.80 per peak automobile per weekday.[10] The total number of automobiles removed by the rapid transit system on

---

of the transportation model see, Coverdale and Colpitts [1968], p. 71, and Los Angeles Regional Transportation Study, *Base Year Report*, 1960, vol. 1.

[9] This figure is determined by assuming that the 307,000 weekday passengers using rapid transit results in 256,000 automobiles being removed during the peak hours. The 1980 employment in Los Angeles County is expected to be 3,512,250. Using the information from the 1958 Coverdale and Colpitts Report which showed that 80 percent of those employed in the Los Angeles area travel by automobile during the peak hours and that each automobile carries 1.2 passengers, the number of autos on the streets during the 1980 peak hours is estimated at 4,683,000.

[10] The SCRTD estimated the yearly cost of the complete bus and rail system at $135,700,000.

an average weekday in 1980 is 288,833—with 256,333 removed during peak hours and 32,500 during the remaining 20 hours. By 1980, an estimated 4,683,000 autos will be used during the peak hours.[11] If the number of automobiles used during the *peak* hours increases at three percent per year, the rapid transit system will remove less than two years' automobile growth.[12] Less than 50,000 peak-hour automobiles would be diverted from the central business district, since only 23 percent of the peak-hour automobile trips diverted to transit have the central area as their destination.[13]

EVALUATION OF PASSENGER ESTIMATES

The passenger estimates made by Coverdale and Colpitts are extremely optimistic, as are most passenger and revenue estimates made for other transit systems. For example, before the Oakland–Fremont line opened in the San Francisco Metropolitan Area, the management of the Bay Area Rapid Transit System (BART) estimated that the line would carry 26,000 passengers per day. By November 1972 the line carried only one-half that number.[14]

One method of analyzing the SCRTD passenger estimates is to compare the proposed system with current traffic patterns. This method was used by Coverdale and Colpitts in 1968, when they likened the traffic pattern of the proposed rail system to be more "... comparable to a commuter railroad than to a conventional rapid transit system as now exists in other cities in that a high degree of travel occurs in rush hours and the average trip length is longer" [SRI 1968, p. IV–ii]. This confirmed their previous study, completed in 1959, where they found that five out of every six bus riders to and from the CBD came from within a 10-mile circle and 20 percent of all riders came from within a 5-mile circle centered on Broadway and 7th Streets [Coverdale and Colpitts 1959, p. A–II].

In light of these data, the DeLeuw Report correctly concluded in 1964 that although "rail rapid transit may be appropriate for the inner areas, it is clear that beyond the 10-mile circle the number of rush hour trips to and from the CBD at the present time is too small and too widely dispersed geographically to justify a high type of rapid transit service" [DeLeuw 1964, p. 15]. Given this pattern of short-length trips to the CBD, the SCRTD five-corridor system, with its focus on the CBD and routes longer than 10 miles, seems designed for a nonexisting passenger demand. This conclusion is further supported by the fact that in 1967 all but two SCRTD bus lines in the San Fernando Valley were losing money. Most bus lines in the outlying areas were unprofitable [Citizens' Advisory Council 1968, p. 69].

The SCRTD estimated that 72.5 percent of its rapid-transit passengers will be former automobile users. This figure is extremely high in light of the experience of other transit systems. The Yonge Street subway in Toronto and the Congress Street Rapid Transit in Chicago which were opened in the 1950s diverted less than 13 percent of their passengers from automobiles [Meyer et al. 1965, p. 100]. No other rapid transit system has had the passenger diversion from autos that the SCRTD expects. Even the BART system expects to attract only 30.3 percent of its passengers from automobiles. The small role that public transit plays in the Los Angeles area, where over 95 percent of the daily trips are taken by automobile, is another reason for doubting the SCRTD's passenger estimates.

Since the rail system is more nearly comparable to a commuter railroad than to a conventional rapid transit system, and since the users of North American suburban commuter railroads tend to have higher incomes than other travelers and residents of a region, one could question the welfare implications of having lower-income groups subsidize the high-

---

[11] Employment in Los Angeles County is estimated at 3,512,250 for 1980. Eighty percent travel during the peak hours by automobiles and average automobile occupancy is 1.2 people. 1980 employment times the number who travel by automobile during peak hours (0.80) divided by people per automobile (1.2) times the number of trips (2).

[12] In Chicago the Dan Ryan and Kennedy rail lines opened in late 1969 and early 1970, respectively. Their opening did not significantly reduce the number of cars from the parallel freeways, as the following table (average daily vehicle counts at peak points) shows:

Year	Dan Ryan	Kennedy
1968	122,300	103,000
1969	126,100	108,200
1970	121,500	104,300
1971	144,100	109,200
1972	159,000	117,000

Source: Hilton [1974], p. 69. See this source for similar results in other cities.

[13] SCRTD, "Appendix B to the Final Report," Table IV–B. The net number of automobiles diverted from the CBD may be less than zero because, "If the mass transit favored downtown disproportionately, it will induce such a rate of development within downtown ... that the effect of mass transit in reducing travel to downtown by private vehicle will be more than offset by the increase of total trip demands" [Contini 1969, p. 6].

[14] Hilton [1974], p. 73.

income group's transportation. The Los Angeles system was to be financed by a one-half of one percent sales tax which would last for almost 50 years. This tax stream, discounted at six percent, would have a present value of $400–$2,000 for families with yearly taxable expenditures of $5,000–$25,000, regardless of whether or not they used the service.

CONCLUSION

Because of the interest in rapid transit for solving a city's transportation problems, a detailed investigation of the cost-benefit study computed for Los Angeles can provide valuable insight to an agency contemplating such a system for its own area. The Stanford Research Institute demonstrates that the benefits are often incorrectly calculated, while not all costs are considered. Further investigation is also needed to estimate passenger demand, since the number of passengers greatly influences the benefits to be derived from the system.

If Los Angeles, or any other city, is planning to introduce a rapid transit system, the difficulties of using cost-benefit analysis raised in this paper must be faced.

THOMAS PETERSON
Assistant Professor
Department of Economics
Central Michigan University

References

Assembly Interim Committee on Transportation and Commerce. 1965. *Southern California Rapid Transit Financing*. State of California. September 15–16, 1965.

Carlin, Alan, and Wohl, Martin. 1968. *An Economic Re-Evaluation of the Proposed Los Angeles Rapid Transit System*. Santa Monica, California, Rand Corporation, September 1968.

Citizens' Advisory Council on Public Transportation. 1968. *Improving Public Transportation in Los Angeles*. Los Angeles.

Contini, E. 1969. "Transportation." In *Agenda for Los Angeles Area in 1970*, W. Hirch and Samuel Hale. Los Angeles: Institute of Government and Public Affairs, University of California.

Coverdale and Colpitts. 1959. "A Study of Public Transportation Needs in the Area Served by the Los Angeles Mass Transit Authority." Los Angeles, May 5, 1959.

—— and ——. 1968. "Estimates of Traffic Revenues and Expenses." Appendix B to the *Final Report*. SCRTD, Los Angeles.

DeLeuw, Cather and Company. 1964. "Report on Automobile Club of Southern California on Public Transportation in Los Angeles." San Francisco.

Haveman, R. H., and Krutilla, J. V. 1968. *Unemployment, Idle Capacity and the Evaluation of Public Expenditures*. Baltimore: Johns Hopkins Press.

Hilton, George W. 1974. *Federal Transit Subsidies*. Washington, D.C.: American Enterprise Institute.

Hirshleifer, Jack, et al. 1960. *Water Supply: Economics, Technology, and Policy*. Chicago: University of Chicago Press.

McKean, Roland N. 1958. *Efficiency in Government through Systems Analysis*. New York: Wiley.

Meyer, John, et al. 1965. *The Urban Transportation Problem*. Cambridge: Harvard University Press.

Peterson, Thomas C. 1970. "An Economic Evaluation of the Southern California Rapid Transit District: Its Proposed Solution to the Transportation Problem in Los Angeles." Ph.D. thesis, University of California, Los Angeles.

Southern California Rapid Transit District. 1968. *Final Report*. Los Angeles, May 1968.

Stanford Research Institute. 1968. "Benefit/Cost Analysis of the Five Corridor Rapid Transit System for Los Angeles." Prepared for Southern California Rapid Transit District. Menlo Park, California, May 1968, mimeo.

Wohl, Martin. 1970. "Users of Urban Transportation and Their Income Circumstances." *Traffic Quarterly* 24, No. 1 (January 1970).

CASE

31 BENEFIT-COST ANALYSIS OF A CURBSIDE RECYCLING PROGRAM*

The City of West University, an incorporated community located within the boundaries of Houston, Texas has established a curbside recycling program for household trash. The program provides for weekly curbside pickup of all normally recyclable materials from each household in the community. In February, 1973, the City of West University began a once-a-week curbside pickup of recyclable material from each home in the city. Citizens desiring to participate are required to remove labels from bottles and cans, remove metal lids from bottles, and rinse the containers free of food. Materials must then be segregated into six separate categories: tin and bimetal, aluminum, colored glass, clear glass, newsprint, and mixed paper. The collection crews inspect sorted items prior to pickup to insure proper cleaning and sorting. The items are then deposited into bins of the trucks that normally serve the city four days per week after normal garbage collection. Materials are hauled to a central location for storage until delivery to the purchasers.

Currently 40 percent of the population participates at least one day a month to some extent. However, only 10 to 15 percent of the households are engaged in regular recycling of all six categories. In its first full year of operation, the program recognized a small book profit from operations of $1,500.

ANALYTICAL FRAMEWORK

The following items were identified as relevant costs and benefits to be analyzed:

Costs	Benefits
Incremental labor	Revenue from sale of materials
Incremental cost of trucks, including fuel and maintenance	Savings from reduced regular garbage collection, including reduced expenses for labor, trucks, fuel, maintenance, administration and overhead
Facilities and overhead	Savings in cost of land for landfill due to reduced garbage deposits
Storage and hauling	Societal savings in terms of energy and natural resources, to the extent not reflected in recyclable material prices
Administration	
Advertising and promotion	

After discussions with City officials it was apparent that many of the costs and benefits tended to offset each other. For instance, there has been no net increase or decrease in the cost of the sanitation program (due to the recycling effort) for administration, facilities and overhead. In addition, the same crews and trucks are utilized for recyclables collection as well as for routine garbage pickup. The Sanitation Department has determined that seventeen round trips per week to the landfill have been eliminated as a result of reduced general garbage collections. This net saving in expenses associated with truck use, fuel, and maintenance has been almost exactly offset by a corresponding increase in these costs due to recycling collections. There has also been no increase in labor costs. The four, four-man crews finish regular collections at 2:30 P.M. each afternoon and make recycling collections from 2:30 to 4:30 P.M. The ability of the existing crews to complete regular as well as recycling pickups during normal 8-hour days results from the quicker pickup of regular refuse (because of recycling) and some pre-existing slack which existed in the collection process.

Hence, the enumeration of costs and benefits can be reduced to the following:

Costs	Benefits
Storage and hauling	Revenue from sale of recycled material
Advertising	Savings in the cost of landfill acreage
	Societal savings due to recycled material usage

QUANTIFICATION OF COSTS AND BENEFITS

Since the only net costs are for advertising, bin rental, and bin hauling, the total annual cost may be simply computed. Approximately $300 per year has been spent on the printing of information regarding

---

*This case was adapted from R. Charles Moyer and David Dewan, "Analysis of a Recycling Program," *Baylor Business Studies* (October, 1975), pp. 15-20. Adaptation to case by R. Charles Moyer.

the program that is included in the monthly bills to each household. Storage and hauling of newspaper has no explicit cost to the city, since the purchaser supplies the bins and handles the hauling himself. The cost of this service is reflected in the rate paid to the city. Aluminum is stored in plastic bags provided by the processor (at no charge) and pickup is provided free. Glass is stored in two 20-cu. yard containers rented by the City for $55 per load. Tin and bimetal are stored in one 40-cu. yard bin rented for $55 per month. This bin is delivered to the purchaser once a month at a $55 charge per delivery. These annual costs are summarized in Table 1.

A considerable portion of the benefits is received from the revenue generated from the sale of collected materials. Table 2 summarizes the annual collections in terms of quantity and revenue. The prices listed are the most conservative, in that they reflect lowest expected prices. The amounts collected are historical values. Currently, about 1,200 tons per year of material are being recycled, from which the City receives approximately $9,570.

Table 1 Summary of Costs

Item	Cost/Year
Bin rental	$1980
Hauling	1980
Advertising	300
Total	$4260

Merger Regulation

Table 2 Annual Collections and Revenue

Item	Amount (lbs.)	Price/lb. ($)	Revenue ($)
Newspaper	1,740,000	$0.004	$3,480
Glass	240,000	.01	2,400
Tin and bimetal	132,000	0.015	1,980
Mixed paper	240,000	0.0015	360
Aluminum	9,000	0.15	1,350
	2,361,000		$9,570

The 1,200 tons per year savings in rubbish to be dumped at the landfill translates into a significant benefit, as a result of the high cost of the land used for landfill. Because of recycling, approximately 9,300 cubic yards per year of waste does not enter the landfill—a 24 percent savings. This translates into a savings of 0.38 acres/year and, with the cost of new landfill acreage at $8,000 per acre, the dollar savings amounts to $3,040 per year.

Questions for Discussion

1. Given the data from the West University projects, does this recycling program seem justified in a benefit-cost analysis framework?
2. What factors make this program unique? Under what conditions would this type of program be successful in other communities?
3. What additional costs and benefits might have been included in the analysis to make it more complete?

Chapter 10 Externalities and Income Distribution

READING

32 PRICE ELASTICITIES OF DEMAND AND AIR POLLUTION CONTROL

Robert E. Kohn*

I Introduction

IN the economic literature on externalities, two separate approaches to pollution control are distinguished; (1) government regulations to enforce control and (2) tax and subsidy schemes to stimulate voluntary abatement.[1] The dichotomy, however, is not always sharp. Enforced controls impose changes on economic activities which may increase costs and induce voluntary shifts away from pollution intensive activities. For example, a limitation on the sulfur content of industrial coal might stimulate the substitution of cleaner burning natural gas. In addition, the higher production costs associated with the shift to low sulfur coal or to natural gas may add to the prices of related outputs, reducing the demand for these products. In turn, substitutions among outputs may occur which will further alter the levels of production and consumption activities from what they would be in the absence of pollution control.

Cost-effectiveness models for achieving environmental goals generally ignore induced voluntary abatement. As a consequence, the proposed solutions may be incorrect in that (a) the environmental goals would be exceeded and (b) the total cost of control would not be a minimum cost. This paper presents an air pollution control model in which *both* required control activity and the induced voluntary adjustments in consumption and production levels are taken into account.

II The Cost-effectiveness Model with Fixed Production and Consumption Levels

The writer has developed a linear programming model for air pollution control (Kohn, 1969, 1971a, 1971b, 1971c, 1972). The requirements in the model are a set of maximum allowable annual emission flows for each pollutant.[2] The variables represent activity levels of individual air pollution control methods. A *least cost* set of control method activity levels is determined which satisfies the requirements on annual emission flows. A set of production and consumption levels which are the source of air pollution provides a constraint on total control activity.

This model, which is formally defined in appendix 1, was previously implemented using data for the St. Louis Airshed. Ninety-four pollution source categories and more than three-hundred control methods — including the ninety-four existing control methods —

Received for publication August 26, 1971. Revision accepted for publication June 26, 1972.

* This research was supported by National Science Foundation grant no. GS–2892. The writer is grateful for the constructive criticism of this paper from Professors T. Bergstrom and J. Hollenhorst and an anonymous referee.

[1] In addition to control by directive or regulation and a variety of incentive systems (subsidies, fees, sale of emission rights), there also may be the possibility of collective goods for reprocessing wastes or enhancing assimilative or productive capacities of the environment. See Davis and Kamien (1969).

[2] Air quality goals are usually expressed as concentrations — parts per million or micrograms per cubic meter. To determine the total annual emission flow, in pounds, for each pollutant corresponding to the legal goal for that pollutant, the *proportional model*, as defined by the Environmental Protection Agency (1971, p. 15490), is used.

were included. It was found that by 1975, the estimated least cost of achieving the allowable emission flows would be 35.3 million dollars a year. However, it was assumed that the projected production and consumption levels are fixed and would not be affected by the control method solution. In this paper, the impact of pollution control on prices and subsequent reductions in the levels of production and consumption are estimated and incorporated in the model.[3]

III Demand Feedbacks and Imputed Costs

It is assumed that the costs of abatement are added to the prices of related outputs. Each control method unit cost is divided by the sales value of the corresponding quantity of output to estimate the proportional increase in price. This ratio is multiplied by the price elasticity of demand for that output to determine the proportional decrease in output. The model is set up in such a way (see appendix 1) that the proportional decrease represents the numerical reduction in a production or consumption level per unit of control method activity.

It is assumed that the induced changes in production and consumption levels, although voluntary, are distortions of economic choice and should be assigned a cost.[4] Accordingly, each induced change in output per unit of control method activity is multiplied by the control method cost to estimate the imputed economic cost of the "distortion." This is a maximum value because part of the adjustment might occur at a lower incremental cost.

Whereas the costs of abatement in the model are economic costs, only *private* accounting costs are used to determine demand feedbacks and imputed costs of output adjustments. For example, the economic cost of converting coal stokers to natural gas includes a "scarcity premium" for the natural gas (Kohn, 1971b, p. 616). Because this is a cost that will be borne by future users of synthetic gas, it does not increase current (1975) prices.

Reductions in the output of final and intermediate goods and services are examined in this model. These include the decrease in the consumption of automobile services when the costs of operating an automobile increase, the reduction in demand for the outputs of industrial plants which use coal when the costs of burning coal increase, the decline in the output of electricity when the power generating costs increase, etc. Although declines in production and consumption are likely to cause reductions in related economic activities, such secondary or derived reductions are not included in the model.[5] In addition, the possibility that the consumption of alternative goods and services will increase (the case when the price elasticities of demand of the reduced outputs exceed unity), or decrease (the case when the price elasticities of the reduced outputs are less than unity) is not considered. The possibility of input substitution by producers is also ignored. Energy substitutions, i.e., natural gas for coal or electric power, are theoretically included in the basic set of control methods. To the extent that there are net reductions in final goods and services, the model incorporates the proposition that there is a trade-off between the output of final goods and cleaner air.

IV Implementation of the Model

The implementation of a model which purports to represent *all* polluting activities in an airshed, their control, and the resulting market impact of abatement is not tidy. Tables 1 and 2 illustrate the type of data used to estimate demand feedbacks and some of the required simplifying assumptions.

The assumption of proportionality is frequently invoked. For example, it is assumed that industry sales are proportional to the quantity of fuel burned or electricity consumed, industrial waste generated is proportional to total sales, etc. Moreover, the proportional relationships, often based on 1967 prices and technology, are assumed equally applicable to the year 1975.

The use of average cost figures to represent a variety of producers and consumers is common in the model. For example, a single sales value represents total automotive purchases per gallon of gasoline consumed. There is the further problem that the purchase of control devices for automobiles represents both capital

---

[3] Leontief (1970) examines the *increases* in production and consumption levels, associated with pollution abatement. The Leontief repercussions are treated as feedbacks in the cost-effectiveness model in Kohn (1973).

[4] An argument can be made that reductions in polluting activities promote economic efficiency and need not be assigned a cost. However, control costs here are imposed on pollution sources according to *cost-effectiveness*, not pollution damage caused.

[5] Both primary and secondary adjustments are considered by Leontief (1970).

TABLE 1.—SELECTED CONTROL METHOD COSTS AND ESTIMATED INCREASES
IN SALES VALUE OF RELATED OUTPUTS

Air Pollution Control Method	Control Method Cost	Sales Value (before control) of Output Corresponding to One Unit of Control Activity	Proportional Increase in Sales Value	References Consulted
Substitution of number one for number two diesel fuel in buses	$.014 per gallon of diesel fuel consumed	$4.20 in bus revenue per gallon of diesel fuel consumed	.0033	Kohn (1969, p. 65). Chairman, Bi-State Transit Company.
Exhaust control device for 1970 to 1975 automobiles	$.018 per gallon of gasoline consumed	$2.00 in total automobile operating costs per gallon of gasoline consumed	.0090	Kohn (1969, p. 58), *The Midwest Motorist* (1970, p. 4).
Conversion of travelling grate stokers (equipped with settling chambers) in the stone, clay, and glass industry, from coal to natural gas	$4.46 per ton of coal replaced by gas	$5100. in stone, clay, and glass industry sales per ton of coal burned in travelling grate stokers (with settling chambers) by this industry	.0009	Kohn (1969, p. 124). U.S. Bureau of the Census (1966, p. 7–92), U.S. Bureau of the Census (1971b, p. 26–15).
Low sulfur coal for pulverized coal furnaces (equipped with electrostatic precipitators) in the primary metals industry	$2.50 per ton of high sulfur coal replaced	$8550. in primary metal sales per ton of coal burned in pulverized coal furnaces (with electrostatic precipitators) by this industry	.0003	Kohn (1969, p. 144). U.S. Bureau of the Census (1966, p. 7–92). U.S. Bureau of the Census (1971b, p. 26–15).
Desulfurization process at the Sioux Power Plant of Union Electric Company	$1.27 per ton of coal burned ($.0005 per kilowatt hour of electricity produced)	$5.65 in chemical industry sales per kilowatt hour purchased from the Sioux Power Plant	.0001	Kohn (1969, p. 287). Executive, Union Electric Company. U.S. Department of Commerce (1970, p. 26–15).
ibid.	ibid	$.0865 in *total* household purchases of electricity per kilowatt hour delivered to households by the Sioux Plant	.0058	*St. Louis Commerce* (1967, p. 56). Union Electric Company (1968, p. 26).
Landfill disposal of industrial waste currently burned on site	$11.16 per ton of waste burned on site	$27,000. in industrial sales per ton of waste burned on site	.0004	Kohn (1969, p. 330). U.S. Bureau of the Census (1971b, p. 26–14).
Baghouse Collectors for electric arc furnaces	$.31 per ton of steel produced	$86.00 per ton of steel	.0036	Kohn (1969, p. 358). *Metal Statistics* (1968, p. 285).
Electrostatic precipitators to upgrade dust collection efficiency from 96.4 per cent to 99.6 per cent in a specific cement plant	$.11 per barrel of cement produced	$3.20 per barrel of cement	.0344	Kohn (1969, p. 397). U.S. Bureau of the Census (1971a, p. 32B–15).

Externalities and Income Distribution

TABLE 1. — *Continued*

Air Pollution Control Method	Control Method Cost	Sales Value (before control) of Output Corresponding to One Unit of Control Activity	Proportional Increase in Sales Value	References Consulted
Incorporate double contact process in existing sulfuric acid plants	$.82 per ton of acid produced	$18.50 per ton of acid produced	.0450	Kohn (1969, p. 393). U.S. Bureau of the Census (1971a, p. 28A–24).

TABLE 2. — SELECTED PRICE ELASTICITIES USED IN THE MODEL

Outputs	Elasticity [a]	References Consulted [b]
Bus Transportation	−1.2	Houthakker and Taylor (1970, p. 115)
Cement Industry	− .3	Loescher (1959, p. 79).
Chemical Industry	−1.0	estimated.
Electricity to Households	− .5	Fisher (1962, p. 96) Houthakker and Taylor (1970, p. 87).
Ferrous Metals	−1.0	Broude (1963, p. 130).
Food	− .3	Powell (1966, p. 672).
Furniture	−1.0	Houthakker and Taylor (1970, p. 80).
Lead Smelting	− .5	estimated.
Leather	− .9	Houthakker and Taylor (1970, p. 67).
Paper	− .6	Houthakker and Taylor (1970, p. 86).
Printing	− .4	Houthakker and Taylor (1970, p. 123).
Petroleum	− .3	Houthakker and Taylor (1970, p. 112).
Services	− .4	Powell (1966, p. 672).
Textiles	− .7	Powell (1966, p. 672).
Transportation Equipment	−1.0	Chow (1957, p. 48).

[a] Long-run price elasticities are used, when available.
[b] Price elasticities are either taken from or based on data in the references cited. In some cases elasticities provided by different references are averaged.

and annual maintenance expenditures. The two are aggregated here and a single price elasticity of demand is used.

Many of the production activities in the model pertain to intermediate goods. Because the literature on the price elasticity of demand for intermediate goods is sparse, it was necessary to estimate many of the elasticities. In some cases, these were based on price elasticities for final goods, as estimated by Houthakker and Taylor (1970). Certainly, errors were introduced by using national elasticities to determine the demand effect of purely local price increases, although for outputs such as bus transportation, electricity, and cement, the national and local price elasticities of demand might be similar. For certain industries, such as chemical and ferrous metals, the price elasticity of demand for local producers was arbitrarily assumed to be unity, although it is likely that the price elasticity for these outputs on a national level might be less elastic. In some instances when appropriate price elasticities of demand for the United States economy were not available, estimates from an Australian study (Powell, 1966) were reluctantly used.

The production and consumption categories commonly used in air pollution control models relate more to fuel use than final outputs (e.g., coal burned in travelling grate stokers equipped with settling chambers, coal burned in pulverized coal furnaces equipped with electrostatic precipitators, coal burned in a specific power plant, etc.) Thus, to estimate the output effect associated with the control of fuel combustion, it was necessary to allocate coal and power use according to individual users. This aspect of the research, which necessitated further reliance on averaging and assumptions of proportionality, is discussed in appendix 2.

The output effect can be illustrated using data from tables 1 and 2. When number 2 diesel fuel in buses is replaced by number 1 diesel fuel, to reduce sulfur dioxide and particulates, it is assumed that bus fares will increase 0.33 per cent. Given a price elasticity of demand for bus services of −1.2, the consumption of bus services will decline an estimated

Decision Making in the Public Sector

0.4 per cent. The imputed cost associated with the induced reduction of 0.004 gallons of diesel fuel per control method activity unit is (.004) ($.014), or $.000056.

V Adjustments in Consumption and Production Levels Associated with the Solution of the Original Model

The control requirements and total cost of abatement under the assumption of fixed production and consumption levels, are presented in column 1 of table 3. The direct abatement of each pollutant is the projected emission flow in 1975, in the absence of control, less the allowable annual flow. These reductions in annual emissions are achieved at an annual cost of 35.3 million dollars. When the anticipated changes in production and consumption levels associated with *this* control method solution are introduced and calculated, the cost and reductions in emission flows in column 2 of table 3 are determined.[6]

As a consequence of voluntary changes in production and consumption levels, carbon monoxide emissions are reduced 23.6 million pounds, hydrocarbons are reduced 5.0 million pounds, etc.

Because of the decline in production and consumption, the maximum control method activity levels are lower. For each pollutant, the total direct abatement is less in column 2 of table 3 than in column 1, as is the total cost of direct abatement.[7]

The excess abatement of a pollutant is the sum of the direct abatement and the indirect abatement from the output effect, less the required abatement for that pollutant from column 1. As a consequence of voluntary adjustments in polluting activities, air quality superior to the target goals would be attained.

VI Results of the Revised Model and Conclusions

In the revised model incorporating feedbacks on production and consumption levels, there is no excess abatement and the total cost of pollution control declines from 35.4 to 34.9 million dollars. For the most part, this consists of declines in automobile control costs and in the costs of controlling industrial coal combustion. Two dissimilar effects are at work here. The voluntary abatement associated with automotive control devices reduces the necessary activity levels for these control methods. Alternatively, the relatively small output effect associated with control methods for industrial coal combustion makes these control methods relatively less efficient — although this *alone* would not account for their reduced activity levels.

The major changes in consumption and production levels are a reduction of 0.7 per cent in the consumption of gasoline, a reduction of 0.3 per cent in coal combustion by power plants — almost entirely because of reduced demand for power by households, and a 3.4 per cent decrease in the manufacturing of sulfuric acid. The increased prices of industrial products associated with the control of coal burning and power plants result in an insignificant output effect. In general the costs of pollution control associated with heat and power inputs add little to the final prices of related outputs.

The voluntary adjustments in polluting activities which may result in improved air quality or in lower costs of abatement, should be of interest to policy makers.[8] The interdependency between abatement and consumption in this model relates to the economic literature on Pareto optimal combinations of abatement expenditures, consumption adjustments and air quality goals (see Dolbear 1967, Donaldson and Victor, 1970, Meyer, 1971). Because the imposition of control methods operates as a tax on selected polluting activities, this work is relevant to economic research on efficient and inefficient pollutant taxes (see Zerbe, 1970, Ruff, 1972). Although the present model may not yield a Pareto optimal combination of abatement expenditures and consumption adjustments, even with optimal air quality goals (see footnote 4), it does yield a least-cost solution, given the assumption that no other taxing schemes are feasible.

---

[6] Each control method activity level in the original solution was divided by the induced proportional change in output plus one. The values in column 2 of table 3 were calculated from this revised set of activity levels.

[7] The increase in the sum of direct plus imputed costs in column (2) would not be possible in an integer programming solution. The fact that certain sources are not completely controlled indicates that there are imputed costs not offset by reductions in direct costs. The problem of divisibility is discussed in Kohn, (1971d).

[8] In fact, it appears that part of the rationale for controlling the sulfur content of coal burned in the St. Louis Airshed was to stimulate vountary conversions to natural gas and fuel oil. The controversy over low sulfur regulations in the St. Louis Airshed is examined in Kohn (1971b).

Externalities and Income Distribution

TABLE 3.—LEAST-COST SOLUTION FOR AIR POLLUTION CONTROL IN THE ST. LOUIS AIRSHED IN 1975 FOR TWO MODELS
(millions of dollars and millions of pounds)

	Original Solution Assuming No Decline in Production or Consumption Levels (1)	Original Solution Allowing for Decline in Production and Consumption Levels (2)	Revised Model Incorporating Decline in Production and Consumpiton Levels (3)
Annual Cost of Direct Abatement	$35.3	$35.2	$34.7
Imputed Cost of Shifts in Production and Consumption	$ 0	$ .2	$ .2
Direct Abatement of Carbon Monoxide	1867.0	1866.9	1843.8
		(millions of pounds)	
Reduction in Carbon Monoxide from Decline in Production and Consumption Levels	0	23.6	23.2
Excess Abatement	0	23.5	0
Direct Abatement of Hydrocarbons	524.3	524.2	519.3
Reduction of Hydrocarbons from Decline in Production and Consumption Levels	0	5.0	5.0
Excess Abatement	0	4.9	0
Direct Abatement of Nitrogen Oxides	111.9	111.4	110.6
Reduction of Nitrogen Oxides from Decline in Production and Consumption Levels	0	1.4	1.3
Excess Abatement	0	.9	0
Direct Abatement of Sulfur Dioxide	989.2	985.2	984.7
Reduction of Sulfur Dioxide from Decline in Production and Consumption Levels	0	4.5	4.5
Excess Abatement	0	.5	0
Direct Abatement of Particulates	163.8	163.6	163.4
Reduction of Particulates from Decline in Production and Consumption Levels	0	.4	.4
Excess Abatement	0	.2	0

APPENDIX 1

The Cost-Effectiveness Model with Demand Feedbacks

For any airshed, it is assumed that there is a set of allowable annual emission flows. This is represented by a $(P \times 1)$ vector, a.

The sources of air pollution are the various production and consumption activities in the airshed. The levels of these M activities are elements of an $(M \times 1)$ vector, s. The abatement technology is represented by an $(N \times 1)$ vector, x whose element x_j is the activity level of an air pollution control method uniquely defined for, and measured in the same units as, a corresponding pollution source, s_i. For each polluting source, one or more control methods are defined, the first of which is the existing control (which may represent noncontrol) method.

The vectors, a and s, are related to the choice vector x by two matrices U and E. The set of feasible solutions to the linear programming model is defined by

$$E x \leq a$$
$$U x = s \qquad (1)$$
$$x \geq 0$$

where E is a $(P \times N)$ matrix whose element e_{ij} is the emission flow of pollutant i per unit of control method j and U is an $(M \times N)$ matrix whose element u_{ij} is unity when the jth control method is defined for the ith source and zero otherwise. Since the ith row of the U matrix corresponds to the ith pollution source, there are as many 1's in that row as there are control methods (and combinations of control methors) for the ith source.

The cost of pollution abatement is $c\,x$, where c is a $(1 \times N)$ row vector whose element, c_j, represents the value of resources used up per unit of control method activity j. For convenience, each existing control method is assigned a zero cost while the cost of an alternative control method is the incremental cost for augmenting or replacing the existing control method. The optimal solution of the linear programming model is the vector x which minimizes $c\,x$ and satisfies the requirements set (1).

Consider a simple one-pollutant example. The allowable annual flow of particulates in an airshed is 0.8 million pounds. A cement plant producing 2.5 million barrels of cement a year is currently equipped with a dust collector such that its emission rate is 2 pounds of particulates per barrel of cement produced. An alternative control device costing an additional 0.14 dollar per barrel of cement to operate would involve emissions of 0.5 pound of particulates per barrel, while a second alternative costing 0.18 dollar per barrel more would reduce emissions to 0.2 pound of particulates per barrel. The least cost combination of control methods is the solution of

231

Decision Making in the Public Sector

Minimize $\$.00 x_1 + \$.14 x_2 + \$.18 x_3$

Subject to $2.0\ x_1 + .5\ x_2 + .2\ x_3 \leq 800{,}000$
$1.0\ x_1 + 1.0\ x_2 + 1.0\ x_3 = 2{,}500{,}000$
$x_1,\ x_2,\ x_3 \geq 0$

(The optimal solution is $x_1 = 0$ barrels, $x_2 = 1{,}000{,}000$ barrels, $x_3 = 1{,}500{,}000$ barrels, total cost = 410,000 dollars per year.)

The interaction of the control method solution with production and consumption levels, via the output effect, is incorporated in the model by subtracting Vx from the s vector:

$$U x = s - V x \qquad (2)$$

The output-effect matrix V has dimensions $(M \times N)$ and its elements are:

$$v_{ij} = (c^*_j / p_i)(\partial_i)(u_{ij}) \qquad (3)$$

where c^*_j is the private cost of abatement per unit of control method activity, p_i is the total value of output associated with one unit of the ith production or consumption level, ∂_i is the price elasticity of demand for this output, and u_{ij} is the ij^{th} element of the previously defined distributive matrix U.

Thus, (c^*_j / p_i) is a proportional increase in selling price which, when multiplied by the price elasticity of demand, determines a proportional decrease in production or consumption level i. When the jth control method is not defined for the ith source, u_{ij} is zero; consequently there are zeros in corresponding entries of the U and V matrices. (This would not be the case if cross elasticities of demand were included.)

Observe that the element v_{ij} of the V matrix is equivalent to a proportion, $\Delta x_j / x_j$, and that the matrix product $V x$ is an $(M \times 1)$ vector whose i^{th} entry is the sum of Δx_j's associated with activity levels of control methods defined for the ith source. Since corresponding control methods and source levels are defined in the same units, this sum is equal to Δs_i. Its operation in the model is such that, although it is a proportion, the coefficient v_{ij} can be interpreted as the reduction in the ith source level per unit of the jth control method activity.

The calculation of v_{ij} and its use in the model may be illustrated in the simple problem noted earlier. If the value of one barrel of cement is $3.20 and the price elasticity of demand for cement is $-.3$, the decline in cement production per unit of control method activity is $(\$.14/\$3.20)(.3)$ for x_2 and $(\$.18/\$3.20)(.3)$ for x_3. The revised problem is

Minimize $0 x_1 + \$.14\ x_2 + \$.18\ x_3$

Subject to $2.0 x_1 + .5\ x_2 + .2\ x_3 \leq 800{,}000$
$1.0 x_1 + 1.013 x_2 + 1.017 x_3 = 2{,}500{,}000$
$x_1,\ x_2,\ x_3 \geq 0$

(The optimal solution is $x_1 = 0$ barrels; $x_2 = 1{,}025{,}172$ barrels; $x_3 = 1{,}437{,}071$ barrels; total cost of required control = 402,197 dollars.) [9]

Although the shifts in consumption and production activities induced by abatement costs are voluntary, they are deviations from the levels that would prevail in the absence of regulations and consequently should be assigned some economic cost. The decreased output associated with a control method activity level times the unit private cost which induced the decrease, or $(v_{ij})(x_j)(c^*_j)$, would represent the maximum social cost of the reduction. For all control methods this cost is $t\ V\ C^* x$, where t is a $(1 \times M)$ matrix of ones and C^* is an $(N \times N)$ diagonal matrix whose non-zero diagonal entry is c^*_j.

The revised model with augmented objective function and with all x coefficients transferred to the left-hand side is

Minimize $[c + tVC^*]\ x$

Subject to $\quad E\ x \leq a \qquad (3)$
$[U + V]\ x = s$
$x \geq 0$

In the numerical example above, the objective function would be augmented by $(.013)(\$.14) x_2$ plus $(.017)(\$.18) x_3$. While this does not alter the optimal control method solution of this simple problem, it does add 6,263 dollars to the least cost sum.

APPENDIX 2

Demand Feedback on Coal Combustion in Industry and Electric Utility Furnaces

Among the pollution sources in the model are fourteen categories of industrial furnaces and six individual power plants. The cost of controlling pollution from these sources will increase prices of outputs which require combustion and electric power inputs. The output effect, here, is a weighted average of proportional increases in prices times price elasticities of demand for individual users of coal and power. For the ith source and j^{th} control method,

$$v_{ij} = [\sum_k (c_j^{**}\ Y_{ik}/S_k)\ \partial_i\ Y_{ik}] / \sum_k Y_{ik}, \qquad (4)$$

where Y_{ik} represents tons of coal burned per year in furnace category i by the kth industry or kilowatt hours of electricity per year from the ith power plant used by the kth industry, commercial or household sector. The symbols v_{ij} and ∂_i are defined in appendix 1. In the case of industrial furnace categories, c_j^{**} is the same as c^*_j in appendix 1, while in the case of electric power plants, c_j^{**} is equal to private control method cost per ton of coal burned, c^*_j, divided by a constant which represents kilowatt hours produced from one ton of coal by the ith power plant. The symbol S_k represents the value of annual shipments of the kth industry corresponding to Y_{ik} in coal combustion or power use. For households, S_k represents the retail value of electricity purchased in a year. Selected values of c_j^{**}, S_k/Y_{ik}, and $c_j^{**} Y_{ik}/S_k$ are shown in table 1.

In implementing the model it was assumed that the proportion of an industry's projected coal consumption burned in a particular furnace category would be the

---

[9] There is an implicit assumption here that for any production activity, marginal costs of production as well as abatement are constant over the range of declining output. For those sources where the optimal control method solution is divisible (i.e., two non-zero control method activity levels in a single row as in the example above) there is the implied but unlikely assumption that there will be two separate prices for the same production or consumption activity. Fortunately (see Kohn 1971d), the occurrence of divisibility in the solution is restricted to P (pollutants) rows in number. (This defect in the model could be eliminated with integer programming.)

same for every industry. Similarly, the proportion of power delivered to the separate industries and to the commercial and household sectors was assumed to be the same for each power plant. While the methodology implies that different power plants in the same system would have to charge different prices for electricity, any price increase could, in fact, be averaged among all customers, and assuming constant price elasticities of demand, result in the same overall reduction in power use. However, there is also the assumption, that the power plant responsible for the rise in price would be the one cut back, which may be unrealistic. (It should be noted that under some conditions load shifting between power plants may be a useful strategy for air pollution control. This approach, which is not included in the present model, is examined by Sheppard (1970). While these simplifying assumptions could be avoided, this would add considerable complexity to the model.

The reduced demand for electricity by industry is based on the increase in prices of industrial products. This understates the reduction in power use because it ignores the possibilities for input substitutions by industrial customers. A more satisfactory analysis of reduced industrial demand for electricity might have been achieved by estimating the proportional increase in the cost of power for each industry and applying price elasticities of demand for electricity by industrial sectors from Fisher (1962, p. 135).

REFERENCES

Broude, H. W., *Steel Decisions and the National Economy* (New Haven: Yale University Press, 1963).

Chow, G., *Demand for Automobiles in the United States* (Amsterdam: North-Holland Publishing Company, 1957).

Davis, O. A., and M. I. Kamien, "Externalities, Information and Alternative Collective Action," *The Analysis and Evaluation of Public Expenditures: The PPB System*, A Compendium of Papers Submitted to the Subcommittee on Economy in Government of the Joint Economic Committee, Congress of the United States, vol. 1, Washington, D.C., 1969, 67–86.

Dolbear, F. T., Jr., "On the Theory of Optimum Externality," *The American Economic Review*, 62, 1 (Mar. 1967), 90–103.

Donaldson, D., and P. Victor, "On the Dynamics of Air Pollution Control," *Canadian Journal of Economics*, 3, 3 (Aug., 1970), 422–431.

Environmental Protection Agency, "Requirements for Preparation, Adoption, and Submittal of Implementation Plans," *Federal Register*, 36, 158 (Aug., 14, 1971).

Fisher, F. M., *A Study in Econometrics: The Demand for Electricity in the United States*, (Amsterdam: North-Holland Publishing Company, 1962).

Houthakker, H. S., and L. D. Taylor, *Consumer Demand in the United States: Analyses and Projections*, 2nd ed. (Cambridge: Harvard University Press, 1970).

Kohn, R. E., "A Cost-Effectiveness Model for Air Pollution Control with a Single Stochastic Variable," *Journal of the American Statistical Association* (Mar. 1972).

———, *A Linear Programming Model for Air Pollution Control in the St. Louis Airshed*, unpublished doctoral dissertation. Washington University, St. Louis, Missouri, 1969.

———, "Air Quality Goals, the Multi-Product Production Function, and the Opportunity Cost of Capital," *Southern Economic Journal*, (Oct. 1971a), 156–160.

———, "Application of Linear Programming to a Controversy on Air Pollution Control," *Management Science* (June, 1971b), 609–621.

———, "Input-Output Analysis and Air Pollution Control," in *Economics of the Environment* (New York: National Bureau Committee for Economic Research) (forthcoming, 1973).

———, "Joint-Outputs of Land and Water Wastes in a Linear Programming Model for Air Pollution Control," *Proceedings of the Social Statistics Section, Annual Meeting, 1970* (Washington, D.C.: American Statistical Association, 1971c), 207–214.

———, "Optimal Air Quality Standards," *Econometrica* (Nov. 1971d).

Leontief, W., "Environmental Repercussions and the Economic Structure: An Input-Output Approach," this REVIEW (Aug., 1970) 262–271.

Loescher, S. M., *Imperfect Collusion in the Cement Industry* (Cambridge: Harvard University Press, 1959), 79.

Metal Statistics, 1968, American Metal Market Company, New York, 1968.

Meyer, R. A., Jr., "Externalities as Commodities," *The American Economic Review*, 61, 4 (Sept. 1971), 736–740.

Powell, A., "A Complete System of Consumer Demand Equations for the Australian Economy Fitted by a Model of Additive Preferences," *Econometrica*, 34 (July 1966), 672.

Ruff, L. E., "A Note on Pollution Prices in a General Equilibrium Model," *American Economic Review*, 62 (Mar. 1972), 186–192.

St. Louis Commerce, March 1, 1967.

Sheppard, D. S., "A Load Shifting Model for Air Pollution Control in the Electric Power Industry," *Journal of the Air Pollution Control Association*, 20 (Nov. 1970), 756–761.

The Midwest Motorist, February–March, 1970.

Union Electric Company, *1967 Annual Report*, St. Louis, 1968.

U.S. Bureau of the Census, Census of Manufactures, 1963, *Volume I, Summary and Subject Statistics* (Washington: U.S. Government Printing Office, 1966).

U.S. Bureau of the Census, Census of Manufactures, 1967, *Volume II, Industry Statistics, Part 2, Major Groups, 25–33* (Washington: U.S. Government Printing Office, 1971a).

U.S. Bureau of the Census, Census of Manufactures, 1967, *Volume III, Area Statistics, Part 1, Alabama-Montana* (Washington: U.S. Government Printing Office, 1971b).

Zerbe, R. O., "Theoretical Efficiency in Pollution Control," *Western Economic Journal*, 8 (Dec. 1970), 364–376.

READING
33 THE DISTRIBUTION OF COSTS AND DIRECT BENEFITS OF PUBLIC HIGHER EDUCATION: THE CASE OF CALIFORNIA*

W. Lee Hansen

Burton A. Weisbrod

ABSTRACT

This paper explores the general nature of income redistribution effects of the financing of public higher education in California. The amount of available subsidy (full cost less student charges) varies dramatically among the three higher education systems—University, State College, and Junior College. Since eligibility for the higher-subsidy institutions is positively related to family income level, and since actual attendance among those eligible increases as family income rises, the result is that the distribution of subsidies actually favors upper income families.

These subsidies are then compared with total state and local taxes paid. The results show that families with children enrolled in public higher education receive positive net transfers (subsidy less taxes paid) and that these net transfers are an increasing fraction of average family money income.

The public higher education system in the United States provides—or, at least, offers—a public subsidy to young people of college age. The extent to which the young people actually receive the subsidy depends on (1) whether they can qualify for admission, (2) whether they avail themselves of the opportunity to attend, and (3), if they do, what quantity and quality of education they receive. As a result, the amount of subsidy received through the public financing of higher education varies greatly from one person to another. Our objective in this paper is to estimate (1) the amount of subsidies received through higher education, (2) the variation in subsidies received by students depending upon the amount of schooling and the kind of schooling they obtain, and (3) the extent to which these subsidies are received in different amounts by students whose families are at different socioeconomic levels.[1]

Attention is restricted to undergraduate education, and the data used are for public education in California. While higher educational systems

The authors are Professors of Economics and of Educational Policy Studies, The University of Wisconsin.

* This paper is an extension of material contained in Chapter IV of our forthcoming book, *Benefits, Cost, and Finance of Public Higher Education* (Chicago: Markham Publishing Co., 1969). Hereinafter this volume is referred to as *Higher Education*.

1 Little effort seems to have been given to this entire subject. For one interesting and perceptive foray, see Christopher Jencks, "Social Stratification and Mass Higher Education," *Harvard Education Review* (Spring 1968).

differ among states, it would appear that the results for California are broadly characteristic of those for a number of other states.

A knowledge of the magnitude and distribution of subsidies or direct benefits provided through public higher education, or, indeed, through any public program, is important for what it suggests as to appropriate pricing, tax, and expenditure policy. By "appropriate" we mean policies that will be efficient, in the sense of doing the most to raise output, and at the same time equitable, in the sense of doing the most to achieve society's distribution goals, such as providing greater equality of opportunity for young people. We can illustrate some of the possibilities. For those "eligible" for higher education, uniform subsidies may provide a "windfall" to the more financially able while doing little to facilitate college attendance by the less well-off. This might argue for some kind of flexible pricing system in higher education, though much the same effect might be achieved less directly through the tax system. For those "not eligible" for public higher education, the provision of other kinds of subsidies or direct-benefit programs may not only yield substantial societal benefits but also help to achieve greater equality, not only of educational opportunity but of opportunity in general.

SUBSIDIES STUDENTS CAN RECEIVE

The amounts of public higher education subsidies that can be received by college students are determined largely by the costs—instructional and capital—of providing instruction to them.[2] But, in addition, the number of years of instruction received is also relevant. Table 1 indicates how the amount of subsidies received will differ, given various assumed patterns of progression through the educational system in California—a state which, like many others, has three different higher education subsystems. First, the annual as well as the cumulative subsidy in each of the systems is shown (lines 1–6). Second, we have also attempted to show how these subsidies will vary, based on several assumed patterns of transfer from one type of institution to another (lines 7–12). The estimated subsidies at each of the three systems are the sums of average instructional and capital costs per student.[3]

The import of this table should be clear. For those people completing a four-year program, a subsidy of more than $7,100 can be received—but only by those students who qualify, on the basis of their high school records, for the University of California. Those who do not qualify can obtain a maximum subsidy of $5,800 at the State Colleges. And for those eligible only for the Junior Colleges, the maximum is $1,440, on the assumption that they do not later qualify for transfer to the State College system or the University of California. Therefore, depending on a student's "ability" level as determined by high school performance, the maximum amount of subsidy he can receive is fairly well determined.

SUBSIDIES STUDENTS DO RECEIVE

In reality, the matter is even more complex, however, because not all students proceed through an entire four-year course. A sizable number of students drop out at the end of each year, some for academic reasons and

---

2 We restrict our attention to undergraduate education.
3 For additional detail and sources see Tables III-1, 2, and 3 in *Higher Education*.

TABLE 1

PUBLIC HIGHER EDUCATION SUBSIDIES, BY TYPE OF PROGRAM AND YEARS OF COLLEGE COMPLETED, 1965

	Type of Program		1	2	3	4
				Year of College		
1.	University of California—4 Years	Per Year Cost	$1,460	$1,460	$2,110	$2,110
2.		Cumulative Cost	1,460	2,920	5,030	7,140
3.	State Colleges—4 Years	Per Year Cost	1,350	1,350	1,550	1,550
4.		Cumulative Cost	1,350	2,700	4,250	5,800
5.	Junior Colleges—2 Years	Per Year Cost	720	720	— —	— —
6.		Cumulative Cost	720	1,440	— —	— —
7.	Junior College—2 Years, and University of California—2 Years	Per Year Cost	$ 720	$ 720	$2,110	$2,110
8.		Cumulative Cost	720	1,440	3,550	5,660
9.	State College—2 Years, and University of California—2 Years	Per Year Cost	1,350	1,350	2,110	2,110
10.		Cumulative Cost	1,350	2,700	4,810	6,920
11.	University of California—2 Years, and State College—2 Years	Per Year Cost	1,460	1,460	1,550	1,550
12.		Cumulative Cost	1,460	2,920	4,470	6,020

Source: Based on Tables III-1, III-2, and III-3, in *Higher Education*.

others for a variety of personal reasons. Thus, not everyone can or does choose to avail himself of the full amount of the subsidy for which he is potentially qualified. Equally important, there are others who, through lack of interest in public higher education, receive no subsidy whatsoever. These are people who join the work force immediately, enter military service, decide not to go on to college for other reasons, or enroll in private colleges.

The actual distribution of subsidies received by students entering each of the various segments of higher education in California is rather difficult to determine, given the paucity of data on attrition and transfer patterns. On the basis of fragmentary data, however, the approximate patterns of progression are indicated in Table 2.

It is quite clear that attrition at the Junior College level is by far the highest, reflecting the fact that a number of its programs require only one year of schooling; that for some students Junior College provides a stepping stone to a State College or University campus; and that for others, Junior Colleges serve an important function of giving young people a chance to survey the opportunities better before rushing into a job choice.

The rate of attrition at the State Colleges is somewhat lower, and attrition at the University of California is the lowest, largely as a result of its greater selectivity in admissions. Its first-year attrition rate—15 percent—seems rather high, but the four-year completion rate of 55 percent is within the range for most other comparable four-year institutions. However, an additional 3 percent of the initial entrants to the University of California completed their work at a State College, and some others undoubtedly graduated from colleges outside the California system of public higher education.

What can we now say about the distribution of the subsidies to students eligible to enter each of the three different systems? The data in Table 3 attempt to answer this question by showing the distribution of all high school graduates by the percent who are eligible and who say they plan to enroll or not enroll at each type of college.

TABLE 2

ESTIMATED PROGRESSION PATTERNS THROUGH PUBLIC HIGHER EDUCATION SYSTEMS IN CALIFORNIA, 1965

	UC System			SC System			JC System		
Year of School	Non-transfer	Transfer to SC	Transfer to JC	Non-transfer	Transfer to UC	Transfer to JC	Non-transfer	Transfer to UC	Transfer to SC
1	85	—	—	80	—	—	70	—	—
2	70	5	—	60	—	—	30	—	—
3	60	4	—	55	8	—	—	2	8
4	55	3	—	50	6	—	—	2	6

Source: Based on a variety of published and unpublished data on patterns of student progression and transfer, as well as on oral conversations with experts on this subject. Subsequent to the preparation of this table and the analysis upon which it is based, we came upon some additional data on transfer patterns among systems; see Coordinating Council for Higher Education, *Feasibility and Desirability of Eliminating Lower Division Programs at Selected Campuses of the University of California and the California State Colleges* (mimeo), January 6, 1967 (this is a preliminary version of the report). The difference between the actual and our estimated patterns of transfer appear to be relatively minor and do not affect the general conclusions we have drawn.

Decision Making in the Public Sector

TABLE 3

ESTIMATED DISTRIBUTION OF ALL HIGH SCHOOL GRADUATES BY ELIGIBILITY FOR HIGHER EDUCATION AND BY TYPE OF HIGHER EDUCATION THEY PLAN TO OBTAIN

Eligibility	Plans to Attend by Type of Higher Education					
	UC	SC	JC	Other	None	All
University of California	5	4	5	3	2	19
State Colleges	—	2	8	2	4	17
Junior Colleges	—	—	31	4	26	64
All	5	6	44	9	32	100

Source: Based on Coordinating Council for Higher Education, *Financial Assistance Programs*, 67–13 (Revised) October 31, 1967, Tables I-2 and I-3, pp. I-9 and I-10.

The extent to which students do not avail themselves of the opportunity to go to the "highest quality" (highest subsidy) college or university segment open to them is indicated by reading across each of the rows. Although 19 percent of all students are eligible for the University of California,[4] only 5 percent plan to enroll at a University campus, with 4 percent going to State Colleges, another 5 percent to Junior Colleges, 3 percent to other institutions, and 2 percent not expecting to enroll in any institution of higher education. Of those eligible for the State Colleges, approximately 2 out of 17 percent eligible plan to enroll, with another 8 percent going to the Junior Colleges, and 4 percent not enrolling at all. And, for the Junior Colleges, only half of the 64 percent eligible plan to enroll. Thus, only 55 percent of the total plan to enroll in public higher education.

Whatever their reasons, many high school students enroll at public institutions which are lower in presumed quality than those for which they are eligible, with a sizable fraction of high school graduates not enrolling in any public institution whatsoever. Of these latter, however, it must be remembered that some go to private institutions in the state or to colleges out of state.

DISTRIBUTION OF AMOUNTS OF SUBSIDIES THROUGH HIGHER EDUCATION

We can now construct a rough distribution of the percentage of an age cohort of high school graduates who will receive different amounts of public subsidies for higher education. This is summarized in Table 4. The rather startling conclusion is that while a small proportion—9 percent—receives rather large subsidies, exceeding $5,000, more than half of California's young people receive under $750 in total subsidy from higher education. And a substantial fraction—41 percent—receive no subsidy at all. This group is divided between those who obtain no higher education whatsoever—almost 80 percent—and those who plan to attend private colleges within California or colleges outside the state—about 20 percent.

In short, there is a highly unequal distribution in the amounts of public subsidies actually received, even though California prides itself on the

---
4 Note that these figures differ somewhat from other data on eligibility, as indicated by the Master Plan, for example.

TABLE 4

ESTIMATED DISTRIBUTION OF PUBLIC SUBSIDIES FOR HIGHER EDUCATION BASED ON AMOUNT RECEIVED DURING PERIOD ENROLLED

Amount of Subsidy	Percentage of Persons Receiving
0	41
$1–749	14
$750–1,999	30
$2,000–3,499	3
$3,500–4,999	3
$5,000–6,499	6
$6,500 +	3
	100

Source: Developed from data in Tables 1, 2, and 3.

wide access to higher education it provides and on the high enrollment ratios which are presumably a reflection of this. Moreover, there is little reason to believe that the distribution of public subsidies through the system of higher education is less unequal in other states than it is in California. No state has as widely accessible a junior college system as does California; thus, other states have larger proportions of young people who obtain no college education whatsoever.

DISTRIBUTION OF SUBSIDIES BY FAMILY INCOME

What can be said about the distribution of the subsidies provided through higher education in terms of the students' family income levels? While this is a somewhat more difficult question to answer with the available data, we have been able to restructure one set of data to shed light on this question.

It is useful, to begin with, to gain an idea of the patterns of college-going by level of family income. These are presented in Table 5, where columns 3–6 show the family income distributions for all California public college students in 1964, column 2 shows the income distribution for families without children in California public higher education, and column 1 shows the distribution for all California families.

The distributions by family income clearly differ among the groups shown. Median family incomes (see bottom row of table) are highest for parents of University students, followed by State College student families and Junior College student families. Lowest of all is the median for all families without children in the California system. These patterns are about what one might expect and, in general, conform to the patterns shown in other surveys.[5] Thus we conclude that access to subsidies is positively related to levels of family income, with the highest single-year subsidy going

---

[5] For example, see the Wisconsin data in L. J. Lins, A. P. Abell, and D. R. Stucki, *Costs of Attendance and Income of Madison Campus Students, The University of Wisconsin, 1964–1965 Academic Year*, Office of Institutional Studies, January 1967; I. M. Boyak, A. P. Abell, and L. J. Lins, *Costs of Attendance and Income of University of Wisconsin–Milwaukee Students, 1964–1965 Academic Year*, Office of Institutional Studies, March 1967; and L. J. Lins, A. P. Abell, and R. Hammes, *Costs of Attendance and Income of University of Wisconsin Center Students, 1964–1965 Academic Year*, Office of Institutional Studies, May 1966.

TABLE 5

DISTRIBUTIONS OF FAMILIES BY INCOME LEVEL AND TYPE OF COLLEGE OR UNIVERSITY, CALIFORNIA, 1964 (in percents)

Income Class	All Families (1)	Families With Children in California Public Higher Education (2)	Families with Children in California Public Higher Education Total (3)	JC (4)	SC (5)	UC (6)
$0–3,999	16.1	17.0	6.6	8.1	4.1	5.0
$4,000–5,999	14.8	14.9	13.0	15.9	10.2	7.5
$6,000–7,999	18.9	19.0	17.6	19.6	17.0	11.1
$8,000–9,999	18.1	18.3	16.4	16.9	17.2	13.1
$10,000–11,999	12.4	12.1	15.8	14.4	19.9	13.3
$12,000–13,999	7.4	7.3	8.8	17.2	10.8	11.3
$14,000–19,999	7.9	7.5	13.0	11.1	13.0	20.3
$20,000–24,999	1.8	1.6	3.4	2.6	3.3	6.6
$25,000+	2.6	2.3	5.4	4.2	4.5	11.8
Total	100.0%	100.0%	100.0%	100.0%	100.0%	100.0%
Median Income	$8,000	$7,900	$9,560	$8,800	$10,000	$12,000

Source: Col. (1)—Letter from Office of Legislative Analyst, California Legislature, in *Tuition for California's Public Institutions of Higher Education,* Joint Committee on Higher Education Hearings, October 13 and 16, 1967; see Tab T, Table 1.
Col. (2)—Percentage distribution of Col. (2), calculated by authors.
Col. (3)—Weighted average of Cols. (4), (5), and (6).
Col. (4), (5), (6)—Edward Sanders and Hans Palmer, *The Financial Barrier to Higher Education in California* (Claremont: Pomona College, 1965), Table M, p. 21, which relates to distribution of parent-supported students only.

Externalities and Income Distribution

to UC students (and their families) who already have the highest (median) family incomes ($12,000).[6]

We can present some crude figures to illustrate the association of family income and subsidies received, by comparing median family incomes for the groups shown in Table 5 with the amounts of the subsidies going to each of these groups. Table 6 presents this information, where median income of families of various types is shown in line 1, the one-year subsidy received is given in line 2a, and the subsidy as a percentage of family income is presented in line 2b. Because students first enrolling at each type of institution do not remain in college equally long, the average number of years they are enrolled is also shown, in line 3. The total subsidy received is shown in line 4a, and the percentage of family income that the subsidy constitutes is in line 4b. Because students transfer among the three higher education systems, the average subsidy is not simply the product of the average subsidy in a particular system and the average number of years of schooling obtained by students who *begin* their schooling in that system. As indicated by line 2b, the values of the single-year subsidies vary from zero percent of family income for those without children in public colleges and universities (some of these people may have children in private colleges or in public colleges not in California), to 14 percent of family income for those with State College enrollees. Whereas the average over-all subsidy is equal to 9 percent of money income for all parents of publicly-enrolled college students (line 2b, column 3), the subsidy climbs to 18 percent of single-year family income when we take account of the number of years that the educational subsidy is received (line 4b, column 3). But because, as noted before, the amount of schooling received differs, the average total subsidies (line 4a) rise far more sharply than the single-year subsidies, as we contrast the families with children enrolled in California Junior Colleges, State Colleges, and University campuses. These patterns of subsidies raise serious questions about the equity of the current system for financing public higher education in California.

At the same time, however, the distributions of students by parental income (as shown by each of the columns in Table 5) are so wide for each type of system—University of California, State College, and Junior College—that any strong conclusions about the "class-serving" nature of the entire system of higher education in California cannot be drawn. While there is a tendency for the higher subsidy schools to draw a higher-income clientele, the overlap of the distributions is still very substantial.

Some added light can be thrown on the equity issue by a restructuring of recent data presented by the California Coordinating Council for Higher Education.[7] The data from several of its tables have been combined to show how eligibility and plans for higher education enrollment vary systematically with income.

We show in Table 7 the percentages of all graduating high school seniors eligible to attend the University of California, and the University and the State Colleges. Approximately 80 percent of the high school

---

[6] Were we to relate the data shown in Table 5 to the data on subsidies received over the entire college stay, the differences in the subsidies received would be accentuated. The reason is that University of California students are more likely to complete four years than are State College students, and the latter are more likely to complete four years than the vast bulk of the students who begin at **Junior Colleges.**

[7] Coordinating Council for Higher Education, *Financial Assistance Programs,* 67-13 (Second Revision) October 31, 1967, Table I-2, p. I-9; Table I-3, p. I-10; and Appendix Table B-3.

TABLE 6

AVERAGE FAMILY INCOMES AND AVERAGE HIGHER EDUCATION SUBSIDIES RECEIVED BY FAMILIES, BY TYPE OF INSTITUTION CHILDREN ATTEND, CALIFORNIA, 1964

	All Families	Families Without Children in California Public Higher Education	Families with Children in California Public Higher Education Total	JC	SC	UC
	(1)	(2)	(3)	(4)	(5)	(6)
1. Average family income[a]	8,000	7,900	9,560	8,800	10,000	12,000
2. Average higher education subsidy per year[b]						
a. Amount in dollars	—	0	880	720	1,400	1,700
b. Percent of Line 1	—	0	9	8	14	13
3. Average number of years of higher education completed[c]	n.a.	n.a.	n.a.	1.2	2.6	2.8
4. Average total higher education subsidy[c]						
a. Amount in dollars	—	0	1,700	1,050	3,810	4,870
b. Percent of Line 1	—	0	18	12	31	41

[a] Median incomes from Table 5.
[b] Average subsidies are based on the distribution of enrollment by year of school and on distribution of enrollment by type of institution.
[c] Average number of years and average subsidies are based on the assumption that entering students progress through the various types of institutions shown in Table 2, that students are distributed among the various types of institutions as shown in Table 3, and that the various subsidies are those shown in Table 1. Because students transfer among the three higher education systems, the average subsidy shown in line 4a is not obtained simply by multiplying line 2a by line 3.

TABLE 7

DISTRIBUTION OF HIGH SCHOOL GRADUATES BY ELIGIBILITY FOR PUBLIC HIGHER EDUCATION IN CALIFORNIA, BY TYPE OF EDUCATION AND FAMILY INCOME (in percents)

	Percentage Distribution of High School Graduates by Eligibility for	
Family Income	University of California	University of California and State Colleges
	(1)	(2)
$0–3,999	10.7	28.0
$4,000–5,999	11.5	26.3
$6,000–7,999	11.9	30.5
$8,000–9,999	16.2	33.2
$10,000–12,499	19.4	37.1
$12,500–14,999	22.5	39.8
$15,000–17,499	27.9	45.4
$17,500–19,999	29.5	45.1
$20,000–24,999	33.3	46.1
$25,000 +	40.1	54.3
Not reported	13.3	28.0
All	*19.6*	*36.3*

Source: Based on data from CCHE, *Financial Assistance Programs*, 67–13 (Second Revision) October 31, 1967, Table I-2, p. I-9; Table I-3, p. I-10; and Appendix Table B-3.

Note: Excluded from the sample of 8,162 were 302 students planning vocational training, 38 nonrespondents on enrollment plans, and 20 for whom eligibility was indeterminate.

graduates do not qualify for the substantial University subsidies because of the academic entry requirements. Even more interesting is the fact that the percentage of all students qualifying for the University of California (column 1) rises quite dramatically by family income level—from about 10 percent in the lowest income bracket (under $4,000) to 40 percent in the highest (over $25,000). Thus, the correlation between high school achievement and family income—and all that it reflects—is startling indeed. This pattern persists as we widen our view to include those eligible for both the University and State Colleges (column 2). But a close examination of the differences between the two columns shows that the percentage of those eligible only for the State College system is roughly constant at all income levels; thus, University eligibility requirements account largely for the unequal distribution of opportunity.

The extent to which family income influences the distribution of those eligible who *plan* to attend each level of higher education emerges from Table 8. For the University (column 1) a larger fraction of upper- than lower-income students plan to attend; the same holds for the combined University–State College system group (column 2); and the pattern continues—though in somewhat muted fashion—when we consider all high school graduates (column 3). Actually, these results are somewhat deceptive since those eligible for a "higher" system can attend a "lower" system. Indeed, when we compare the percent of University-eligible students planning to attend one of the three public systems, we find that the proportion

Decision Making in the Public Sector

TABLE 8

COLLEGE ATTENDANCE PLANS OF CALIFORNIA HIGH SCHOOL GRADUATES, BY FAMILY INCOME AND HIGHER EDUCATION SEGMENT, 1966

Family Income Level	Percent of UC Eligibles Planning to Attend UC (1)	Percent of UC-SC Eligibles Planning to Attend Either UC or SC (2)	Percent of All California High School Graduates Planning to Enroll in UC, SC, or JC (3)
$0–3,999	30.4	22.5	53.1
$4,000–5,999	26.1	29.7	56.1
$6,000–7,999	23.4	28.1	56.3
$8,000–9,999	21.5	36.5	60.0
$10,000–12,499	25.3	32.6	62.0
$12,500–14,999	26.2	37.5	64.6
$15,000–17,499	26.9	32.1	63.4
$17,500–19,999	33.3	45.7	64.2
$20,000–24,999	45.4	52.0	68.2
$25,000 +	46.7	47.8	57.8
No response	30.5	30.1	47.9

Source: Same as Table 7.
Note: UC (University of California); SC (State Colleges); JC (Junior Colleges).

is fairly constant with respect to family income, at about 70 to 75 percent (these data are not shown in the accompanying tables). Much the same kind of pattern emerges for both the University and State College eligibles who plan to undertake higher education. The point, however, is that enrollment in a lower system—often dictated by family income considerations—implies a reduced level of subsidies.

WHO PAYS THE TAXES?

Having now shown the extent to which families in different income groups are awarded subsidies through the fiscal system by virtue of the provision of higher education, we turn in this section to develop estimates of the state taxes alone, and the combined state and local taxes, that are paid by families at each income level. The objective is to provide a basis for comparing the subsidies received with the tax payments made. Such information is essential in assessing the equity of the current methods of financing higher education in the State of California.

Our approach is to estimate the incidence of the most important state and local taxes by family income level, so as to note the absolute amount of taxes paid at each income level. We can then compare this amount with the subsidy received and note any differences. But we still have no real way of determining how much of whatever taxes are paid reflect support for higher education, as against the many other services provided by state and local governments.

The average amount of taxes paid at each income level as well as the effective tax rate, for California state taxes alone and for state and local taxes combined, is shown in Table 9. The most important finding is that

Externalities and Income Distribution

TABLE 9
ESTIMATED TAX BURDENS BY INCOME CLASS, CALIFORNIA, 1965

Adjusted Gross Income Class	State Taxes Only Per Family[a]	Effective State Tax Rate[b]	State and Local Taxes Per Family[c]	Effective State and Local Tax Rate[b]
	(1)	(2)	(3)	(4)
$0–3,999	$ 104	5.2	$ 474	23.7
$4,000–5,999	132	2.6	527	10.5
$6,000–7,999	161	2.3	576	8.2
$8,000–9,999	221	2.4	696	7.7
$10,000–11,999	301	2.7	833	7.6
$12,000–13,999	389	3.0	984	7.6
$14,000–19,999	539	3.2	1,228	7.2
$20,000–24,999	865	3.8	1,758	7.8
$25,000 +	2,767	5.5	4,093	8.2

Sources: Personal income, sales, cigarette and beverage taxes by income level were obtained from Letter from Office of Legislative Analyst, State of California in *Tuition for California's Public Institutions of Higher Education*, Joint Committee on Higher Education, Hearings, October 13 and 16, 1967; see Tab T, Table 1. State gasoline taxes and local property taxes were based on itemized tax deductions reported on state income tax returns, 1965, and summarized in Franchise Tax Board, *Annual Reports, 1965* and *1966*, Table 13. Local sales taxes were assumed to be distributed in the same manner as state sales taxes above. Since local sales tax revenues in 1965 equaled one-third of state sales tax revenues, this factor was applied to the estimated amount of state sales taxes in each income level.

[a] Personal income, states sales, cigarette, and alcoholic beverage taxes only.
[b] Taxes as a percent of estimated mean income of each income class. The mean of the highest income interval was arbitrarily assumed to be $50,000
[c] State taxes include personal income, sales, cigarette, alcoholic beverage, and gasoline taxes. Local taxes include local sales and property taxes.

while the state tax structure (column 2) seems to be somewhat progressive—that is, the effective tax rate rises with income—except in the lowest income classes, the combined state and local tax structure (column 4) is regressive below $8,000 and is essentially proportional above that level.[8]

We return now to our major task of this section which is to compare the amounts of taxes paid with the subsidies received by families with children enrolled in college, so that we can observe the extent to which broad groups of families do or do not receive net subsidies through higher education. In making such a comparison we once again remind the reader that this involves comparing *all* taxes with benefits received from higher education *alone*. As shown by Table 10, the annual value of higher education subsidies (line 2) received by a family with a single child enrolled in a public college exceeds the total amount (line 3) of all state and local taxes they pay, by rather substantial amounts. On an over-all basis the average higher education subsidy is $880 per year (line 2, column 3), in contrast to total state and local taxes paid of $740 (line 3, column 3); this results in an annual net transfer of $140 from all taxpayers to parents of college students. But this average conceals wide differences by type of college. For families with a child at one of the State Colleges or one of the University campuses, the net transfers range from $670 to $810 per year. Meanwhile, however, families without children or with children not enrolled in public institutions of higher education receive no subsidy whatsoever,

[8] The recent changes in the California state income tax structure have increased, but only slightly, the over-all progressivity of the state tax structure.

TABLE 10

AVERAGE FAMILY INCOMES, AVERAGE HIGHER EDUCATION SUBSIDIES RECEIVED, AND AVERAGE STATE AND LOCAL TAXES PAID BY FAMILIES, BY TYPE OF INSTITUTION CHILDREN ATTEND IN CALIFORNIA, 1964

	All Families	Families Without Children in California Public Higher Education	Families with Children in California Public Higher Education Total	J. C.	S. C.	U. C.
	(1)	(2)	(3)	(4)	(5)	(6)
1. Average family income[a]	8,000	7,900	9,560	8,800	10,000	12,000
2. Average higher education subsidy per year[b]	—	0	880	720	1,400	1,700
3. Average total state and local taxes paid[c]	620	650	740	680	770	910
4. Net transfer (Line 2 — Line 3)	—	−650	+140	+40	+630	+790

[a] From Table 5.
[b] From Table 6.
[c] Total state and local tax rates from Table 9 were applied to the median incomes for families in each column.

while they pay an average of $650 in state and local taxes. This is not to suggest that such families should pay no state and local taxes, for some may have benefited in the past, others may benefit in the future, and still others may have opted for more expensive nonpublic California higher education. In any event, as is evident from a comparison of line 4 and line 1, the current method of financing public higher education leads to a redistribution of income from lower to higher income families; indeed, there is very substantial progressivity in the resulting pattern of transfers.

CONCLUSION

The general nature of the redistributive effects of the current method of financing public higher education in California is clear. Some low-income persons have benefited handsomely from the availability of publicly-subsidized higher education. But on the whole, the effect of these subsidies is to promote greater rather than less inequality among people of various social and economic backgrounds, by making available substantial subsidies that lower income families are either not eligible for or cannot make use of because of other conditions and constraints associated with their income position. To overcome the effects of the present system would require a substantial overhaul of the pricing system in public higher education, a realignment of the tax structure, and/or a broadening of the eligibility base for public expenditure programs. With respect to the latter alternative, eligibility for public subsidies to young people might well be expanded so as to embrace all young people—not only those who go on to college but also those who opt for alternative ways of expanding their earning power, such as apprenticeship or on-the-job training, or even investments in businesses. In any case, it is clear that whatever the degree to which our current higher education programs are rooted in the search for equality of opportunity, the results still leave much to be desired.

CASE
34 CALCULATION OF AN EFFLUENT CHARGE: CASE OF PPG INDUSTRIES IN BARBERTON, OHIO

The PPG Barberton Chemical Plant has been a major polluter of both water and air since its founding in 1899. A major product of the Barberton Plant is soda ash that is produced from the interaction of salt and limestone (solvay process). In addition, the production process also creates a waste which largely consists of unused chloride ion from salt and calcium ion from limestone.

The discharge of the wastes into the Tuscawaras River is controlled in relation to the current in order not to create extreme variations in the concentration of the pollutant in the river. The Ohio Department of Health, following an analysis of the entire river basin, concluded that:

> ... the discharge of these wastes renders the water of entire length of the Tuscawaras River unsuitable for most uses and a significant portion of the Muskingum River unsuitable for use as public water supply.[1]

To add to the problem, the polluted water of the Tuscawaras infiltrates into the ground waters adjacent to the river bed and seriously degrades the ground water quality. The ground water supply of the city of Massillon is a prime example because the city has experienced a sharp rise in the level of chloride in the ground water serving the community. The chloride level has risen from 20 mg/l in 1961 to 170 mg/l in 1968.

A map of the Muskingum River Basin shown in Appendix 1 depicts the area directly affected by the pollutant discharge of the PPG Barberton Plant. The course of the Tuscawaras is traced from the upper most extreme (Barberton) through Massillon to the joining of the Muskingum and finally the Ohio River.

The city of Massillon submitted a formal complaint to the Ohio Water Pollution Board in 1966. This complaint fostered an inquiry into the present condition of the Muskingum Valley Watershed. The Division of Engineering, Ohio Department of Health, submitted a "Report and Recommendations on Water Quality for Muskingum River Basin" in October, 1968.

[1] Division of Engineering, Report and Recommendations on Water Quality for Muskingum River Basin, Ohio Department of Health, October, 1968, pp. 1-24.

Table 1 shows a summary of the water quality of the Tuscawaras River Sub-Basin in 1967. As can be seen in Table 1, the concentration of dissolved solids and chlorides increased substantially from the Akron Diversion Dam (upstream of the PPG Plant) to Clinton. Chloride concentration, of major concern to the city of Massillon, increased from a maximum of 56 mg/l at Akron Diversion Dam to a maximum of 7,650 mg/l at Clinton and 5,450 mg/l at Massillon.

Barberton is not the only polluter of the Tuscawaras River Sub-Basin as is shown in Table 2. All the facilities listed are upstream from Massillon, and thus have an effect on the concentration of pollutants at that point. According to the Ohio Department of Health:

> ... in the Tuscawaras River Sub-Basin, new or additional waste treatment or control measures are

Table 1 Summary of Water Quality Data—1967

Main Stem

Station	Akron Diversion Dam		Clinton	
Constituents	Min	Max	Min	Max
Dissolved Solids MG/L	332	411	317	9,999
Chlorides MG/L	19	56	500	7,650
Sulfates MG/L	62	160	105	1,400
Alkalinity MG/L	77	181	72	195
pH (index)	7.5	8.5	6.9	8.4
BOD (5 day) MG/L	0.5	4.2	0.0	8.4
TOC MG/L	2.3	8.9	5.3	23.9
Dissolved Oxygen MG/L	7.0	13.0	6.3	10.5

Station	Above Massillon		Below Massillon	
Constituents	Min	Max	Min	Max
Dissolved Solids MG/L	2,290	8,712	1,826	6,961
Chlorides MG/L	765	5,450	530	2,970
Sulfates MG/L	35	1,875	88	160
Alkalinity MG/L	79	216	75	144
pH (index)	6.3	8.3	6.4	7.8
BOD (5 day) MG/L	2.0	8.0	1.7	10.4
TOC MG/L	5.1	13.3	4.9	11.0
Dissolved Oxygen MG/L	2.7	10.0	1.5	11.4

Source: Ohio Department of Health, Tuscarawas River Sub-Basin.

Table 2 Industrial Wastewater Pollution Control Facilities Muskingum River Basin

Tuscarawas River Sub-Basin

Plant Name	Location	Receiving Stream
Midwest Rubber Reclaiming Co.	Barberton	Wolf Creek
Minnesota Mining & Mfg. Co.	Copley Twp. Summit County	Pigeon Creek
Morton Salt Co.	Rittman	Cheppewa Creek— Underground
Ohio Brass Co. Barberton Division	Barberton	Wolf Creek
Ohio Match Co.	Wadsworth	Mill Creek
Packaging Corp. of America	Rittman	River Styx
PPG Industries, Inc. Chemical Division	Barberton	Tuscarawas River

Plant Name	Type of Industry	Critical Constituents
Midwest Rubber Reclaiming Co.	Rubber Reclaiming	Suspended Solids
Minnesota Mining & Mfg. Co.	Chemical	Metals, Suspended Solids
Morton Salt Co.	Chemical	Chlorides
Ohio Brass Co. Barberton Division	Ceramic	Suspended Solids
Ohio Match Co.	Matches— Chemical	Suspended Solids
Packaging Corp. of America	Paper Mill	Oxygen Demand, Suspended Solids
PPG Industries, Inc. Chemical Division	Chemical	Dissolved Solids, Suspended Solids, Chlorides

Source: Ohio Department of Health.

required in 38 industries. Eighteen of these establishments have organic demand waste of which sixteen are dairy products. The wastes from seven others consist mainly of inert suspended solids and another six are spent acid pickling liquors. By far, the most significant industrial wastes loads of the area are the suspended and dissolved solids, particularly chlorides discharged to the upper reach of the Tuscawaras River from the Chemical Division, PPG Industries, Barberton.[2]

PPG is specifically identified by the Ohio Department of Health as the major source of chloride pollution to the Ohio Sub-Basin.

The Water Pollution Control Board of Ohio (Department of Health) set criteria for stream-water quality for various uses, effective October 10, 1967. Water use is divided into six classes, and criteria are set for each class. The six uses are as follows:

[2]*Ibid.*, pp. 2-3

Externalities and Income Distribution

1. For Public Water Supply
2. For Industrial Water Supply
3. For Aquatic Life A
4. For Aquatic Life B
5. For Recreation
6. For Agricultural Use and Stock Watering[3]

The Department of Health, upon completion of its study of the Muskingum River Basin, concluded the following:

> ... tentatively, for the protection of the water supplies in this area, it is recommended that chloride criteria for the Tuscawaras River at Massillon be established as 750 mg/l as Cl by 1972 and 500 mg/l as Cl by 1975. In addition, future desired uses of the Tuscawaras River water may require further limitations of chloride discharges.[4]

The above criteria apply to the Water Pollution Control Board's water use class one for Public Water Supply. This standard was adopted by the Board for the area in question (Tuscawaras River at Massillon) and is in effect at the time of this case. PPG was named the major offender and was ordered to comply by the prescribed dates or "risk possible repeal of license to discharge wastes into public waters."[5]

The company stated that it was in the process of installing water pollution control devices that would bring the chloride ion concentration to a level of 1200 mg/l by 1975, at which time the soda ash operation at Barberton would be phased out and replaced by manufacturing of other (nonpolluting) products. The pollution level proposed by PPG is considerably higher than that recommended by the Department of Health, but it will take until 1977 for the chloride ion concentration to fall below the prescribed maximum.

PPG stated at the Muskingum River Basin hearings that to meet the standards set by the Water Pollution Control Board it would be forced to reduce production of its soda ash product by one-third, thus jeopardizing the future of PPG Barberton operations. In May of 1971, PPG announced that because of "too stringent" water pollution control laws, it would close its soda ash operations and lay off 1,000 employees by 1972.

The problem is the pollution of a public waterway that affects a number of downstream users (particularly the city of Massillon). The alternatives are three: (1) force PPG to comply with the standards by the prescribed dates, thus forcing a closing of the soda ash operations and lay-off of 1,000 employees, (2)

[3]Water Pollution Control Board, *Criteria for Stream-Water Quality for Various Uses*, Ohio Department of Health.
[4]Division of Engineering, *op. cit.*, p. 22.
[5]*Ibid.*, p. 22.

Decision Making in the Public Sector

allow PPG to continue to pollute beyond the prescribed dates set by the Water Pollution Control Board, thus allowing PPG to adjust its operations over time in order to comply with the Board's standards, or (3) assess a pollutant tax based on emissions over a prescribed level, or based on actual effort of the firm to comply with the water quality standards.

CALCULATION OF AN EFFLUENT CHARGE FOR PPG INDUSTRIES

The loss to society due to the shutdown of PPG is fairly well defined. The PPG Barberton Plant contributed nearly $47 million to northeastern Ohio in 1969; 2,200 employees received $20.6 million in wages; purchases for supplies amounted to $13.3 million; utility and hospital expenditures exceeded $11.6 million; and state and local taxes totaled $1.1 million. The soda ash operation represents about 50 percent of the entire PPG plant operation. Thus, it may be estimated that the northeastern Ohio community would lose $23.5 million (50 percent of 47 million) if the soda ash plant were closed.

Specifically, the Barberton community will be greatly affected. Mr. Cox, Mayor of Barberton, said that, "the lay-off of 1,000 employees will cost the community $10.5 million in total payroll, $250,000 in real estate taxes, and $120,000 in income taxes annually."[6] Mr. Clarence Cox, Superintendent of Barberton Schools stated:

> ... the loss of $250,000 in revenue to the school system means a reduction of 25 teachers, and increase in class size ... in all, a 7.5 percent reduction in income at a time when inflationary factors are escalating our costs.[7]

Mr. J. W. Deibel, President of the Barberton Chamber of Commerce stated:

> While the loss of 1,000 jobs is a serious blow to the area, the full impact is even greater than most realize. According to statistics available, 1,000 jobs in manufacturing generate income to support 3,120 other people; make payments on mortgages or rents on 1,160 homes or apartments; create ownership of 1,190 passenger cars; make available $3,300,000 in bank deposits; and pump $4,000,000 annually into retail sales which is sufficient to support 40 area retail establishments.[8]

[6]Mayor Cox, Mayor of Barberton, March 2, 1972.
[7]Mr. Clarence Cox, Superintendent of Barberton Schools, March 3, 1972.
[8]J. W. Deibil, Pres. of the Barberton Chamber of Commerce, March 3, 1972.

Mr. D. Coupland, President of the Chemical Workers local stated:

> ... all hourly employees with up to seventeen years service will have to be terminated. The hourly employees affected have a cumulative total of 4,237 years of service, and the salary employees about the same.[9]

The loss of $23.5 million annually to the northeastern Ohio community resulting from the PPG closing is probably the best measure (although conservative, for qualitative factors such as large class size and fewer instructional aids in the schools are not valued) of the loss to society from shutdown of soda ash operations. Utilizing the $23.5 million and converting to a daily basis (270 working days annually) would result in a loss to the community in excess of $87,000 per day, which could be considered the social benefit to the community of keeping PPG operating.

The measurement of the loss to society or the social cost to society due to PPG's water pollution is less well defined. One determination of the social cost of pollution might be the cost of cleaning it up or of meeting the standards set by the Water Pollution Control Board. In the case of PPG, this cost was stated by Mr. Widing at the Muskingum River Basin Hearing in 1968 as cutting back soda ash operation by one-third. This may be computed as 1/3 x 1500 tons/day x $30/ton = $15,000/day. But if this is to be taken as the correct cost, it must be assumed that the standard set by the Board does reflect the social cost correctly. This may not be the case as is stated by Ronald H. Coase:

> ... there is no reason to suppose that the restrictive and zoning regulations made by a fallible administration subject to political pressures and operating without any competitive check will necessarily be those which increase the efficiency with which the economic system operates.[10]

According to Mr. Fredo and Mr. Macklin, sanitary engineers from the Ohio State Department of Health and the Summit County Department of Health, respectively, there is no present way to determine the actual social cost in a pollution situation such as the one created by PPG. There is no defined cost for the treatment of water in this case. The damages here are of a general health and nuisance nature.[11]

Thus, the assignment of pollution charges becomes somewhat arbitrary. In a pollution situation analo-

[9]Mr. D. Coupland, President of the Chemical Workers Local, Barberton, Ohio, March 2, 1972.
[10]Ronald Coase, "The Problem of Social Cost," the *Journal of Law and Economics*, University of Chicago Law School, October, 1960, p. 18.
[11]Division of Engineering, *op. cit.*, p. 16.

gous to this one, the Nixon Administration proposed a flat tax rate per unit of pollutant emitted. This method of pollution control is superior to the present method (pollution standards) in optimizing the allocation of resources only to the extent that the amount of the pollution tax represents the true social cost.

Although the exact damage in cases like this is impossible to assess, an attempt will be made to define two methods to determine a pollution tax that is workable and which as closely as possible reflects the true social cost. The first method for this case in water pollution is a tax on emissions as follows:

1. Determine what the present uses of the polluted water are.
2. Determine the degree of damage in dollars for each incremental amount of pollutant above the "safe" level (this is to take into account the capacity concept) for each of the uses determined in step 1. This is the arbitrary part. This could be handled by a federal agency and set up in the form of a tax schedule similar to the income tax rate schedule. Due to its inherently arbitrary nature it would have to be accepted on the basis of authority as is our income tax schedule.
3. Determine a weighting factor to apply to the pollution tax for each of the uses in step 1. For example, if it was determined by the planning board in control that the Tuscawaras River was to be used only for industrial purposes, the weighting factor for the damage to industrial users would be 1.00. The weighting factor for damage to fish and swimmers would be 0. The weighting factor could take on values anywhere between 0 and 1 depending upon the degree of public use of the river that the planning board deems proper.
4. Determine the concentration of the particular water pollutant attributable to each polluter. This is not difficult since in most situations the number of concerns emitting the particular pollutant we are measuring (in this case chloride) is not large.
5. This process (steps 2-4) is repeated for each type of pollutant found in the water. Thus a separate tax is levied upon a polluter for each of his specific pollutants.

This above process when applied to the PPG case would proceed as follows:

1. Determination of users Mr. Warren R. Bradlee, chief civil engineer for the consulting firm of Ford, Bacon, and Davis stated in his testimony at the aforementioned hearing:

A principal use of surface waters in the Muskingum Basin is for industrial water supplies, with cooling water for electric power generation accounting for about three quarters of the total amount. Manufacturing plants, particularly primary metal industries, are the second largest industrial users. Relatively small quantities taken mostly from the minor streams are used for irrigation and livestock watering. No potable water supplies are taken from the main stem of the Tuscawaras-Muskingum River Basin. An important function of the main stream is to receive and assimilate waste waters from municipalities and industries. Other important uses of the surface waters and streams of the basin are for recreation and the support of fish and wildlife.[12]

2. Determination of Damages In his same testimony Mr. Bradlee relates his findings concerning the harm from excessive chloride concentration:

The principal effects of the high chloride concentration in the upper sections of the main stem of the river system are the diminution of fish life, and some limitations in the use of the streams for water supplies. At the higher concentrations, changes occur in natural stream vegetation and biota, and recreational usage of the stream is impaired. Water containing over 250 ppm chloride ion is unsuitable for use as a potable supply. The use of this water for cooling purposes usually requires non-corrosive metals in heat exchangers, condensers, and similar equipment. The incremental costs involved are not a significant part of total production cost.[13]

From the report of the firm of Roy F. Weston, environmental scientists and engineers:

Dissolved chloride concentrations of more than about 0.2 to 0.5 per cent in the water are toxic to fish, wildlife and plant life. Extreme fluctuations in salinity are perhaps even more hazardous to the aquatic community.[14]

The following pollution tax rate values are assigned as examples (note that payment is to be made only on that amount of pollution above the threshold values):

For industrial water suppliers—[$1/(milligram cl/liter of water)]/day for concentrations above 1500 parts per million.

For irrigation and livestock watering—[$.50/(milligram cl/liter of water)]/day for concentrations above 500 parts per million.

---

[12]Mr. Warren R. Bradlee, Chief Civil Engineer for the Consulting Firm of Ford, Bacon, and Davis, testimony at the Muskingum River Basin Hearing, 1968, p. 170.
[13]*Ibid.*, p. 171.
[14]Firm of Roy Weston, Environmental Scientists and Engineers, Report to Muskingum River Basin Hearing, 1968, p. 413.

Decision Making in the Public Sector

For swimming—[$.75/milligram cl/liter of water)]/day for concentrations above 800 parts per million.

For support of fish and wildlife—[$.25/(milligram cl/liter of water)]/day for concentrations above 1000 parts per million.

3. Determination of Weighting Factors Let us suppose that the Tuscawaras River is to be set up as primarily an industrial river with secondary consideration given to irrigation and the livestock watering and to the support of fish and wildlife (which means that only the coarser fish could survive). Weighting factors for:

Industrial damage = 1.0
Irrigation and livestock watering = 0.5
Fish and wildlife damage = 0.5
Swimming damge = 0

4. Determination of the Percent of the Pollutant (Chloride) Attributable to Each Polluter PPG is the only significant source of the pollutant chloride on the upper Tuscawaras River basin. Therefore, it can be assigned 90 percent of the damages of chloride pollution (the rest is assumed to result from natural causes).

In order to calculate PPG's pollution tax, assume that there are ten industrial users of water on the Tuscawaras where the average chloride concentration (measured at the intake of each plant) is 1750 ppm (note that parts per million and milligrams/liter are equivalent). This portion of PPG's bill comes to $250/day x 1.0 x 90% = $225/day. Note that the $250 comes from the rate of $1 per milligram per liter over the 1500 ppm standard.

Assume that there are five points on the Tuscawaras where irrigation and livestock watering takes place, and the average concentration is 600 ppm. Thus 600 ppm — 500 ppm (standard yields 100 x $.50/day x 0.5 x 90% = $22.50/day). The case of fish and wildlife damage is slightly different. It is a continuous problem all along the river at every point where the concentration exceeds 1000 ppm. This case could be handled by using integral calculus but it is not felt that a thorough discussion would add anything here, so assume the damage to fish and wildlife is $75/day.

It has been determined that the cost to society from chloride pollution by PPG is $322.50 per day based upon the above calculation technique. A second method of applying a pollutant tax centers on the efforts made by the polluter to meet the water quality standards. The method is described as follows: A determination must be made of (1) the annual investment in water pollution control required to meet the water quality standards, (2) the expenditures required to bring the present water quality within the standards (initial clean-up costs), (3) a realistic amortization period to amortize the initial clean-up costs, (4) the annual amortized cost of initial clean-up, (5) an error term, and (6) the value (in dollars) of annual expenditures on pollution control made by the polluter. Once the above costs have been determined, a pollutant tax could be assessed based upon the efforts made by the polluter to meet the water quality standards. The assessment may be computed as follows: Cost #1 + Cost #4 + Cost #5 — Cost #6 = Annual Pollutant Tax Assessment.

Application of the second method to the case of PPG follows. The Natural Resources Committee has published estimates of the percentage of waste treatment cost to total sales value for a number of products in specific industries. A portion of the data is shown in Table 3.

Table 3

Product	% Waste Treatment Cost to Sales Value
Textiles	2.32
Chemicals	2.81
Petroleum-Refining	1.52
Ferrous Metals	1.05
Paper	15.61

Source: "Water Pollution in the United States," 1955.

The estimates in Table 3 are undoubtedly low, but they could serve as a factor in calculating the annual investment in water pollution control required to meet water quality standards (#1 above). Annual sales value of the PPG Barberton Plant's soda ash production approximates $30 million. Thus, using the percentage waste treatment cost for chemicals listed above, and applying that percentage to annual sales value of $30 million will yield the estimated annual investment in water pollution control required of $843,000.

In a discussion with Mr. Donald Factor, Supervisor of Environmental Control at PPG, he stated the following:

> . . . it is economically not feasible with the present technology to meet the water quality standards set by the Water Pollution Control Board of Ohio. However, if technology were to advance to a point where the standards could be met, initial clean-up costs would be in excess of $3,000,000.[15]

[15] Mr. Donald Factor, Supervisor of Environmental Control at PPG, Barberton, March 4, 1972.

Using $3 million as the estimated initial clean-up cost and establishing the amortization period at 20 years results in an annual amortized cost of initial clean-up of $150,000. An error term will be estimated at 1 percent sales value because of the relative age of the Natural Resource Committee's data. The error term will equal $300,000 (1 percent of $30 million).

Mr. Factor stated, "the company spends approximately $1,000,000 annually on water pollution control."[16] It will be assumed the $1 million is a fair value to be assigned to the annual expenditures made by PPG. Applying the above factors to the equation will result in an annual pollutant tax of $293,000 calculated as follows:

$843,000 (#1) plus $150,000 (#4) plus $300,000 (#5) minus $1,000,000 (#6) equals $293,000 (annual pollutant tax).

The above pollutant tax assessment (on a per day basis) would amount to a $1,080 per day (270 working days) cost to the polluter (PPG).

SUMMARY OF CASE

The two methods proposed as a basis for computing the social costs of pollution so as to determine what amount to assess the polluter (PPG) yield significantly different per day costs. An effluent tax based upon the cost to society from emissions of chloride by PPG would be $322.50 per day. An estimate of the actual cost of abatement of pollution to the polluter (PPG) amounts to $1,080 per day.

This large discrepancy in estimated social costs may partly be explained by the fact that the first method (tax on emissions) only estimated the cost of chloride pollution, while the second method included the cost

[16]Ibid.

Externalities and Income Distribution

of all water pollution. Also, it is not the intent of this case to devise a self-contained method of computing a pollutant tax, only to recommend an approach which would allow the polluter to adapt operations over time to meet pollution standards and also force the polluter to internalize the social costs (through assessment of a pollutant tax).

The estimated social cost using the above methods was $322.50 per day and $1,080 per day, respectively. However, it must not be concluded that the polluter should be restrained from polluting solely because of the alleged harm he has inflicted. As noted by Ronald H. Coase in his article, "The Problem of Social Cost":

> The problem of dealing with harm is not just restraining those responsible for it. What has to be decided is whether the gain from preventing the harm is greater than the loss which would be suffered elsewhere as a result of stopping the action which produces the harm.[17]

Questions for Discussion

1. In view of the hardship upon PPG in meeting the Pollution Board's standards, should PPG have been forced to comply?
2. What is the social cost to society due to PPG's water pollution?
3. What will society lose when PPG carries out its shutdown?
4. Would PPG have discontinued the soda ash operations due to economic reasons regardless of the demands of the Ohio Water Pollution Control Board?
5. Based upon the cost to polluters of clean-up, should they be entitled to tax credit or subsidies for pollution control?

[17]Ronald Coase, op cit. p. 27.

Source: Ohio Department of Health.

MUSKINGUM RIVER DRAINAGE BASIN
GENERAL REFERENCE MAP
OHIO DEPARTMENT OF HEALTH

CASE
35 THE COST OF POLLUTION CONTROL AT THE TIMKEN COMPANY*

A recent survey conducted by The Conference Board for the Environmental Protection Agency found that for water pollution abatement alone, over a 5-year period, 1965 to 1969, 500 plants spent a total of $315,064,000.[1] Moreover, these expenditures increased over the 5-year period by more than 239.5 percent.[2] The information gathered in the survey was developed from a survey of manufacturing establishments in seven major industry categories which accounted for 92.3 percent of the water used and discharged in 1968 by all manufacturing industries included in the 1967 census of manufacturers report, *Water Use in Manufacturing*.[3] In addition, the survey found that in 1969, among the 500 plants reporting expenditures for construction of abatement facilities, 463 or 92.6 percent noted expenditures for operation and maintenance totaling $65,405,000.[4]

Another survey conducted by McGraw-Hill found that American business must spend a total of $22.8 billion in the years ahead to bring all of its existing facilities up to meet all present pollution control standards.

Also, pollution control spending will account for 5.3 percent of planned 1972 capital investment expenditures.[5]

The Timken Company, with headquarters in Canton, Ohio, manufactures tapered roller bearings, fine alloy steel, and removable rock bits. The company operates several bearing plants domestically in Ohio, as well as a new plant under construction in Gaffney, South Carolina. Foreign bearing plants are located in Australia, Brazil, Canada, England, France, and South Africa. The steel producing facilities are located in Canton and Wooster, Ohio, while the rock bit operations are located in Colorado Springs, Colorado.

It is The Timken Company's policy to establish and administer programs to eliminate pollution of any type derived from any of its manufacturing processes even though the cost of such programs cannot be returned or recovered.

Twenty-five years before the Water Quality Act of 1965 and the Federal Air Quality Act of 1967, The Timken Company began treating some of its pollution problems. In the 1930s, The Timken Company, realizing that waste pickle liquor should not be dumped in a raw condition into neighboring streams, drained such waste materials into a settling pond, where it leached into the ground. The Timken Company later developed a system for disposing of the waste pickle liquor by neutralizing it with lime in large pits and then hauling it to a slag disposal area. By 1948, it was decided that this system was inadequate. A large area was purchased to build a settling pond which, for 15 years, served to keep not only the streams of the area but also the underground water free of pickle liquor pollutant. An acid neutralizing plant was then built in 1948 at a cost of $90,000 to completely neutralize the waste pickle liquor before it was pumped to the settling pond. The plant was expanded in 1960, and by 1965, The Timken Company was neutralizing approximately 18.3 million gallons of waste acid annually.

After World War II, The Timken Company became involved in methods of preventing mill scale, oil, and grease pollution from entering the area streams. In 1947 and 1957, the company built process water ponds to reduce stream pollution as well as to conserve water. With the installation of these ponds, it became possible to pump water from sewers, which formerly ran into streams, into these ponds. Here the mill scale settled out, and the grease and oil accumulated on the surface where it was pumped into large tank trucks and hauled away.

About every 2 to 3 years, it is necessary to drain these ponds, mechanically remove the accumulated residue on the bottom, and haul it to a slag dump

---

*This case has been developed by G. William Trivoli based upon research by Richard Caldas and Dennis Arnold, both of The Timken Company, and upon an interview with Mr. George L. Deal, Vice President-Finance and Chairman-Finance Committee, The Timken Company.

[1] Leonard Lund, "Industry Expenditures for Water Pollution Abatement" (New York: The Conference Board, Inc., 1972), pp. 1, 5.
[2] *Ibid.*, p. 5.
[3] *Water Use in Manufacturing*, Bureau of Census for 1967, Census of Mfgrs. Report (Washington, D.C.: Department of Commerce, December, 1967).
[4] Lund, *Op. cit.*, p. 14.
[5] Fifth Annual McGraw-Hill Survey of Pollution Control Expenditures," Economics Dept. (New York: McGraw-Hill Publishing Co., 1972), pp. 1-4.

Decision Making in the Public Sector

area. All the water that is pumped to these ponds is pumped out and back to the mill for reuse. It is estimated that 23.6 million gallons of water are saved each day by means of these recirculating processes. Timken's major pollution control investments are listed in Table 1 for the years 1961 through 1971.

In 1950, an oil disposal plant was built at a cost of $50,000, halting the pumping of soluble oil into area streams. This plant separates soluble oil from water and processes other waste oils. The Timken Company processes approximately 15 million gallons of oil per year, reclaiming about 238,000 gallons of oil of suitable burning quality.

The company's first effort in collecting air pollutants was in 1953 when an air cleaning system was installed for the hot scarfing of steel. This system, installed to improve working conditions and to combat air pollution, was replaced in 1964 with a better designed system at a cost of $225,000. This system removes an average of three tons of dust per day.

A new bearing plant under construction in Gaffney, South Carolina, will have the most modern equipment to conserve water and to prevent air as well as water pollution. The process water system will operate on the closed loop principle in which pollutants introduced into the water during usage are recycled within the operations.

There are a number of other improvements that have been made through the years by The Timken Company to control air and water pollution. Some of these include establishing pollution control committees at each plant and forming a corporate group to study the legal and technical aspects of pollution as they apply to The Timken Company. Also, a new lab area has been created to monitor and test air and water samples. In addition, the company has replaced its steam locomotives with diesels, installed smoke detection equipment on soaking pits, improved fuel-air ratio controls for heating furnaces, and installed dust collection systems for grinders.

TIMKEN'S POLLUTION INVESTMENT DECISION PROCESS

The Timken Company is somewhat unique in that it has a company finance policy against outside borrowing for its domestic operations. This policy was "violated" only once in the early 1950s when it borrowed $25 million from five banks to finance a take-over of the outstanding minority interests of its British operations. The chief financial officer of Timken, Mr. George L. Deal, stated that the banks were most anxious to make the loan to the firm despite the fact that Timken had never before sought a loan.

With the emergence of the increasing pollution regulation, both Federal and regional, the firm's investments in pollution-control equipment rose markedly throughout the 1960s (See Table 1 for the trend 1961-71). The firm's policy regarding pollution-control investments was that they must "abide by the law," thus they attempted to have necessary equipment installed and operating prior to the relevant regulatory deadline.

Timken has developed what its management feels to be a good statistical model of its entire U.S. operations. Into the model, they feed all the relevant inputs such as price controls, investment credits, wage settlements, supplies, depreciation, and sales forecasts. Various anticipated capital expenditures are also fed into the model to observe the effects upon overall working capital based upon anticipated sales forecasts. Top management in conjunction with its engineering staff work out an appropriate capital budget for the next fiscal year as well as a tentative long-range capital budget for 5 years.

Based upon capital expenditure requests from all departments and plants, the total desired capital investments may total, say, $50 million for the 1973-74 period. The finance people utilize a discounted cash flow approach to analyze the lengthy list of project requests in light of the anticipated internally generated revenues, and decide that only a $35 million total capital budget can be approved for fiscal 1973-74. It is now up to the individual department heads and plant managers to trim back their requests.

Table 1 Major Pollution Control Equipment Expenditures at the Timken Company (1961-1971)

Date	Description	Type of Pollution Control	Installation Cost
1961	Dust Control Unit Melt Shop	Air	$ 270,000
1964	Dust Control Unit Hot Scarfing	Air	225,000
1966	System Waste Oil Collection	Water	185,000
1968	Dust Control Unit Melt Shop	Air	850,000
1970	Dust Control Unit Melt Shop	Air	725,000
1970	Recirculating System	Water	250,000
1970	Sanitary Sewer System	Water	350,000
	Total 1961-1970		$2,855,000
1971	Dust and Fume Control Unit	Air	150,000
1971	Boiler House Air	Air	1,000,000
	Total 1961-1971		$4,005,000

Finally, a tentative schedule of investment projects is developed for planning purposes, which shows a breakdown on a single sheet the total capital investments for each of the firm's many units under the following categories:

1. Carry-over from previous year (unspent capital investment funds)
2. Additional (new) Production Equipment & Tooling
3. Building Projects
4. Replacements or Modification of Existing Equipment
5. Rebuilding of Existing Equipment
6. Tooling
7. Leased Equipment and Facilities (For planning purposes this is treated with capital expenditures, thus capitalized and depreciated.)
8. Miscellaneous Investments
9. Environmental Control and Safety

Under the final category, Environmental Control Investments, the engineering staff must examine each plant's needs and requirements. They must determine the existing pollution problems, the legal requirements, and the technical feasibility of meeting those standards. Pollution control investments must come out of the plant's overall capital investments budget. Suppose a single unit is budgeted for $2.3 million, all the above listed categories of investment being included. If a particular unit has an especially difficult pollution problem and is in need of substantial capital improvement, it may request that there be a reconsideration by the firm's capital planning committee. For example, let us say that they need an additional $600,000 to meet an environmental control order from the capitol, Columbus. This project may be put back into this plant's budget, then a decision must be made as to the integrity of the overall $35 million capital budget limit. Thus, the overall budget may be increased to $35.6 million. But, once the capital budget for the next fiscal year is finalized, it becomes official and cannot under any circumstances be altered in any material way.

At the present time, Timken has no means of rationally evaluating pollution-control investments that make no positive contribution to profitability. Their attitude is that they must meet the government standards; as long as there is a known technical solution and it is physically possible to meet the government-imposed deadline, the firm makes every effort to make the necessary investments.

There has been some attempt by government to lower the cost of capital for firms investing in pollution control equipment. The two major methods that have been utilized are (1) a tax break on the corporate income tax for pollution control facilities and (2) issuance of tax exempt industrial revenue bonds by various state governments.

The state of Ohio, for instance, provides financial assistance to industries attempting to meet federal and state air pollution standards through the Ohio Air Quality Development Authority (OAQDA) and for water pollution standards through the Ohio Water Development Authority (OWDA). The method of financing is through the sale of revenue bonds either by OAQDA, for air pollution abatement, or OWDA for water pollution for each project. The usual retirement period of the bond is between 10 and 12 years. The private firm, in semi-annual payments, retires the debt, after which time the facility reverts to the firm unless otherwise specified in the agreement.

The interest rate on the bond is determined by the existing municipal bond market conditions at the time of sale. The credit of the firm involved must be sufficient to secure the bond sale since the credit of the issuing state is not pledged behind the issue. The bonds are a tax-free issue, that is, the interest paid to bondholders is nontaxable.

Since The Timken Company finances all capital expenditures out of retained earnings, there is no question that pollution-control investments reduce otherwise profitable investments in new plants or equipment. The firm presently is conducting a study of the feasibility of utilizing industrial revenue bonds to finance its pollution-control equipment. This would be a substantial change in the corporate financial policy, but it has been estimated that these bonds could result in a cost of capital savings of as much as 2 percent under the prime interest rate.

POLLUTION CONTROL: THE COST TO THE TIMKEN COMPANY

The Timken Company has spent in excess of $4 million since World War II on air and water pollution equipment. These expenditures include funds for research and experimentation, dust collectors, fans and controls, installation of a chemical precipitation plant, pumps, settling ponds, acid neutralization, and oil disposal systems.

Pollution-control equipment accounts for an increasingly significant share of Timken's total operating cost. Conservative operating costs for some of the major pollution control equipment at The Timken Company during the period of 1968-1970 shown in Table 2 indicates that the operating costs for major pollution-control equipment are significant. Operating costs averaged about $415,000 per year over the 3-year period for just the four pollution control units shown.

Table 2 Operating Cost of Some Major Pollution Control Equipment at the Timken Company (1968-1970)

Description of Equipment	Type of Pollution Control	Operating Cost - Dollars 1968	1969	1970	Total
Dust Control Units Melt Shop	Air	$183,000	$191,800	$179,700	$554,500
Dust Control Unit Hot Scarfing	Air	43,800	58,300	47,600	149,700
Acid Neutralizing & Oil Disposal Systems	Water	134,800	186,200	160,700	481,700
Settling Ponds	Water	20,000	20,000	20,000	60,000
Total		$381,600	$456,300	$408,000	$1,245,900

Table 3 Summary and Analysis of Data Contained in Tables 1 and 2

($ Thousands)

	1968	1969	1970	Average 1968-1970	1971
(1) Sales	351,427	399,396	389,195	380,006	410,613
(2) Expenditures for Plant and Equipment	28,777	24,456	48,714	33,982	37,000
(3) Cost of Goods Sold	228,482	271,542	271,436	257,153	273,218
(4) Profits (B.T.)	68,840	70,292	55,765	64,966	72,597
(5) Expenditures for Major Pollution Control Equipment	(1968-70 = 2,175)			725	1,150
(6) Cost of Operating Major Pollution Control Equipment	382	456	408	415	NA*

	Data Comparison	
	Total Operations Average 1968-1970	Domestic Operations, 1971
(1) Expenditures for Major Pollution Control Equipment ÷ Total Sales	.19%	$\frac{\$1,150}{410,613} = .28\%$
(2) Expenditures for Major Pollution Control Equipment ÷ Total Expenditures for Plant and Equipment	2.13%	$\frac{\$1,150}{37,000} = 3.10\%$
(3) Expenditures for Major Pollution Control Equipment ÷ Profits (B.T.)	1.11%	$\frac{\$1,150}{72,597} = 1.58\%$
(4) Operating Costs for Major Pollution Control Equipment ÷ Average Total Sales	.11%	NA*
(5) Operating Costs for Major Pollution Control Equipment ÷ Cost of Goods Sold	.16%	NA*

*NA = Data Not Available

Table 4 Consolidated Net Sales of the Timken Company by Major Classifications of its Products for Period 1967-71

(In Thousands of Dollars)

Date	Total Sales	Bearings, Rock Bits and Sundry	Percent of Total	Steel	Percent of Total
1967	$355,056	$271,000	76.32%	$84,056	23.68%
1968	351,427	265,433	75.53	85,994	24.47
1969	399,396	308,073	77.13	91,323	22.87
1970	389,196	314,402	80.78	74,794	19.22
1971	410,613	322,002	78.42	83,611	21.58

Source: Form 10-K, Annual Report Pursuant to Section 13 or 15(d) of the Securities Exchange Act of 1934, for fiscal year ended December 31, 1971, File No. 1-1169, pp. 2-3.

Tables 1 and 2 above indicate that, in addition to the initial cost of pollution-control equipment, approximately 10 to 25 percent of the initial cost is spent annually to operate the equipment. For example, the dust control unit for the hot scarfing operations, which initially cost $225,000, costs approximately $50,000 to operate annually, or almost 25 percent of the initial cost.

A summary and analysis of the data from Tables 1 and 2, including figures from the Consolidated Income Statement and Statement of Sources and Application of Funds from The Timken Company Annual Report is shown in Table 3. Analyzing the summary of data shown in Table 3, the following conclusions may be drawn regarding the cost of pollution control at The Timken Company:

1. An average of $725,000 per year has been spent for new major pollution-control equiment during 1968 to 1970.
2. An average of $415,000 per year has been spent for operating major pollution-control equipment during 1968 to 1970.
3. An average total of $1,140,000 per year has been spent on major pollution-control equipment during 1968 to 1970.
4. An average of $.19 out of every $100 of sales has been used for purchasing new major pollution-control equipment during 1968 to 1970.
5. An average of $2.13 out of every $100 spent for plants and equipment has been used for purchasing new major pollution control equipment during 1968 to 1970.
6. An average of $1.11 out of every $100 of profit has been used for purchasing new major pollution-control equipment during 1968 to 1970.
7. An average of $.11 out of every $100 of sales has been used for operating major pollution-control equipment during 1968 to 1970.
8. An average of $.16 out of every $100 spent for operating costs has been used for major pollution-control equipment during 1968 to 1970.

All the above calculations are necessarily based upon Timken's consolidated statements (see Appendix 1); however, all the major pollution control expenditures were made on domestic operations. This tends to understate most of the percentages listed in Table 3 under Data Comparison. Information contained in the 10-K statements filed with the SEC indicates that bearings constitute the firm's principal product, and approximately 39 percent of the steel they produce each year is used in its bearing and other operations. A consolidated net sales breakdown for the firm is shown in Table 4 by the major classifications of its products over a 5-year period beginning with 1967. Also included in Table 4 is the net income from operations outside the U.S. over the same period.

The bearing business is highly competitive. Although Timken competes with some 60 domestic manufacturers of bearings, it has been able to maintain a dominant position in the market. Timken owns a number of U.S. and foreign patents relating to certain of its products. While the firm regards these patents as important, it does not deem its business as a whole to be materially dependent upon any one patent or group of patents.

Decision Making in the Public Sector

Appendix I The Timken Company and Subsidiaries
Consolidated Balance Sheets

Assets

	Dec. 31, 1971	Dec. 31, 1970
Current Assets		
Cash	$ 15,261,616	$ 9,873,460
Short-term investments—at cost, which approximate market value	25,976,167	19,789,821
Trade receivables, less allowances, 1971—$758,751; 1970—$715,182	44,004,551	45,287,085
Inventories—at lower of cost (first-in, first-out method) or market:		
Finished products	$ 62,864,924	$ 53,245,545
Work in process and raw materials	55,174,417	54,104,069
Manufacturing supplies	12,135,139	12,982,083
	$130,174,480	$120,331,697
Total Current Assets	$215,416,814	$195,282,063
Property, Plant and Equipment—at cost		
Land and buildings	$102,460,912	$ 98,313,976
Machinery and equipment	316,244,141	293,161,354
	$418,705,053	$391,475,330
Less allowances for depreciation	217,423,473	201,778,806
	$201,281,580	$189,696,524
Miscellaneous Receivables and other Assets	3,407,519	4,128,788
Deferred Charges and Prepaid Expenses	556,389	537,342
	$420,662,302	$389,644,717

Liabilities

Current Liabilities		
Accounts payable and accrued expenses	$ 26,701,030	$ 23,711,078
Salaries, wages and payroll taxes	14,120,089	7,855,928
Bank loans	1,070,143	5,173,530
Accrued taxes	5,307,417	4,821,133
Income taxes	19,016,468	13,521,759
Total Current Liabilities	$ 66,215,147	$ 55,083,428
Deferred Income Taxes	3,945,000	2,935,000
Capital and Earnings Invested in the Business		
Common Stock without par value: Authorized—12,000,000 shares Issued including shares in treasury—10,654,072 shares		
Stated capital	$ 43,905,122	43,905,122
Earnings invested in the business	306,859,676	287,908,943
	$350,764,798	$331,814,065
Less cost of Common Stock in treasury (1971—7,967 shares; 1970—6,167 shares)	262,643	187,776
Total Capital and Earnings Invested in the Business	$350,502,155	$331,626,289
	$420,662,302	$389,644,717

Questions for Discussion

1. The fact that The Timken Company has been engaged in installing and operating pollution control equipment for the past 30 years, long before governmental action, is certainly laudatory. But, if their competitors were not also involved in installing such equipment, then would they not possess a competitive "edge" over The Timken Company? Discuss the implications of the above problem, as well as the effects of uneven pollution standards or enforcement. Does the game theory model of behavior help in your analysis of voluntary vs. compulsory pollution control investments?

2. A number of corporate planners have indicated

Externalities and Income Distribution

that they are reluctant to authorize installation of pollution control equipment for fear that it may become obsolete in a few years. What would be the impact upon a firm such as The Timken Company, that already has a substantial investment in air and water pollution abatement equipment, of a raising of acceptable pollution level standards by governmental agencies? Explain.

3. In light of the economics of social costs and the effluent charge concept, how much should The Timken Company be spending on pollution control? Explain.
4. Has The Timken Company done enough in the area of pollution control, given the existing technological and legal climate? Explain.